BEST LITTLE STORIES

— *from the* —

WHITE HOUSE

Imposing but stark-looking in wintertime was the President's House of the 1840s, still the largest home ever built in America. By the time John Plumbe (1809–1857) took this daguerreotype of the Executive Mansion's south side, circa 1846, Thomas Jefferson, Dolley Madison, the British, and Andrew Jackson, among others, had come and gone. (American Memory Collections, Library of Congress)

BEST LITTLE STORIES

from the

WHITE HOUSE

Second Edition

C. Brian Kelly

with **First Ladies in Review**
by **Ingrid Smyer**

CUMBERLAND HOUSE
NASHVILLE, TENNESSEE

Other books by C. Brian Kelly

Best Little Stories from the Civil War (with Ingrid Smyer)

Best Little Stories from World War II

Best Little Stories from the American Revolution (with Ingrid Smyer)

Best Little Ironies, Oddities, & Mysteries of the Civil War (with Ingrid Smyer)

Best Little Stories from the Wild West (with Ingrid Smyer)

Best Little Stories from Virginia (with Ingrid Smyer)

Best Little Stories from the Blue and the Gray (with Ingrid Smyer)

BEST LITTLE STORIES FROM THE WHITE HOUSE
PUBLISHED BY CUMBERLAND HOUSE PUBLISHING
431 Harding Industrial Drive
Nashville, Tennessee 37211

Cover design: Gore Studio, Inc., Nashville, Tennessee

Library in Congress Cataloging-in-Publication Data
Kelly, C. Brian.
  Best little stories from the White House / C. Brian Kelly. With First
ladies in review / by Ingrid Smyer. — 2nd ed.
    p. cm.
  Includes index.
  ISBN 1-58182-466-1 (pbk. : alk. paper)
  1. White House (Washington, D.C.)—Anecdotes. 2. Presidents—United States
Anecdotes. 3. Presidents' spouses—United States–Anecdotes. 4. Presidents-
United States–Family–Anecdotes.
  I. Smyer-Kelly, Ingrid, 1927–   . First ladies in review. II. Title. III. Title: First
ladies in review.
  F204.W5K45 2005
  975.3–dc22

                                                        2005016618

Printed in Canada
2 3 4 5 6 7 8 — 10 09 08 07

For our mothers,
Claire and Ingrid

Contents

III. Ends   263

IV.   As for the Future White House   335

V.   First Ladies in Review   341

Introduction

IT WAS AN IRISHMAN FROM County Kilkenny, a "house carpenter," a resident of young America for all of seven years, who designed and built the White House. He built it twice, actually.

Apparently apocryphal is the old saw that Thomas Jefferson submitted a design under false initials in the competition for the architectural honors—and then was passed over. One way or the other, though, Irishman James Hoban was the choice who emerged.

He worked under the close supervision of George Washington, with Jefferson occasionally dropping by. Washington, very much involved with the creation of the entire federal city bearing his name, scrutinized the plans and the site selection, then watched over construction of the "President's House" as the first public building to begin rising in that city. The Master of Mount Vernon never did live in it. Jefferson, on the other hand, did.

Hired slaves began excavating the site in 1791, it seems. Stonecutters from Scotland later cut and finished many of the sandstone blocks making up the outer walls of the future "White House." The stone itself was native; it came from a quarry at Aquia Creek, across the Potomac River in Virginia. Hired slaves worked over there, too. And speaking of which—What ironies, what bittersweet history, here, this one thread: African-Americans and the White House! At first slaves were hired out by their masters, the money going into their masters' pockets, to help build it. Later, for generations and through several presidents, slaves worked and lived here, right under its roof. Here, too, Lincoln then agonized over the Emancipation Proclamation (with an unlikely friend's help), and here after the Civil War, paid black workers became a permanent part of the staff (mostly as servants, true). In those postbellum years also, a onetime slaveowner would reside here with his daughter and presidential son-in-law. And here, as late as 1901, Teddy Roosevelt would take heat for inviting the distinguished Booker T. Washington to dinner. And then (in the late 1920s yet!), Herbert Hoover's wife, Lou, thought she was being politically correct, if you will, and indeed was breaking tradition by entertaining a black congressman's wife at a small tea—small and quite separate, that is, from the one she held for the congressional wives in general. Here, in the White House also, Woodrow Wilson's housekeeper insisted that black and white staff members take their in-house meals at separate tables. Surely another extreme altogether, Eleanor Roosevelt's housekeeper fired the white domestics and replaced them with blacks.

In the beginning, though, the site chosen for the mansion was a piece of the large presidential park envisioned by the Frenchman planning the entire city, Pierre L'Enfant. By 1792, however, his conception of a European-style "palace" as the presidential home had been turned down. Too grandiose by far for the young, so democratic republic. Even so, this would be the grandest home in America for many years, perhaps its largest until the Civil War.

It would be eight years under construction before its first presidential occupant, John Adams, could move in . . . and even then, its interior rooms and many other features were far from finished. You could almost argue, in fact, that it wasn't finished, truly, until yesterday. And . . . who knows what they may do to it tomorrow, as it has undergone so many changes, additions, improvements, and even subtractions in its two-hundred-year history. The fact is, the White House we see today is not the White House of yore.

Just about every president or first family has made some lasting change here, whether of small scale or large. The Benjamin Harrisons put in electricity and Chester Arthur the small elevator to the second-floor family quarters. Others contributed in more visible and far-reaching ways. Jefferson it was, third president and second official White House occupant, who oversaw the planning and construction of the structure's early east and west wings. Nice touch, too! After the British burned the place down in 1814, leaving only a gutted shell, really, Irishman James Hoban and his construction crews had to come back and build the White House all over again, with various changes from the original model. Later, much later, of course, it was Teddy Roosevelt who removed the large greenhouses that had grown at the west end—unsightly blisters, too, to judge by the photos still remaining—and added the West Wing that now houses the famous Oval Office. William Howard Taft, though, actually installed the Oval Office . . . but not the one so often pictured or cited today, since Franklin Delano Roosevelt moved Taft's creation from one side of the West Wing to the other, to face on the Rose Garden. And speaking of the Rose Garden, Jack Kennedy redesigned and rebuilt it, with friend Bunny Mellon's help (Mrs. Paul Mellon). Some years before, of course, threatened with the physical collapse of ceilings and other old sections, the Harry Trumans had overseen the most extensive White House restoration job since right after the British "visited" the Executive Mansion in 1814. So extensive was the Truman reconstruction that the entire interior was taken out, much of it piece by carefully marked piece—a truck or bulldozer could have driven through the empty space inside—and then much was meticulously replaced in proper place, or replicas were substituted. Important, too, steel supporting structure now replaced the old, weakening materials of the nineteenth century.

The result today, after all the changes over two centuries, is a stately and graceful home of 132 rooms, situated on an eighteen-acre "plot" in the middle of Washington, D.C., and maintained, at a recent count, by a staff of 115. It sounds like it could be a hotel, so many employees and rooms (and under Eleanor and FDR, it sometimes did resemble one, so many visitors came and went all the time). It sounds by description that it could be massive and overwhelming on the one hand, and by its history could be a jerrybuilt hodgepodge creation on the other hand (all those changes and additions!). But in fact it is none of the above. Inside, it is surprisingly pleasing and *under*whelming, if you will, in its proportions. Outside, grand, yes, but no hotel, no monolith . . . rather, just about right. It is difficult to believe this graceful and elegant building—where John and Abigail Adams once found just six rooms to be livable—actually holds a total of 132 rooms.

But we are not come here to write only about bricks and mortar, but rather we write about its people over the years, presidents and first ladies very much included, yes, but many others, too—those who lived here (and a few who died here), who worked here, visited here, even wedded or were born here. Ours is history in small bursts, or vignettes, yes, but we hope something of the presidential home's soul becomes visible in these pages also.

First ladies, first family . . . call it America's First Home, just what it has been for two hundred years as of fall 2000. That was the time of year when John Adams moved in—in 1800. Eight years before that, of course, came the laying of the White House cornerstone, on

October 13, 1792. It's a shame, yes, but George Washington, with business out of town, did miss it. True.

It was a Saturday. The crowd collected first at a Georgetown hostelry, the Fountain Inn. They then walked—about a mile—to the building site, led by Freemasons arranged according to Masonic rank.

James Hoban of course was there.

After the first group came those very important men, the voices of authority locally, the commissioners assigned earlier to help George Washington find and lay out the ten-square-mile site for the new federal city on the Potomac between the ports of Alexandria on the Virginia side and Georgetown, across and up the river a ways, on Maryland ground. They, the three commissioners, together with active partner Washington, had supervised the site selection, the architectural and construction contract awards, and now would oversee the construction itself of the President's House.

After the Federal district's commissioners (Thomas Johnson, Daniel Carroll, and David Stuart) came the local gentry, followed by workers and artisans, and all gathered, it now is thought, at the southwest corner of the recently laid-out foundation. After suitable speechifying, Master Mason Collen Williamson wedged the freshly mortared cornerstone into its designated niche—trapped underneath was a brass plate noting "This first stone of the President's House . . ." was laid down in the seventeenth year of independence. It also said, in Latin, *Vivat Respublica*—"long live the Republic!"

There was no intention, when they laid the cornerstone and began to build, to call it the White House. But once the edifice was up and standing, a large, large block in a near-naked landscape, no real city yet surrounding it but only some farmland framed by still wild-looking countryside, and once those great chunks of hand-cut sandstone forming its walls were whitewashed, it became obvious. This was, and must be, even by the time of Jefferson's tenure as the second official occupant, the "White House." So obvious, what else to call it, really? And yet not until one hundred years later was it made official. On Theodore Roosevelt's stationery and other documentation at last appeared that designation so well known today. Henceforth and forevermore. The White House.

C. Brian Kelly and Ingrid Smyer
Charlottesville, Virginia

BEST LITTLE STORIES

from the

WHITE HOUSE

Back in 1917, the presidential Inauguration Day still fell on March 4 every four years, rather than January 20. Here, Woodrow Wilson is seen riding to his second inauguration with his second wife, Edith. His first wife, Ellen, died in the White House during his first term.

I: Beginnings

I pray heaven to bestow the best blessings on this house, and all that shall hereafter inhabit it. May none but honest and wise men ever rule under this roof!

—John Adams,
first Official White House occupant,
in a letter to his wife, Abigail.

One Dread Moment

THERE WAS THAT ONE MOMENT . . . the very first moment in the Oval Office just vacated by the man before him. Only bare furniture to greet the newcomer. Bookshelves, but no books. Walls, but no pictures. A big desk . . . but empty. Totally empty!

The nation! The nation was in crisis, and here he was, the new president, alone in his wheelchair. "Here he was, without even the wherewithal to make a note—if he had a note to make," wrote aide Rexford Tugwell.

All alone in the empty, power-laden room, with an awaiting world beyond the bare walls poised to hear his proclamations, and now, of all times, "for a few dreadful minutes he hadn't a single thought."

Ever since his landslide election four months before, polio-crippled Franklin Delano Roosevelt had been pointing toward this very moment—his first day at work as the new president.

It had been a strange and pressure-filled interregnum since Election Day 1932.

First, he was down with the flu for about five days. Then there was a tense meeting at the White House with outgoing President Herbert Hoover just a week after the election. Discussing European hopes of canceling huge World War I debts to the United States, Hoover directed almost all his conversation to FDR aide Raymond Moley, not to FDR himself. Hoover, indeed, found his political adversary to be "amiable, pleasant, anxious to be of service" but also "badly informed" and lacking in "vision."

Democrat FDR often nodded, wrote biographer Nathan Miller. Not in agreement, as Republican Hoover thought, but merely to signify his understanding.

And so they parted, with Hoover expecting FDR's endorsement of various proposals to avert the latest crisis of the Great Depression. Much to Hoover's amazement, FDR instead "went public" with contradictory views of his own. The hostility between the two only deepened as a result.

In those days, the lapse between Election Day and the presidential inauguration stretched from early November to March 4, a hiatus of power too long for the modern world and since corrected—inaugurations now are scheduled on January 20 of the year following the presidential election.

During the long 1932–33 interregnum, FDR often gave the appearance of that "amiable, pleasant" man simply awaiting his turn at the bat, although some critics felt he should show more concern for the ailing nation, put his shoulder to the wheel, and help Hoover deal with the nation's ever-growing economic crisis. As the year 1932 ended, the critical problem was the nation's faltering banking system.

Roosevelt may have appeared unconcerned, but that wasn't entirely so, added FDR biographer Miller: "Behind the scenes . . . Roosevelt and his advisers were working up a comprehensive legislative program that contained the basic outline of the New Deal." But a New Deal to be revealed only when FDR took office in March 1933. A New Deal, some still will argue, already laid out in concept by the unpopular, ill-fated President Hoover himself.

Well into the new year, with many banks closing their doors, FDR cruised the Bahamas in Vincent Astor's yacht and came ashore in Miami, "tanned and happy," for a conference with aide Moley—and a public appearance with the mayor of Chicago, Anton Cermak. From an open touring car that evening, the president-elect delivered a few remarks in the city's Bay Front Park, then turned to greet Cermak.

"Just then I heard what I thought was a firecracker, then several more," FDR said later.

Not twenty feet away was a man shooting at FDR with a pistol . . . but Cermak, in the line of fire, suddenly had stains of blood all over his shirt. He had been shot instead.

Roosevelt wouldn't let his car speed away without gathering in the wounded Cermak first. He held Cermak in his arms as the open car raced for Jackson Memorial Hospital. He kept telling Cermak: "Tony, keep quiet—don't move. It won't hurt you if you keep quiet."

Roosevelt stayed at the hospital until Cermak came out of emergency surgery. Only then would FDR return to the Astor yacht for the night. There, members of his entourage, shaken by the evening's events, were up all night, restless, still excited, talking. But not FDR. Acting perfectly normal, he went to bed and slept with no apparent disturbance.

Cermak died a few days later, but until his inauguration, FDR continued to exude the same unflappable, confident air. With the bank crisis at high pitch by inauguration time in March, the Hoovers perfunctorily entertained the Roosevelts at the White House the afternoon before the inaugural ceremonies. While family members sipped tea in the Red Room, Hoover and Roosevelt argued in an adjoining room over the proper response to the latest bad news. Again, FDR refused to go along with a Hoover plan, this one to act jointly in an effort to discourage the bank closings spreading across the country.

Supposedly, FDR told Hoover, "If you haven't the guts to do it yourself, I'll wait until I'm president to do it."

During the night, the governors of New York and Illinois closed the banks in each state. On Inauguration Day, the entire nation's banks were closed or closing. While riding to the Capitol with his successor, Hoover wouldn't speak to him. In his inaugural address shortly afterward, the confident FDR delivered that famous, still-remembered line: "The only thing we have to fear is fear itself."

That evening, while Roosevelt family members attended the inaugural ball, FDR stayed "home" in the White House. He spent a quiet evening in the Lincoln study (recently decorated by Hoover's wife, Lou) with old friend and aide Louis Howe. It was the next morning that FDR reported for duty at the Oval Office for the first time . . . and felt that one tiny moment of helplessness. But only for a moment, for in seconds, recalled his aide Tugwell later, FDR began searching the desk for a call button, and when he couldn't find it, he simply yelled.

Two staffers came running. FDR was on his way, and that very evening, he "signed the necessary documents calling Congress into session and proclaiming a four-day national bank holiday," wrote biographer Miller. The New Deal itself was off and running. The crippled country had a new man at the helm—himself crippled, but brimming with confidence.

Day in the Life of . . .

ALMOST NINE O'CLOCK INAUGURATION MORNING, and the president-elect was nowhere in sight. Where could he be? A worried aide pressed the incoming president's wife for his whereabouts. "I guess he's still in bed," she replied.

Startled, the aide ventured into the darkened bedroom at Blair House, the government's official guest quarters across Pennsylvania Avenue from the White House. It was a quiet room—no lights, curtains drawn.

"Governor?"

"Yeah?" came a voice.

"It's nine o'clock."

"Yeah?"

"You're going to be inaugurated in two hours."

"Does that mean I have to get up?"

Of course he did get up, dress and go on to the inaugural ceremonies, but . . . still asleep the morning of his own inauguration? Actually, that was his way, his style.

A day or so later, now the official occupant of the White House, he was told the presidential day customarily began with meetings at 7:30 A.M.

Oh, no! Not for this president, it wouldn't! The meetings could darn well go on without him. Because he wouldn't be there until nine o'clock in the morning, thank you.

A lazy-bones president? Was Calvin Coolidge to be his role model for working the new job? Coolidge, after all, knocked off and took a nap most afternoons—not just a a few winks on the nearest couch, but a real, full-fledged nap, pajamas and all. This new president, in fact, announced plans to hang a portrait of Coolidge in the cabinet room in place of Harry Truman's portrait.

Coolidge, in fact, was a favorite presidential predecessor, so far as this White House newcomer was concerned. Well remembered was the taciturn New Englander's refusal to tamper with the nation's well-being by being overactive and meddlesome as president. Awakening from his famous nap, the sometimes-mischievous Coolidge would pose a rhetorical question: "Is the country still here?"

That was a view that had appeal to the newcomer, but the latest president to take office would prove no lazybones, no taciturn, nap-taking Coolidge. Far from that model, he would be noted for a tough, demanding schedule that belied his age; for his communication with the public; and for his determination to do things his own way, whether in policy decisions or personal attitude.

For instance, he revered the office and traditions of the office of president. From Day One, he never appeared in the Oval Office without jacket and tie. An aide one time noticed he was hot, was perspiring, and suggested he discard the jacket. "Oh, no," said this president, "I could never take my coat off in this office."

From the very beginning of his presidency, this latest successor to Calvin Coolidge began his day by meeting his vice president and White House chief of staff at nine in the morning. Ronald Reagan, Republican, former movie actor, former governor of California, and now the nation's oldest president ever, then plowed through a day of work and other activity that went on and on . . . and on.

His typical workaday began with a wake-up call by the White House operator at 7:30 A.M. He then browsed through the news-papers, caught up on his favorite comics and looked over the "daily packet of press clips, a compilation of important news items pre-pared by the White House staff," recalled former Reagan domestic policy adviser Dinesh D'Souza in his book *Ronald Reagan: How an Ordinary Man Became an Extraordinary Leader.* Added D'Souza: "Then the Reagans [Ronald and wife Nancy], together with their cocker spaniel *Rex,* a gift from William F. Buckley Jr. and his wife, Pat, would have their standard breakfast of juice, toast, and decaffeinat-ed coffee and watch the morning news shows. Occasionally the staff taped a particular segment that they thought Reagan should see."

Arriving at the Oval Office exactly at 9 A.M., Reagan "never returned to the residence until the end of the day," wrote D'Souza also. "His critics said he was 'prone to nodding off' during the after-noon, but contrary to the popular rumor, there is no evidence that he took naps in his office. . . . All those who worked with Reagan confirm that he worked a full day without interruption."

While he sometimes did nod off during the day to offset jet lag caused by a strenuous trip, he normally worked while traveling.

Hard-working President Ronald Reagan sometimes did take a break. Here, Secretary of State George Schultz watches as Reagan shows off his putting style aboard Air Force One. (Courtesy Ronald Reagan Library)

"Others on *Air Force One* might be chatting or having a drink, but Reagan would sit by himself, reading or putting finishing touches on his next speech. Larry Speaks, his press secretary, writes that Reagan had enormous stamina and could keep working when his much younger staff was thoroughly exhausted."

Those daytime meetings, incidentally, like those of any president, primarily were with "cabinet members, staff, congressmen, representatives of various groups, and foreign visitors." Reagan would take an hour or so in the late morning to "catch up on his reading or answer correspondence."

He lunched at his desk, usually light fare such as soup and fruit—"once a week he dined with [Vice President] George Bush."

Then came an afternoon of more meetings. A methodical man, Reagan kept close track of his appointments. The day's schedule was printed on green stationery, and he checked off each meeting with a pencil once it was over. "He would conclude each meeting a few minutes before time was up, clear off his desk, and prepare for the next one. He did everything on time; he hated to keep people waiting. Aides observed that the president took evident satisfaction in the regularity of his regimen and the brisk thoroughness with which he discharged his responsibilities."

In a long, tedious meeting he was known to doodle on a blank pad. If the participants became too confrontational or the meeting really dragged, he often reached into a jar to pull out a few jelly-beans. "This could be an entirely casual gesture, but his aides soon learned that it sometimes conveyed Reagan's impression that the participants were getting overly heated or technical. It could also be a signal that the topic at hand was exhausted, and it was time to move on."

Some days, of course, he enjoyed the break in routine afforded by an out-of-town speech or function. Most of the time, however, Ronald Reagan, the oldest president, worked through the nine-to-five day at his desk . . . and still didn't quit. "Around 5 P.M., when Reagan had concluded his appointments, he cleaned his desk and assembled a pile of reading material to take home."

Before going back to work "at home"—the family quarters upstairs—however, Reagan took time for his daily workout. He changed clothing and turned to a bedroom converted into an exercise gym, added the D'Souza account. There, he "worked out with weights for thirty to forty-five minutes." Reagan was such a "believer" in daily exercise, he took portable workout equipment with him when traveling.

By now on a routine day at the Reagan White House it was time to consider dinner. If the first couple had no obligations such as a state dinner, wrote D'Souza, "the Reagans were just as happy to eat an early dinner from portable tables—meat loaf or chopped steak and mashed potatoes, and macaroni and cheese were Reagan's favorites—while watching the evening news simultaneously on all three networks."

About once a week, they would watch an old movie—they didn't care for "the vulgarity and sexual explicitness of contemporary films."

More often in the evenings, Ronald Reagan simply went back to work . . . this time in an upstairs study. "He trusted his subordinates to include everything that he needed to read and never stopped until he had gone through it all. During this time, he could not be disturbed. When he finished his briefing papers, Reagan did some casual reading in bed—a magazine about horses or a novel by Tom Clancy or Louis L'Amour—before falling asleep around 11 P.M."

End of day in the Reagan White House, a full day even if he did refuse to start his daily schedule with a 7:30 A.M. meeting.

Additional note: Not only was Ronald Reagan the oldest president, he was the first president to survive wounding by a would-be assassin. (True, Teddy Roosevelt was also shot and—in his case slightly wounded—but only while campaigning as a former president for a return stay in the White House.)

It happened early in Reagan's first term as president. A mentally disturbed young man, John Hinckley, shot him outside the Washington Hilton Hotel on March 30, 1981, also wounding Press Secretary James Brady, Secret Service Agent Timothy McCarthy and Washington police officer Thomas Delahanty.

Reagan would have died within minutes if Secret Service Agent Jerry Parr hadn't ordered the presidential limousine to rush Reagan straight to George Washington University Hospital. The president at first didn't realize he actually had been wounded, but he felt pain in his chest and Parr saw blood in his mouth.

As events turned out, a remarkably resilient Reagan would recover from his wound with hardly a pause in his presidential career. Not only recover fully, but inspire his countrymen by the indefatigable spirit and good humor he displayed in the face of his temporary adversity. As usual, too, recalled D'Souza, Reagan spontaneously came up with one quip and memorable one-liner after another.

Among his best known:

- Arriving at the hospital, he told the doctors greeting him: "Please tell me you're Republicans."
- After emergency surgery, he recalled the famous W. C. Fields line: "All in all, I'd rather be in Philadelphia."
- Telling his wife Nancy about the unexpected shooting, an old Jack Dempsey line: "Honey, I forgot to duck."
- When a nurse held his hand: "Does Nancy know about us?"
- When three aides came to visit: "I should have known I wasn't going to avoid a staff meeting."
- To aide Michael Deaver (the same who awoke Reagan the morning of Inauguration Day and who suggested doffing his jacket one hot day): "Who's minding the store?"

- To the doctors and nurses as he left the hospital: "If I had this much attention in Hollywood, I'd have stayed there."
- And finally, a year later, returning to speak before the same group that he had addressed the day of the shooting, was he afraid? "No, but I'm wearing my oldest suit today." And to the audience: "I know you all understand how happy I am to be back, but if it's all the same to you, when I finish speaking, I think I'll slip out the back door this time."

Passing the Baton

PASSING THE BATON—OR TAKING it in hand—has not always been a smooth and easy moment for the various presidents occupying the White House, one after the other like runners in a relay race. Definitely one of the rougher such transfers was the Truman-Eisenhower Inauguration Day episode of January 20, 1953.

Tradition called for incoming President Dwight D. Eisenhower to pick up outgoing President Harry S. Truman at the White House for the short trip by limousine to the Capitol for Ike's swearing-in as Truman's successor. They had not been in touch since a short meeting the previous November, except for a recent Eisenhower offer to send the departing Truman home to Independence, Missouri, aboard the official presidential airplane of those days, the (what else?) *Independence.*

Ike had read a newspaper story saying that the Trumans, Harry and Bess, planned to take a train back to Missouri. The incoming president then, on January 15, sent Truman a telegram saying, "it occurs to me that it may be much more convenient for you and your family to make the trip in the *Independence* rather than the Pullman."

Truman never replied. The fact is, he was still burning over the 1952 campaign—the loss to the Republican ticket headed by Eisenhower, the GOP jibes about the "mess in Washington," and charges that the Democratic Truman administration had been "soft on Communism." Truman also was nettled by Eisenhower's critiques of foreign policy decisions he had helped to carry out as chairman of the Joint Chiefs of Staff. Irritating also was Eisenhower's vow to go to Korea if elected, as if he somehow could end the festering Korean War, as if the pledge were anything more than pure political rhetoric.

Then, too, there had been that post-election meeting in November, all of twenty minutes devoted to the coming transfer of power.

Eisenhower, once an admirer of the former senator from Missouri, had his own list of complaints by the end of his 1952 campaign against Democrat Adlai Stevenson. By that time, wrote Eisenhower biographer Stephen Ambrose, the publicly affable Ike really "disliked" Harry Truman. "He thought the President was guilty of extreme partisanship, poor judgement, inept leadership and management, bad taste, and undignified behavior. Worst of all, in Eisenhower's view Truman had diminished the prestige of the office of the President of the United States."

Truman didn't really help matters with his post-election telegram to Eisenhower proposing a transition conference at the White House and offering the presidential plane *Independence* for the trip to Korea—"if you still want to go." (No thanks, replied Eisenhower, he would be happy to go by any military aircraft that might be available. He did go, he toured the front lines, and he concluded the stalemated Korean War should be ended as quickly as possible, without mounting a highly uncertain and costly offensive to liberate North Korea from Communist rule.)

No surprise, then, that the meeting in the White House November 29 was a frosty one. Wrote Secretary of State Dean Acheson afterwards: "The good nature [Eisenhower's] and easy manner tending toward loquacity were gone. He seemed embarrassed and reluctant to be with us. Sunk back in a chair facing the President . . . he chewed the earpiece of his spectacles and occasionally asked for a memorandum on a matter that caught his attention."

Before the difficult session was over, added the Ambrose account, "Truman offered to leave some portraits in the Oval Office. Eisenhower curtly told him no thanks." Eisenhower did accept a world globe that he had given Truman at the Potsdam conference in newly defeated Germany just before the end of World War II.

Truman also offered suggestions on organizing the White House staff but later confided to his diary, "I think all this went into one ear and out the other."

And it surely did. As a career army officer, general, leader of the Allied conquest of German-occupied Europe, chairman of the Joint Chiefs, then president of Columbia University for a short time, Eisenhower did have some expertise of his own in organizing a staff.

All of which was an unhappy and difficult prelude for both men to contend with as Eisenhower's limousine arrived at the North Portico of the White House the morning of Inauguration Day 1953 to pick up Truman for the ride to the Capitol and the ceremonial transition of power.

Things did not go well from the start.

Come inside for coffee, Mr. President-elect?

No, Ike would stay in the limo and wait for Truman to come out.

One onlooker was longtime Chief Usher J. B. West, and he later wrote: "I watched the two grim-faced men step into the special, high-roofed limousine [General Eisenhower refused to wear a tall silk hat, for which the limousine was designed], and I was glad I wasn't in that car." As West noted also, Bess Truman already had given Mamie Eisenhower a tour of the White House. "The two ladies . . . had known each other for years and were much more cordial than their husbands."

Meanwhile . . . that frosty, frosty ride to the Capitol.

By Truman's later account, noted Ambrose, Eisenhower "broke the silence" by saying he had avoided Truman's own inauguration in 1949 "out of consideration for you, because if I had been present, I would have drawn attention away from you."

Possible translation: I would have been the star of the show, not you.

Was the remark really meant that way? Probably not, but it wasn't overly tactful, either. Truman, still by his own account, was quick to bat down Ike's apparent pretensions. "Ike, I didn't ask you to come—or you'd been there."

For his part, Eisenhower later denied there was such an exchange, but he did recall another conversational gambit the two men fell into while riding up to the Capitol. Eisenhower asked who had ordered his army-officer son John Eisenhower back home from duty in Korea to attend the inaugural events.

By Ike's version of this exchange, Truman simply said, "I did."

Truman's later version: "The President of the United States ordered your son to attend the Inauguration. The President thought it was right and proper for your son to witness the swearing in of his father to the Presidency."

Minutes later, they were making their way through the Rotunda of the Capitol with a bevy of aides and dignitaries, heading for the ceremonial platform at the east front—and their separate destinies. Outside, the largest inaugural crowd to date anxiously and excitedly awaited Eisenhower, the first Republican to ascend to the Presidency since Herbert Hoover's election of 1928, twenty-four years earlier. In between had come the depression, FDR, World War II, and . . . Harry Truman.

The Trumans, by the way, did stick to their plan and returned home to Independence by train.

Three days after the inauguration, President Eisenhower sent citizen Truman a letter thanking him for the "very many courtesies you extended to me and mine during the final stages of your Administration." Ike specifically and "especially" extended his thanks "for your thoughtfulness in ordering my son home from Korea."

Further, ". . . and even more especially for not allowing him or me to know that you had done so." Translation needed?

That was their last communication, reported Ambrose in his two-volume biography *Eisenhower,* "until after Eisenhower himself left the presidency."

Additional notes: Quite a contrast would be the entirely amicable transfer of power between outgoing Democrat Lyndon B. Johnson and incoming Republican Richard M. Nixon in 1969. "On January 20, 1969, I worked in the White House as usual, directing the astonished staff to arrange the most unusual transfer of power any of us had witnessed," wrote Chief Usher West in his book *Upstairs at the White House: My Life with the First Ladies.*

West served as chief usher from partway through the FDR years to the first weeks of the Nixon stewardship. He had seen the great and the near-great of both political parties come and go, as occupant and visitor, but never had he seen anything quite like this:

From election day onward, the transition of administrations had been carried on without a hitch. The mood of the switch over was evident from that first greeting between Claudia (Lady Bird) Johnson and Thelma (Pat) Nixon on November 10, at the White House door. They embraced and kissed each other.

The Nixons were back several times before the Inauguration, visiting, measuring, planning their lives there. You could hardly believe they were of different political parties, much less that Richard Nixon and Lyndon Johnson had once been bitter campaign opponents.

West had seen the White House change hands four times before. Both FDR and John F. Kennedy died in office and were succeeded by their vice presidents, Truman and Johnson. Then there had been the two politically shaded passings of the baton, Truman to Eisenhower and Eisenhower to Kennedy.

Now, on this January morning in 1969, the Johnsons were having the Nixons in for breakfast. For that matter, the respective vice presidents also were on the guest list—outgoing Hubert Humphrey and incoming Spiro Agnew and their families. Wrote West later: "All gathered in the Red Room to drink orange juice and coffee, and nibble on sweet rolls and toast. At 11:30, laughing and cordial, the group set out for the Capitol. President Johnson, who had delivered his own inaugural address in a business suit, even wore a cutaway coat and striped trousers to please Mr. Nixon."

Not only that, but two Nixon "family members" had been allowed to spend the previous night at the Johnson White House. When Dick and Pat arrived inauguration morning, the Nixon dogs Pasha (Yorkshire) and Vicky (poodle) ran out to greet them. Growled one onlooking staff member, "A dog's welcome to the White House—that's what they'll write."

But nobody did, West later reported . . . until he and collaborator Mary Lynn Kotz did.

Jackie's Painful Tour

THE SMALL ELEVATOR EDGED UPWARD to the second floor, the family quarters. As the door slid open, the young woman inside—years younger than any first lady of the twentieth century—girded herself by taking a deep breath.

Down the hall ahead Mamie Eisenhower was waiting. And waiting. She did not advance a step as Jacqueline Kennedy emerged for a preinaugural tour of the private family rooms above the ceremonial and social realms of her future home, the White House.

It was not a friendly, relaxed encounter between the old and the new that December morning in 1960. For one thing, Mamie Eisenhower was determined to be alone while she showed her successor around. "Please have the rooms in order, but no servants on the upstairs floors," she had instructed Chief White House Usher J. B. West.

The time for the visit was set for noon and at 1:30 sharp, Mamie Eisenhower planned to leave the premises for another engagement. As the wife of a onetime general, college president, and now president of the United States, even a lame duck president, she often could be imperial in her manner. Add to that tendency the outgoing "first couple's" distinct feeling that Democrat John F. Kennedy's narrow election victory over the Republican vice president Richard M. Nixon was a repudiation of the Eisenhower record.

While more friendly feelings emerged later, Ike was known in 1960 to consider JFK as a "young whippersnapper" and to have objected (in a letter to a friend) to any notion "that we have a new genius in our midst who is incapable of making any mistakes." To make matters worse for the youthful Jackie Kennedy, her visit came only two weeks after her cesarean delivery of John F. Kennedy Jr. at nearby Georgetown Hospital. She looked thin and pale, and she had requested a wheelchair for the intimate White House tour. Obviously, someone would have to push her along.

"Oh, dear," Mamie had said at that news. "I wanted to take her around alone."

Mamie's solution was to have a wheelchair on hand but tucked out of sight. "It will be available if she asks for it," she instructed.

Jackie arrived at the south entrance shortly before noon, seated informally in the front seat of a station wagon driven by a Secret Service agent. Chief Usher West escorted her inside—past the Diplomatic Reception Room where she entered and through the hall beyond to the elevator. Silently, she looked all around, obviously absorbing details, but also "somewhat ill-at-ease."

Upstairs, she had to advance to take Mamie Eisenhower's proffered hand. "Hello, Mrs. Kennedy," said the outgoing first lady. "I do hope you are feeling much better now. How is the baby?"

As West bowed out of the picture, Mamie then led the way for her special guest, both of them on foot—no wheelchair.

An hour and a half later, two rings of the buzzer in West's office signified that the first lady was descending in the elevator. Two first ladies, in fact.

Their respective cars were waiting at the south entrance. Mamie quickly left in her chauffeur-driven Chrysler limousine for her card-game engagement, and Jackie "walked slowly" to her station wagon.

As West briefly made arrangements to send Jackie blueprints and photographs of the rooms that she soon would be redecorating, he wrote later, "I saw pain darken her face."

It wasn't until the Kennedys had settled in at the White House weeks later that West learned just how difficult the White House tour had been for the new first lady. She asked him one day if he had known about the request for a wheelchair. When he told her yes, she was dumbfounded. "Then why didn't you have it for me? I was so exhausted after marching around this house for two hours that I had to go back to bed for two whole weeks!"

West explained that it had been there, hidden behind the closet door right by the elevator. "We were waiting for you to request it," he added.

Instead of pain or anger, Jackie reacted with a giggle. "I was too scared of Mrs. Eisenhower to ask," she confided.

In time, Chief Usher West would find the new mistress of his White House realm to be "elegant, aloof, dignified and regal" in public, and in private, "casual, impish and irreverent."

One thing she never was again, though, was "uncertain." Soft-spoken and subtle as she was, her voice often almost a husky whisper, "she had a will of iron, with more determination than anyone I have ever met." Younger than any first lady West served in his thirty years at the White House, from the Franklin Roosevelts to the Richard Nixons, she nonetheless "had the most complex personality of them all."

As he—and the world—soon would learn, the complete Jackie Kennedy and husband Jack would be stamping a fresh new image upon the tradition-bound President's House.

A Most Rowdy Party

HAVING JUST LOST HIS WIFE, Rachel—just about literally, it would seem—to her inordinate fear of living in the White House, the widower Andrew Jackson slowly wound his way to Washington in the gray early weeks of 1829.

It was January 19 when the "Hero of New Orleans" left his beloved Hermitage outside Nashville and boarded a steamboat on the nearby Cumberland River to begin the long journey to the young nation's capital. It would be February 11, about midmorning, before he arrived at his destination, now in an unremarkable carriage drawn by a pair of horses.

In the carriage with the tall, spare Jackson was a single black servant, while ahead rode ten horsemen as an escort. All along the way, people tried to catch a glimpse of their next President . . . and those that did usually saw a serious, soldierly man dressed in a black suit and black tie, a black mourning band on his sleeve, all set off by a white shirt and high beaver hat. Rather than the frontier "ruffian" in buckskins that some of them might have expected, they saw a dignified, even presidential-looking figure.

The Hero, come to succeed John Quincy Adams in the President's House, would spend the preinaugural days before March 4 at the newly opened National Hotel on the northeast corner of Pennsylvania Avenue and Sixth Street and, later, at a hostelry known as Gadsby's. He would spend that time largely engaged in selecting cabinet and other appointees. He had arrived quietly, with little fanfare, and he would quietly await his turn as president as well.

Out in the hinterlands, though, a giant but friendly beast was awakening and preparing to set out for Washington. The people, electrified by Jackson's talk of a "people's government," wanted to be with their hero, the General, Old Hickory, the Great Reformer: Andrew Jackson, by whatever name to call him.

As the hour of his oath-taking approached, they swarmed into town, swamping the hotels and filling the boardinghouses to bursting. "I never saw such a crowd here before," wrote Sen. Daniel Webster of Massachusetts as early as February 19. "Persons have come five hundred miles to see General Jackson, and they really seem to think that the country is rescued from some dreadful danger."

With the changeover in presidents looming closer, Jackson eschewed the customary courtesy call upon outgoing President Adams. For one thing, Jackson (and his supporters) still were smoldering over the "secret understanding" by which Adams had won the presidency four years before. That was when fellow presidential aspirant Henry Clay of Kentucky delivered his considerable backing in the House of Representatives to New Englander Adams, allegedly in return for appointment as Adams's secretary of state. The result was to deny Jackson the presidency, despite the fact that he had won both the popular and the electoral votes in the 1824 election. Since none of the four candidates in that race had won a majority of the electoral votes, however, the final choice for president was up to the House.

Just five days after the House bestowed the presidential mantle upon Adams, he chose Clay for the prestigious post overseeing America's foreign affairs. Jackson reacted vehemently. "The Judas of the West [Clay] has closed the contract and will receive the thirty pieces of silver," fumed Jackson. "His end will be the same. Was there ever witnessed such a bare faced corruption in any country before?"

Importantly, too, recalled historian Robert V. Remini in his biography *The Life of Andrew Jackson,* the entire affair launched Jackson upon his crusade for reform in government—and the campaign that really did win him the presidency in 1828. Thus was set in motion "a movement that changed the course of American political history, a movement that historians would call 'Jacksonian Democracy.'"

By 1829, moreover, Jackson had developed a far more personal animus against Adams. As Remini explained, the touchy Jackson was furious over "the slanderous articles about his marriage that appeared in the Washington newspapers." The recently widowed president-elect blamed Adams for failing to quash such attacks impugning the integrity of his late wife, Rachel. It of course was "ridiculous to think the President could control the partisan press" and Jackson, angry or not, should have paid the courtesy call on the outgoing White House occupant, Remini also noted.

For his part, Adams "decided to boycott" the Jackson inauguration on March 4 and even moved out of the White House the night before.

What came about that next, boisterous day was an inaugural event never to be forgotten by presidential and White House historians.

On that bright, sunshiny day Jackson delivered his inaugural address and took his oath of office (in that order, yes) before a huge, rambunctious crowd gathered before the East Portico of the Capitol, an outdoors event that would be both a historical "first" and a precedent for future inaugural ceremonies. "The open-air ceremony was scheduled because of the vast numbers of people jammed into the city and the necessity of giving them an opportunity to witness their Hero's final triumph as he took the oath of office," wrote Remini. Francis Scott Key, who once had watched rockets burst in the air over Baltimore Harbor, was again moved by this sight. "It is beautiful," he said; "it is sublime."

Jackson, still in mourning, still dressed in black, walked up Pennsylvania Avenue between walls of people to the Capitol, where he witnessed the indoor swearing-in of South Carolina's John C. Calhoun as vice president. Then it was outside, to the East Portico and the roaring crowd of fifteen to twenty thousand souls. One moment dark-looking, the carpet of people stretched out before the president-elect quite suddenly turned bright as the men in the assemblage doffed their dark hats and all looked upward with "radiant" faces, recalled one witness.

Still for a moment, perhaps taken aback, Jackson bowed low to his fans—to "the majesty of the people," said a history of Washington's first forty years.

Apparently happy with Jackson's short inaugural speech (less than ten minutes in length), the crowd resumed its roar of approval, then quieted once more as Chief Justice John Marshall administered the oath of office. That done, Jackson raised and kissed the Bible. As the onlookers then broke out in screams and cheers, Jackson again bowed to his people.

Now, quite suddenly, there was no holding them back. With a surge that broke a restraining ship's cable across the portico steps, they washed up and over the stairway, and the ceremony's marshals had to drag Jackson to safety inside.

He then managed to leave the building, mount an awaiting white horse, and ride down Pennsylvania Avenue to the President's House, as it was still formally known, for the public reception scheduled to be held there. This, too, was no easy task, since the street and sidewalks were jammed with his excited well-wishers—all headed for the same destination, it appeared.

"Such a cortege as followed him!" wrote Margaret Bayard Smith, onlooking wife of a U.S. senator from Maryland. "Country men, farmers, gentlemen, mounted and dismounted, boys, women, and children, black and white. Carriages, wagons and carts all pursuing him to the President's house."

And it was at the White House itself that the climactic moments

So great was the excitement and so crowded was the White House for Andrew Jackson's inauguration in 1829 that "Old Hickory" himself had to be led away to quieter, safer premises. (By Robert Cruikshank, artist (1789–1856); American Memory Collections, Library of Congress)

came—came with the crash of broken crockery and glassware; with barrels of punch and pails of liquor upset and spilling on floors; with men in muddy boots standing on fabric-covered chairs and, literally, with people leaping out of the windows to partake of the refreshments that staff members wisely moved outdoors. Never again have those hallowed walls seen a "party" quite like the one that greeted the "people's President" Andrew Jackson on that March fourth of 1829.

The high and mighty mixed with "the most vulgar and gross in the nation" for the occasion, opined Supreme Court associate justice Joseph Story. "The reign of KING MOB seemed triumphant," he said. "The Mob broke in, in thousands," added South Carolina's Senator James Hamilton Jr. And among the throngs were "many fit subjects for the penitentiary."

Also shocked was Margaret Smith, who agreed it had been quite a scene. "The Majesty of the People had disappeared, and a rabble, a mob, of boys, negroes, women, children, scrambling, fighting, romping," she later wrote. "What a pity, what a pity."

Once more, Jackson himself almost had been overwhelmed and trampled under. Friends formed a protective circle around him, and he eventually escaped the frenzied scene at his future home for the much quieter confines of his hotel lodgings.

The party, in the meantime, simply went on without him. And not all were totally dismayed—Senator Hamilton, for instance, later said that "notwithstanding the row Demos kicked up, the whole matter went off very well."

Perhaps he meant the inaugural events as a whole. For that matter, the contemporary publication the *Argus of Western America* reported two weeks later that it had been "a proud day for the people." In the view of the *Argus,* "General Jackson is their President. Plain in his dress, venerable in his appearance, unaffected and familiar in his manners, he was greeted by them with an enthusiasm which bespoke him the Hero of popular triumph."

Mrs. Smith, for her part, later granted that it was the people's day, with the people's president taking office, and the people would rule, but she also offered a word for the ages: "God grant that one day or other, the People do not pull down all rule and rules."

The newly widowed Jackson of course did not attend the inaugural ball held in his honor at the Washington Assembly Rooms that night. He rested, attended a quiet dinner with Calhoun and others, then retired early. For him, and him alone, there would be a presidency to take on the very next day.

Additional note: Andrew Jackson couldn't move into the White House for six days after its inaugural ordeal. Repairs, you know. But when he did, he took up residency with vigor, innovation, and vengeance. Please thank Andrew Jackson for the impetus that brought about actual construction of the long-planned North Portico, today's front entrance, in effect. He also added long wings on either side of the building, for office spaces, horse stalls, and carriage spaces. No oval office as yet, but there, similar to Thomas Jefferson's previously proposed wings, was another early glimmer of today's modern West Wing and center of official presidential activity. Jackson also created the Executive Mansion's first formal garden. In addition, one of the magnolia trees he planted in memory of his late wife, Rachel, has stood by the President's House to this day.

Reportage at Close Quarters

THE PRESIDENT-ELECT, MR. LINCOLN, had proceeded into the capital a week before his expected arrival, without prior announcement, because of the sundry plots against his person that were widely rumored. He was presented to a young reporter in the House of Representatives, at the Capitol building itself, on the Saturday before his inauguration, and noting the fellow's youthfulness, he said, "You are not a member of the House?" To which the young man, Henry Watterson, replied, "No, sir, I only hope to be."

Then came the significant day that all were anticipating, albeit some with considerably more dread than joy—the inauguration on March 4.

The young man, the journalist Mr. Watterson, had been assigned to report on the inaugural events, so he would need a copy of the newly sworn president's speech. He had been told by messenger's note that very morning that a copy of Mr. Lincoln's inaugural address would be made available to him if he would present himself to Ward H. Lamon.

But who was Ward Lamon? Where might he be located? Mr. Watterson had no idea. "I had never heard of him," he wrote in *The Cosmopolitan* magazine in 1909. "The city was crowded with strangers. To find one of them was to look for a needle in a haystack."

The solution, however, was quite obvious: start the search at that mecca of meccas in the capital city of 1861, the Willard Hotel. And so, Mr. Watterson hied himself to those very premises and soon found himself on the second floor, before a myriad of "little dark entry-ways to the apartments facing on Pennsylvania Avenue."

He proceeded down the long corridor connecting them all, and as he did so, he saw a half-opened door. There, just past the doorway, was Mr. Lincoln himself, "pacing to and fro, apparently reading a manuscript."

Eureka!

"I went straight in. He was alone and, as he turned and saw me, he extended his hand, called my name, and said: 'What can I do for you?'"

When Mr. Watterson explained, the president-elect was able to oblige with no further time wasted. "Why," he said, "you have come to the right shop, Lamon is in the next room. I will take you to him, and he will fix you all right."

And so it was that Mr. Watterson soon was striding to a nearby telegraph office, also at Fourteenth and Pennsylvania, but "over the way at the northeast corner," to impart to various newspapers across the nation the contents of Lincoln's all-important message for a fractious, divided nation. The young reporter noticed the Lincoln speech "had been clumsily typeset in some country office and was considerably interlined with pencil marks."

In just two hours, the same young man—acting as an assistant to the veteran reporter L. A. Gobright—was stationed on the wooden platform erected at the East Portico of the Capitol for the Lincoln inauguration. As witness to this most historic event, our youthful journalist was so close to the principal parties that when Mr. Lincoln removed his black silk hat, "I lifted my hand to receive it."

Not to be, however . . . Lincoln's old campaign adversary, Stephen Douglas, that is to say, Senator Douglas, was quicker. He reached over Mr. Watterson's arm, "took the hat and held it during the delivery of the inaugural address which followed."

For such an auspicious occasion, it should be noted, the president-elect wore a black suit and a black tie that emerged from a "turndown collar." He was "tall and ungainly"; he brandished a walking cane, with head either of silver or gold, Watterson couldn't recall which. On the wooden platform was a table holding a Bible, a pitcher of water, and a glass. Mr. Lincoln pulled a manuscript from his breast pocket—the same papers that Mr. Watterson had seen him perusing at the hotel earlier—and laid his cane on it to hold down the paper.

He next took out his steel-rimmed spectacles, and then he was ready.

For the speech that followed, "His self-possession was perfect," Mr. Watterson would write years later. "Dignity, herself, could not have been more unexcited. His voice was a little high-pitched, but resonant, quite reaching the outer fringes of the vast crowd in front; his expression serious to the point of gravity; not a scintillation of humor. Notwithstanding the campaign pictures of Lincoln, the boor, I was prepared to expect much. It is only true to say he delivered that Inaugural Address as though he had been delivering Inaugural Addresses all his life."

The apparently disappointed Mr. Watterson derived one further fact on that fateful day. "To me it meant War."

Subsequent events did indeed mean war, the American Civil War. Astonishingly enough, in mere weeks the same young man who had discovered the president-elect alone in his hotel room, who then had stood so close by during the inaugural ceremonies as to reach for the presidential black silk hat . . . this same young man was the sworn enemy of all that Mr. Lincoln represented and stood so righteously for, the Union.

Henry Watterson, although he later in life became a member of Congress, although he subsequently became the distinguished editor of the *Louisville (Kentucky) Courier* for many years, did raise his hand against Mr. Lincoln and his federal government by joining the armies of the Confederate States of America (CSA) as a soldier in their cause.

His heart, he did later confess, never was entirely with the

Secessionists. And just think, had he been all fire and hatred like some, what awful deed this young man, or another in his place, might have wrought on March 4, 1861. What outcome to the nation's fate? By what fateful chance was assassination avoided then . . . and yet not in April of 1865?

Boardinghouse Manners

WHAT A DIFFERENCE BETWEEN ONE president's inauguration and his successor's, just eight years later! The first in this pairing came on a sunshiny day in a still-primitive capital city boasting all of 316 federal patronage jobs awaiting the new chief executive's pleasure. A capital city of mud and swampland, no real streets, and a handful of houses so rudimentary a contemporary called them "small, miserable huts." A capital city with an incomplete Capitol and an unfinished President's House that had a privy standing outside.

But it was a nice day for March 4 of any year, pleasant and mild enough for the nation's third president—tall, lanky, and for all his democratic leanings, aristocratic in looks and manner—to walk from his boardinghouse quarters to the Capitol for his inauguration. He wore a gray waistcoat over green breeches and gray woolen stockings for the auspicious, long-awaited occasion.

It had been long awaited, too! Not only for Thomas Jefferson himself, but for the entire onlooking nation. The election in November of 1800 had been only the start, rather than the expected finish, of the campaign to fill the young nation's presidency for the third time. The ticket nominally headed by Jefferson had defeated incumbent John Adams and his running mate, Thomas Pinckney, a result unexpectedly producing an awkward tie for the presidency between Jefferson and his running mate, Aaron Burr—seventy-three electoral votes for each.

With that outcome, the entire matter was thrown into the House of Representatives for final disposition. And there it took thirty-six ballots, from February 11 to February 17, 1801, to produce a majority vote electing one man over the other. Fortunately for the nation, the choice in the end was Jefferson.

The distinguished Virginian, the vice president at the time, had spent the winter of political tumult at Conrad & McMunn's tavern and boardinghouse, located at C Street and New Jersey Avenue, with about thirty congressmen from his own Republican party (no relation to the Republicans of today, but a supportive and convivial company for the beleaguered Jefferson, to be sure).

The day of his inauguration, Jefferson walked to the Capitol, just a block or so away. With him was a minor parade of soldiers and civilians, also on foot. Ostentation there was not.

He took his oath of office in the Senate Chamber, packed by nearly a thousand persons, according to one eyewitness. "The Senate chamber was so crowded I believe not another creature could enter," wrote Margaret Bayard Smith, wife of a Jeffersonian-era political journalist who later became a U.S. senator from Maryland.

Conducting Jefferson's swearing-in was his old enemy John Marshall, a fellow Virginian and chief justice of the United States. Jefferson shook hands with his recent rival (and now a bitter enemy, too), the scheming Aaron Burr, the new vice president. Jefferson then read his inaugural address "in a manner mild as it was firm," said Margaret Smith. An address, not so incidentally, calling for unity. "We are all republicans; we are all federalists," he said, in reference both to his party and that of his political opponents.

It was only a short walk back to the boardinghouse, and that is exactly where the new president headed, rather than to the future White House. The President's House, as it still was called, wasn't ready for him, and he wanted to spend some time at his beloved Monticello at Charlottesville, Virginia, anyway.

He sat that night at the bottom of the communal boardinghouse table as usual. By some accounts, there was little excitement over his official ascension to the presidency that very day, except that a visitor from Baltimore, placed right next to Jefferson, was pleased with the coincidence and wished the new president well.

Jefferson allegedly smiled in response and had a ready answer. "I would advise you," he said, "to follow my example upon nuptial occasions, when I always tell the bridegroom I will wait till the end of the year before offering my congratulations."

In sharp contrast to Jefferson's thoroughly plebian inaugural day was the inauguration just eight years later (March 4, 1809) of fellow Virginian James Madison.

While no throwback royalist, by far, Madison rode by coach to his inaugural ceremonies at the Capitol. An estimated ten thousand visitors crowded into the fast-growing federal city for the august occasion, which included a gay, swirling inaugural ball staged that night at Long's Hotel in Georgetown. Madison delivered his maiden address as president in the Hall of Representatives at the Capitol, then held a reception at his own Washington residence.

Jefferson, still holding to his constraints but clearly delighted on Madison's behalf, declined his good friend's offer to ride up Capitol Hill in the coach. Jefferson instead rode his horse in the caravan of well-wishers following the Madison party. Offered a special chair to hear Madison's inaugural address, Jefferson declined that honor, too. "This day I return to the people," he said. And with the people he sat.

Jefferson did attend both the Madison reception and the ball that night. As an interruption, earlier in the day, however, he and Madison had to hurry back to the White House to appear at a surprise reception given in Jefferson's honor as a fond farewell gesture.

The tall, white-haired widower captivated and surprised many onlookers by his obvious mood of relief and gaiety. He and Madison's colorful wife, Dolley—described by the writer Washington Irving as "a fine, portly, buxom dame who has a smile and a pleasant word for everybody"—were the real rivals for the crowd's attention at the ball, rather than the diminutive new president, Madison.

Afterwards, Jefferson reverted to more plebian form: he left Washington quietly, alone on his horse, for the ride back to Monticello, about 120 miles distant. He plugged on through a severe snowstorm and arrived about mid-March. On the way, however, he repeatedly encountered farmers vigorously cheering him on and drinking to his health. And in his native Albemarle County, neighbors rushed to welcome him back from the presidency of his country . . . of their country.

New Boss in Town

SHE MAY HAVE LOVED HER pink. She may have greeted Chief Usher J. B. West and a staff aide in bed her first morning at the White House with a bow of pink satin in her hair and outfitted in "a dainty, pink ruffled bed jacket."

She may indeed have been "feminine to the point of frivolity," as West later wrote. For her, he added, "ruffles and flourishes were something to wear." Further, in West's words also, she was affectionate, sentimental, gay, breezy, and quite open. "[W]e all got to know her better than we did any other First Lady because she let us in on almost everything going on in her life, and she took an interest in everything in ours."

For all that, Mary Geneva Doud Eisenhower—Mamie for short— soon made it clear to one and all on the White House staff that she was boss of the house and all its doings. As West said also, "beneath that buoyant spirit, there was a spine of steel."

Mamie not only knew what to do, but also how to get it done. "As the wife of a career army officer, she understood the hierarchy of a large establishment, the division of responsibilities, and how to direct a staff," explained West. "She knew exactly what she wanted every moment and exactly how it should be done. And she could give orders, staccato, crisp, detailed and final, as if it were she who had been a five-star general. She established her White House command immediately."

As the staff soon found out, even Mamie's husband, the president, had better mind his p's and q's on certain matters, on anything remotely concerning her domain.

For instance, in his second week as president, Ike organized a stag luncheon for various associates, a harmless enough exercise you might think. The staff, not the slightest bit taken aback, made the usual preparations for a stag lunch, complete with stag-lunch menu, with plans for Ike's fifty guests to be seated in the State Dining Room. Strictly routine, nothing to it, everybody thought.

As the day of the luncheon approached, Eisenhower routinely

Gathered at the White House for Christmas Day, 1957, were Ike and Mamie, their son John, his wife Barbara and their children, (left to right) David, Mary, Anne, and Susan. (Courtesy Dwight D. Eisenhower Library)

asked for the proposed menu, then approved it. All plans still on track.

The day of the luncheon, however, Mamie suddenly halted in her daily bedside conference with Chief Usher West. She had been looking over the daily menus. West's book *Upstairs at the White House* relates the rest of the tale.

"What's this?," Mamie asked. "I didn't approve this menu."

"The president did, two or three days ago," West replied.

Whoops, that wouldn't do, as quickly became apparent. Mamie frowned and shook her head.

"I run everything in my house," she declared. "In the future, all menus are to be approved by me and not by anybody else."

Going downstairs "to inspect" the luncheon table a short while later, West's book also related, Mamie found it was set with traditional "President's House" silverware and with green-bordered Lenox china acquired during the extensive White House renovations ordered by the Trumans. In addition, "We had brought up the new banquet chairs purchased by Mrs. Truman."

But Mamie was "aghast" when she saw the size of the new bentwood chairs. "Heavens!" she said, "It looks like we're having a children's party in here!"

The stag luncheon went on, but the next day Mamie told West, "We must do something about those little chairs. They won't do for men at all."

She liked the twenty "high-backed, upholstered" chairs normally kept in the State Dining Room, but "mainly for show." Telling West to "have some more of the big ones made, enough to fit at the banquet table," Mamie handed down her latest edict. "We just won't invite any more people than we can seat."

There would be many more changes ordered by Mamie Eisenhower. After sleeping just one night in Bess Truman's "narrow" bed in the small chamber once known as the first lady's dressing room, Mamie told West to order a king-sized bed—she and Ike would do their sleeping together, thank you.

In short order, the new bed was in place, replete with padded headboard of pink. Mamie moved the pink-and-green curtains from Margaret Truman's former sitting room across the hall to the Eisenhower bedroom and ordered a bedspread made with the same pattern. A bench at the foot of the bed and the bed's dust ruffles were of the same pink hue as the headboard, while the carpet and walls were done in Williamsburg green.

Soon, too, came additional Mamie edicts:

- Personnel working in the official executive offices of Teddy Roosevelt's West Wing (location of the famous Oval Office) and those of the social office ensconced in FDR's East Wing no longer could traipse through the first floor of the White House proper to go from one wing to the other. Go around outside, was her order to members of both staffs. "You're not to use the mansion as a passageway."

- Not only the mansion, but she, herself, was to be treated with respect, in her case with the deference befitting a first lady. "When I go out, I am to be escorted to the diplomatic entrance by an usher," Mamie announced. "And when I return, I am to be met at the door and escorted upstairs."

- As in the army world left behind, one's rank would call for certain protocol. One time Chief Usher West answered the telephone in the Executive Mansion "command post" simply by saying, "West speaking." At the other end was Mamie. "Never call yourself 'West,'" she said. "You are Mister West, and you must insist that everyone refer to you in that way. You must establish your authority with everyone. You are not a servant." The lesser-ranking domestic staff, on the other hand, did not rate the salutations *Mr.* or *Mrs.* When Mamie heard a maid call the maitre d' "Mister Ficklin," Mamie interrupted to say, "You're to address him as Charles."

Among other changes, Mamie scrapped the old U-shaped banquet-table arrangement for formal affairs in the State Dining Room.

For years, that scheme had placed the first lady across from her husband the president, but with her back to many of the guests. From now on, wrote West, "The President and First Lady would sit side by side in the throne-like mahogany chairs at the head of an E-shaped banquet table—just like royalty."

Diminutive in size, Mamie experimented with different approaches to receiving guests at the White House. At first she asked for a platform, "so everyone can see me." But the handshaking as she received guests almost, in her words, "jerked me off the platform." Next she tried standing on the landing of the grand staircase and simply waving at 2,000 or so Shriners' wives in town for a national Shriners convention. For 1,500 Republican women visiting shortly afterwards, she moved down to the first step of the stairs, with four leading GOP women standing immediately behind.

But that wouldn't do, either. She asked to have the GOP ladies stand back two or three more steps—"They're so close, nobody knows who is me!"

As time went on, no detail would prove too minor for Mamie's attention as hostess of the White House. For any important occasion, West reported (and probably for many not-so-important ones), she chose the flowers and selected the linens or place mats, "even the place cards and tiniest souvenirs."

No meddlesome amateur was this friendly, outgoing but absolutely firm woman, either. Said West: "Mamie Eisenhower as a hostess was spectacular. In her diamonds and décolleté gowns, she fairly sparkled. She and the General applied more spit-and-polish, more pomp and circumstance to their lavish, formal entertaining than any other President and First Lady in my White House existence." (For J. B. West, that "existence" covered service with the Franklin D. Roosevelts, the Harry S. Trumans, the John F. Kennedys, the Lyndon B. Johnsons, and the Richard M. Nixons, in addition to Ike and Mamie Eisenhower.)

Before Mamie Eisenhower would leave the premises in 1961, incidentally, she and Ike would host thirty-seven visiting heads of state, "in addition to the usual ten-event 'social season.'" West also noted. For "the General" himself, the crown jewel of the annual social calendar was always the military reception held "for the thousands of top brass in Washington," all come to meet and mingle with the commander in chief and his wife—for them, a favorite evening, just like their old army days.

Additional notes: In addition to her other duties as first lady, Mamie Eisenhower maintained a White House recipes file. Here, courtesy of the Eisenhower Presidential Library and the Internet, is her recipe for sugar cookies:

1½ c. flour	1 c. sugar
1 t. baking powder	2 egg yolks
½ t. salt	1 t. vanilla
½ c. butter	1 T. cream

Mix and sift flour, baking powder, and salt. Cream butter, add sugar slowly and cream until fluffy. Stir in well-beaten egg yolks and vanilla extract. Add sifted dry ingredients alternately with the cream. Chill for one hour, roll and cut in any desired shape. Sprinkle with sugar before baking. Bake in a moderate oven at 350° or 375° for 10 to 12 minutes.

Mamie's Million Dollar Fudge

4½ c. sugar	12 oz. semisweet chocolate bits
pinch of salt	12 oz. German sweet chocolate
3 T. butter	1 pint marshmallow cream
1 tall can evaporated milk	2 c. nutmeats

Boil the sugar, salt, butter, evaporated milk together for six minutes. Put chocolate bits and German chocolate, marshmallow cream, and nutmeats in a bowl. Pour the boiling syrup over the ingredients. Beat until chocolate is all melted, then pour in pan. Let stand a few hours before cutting. It will be better the next day. Store in a tin box.

With cooking considered one of Ike's hobbies, he was known in a select circle for Eisenhower's Barbeque Sauce. Here is that recipe:

¼ c. butter	1½ t. Worcestershire sauce
2 t. salt	1 T. sugar
1 no. 2 can tomatoes sieved	3 t. paprika
2 t. chili powder	1 t. black pepper
¼ cup vinegar	1 small onion, finely chopped
¼ t. Tabasco sauce (or more according to taste)	

Mix the ingredients and simmer for 15 minutes. Use for basting meat or chicken, and serve as sauce for it as well. Makes two cups, enough for 5 pounds of meat or poultry.

Bless This House

LIVING BEHIND THESE IMPRESSIVE, IMPOSING, sometimes intimidating walls all these years have been real people—men, women, children, with very human wants, needs, triumphs, and tragedies. Just like all of us. And the first of these were John and Abigail Adams, the nation's second president and first lady.

Like many Americans in the centuries since, they underwent a job transfer of sorts in 1800 and moved into a new house that was far from finished—the White House. They shared the visions of future grandeur for the President's House—sometimes derisively called the President's Palace—but they also had to deal with concerns such as shopping at nearby stores, putting up the laundry, keeping warm and dry, and hoping that work on the outdoor privy would be complete in time.

John Adams, that stalwart from Revolutionary days, traveled down to Washington from their home at Quincy, Massachusetts, in advance. Abigail was still recovering from one of her persistent "fevers," but her husband was required in his new place of business in the fall of 1800.

Not that he had just been elected president. The fact was that the seat of government was moving from Philadelphia to the new capital "city" of Washington, the term *city* not yet a true description for the scattered edifices beginning to rise from muddy flats by the Potomac River. John Adams already had been through an inauguration—he had weathered that ritual in 1797 alone, with no family present. It was held in Philadelphia before the House of Representatives, and for the occasion Adams wore a plain gray suit in the fashion of his day. He left home the sword that he often had worn as vice president and presiding officer of the Senate.

George Washington, of course, was just leaving the presidency, and like any two rational men he and Adams had struck a small deal beforehand—Adams bought some of his predecessor's furniture. Already, in the nation's infancy, the price of serving in government could be high and inadequately reimbursed. "Every one asks and every one cheats as much as he can," Adams complained of the prices in Philadelphia. In Philadelphia, too, the President's House had not been ready in time for his inauguration.

The night before the inauguration, he slept badly, so he felt awful the next day "and really did not know but I should have fainted in presence of all the world." (Shades of George Bush in Japan two centuries later!) Adams even wondered whether he should simply take his oath and then say nothing, or linger to give a speech. In the end, he did the latter and was off and running in his term as the second president.

Just three years later, on November 1, 1800, he was alone again while moving into the President's House in the new capital. He would be the first president to sleep in the great house by the Potomac—but not the first historic figure to do so. John Marshall, the secretary of state, in need of lodgings, had lain down his head in the unfinished White House for some weeks during late summer.

The next day, November 2, Adams was able to summon Abigail with a somewhat false assurance: "The building is in a state to be habitable, and now we wish for your company."

All well and good sounding, but in fact, with winter coming on, what was "habitable" in the incomplete structure were six damp and drafty rooms. And all around were the mud of construction, worker huts, the debris of unfinished work—and leagues of wild, untamed land lying between Massachusetts and Washington.

For Abigail, the journey of more than 550 miles would take until November 16, unhappily punctuated by a stop in New York to visit their alcoholic son Charles Adams on his deathbed (he died December 1 of cirrhosis of the liver). She and her party became lost outside of Baltimore and approaching the site of the future capital city found "nothing but a forest & woods on the way, for 16 and 18 miles not a village; Here and there a thatched cottage. . . ."

And what she found at her destination itself was far from the grand White House and grand international city of modern times. Georgetown, one mile from the new house, was after every rain "a quagmire." Even without that drawback, it was "the very dirtyest Hole I ever saw for a place of any trade, or respectability of inhabitants."

As for the "transferred" couple's new home, it was big, bigger than anything they had ever occupied, bigger than any house in young America, in fact. "Twice as large," she wrote, as their meeting house in Quincy, but obviously, too, "this House is built for ages to come."

To keep warm and dry, the Adamses had to keep the fireplaces roaring, "or sleep in wet & damp places," but they had trouble with another mundane detail—finding cut wood for the fires. "Surrounded by forests, can you believe that wood is not to be had, because people cannot be found to cut and cart it."

They could turn to coal, but there was the problem of having grates made to fit the fireplaces. "We have, indeed," she wrote like a frontierswoman, "come into a new country."

The prosaic intruded also, in terms of the family laundry. Abigail Adams had to establish a "drying room," and she settled upon an unfinished but large chamber they called the "audience room." Today, the room she chose for her laundry is known as the East Room, where the bodies of seven successors to Adams as president have lain in state.

One might wonder more immediately, though, what John Adams thought that first night alone, as the first of all presidents to sleep in the White House. Whatever he did think, he wrote to Abigail the next day with both the message to come join him and a high and noble sentiment widely quoted ever since: "I pray heaven to bestow the best blessings on this house, and all that shall hereafter inhabit it. May none but honest and wise men ever rule under this roof!"

Steppingstone President

FATE WAS NOT KIND TO the "Old Hero," as William Henry Harrison was called in his day, and it may have been his inauguration that ended his presidential career before it really began. He in effect was a steppingstone president—first to die in office, first to usher in a vice president as the new president, and holder of the shortest presidential term on record—exactly one month, from March 4, 1841, to April 4, 1841.

A steppingstone in another sense also: He was the son of the

Virginia patriot Benjamin Harrison, a signer of the Declaration of Independence, and he was the grandfather of a future president, another Benjamin Harrison.

Coming in between, William Henry Harrison, at age sixty-eight, chose to deliver an inaugural speech of an hour and forty minutes outdoors, wearing no hat and no heavy coat on an unusually bitter, rainy, and cold March day in Washington. He rode his horse down Pennsylvania Avenue, again with no overcoat and with his hat held in his hand. That he caught cold soon after is usually attributed to his inaugural appearance—and to the possibility that the old Indian fighter was no longer quite the man who once had roamed the rough-and-ready Northwest Territory, a huge area that eventually spawned the states of Indiana, Illinois, Wisconsin, and Michigan.

His presidential campaign had stressed—perhaps even exaggerated—his early triumphs, such as his defeat of the Shawnee Indian chief Tecumseh on the Tippecanoe River. With fellow Virginia native

Looking the part of a statesman for the ages in this mezzotint by James R. Lambdin (1807-1889), William Henry Harrison would enjoy, if that is the word, a presidential term of only one month before he succumbed to pneumonia. (American Memory Collections, Library of Congress)

John Tyler on the Whig ticket as vice presidential candidate, Harrison had campaigned in 1840 on the slogan "Tippecanoe and Tyler, too." He used log cabins and cider as symbols intended to stress the frontiersman theme. The Harrison-Tyler combine, in fact, paved the way for many a modern political campaign by trotting out promotional placards, hats, effigies, floats, and similar tools of the present-day political trade. It stressed the stump speech, parades, banners, torches, campaign songs . . . all very familiar today. Tyler and Harrison, however, did not stress their mutual status as sons of Virginia, as indeed, scions of aristocratic Virginia families both born to plantation life far removed from the northwest frontier, both in spirit and geography.

The victorious Harrison was unable to fight off the pneumonia that developed soon after his inauguration. He did act quickly to appoint a distinguished cabinet, with the famed Daniel Webster as secretary of state. When he succumbed to his illness on April 4, John Tyler became the first U.S. vice president to take over the presidency because of a predecessor's death in office.

To the very last, it seems, few in Washington or the country at large quite realized the seriousness of Harrison's feverish sickbed. He himself may have, though. Just two days before his death, he told a woman attending him: "Ah, Fanny, I am ill, very ill, much more so than they think me."

As a footnote to his short White House tenure, it seems that Harrison's wife, the former Anna Symmes, was fated never to spend a day or night in the White House as first lady. Unable to leave their "frontier" home and attend his inauguration due to illness of her own, she never did reach Washington in her brief role as the president's wife. His body came back to her instead.

Early Blow for Lincoln

ABE LINCOLN'S FIRST TERM AS president had hardly begun in early 1861 when the East Room of the White House became the setting for a body lying in state—just as Lincoln's own would lie four years later.

The deceased in this case was a young man, not yet thirty, who had been a friend of the Lincolns in Springfield, Illinois; a campaigner for the presidential nominee; and then a frequent visitor to the White House in early 1861, with the Civil War about to explode. Young Elmer Ephraim Ellsworth even accompanied the president-elect to Washington for the first Lincoln inauguration.

Although an upstate New Yorker by birth, he had "read law" in Lincoln's law office in Springfield, and he was a bit of a celebrity in those prewar years. He and his U.S. Zouave Cadets of Chicago were famous for their tour of twenty cities in 1860, he, especially, as the drill instructor and as author of a *Manual of Arms for Light Infantry.*

Quite fond of the young officer, Lincoln gave him a position in the new administration, as adjutant and inspector general of militia in the War Department. With the outbreak of war, however, Ellsworth hurried to New York City, where he raised the Eleventh New York Volunteer Infantry, or Fire Zouaves, most of the men being recruited from among the city's firemen.

They were sworn in before Lincoln himself in Washington on May 5 and two days later they were busy putting out a fire, but that action was incidental to coming events.

On May 23, Virginia seceded, and across the Potomac from Washington, in Alexandria, Virginia, was a hotbed of Southern sympathizers. Visible from the White House itself was a Rebel flag, and Ellsworth—now Colonel Ellsworth—told Lincoln that he and his Zouaves would see to it that the offending flag disappeared from view.

The next day, May 24, he and his men crossed the Potomac by boat and stormed the Marshall House on today's King Street in downtown Alexandria, the hotel that was defiantly flying the Rebel standard. In the shooting that erupted, both Ellsworth and hotel proprietor James W. Jackson were killed, their violent demise often called the first real bloodshed of the great conflict to come. Ellsworth thus became the first commissioned officer to die in the Civil War, while Jackson was ballyhooed throughout the South as a martyr to the Secessionist cause. And on May 25, Ellsworth's body lay in state in the East Room of the Lincoln White House.

Lincoln, in the aftermath, had to write his first letter of condolence of the war. Addressing Ellsworth's parents, he described the slain officer as "my young friend and your brave and early fallen child."

President . . . In Secret

ANOTHER TIME, ANOTHER DAY, A gentleman from Ohio was sworn in as president of the United States in the White House itself—in secret.

No counterfeit, nor any political neophyte, he was the well-bearded Rutherford B. Hayes, Civil War hero, former congressman, former governor of Ohio, and now nineteenth president.

The history books will say that he was inaugurated on Monday, March 5, 1877. And, true, he was. But, in secret, he also was sworn in as president Sunday evening, March 4, in the Red Room of the White House.

It happened during a resplendent dinner party for thirty-eight of Washington's most distinguished "celebrities," people such as cabinet members and Supreme Court justices. The hosts were the outgoing president and his wife, Ulysses S. and Julia Grant. The dinner, while a "cover" of sorts, was real enough, lavish enough—twenty courses served, along with a variety of drink to fill the six different wine glasses at each plate.

Incoming President Hayes and his wife, Lucy, were there, too . . . but was he still incoming? Or now president? Just two days before, he didn't really know if he would be president at all!

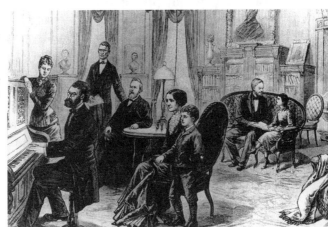

The Hayes family in the White House's music room. On Sunday evenings, cabinet members and senators would join the family in singing favorite hymns. (Rutherford B. Hayes Presidential Center photo)

The explanation is a combination of circumstance. First, the hotly fought election of 1876—the centennial year for America—had been so close that Republican Hayes trailed his Democrat opponent Samuel Tilden in the popular vote but might have the edge in the all-important electoral vote. Yet, here was fresh doubt, not only because of the close popular vote, but also because of charges of chicanery arising in four southern states. An electoral commission investigating both the vote count and the charges of fraud gave its nod to Hayes only at the last possible minute, on March 2.

Now, enter the calendar: Grant's term would expire Sunday, March 4. By tradition, the presidential inauguration was never held on a Sunday; in this case, then, it must await the next day, Monday, March 5. Technically, the country would not have a president in office for twenty-four hours, from noon Sunday to noon Monday. Although it had happened twice before in the nation's early history (James Monroe and Zachary Taylor simply skipped the first day of their respective terms by waiting a day for their inaugurations), such a hiatus would not now be desirable. With all the bitterness engendered by the last-minute decision endorsing Hayes, with street demonstrations cropping up in Washington, Grant felt it would be safer for Hayes to take office officially, if not publicly, on Sunday.

At dinner that night, the guests began their promenade from the East Room, where they had been received, to the State Dining Room for the meal itself. Few noticed Grant and Hayes take another route, to halt in the Red Room. There, flanked by bowers of flowers, Chief Justice Morrison R. Waite administered the oath of office to Rutherford B. Hayes.

If all else was carefully prepared for the occasion, one traditional item was missing—no one had thought to provide a Bible. With no Bible immediately available, the swearing-in proceeded anyway, to be followed the next day by a full-blown inauguration, oath-taking on the Bible and all, at the Capitol.

The president-for-a-day was still president! By the logic dictating the hurried and secret oath-taking the evening before, however, the nation really did go without a President for a while. Not a full twenty-four hours, but for the hours between noon Sunday and the minute of the swearing-in that took place in the Red Room the evening of Sunday, March 4.

Hooting at Owls

FROLICSOME IS NOT HOW THIS president of dour public countenance is best remembered today, not this dedicated citizen . . .

- Who the morning of his inauguration took occasion in his hotel room to dance before his wife while chanting in childish sing-song: "We're going to the White House today; we're going to the White House today."
- Who, perceiving his newly appointed postmaster general Albert Burleson's black umbrella and stiff dignity, quickly nicknamed Burleson "the Cardinal."
- Who entertained his cabinet in their second meeting with a tired joke: to wit, a convert presiding at an especially bitter religious debate was discouraged by the eggs thrown his way, drew a pistol and said, "This damn Job business is going to last just two seconds longer!"
- Who kept other family members close as frequent visitors to his new home, often as overnight guests, but scrupulously refused any of them, even his own brother (or especially his own brother) even a hint of a federal job anywhere.
- Who liked a snappy game of billiards in the evening.
- Who chased up and down the White House corridors playing tag with daughter Nellie. Sometimes it was "rooster-fighting," instead.
- Who, despite his intellectual renown across the breadth of the land, favored for entertainment neither opera nor ballet nor serious theater, but vaudeville, where, said biographer Arthur Walworth, "he could himself become one of the people to whom he was devoting himself."
- Who, unknown to his millions of recent voters, took great delight in operating the presidential home's small electric elevator, a functional box made ornamental with panels of mirrors.
- Who was known to go to his bedroom window at night when awakened by the owls hooting in the magnolia tree outside,

It's 1916, opening day at the ballpark, and there he is—the surprisingly frolic-some Woodrow Wilson, obviously having a good time as he throws out the first ball to open the 1916 season. (National Photo Company Collection, American Memory Collections, Library of Congress)

pause, and then hoot right back. In the morning, he would tell those at the breakfast table he had "hooted the hooters away."

- Who, his first night at the White House, admittedly through no plan of his own, slept in the Lincoln bed "without benefit of nightclothes." (The presidential trunk had temporarily disappeared, it seems. It was delivered at 1:00 A.M., too late to be of any help that night.)

This president did have his idealistic vision, or set of visions, that he thought called for earnest example and a certain public image, which indeed was far less fun-loving than the private man seen by intimates.

Showing his more serious side, he was the first president since James Madison to order no inaugural ball. Why? "He disliked making himself and his family the center of social and commercial aggrandizement," wrote his biographer Walworth. Typically, too, the night of his election, his expression had become "grave" when the early returns indicated he would win. After he had indeed won, tears were in his eyes, he fell into silence, and he spoke of feeling "a solemn responsibility." Still, the next day, he stuck to old habits and went to watch his college team (Princeton) at football practice.

Fierce and bristling, he insisted he must have "a chance to think."

He and his family fled to Bermuda while he took that time to think (and threatened to "thrash" a photographer impudent enough to aim a camera at his daughter Jessie).

His, on the other hand, was "one of the briefest inaugural addresses in the history of the nation," reported Walworth, but also, "one of the most moving".

Despite the schoolmaster's mien, he was a man casual enough to tell his cabinet members in their first meeting with him, "Gentlemen, I thought we had better come together and talk about getting started on our way."

Soon, a week after taking his cabinet seat, the newly appointed Interior Secretary Franklin K. Lane was able to write a friend: "The President is the most charming man imaginable. . . . There had been a particularly active set of liars engaged in giving the country the impression that . . . [he] was what we call out West 'a cold nose.' He is [on the contrary] the most sympathetic, cordial and considerate presiding officer that can be imagined."

So, there you have it—even then, Woodrow Wilson hardly was known to the greater public for frolicsomeness, joviality, or nonchalance. Nor was it yet suspected in early 1913 that his would be one of the most dramatic presidencies of all, both personally and politically, with one crushing blow after another awaiting this surprisingly joyful man.

Prophetic Words Repeated

FOR SLANDERING ANDREW JACKSON'S WIFE, Rachel, one Charles Dickinson was sent to his grave and Jackson was left with a bullet in his chest that would stay there, next to his heart, for the rest of his life.

The old talk—Rachel, don't you know, became a legally divorced woman only after marrying Jackson—surfaced again in Jackson's campaign for president in 1828, and it was with difficulty that Jackson restrained his impulse toward added duels in defense of Rachel's honor.

This was the first nearly popular presidential election—the first in which the voters chose the electors rather than the state legislatures choosing the electors. And the political organization that Jackson built for the election was the beginning, the foundation, of today's Democratic Party.

Rachel, though, was terrified at thoughts of herself as first lady of the land, as hostess of the Jackson White House. "For Mr. Jackson's sake I am glad," she told one well-wisher after his election. "For my own part I never wished it."

In addition, she told a visiting young Virginian, Henry Wise, "I assure you I had rather be a doorkeeper in the house of God than to live in that palace in Washington."

As events turned out, those were prophetic words.

During the election she had held up under the occasional slander, but soon after, "Friends noted a relinquishment of courage, a lapse into melancholy," wrote Jackson biographer Marquis James. Nearly forty years after her marriage to Old Hickory, the hero of New Orleans and Horseshoe Bend, the onetime frontier beauty was, sad to say, grown obese. With her breath coming in a wheeze, she obviously was not well. In November 1828, a local doctor began bleeding her.

All the while, and to her consternation, plans were being laid for Jackson's triumphal trip early in 1829 to Washington and the White House.

There was thought of Rachel staying home, at the couple's beloved Hermitage outside of Nashville, Tennessee, but advisers said it would be best to avoid any seeming retreat from lingering gossip and for both to take their rightful place in the White House.

And so unfurled the banners of preparation—suggestions of travel in a coach drawn by six white horses, of grand farewells, of balls and banquets. Rachel was overwhelmed, engulfed. That is when she told young Wise, recently married into a Nashville family, of her heavenly preference to "that palace" in Washington.

Friends rallied to help the president-elect's wife prepare herself. "The poor woman submitted to be borne off to Nashville to begin the process of measuring and fitting her unstylish form to attire deemed suitable for the first lady of the land," added James in his 1937 biography *Andrew Jackson: Portrait of a President.*

Something terrible happened on the trip into town. By some accounts she overheard a snatch of conversation "lamenting the impossibility of rendering presentable to official society this illiterate country woman." By another account, she ran into more of the old slander about herself and Jackson. Whatever the truth, her friends found her "'crouching in a corner,' terror-stricken and hysterical."

A few days later, she was treated at the Hermitage for muscle spasms of the chest and left shoulder and "irregular action of the heart." Three quick bleedings seemed to help, and Rachel Jackson fell asleep with her pain gone.

For the next three days, with husband Andrew Jackson nearly always by her side, she seemed to be recovering, but on Sunday evening, December 22, "she sat [in a chair before the fire] too long and was put to bed with a cold and slight symptoms of pleurisy," recalled biographer James.

Her doctors brought on a sweat with hot drinks, persuaded Jackson to find sleep for himself, and all retired . . . except for the patient. "Twice she had her maid Hannah help her to the chair by the fire and fill a pipe with tobacco." She sat in her nightdress, and shortly before 10 P.M. was heard to say once more, "I had rather be a doorkeeper in the house of God than to live in that palace." It was the last time she would say it, for twenty minutes later, she cried out, "I am fainting," then collapsed in the maid's arms.

By the time Jackson and others responded to Hannah's screams, the mistress of The Hermitage—but never of the White House—was gone.

Lincoln's Farewell to Herndon

LINCOLN'S LEAVETAKING FOR WASHINGTON WAS done in an atmosphere of foreboding. Much like Christ approaching the Last Supper, Lincoln met with various of his own disciples, and there was much thought—much talk even—of death. This was in the days immediately before boarding the train out of Springfield, Illinois, for the fateful trip east to the White House.

He went, in the first week of February 1861, to visit his stepmother, Sarah Bush Johnston Lincoln, at her homestead in Coles County, Illinois. "Here, in the little country village, he met also the surviving members of the Hanks [his mother's] and Johnston [his step-mother's] families," wrote Lincoln's law partner William Herndon. "He visited the grave of his father, old Thomas Lincoln, which had been unmarked and neglected for almost a decade, and left directions that a suitable stone should be placed there to mark the spot."

The president-elect next stopped at nearby Charleston, official seat of Coles County and site of the fourth Lincoln-Douglas debate. Staying overnight, he spoke in the "public hall," recalling "boyhood exploits." Present were many who knew him in earlier years, even "as the stalwart young ox-driver when his father's family drove into Illinois from southern Indiana [in 1830]." One fellow recounted details of the wrestling match in which a very young Lincoln, fresh from flatboating on the Mississippi with a load of hogs, bested a local champ named Daniel Needham. Also in Charleston, a man showed up with a horse that young lawyer Lincoln had recovered for him in a civil suit.

They all had some sentimental tale to tell, said Herndon, but Lincoln's farewell to his stepmother was especially moving. "The parting, when the good old woman, with tears streaming down her cheeks, gave him a mother's benediction, expressing the fear that his life might be taken by his enemies, will never be forgotten by those who witnessed it."

As for Lincoln, "deeply impressed by this farewell scene . . . [he] reluctantly withdrew from the circle of warm friends who crowded around him, and, filled with gloomy forebodings of the future, returned to Springfield."

But now came a steady stream of old friends and well-wishers there, too. Some came from New Salem, Illinois, where Lincoln had spent six years as a store clerk, town postmaster, county surveyor, and toward the end, student of law. These good citizens, too, had favorite Lincolnesque stories to recall. Hannah Armstrong, whose son was the "Duff" Armstrong whom Lincoln successfully defended in a famous murder trial, came to say goodbye and was "filled with a presentiment that she would never see him alive again."

He tried to laugh off her fears, saying, "Hannah, if they do kill me, I shall never die again."

Strange-sounding talk today, but in the early 1860s the country was on the brink of civil war. Lincoln's election was controversial and often resented—more than talk, there were real plots of assassination brewing even before he took his oath of office.

Preparing to leave Springfield, he of course had to settle affairs with his law partner of many years, Herndon. Lincoln held off this poignant moment until his last day in Springfield.

He appeared in the afternoon, and they went over the books and a few pending affairs of mutual interest, then Lincoln plopped down on an old sofa against one wall and stared for some time at the ceiling. Neither man spoke.

Finally, Lincoln did break the silence. "Billy, how long have we been together?"

"Over sixteen years."

"We've never had a cross word during all that time, have we?"

"No indeed, we have not!"

They talked on—actually, it was Lincoln who rambled on companionably. "He then recalled some incidents of his early practice and took great pleasure in delineating the ludicrous features of many a lawsuit on the circuit."

Lincoln also mentioned that others had tried to take Herndon's place as his partner—"weak creatures," added Herndon in his famous biography of Lincoln, "who, to use his own language, 'hoped to secure a law practice by hanging to his coat-tail.'"

Others have written that Lincoln on this same occasion made oblique reference to Herndon's reputed love of "the bottle," but did not chastise his longtime partner. Others, in fact, have accused Herndon of sometimes embellishing his facts a bit, too. For his part, Herndon strikes a wonderful, sentimental scene and even adds, "I never saw him in a more cheerful mood."

But only for the moment. Lincoln soon gathered his papers and books and prepared to leave. First, though, "he made the strange request that the sign-board which swung on its rusty hinges at the foot of the stairway should remain." It should stay "undisturbed," said Lincoln. He then lowered his voice. "Give our clients to understand that the election of a President makes no change in the firm of Lincoln and Herndon. If I live, I'm coming right back some time, and then we'll go right on practicing law as if nothing had ever happened."

After a last look at their offices, Lincoln went into the outside hall, followed by Herndon. They went downstairs. The mood was somber. "He said the sorrow of parting from his old associates was deeper than most persons would imagine, but it was more marked in his case because of the feeling which had become irrepressible that he would never return alive."

Herndon tried to discount such wild thoughts and cheer him up, while others on the street outside frequently interrupted to say their own farewells to the remarkable local citizen going to Washington as president.

Finally Lincoln broke away. He and Herndon shook hands warmly ..."and with a fervent 'Good-bye' he disappeared down the street, and never came back to the office again."

Auspicious Change

UPON THE ARRIVAL OF TEDDY Roosevelt, his wife, Edith, and their six children in 1901, the White House entered an uncommonly tumultuous era, with teenager Alice, oldest of his children and born of an earlier marriage, the ringleader.

The tone may have been set when she arrived with her blue macaw called Eli Yale and famous for a mean peck "that could crack a whiskey glass," plus her green snake called Emily Spinach.

The menagerie did not stop there. When young Quentin Roosevelt was ill one time, his brothers and sisters smuggled his pony Algonquin to his upstairs room by elevator. "This cheered up the ailing brother immensely but caused consternation among members of the White House staff," wrote Alice's biographer Howard Teichman many years later.

The Roosevelt clan would always be remembered by the staff for other activities, too—such as roller-skating, bicycling, and even stilt-walking throughout the large home at 1600 Pennsylvania Avenue.

And not only staff memories! Alice once persuaded her siblings to "attend" various state dinners—not in any ordinary and visible way, but rather by crawling along under the tables "pinching the knees of friends and begging them for food." Thus there were memories for world leaders to keep, too.

Perhaps there was method to Alice's assignment to a large bedroom and dressing room right across the hall from her parents' bedroom suite! More seriously, Teddy Roosevelt, as one parental dictum, told his daughter that she must delve into a new book every night before bedtime and learn something from it, no matter how late the hour, then tell him the *something* at breakfast the next morning. And indeed she always was well informed.

In the meantime, the Teddy Roosevelt occupancy made history even for so famous an edifice as the presidential home in Washington, D.C. Moving in immediately after the abruptly widowed Mrs. William McKinley's departure, the Roosevelts found drabness the order of the day—an exterior of buff or gray and interior furnishings that Alice called " Late Grant and Early Pullman."

Setting to work with energy and zeal, the Roosevelts discarded potted palms, faded silk screens, old stained-glass windows, and brought in light. They painted and wallpapered. They had a master sculptor from Sicily carve the marble capitals of the outside pillars; they had the famous American architect Stanford White work his magic with the front of the stately building. They added the West Wing, now so well known for its Oval Office, which in point of fact was created by Teddy's successor, William Howard Taft.

Most famously of all, Teddy ordered the outside walls painted white once more. His presidential stationery was given the new heading. And so it *officially* has been ever since—the White House!

Ike's First Presidential Crisis

INAUGURATION DAY FOR DWIGHT D. EISENHOWER—first Republican to come along in a long, long time, what with FDR's unprecedented four election victories and Harry Truman's unexpected election in

1948—was, naturally, a happy day. But a long day for Ike, replete with one minor crisis.

His more public events of January 20, 1953, had begun with a church service at 9:30 A.M., at the National Presbyterian Church. Twenty minutes there. Then came the uncomfortable ride to the Capitol with Harry Truman, replete with their exchange of sharp words.

Eisenhower took his oath of office at 12:32 P.M., it is recorded for posterity. He shook hands with the outgoing Truman and then crossed the platform overlooking the crowds in the east plaza of the Capitol to kiss Mamie Eisenhower, the new first lady. Let it be known that her eyes were full of tears. Perhaps his were, too.

The inaugural parade that soon followed would have stretched for ten miles if all units had lined up at once and stood still for posterity's measurements. In any case, it took more than five hours to pass by the Eisenhower reviewing stand.

Mamie was an appreciative audience, alternately waving, smiling, clapping, blowing kisses, even, it is said, giggling. She, late in the cold afternoon, accepted the offer by the elderly man next to her to share his lap robe for warmth. He was the last Republican to have occupied the White House before Ike . . . before Democrats FDR and Truman, for that matter. He had been ousted way back in 1932. He was Herbert Hoover, by now, in 1953, seventy-eight years in age.

All this time, Ike himself had been standing to review his parade. Salutes every time a new unit passed by flourishing the proud colors. Many units, many salutes, for the general-turned-president.

Then, parade finally over, the new first couple was driven to the White House. They entered their new quarters at an exact moment, 7:02 P.M., the day's unnerving crisis sneaking up to them by now.

For the next three hours, Mamie was busy in their new home preparing for the evening's two inaugural balls. She fully intended to put her best foot forward, and in Ike's eyes, she surely did. "By golly, Mamie," he said when she presented herself to him, "you're so beautiful!"

For Mamie's all-important inaugural appearance that evening, designer Nettie Rosenstein had created a Renoir-pink, rhinestone-studded gown of peau de sole, with an evening bag of matching pink silk adorned with rhinestones, pearls, and beads within a silver frame. As further reported in *Ike and Mamie: The Story of the General and His Lady* by Lester and Irene David, "Beneath the gown's bouffant skirt were taffeta and crinoline petticoats; on her arms, almost to the shoulder, were silk gloves; on her feet, fabric shoes. Taffeta petticoats, gloves, shoes—all were of the pink silk."

Ike now was ready to get dressed, too. It was getting late, time to move on, even after such a long, demanding, exciting, wearing day. And so, finding his way about the unfamiliar quarters they had moved into, he began poking and prying about . . . searching, actually. But he couldn't find the essential item he needed.

"Hey, Mamie," came the plea, "where the hell is my monkey suit?" But no one knew. Neither Mamie nor his valet. "They searched the closets and the still unpacked bags without success while the new president of the United States sat on the bed in his shorts and growled that the first crisis of his administration had already occurred," said the Davids in their book.

The answer to the puzzle finally was supplied by Mamie, her guess right on the mark. His white tie and tails must still be on the train they had taken the day before to reach Washington. And sure enough, when Ike's valet and a Secret Service man "raced" to the railroad station and looked through the Eisenhower car of the day before, there was one errant suitcase awaiting its rightful owner. And it did contain the missing "monkey suit."

And so . . . one crisis averted!

Ike's next crisis was even more minor and easily solved. It came the next day. Early.

He rose at 7 o'clock despite the late night and the long hours of the day before and took the small White House elevator down from the second-floor family quarters to the ground floor. There he encountered Secret Service agent Rufus Youngblood. Ike was itching to get started in his new job as president.

Only one minor problem.

"Would you show me where my office is?" he had to ask. "I want to get an early start."

Coolidge's Favorite Prank

THE SWEARING IN OF CALVIN Coolidge, like that of Harry Truman and of Lyndon B. Johnson, was sudden, without pomp, and totally lacking in advance planning. For hours, in fact, Vice President Coolidge didn't even know his president and fellow Republican, Warren G. Harding, was dead.

Harding, under circumstances that some thought suspicious, died suddenly while traveling on the West Coast. In the East, Calvin and Grace Coolidge were visiting his father's humble farmhouse in Vermont—no telephone, no electricity. Coolidge was notified of his new status at 2:47 A.M. on August 3, 1923. The nearest newspaper reporters then had to travel twenty miles to serve up this national story.

Wasting no time, the Coolidge family quickly gathered—in nightshirts—around a table lighted by a kerosene lamp and bearing the family Bible. As a notary public, Calvin's father legally could swear in his son as president, which he did.

The younger Coolidge then faced the press for the first time as president of the United States. His reaction to the night's events? "I think I can swing it," said the famously taciturn Coolidge.

The Coolidges moved into the White House after a stay at the Willard Hotel in Washington allowing the widowed Mrs. Harding time to pack up and leave. The new man was not quite as dour and reticent as he often is made out to be. While his two teenaged sons, Calvin Jr. and John, gave the White House a breezy sense of youth once again, Coolidge himself was not above an occasional prank.

"He would press all the buttons on his desk and then hide behind a door in his office. Secretaries, military and naval aides, assistants of all sorts, Secret Service men with drawn revolvers would rush in from all directions. Out from behind the door would step the President." So reported Howard Teichman in his biography of Alice Roosevelt Longworth, *Alice*.

Like many presidential families before and after, the new White

He could be taciturn, famously so, and sober in mein ... but Calvin Coolidge also loved his pranks. He favored a good afternoon nap, pajamas and all, as well. (National Photo Company Collection, American Memory Collections, Library of Congress)

House occupants brought a menagerie with them. In this case, the dogs and cats wore collars with White House name tags; a raccoon named Rebecca lived in a special cage; and a flock of chickens was kept in a coop near the august presidential mansion. It was Coolidge's order that only his own chickens would be served at his dinner table. "His command was carried out to the letter, but the Coolidge chickens had a curious minty taste. Investigation showed the chicken coop stood atop an old mint bed planted by Alice's father [Teddy Roosevelt]," wrote Teichman. "The coop was moved immediately."

Additional note: Markus Ring, consultant in dental technology from North Bethesda, Maryland, sheds additional light on Calvin Coolidge's ascension to the presidency. Ring has informed the author that his own brother, the late Gustave Ring, was a Western Union telegraph operator at that time, and he "handled" five telegrams setting the stage for the rustic Coolidge swearing-in.

According to Markus Ring, Coolidge first was notified of Warren G. Harding's death and the passing of the presidential baton "by a

Western Union telegram, sent from Washington, then by messenger in an auto to the Coolidge home."

By this account, the secretary of state instructed Coolidge to take his new oath of office. But then came an exchange of four more telegrams:

Coolidge to Chief Justice (William Howard) Taft: Can my
    father, a Notary, administer the oath?
Taft to Coolidge: Yes.
Coolidge to Taft: What is the exact oath?
Taft to Coolidge: The full oath.

First in Line

FOR HIS FIRST INAUGURATION AS the nation's first president, the Virginian George Washington wore brown broadcloth, a suit that was woven in Hartford, Connecticut, and he had buttons emblazoned with an eagle, its wings spread. He wore his very best white stockings of silk. Silver buckles adorned his shoes. As befitted a general to be hailed even by Napoleon, there also was a dress sword in a scabbard of steel.

Soon after his breakfast on that April 30, the city's church bells began to ring—at first cheerfully, but soon more somberly, it has been observed, since their purpose was a call to prayer.

Naturally, there were the excited crowds. The pomp and ceremony. The official escorts. And the inaugural speech—as the very first, it was likely to be a trend-setter.

The swearing in and speechifying would be at the place where Congress met, true, but this place, in 1789, was not the scene in Washington, D.C., that we know so well today. This inauguration took place in the Federal Hall overlooking Broad and Wall Streets in New York City, since there was no federal city of Washington as yet—and for the official presidential residence following the inaugural festivities, no White House as yet, either.

Although he never would take up residence in the White House himself, George Washington certainly put his own stamp upon the future President's House as an influential adviser on its design, site selection, and construction. Sadly, he died, late in 1799, barely a year before John Adams moved in as the executive mansion's first official resident.

Lincoln Escapes a Trap

DESPERATE, BIZARRE—BUT NO MORE so than shooting a man in a crowded theater. This plot, too, was aimed at that most controversial of American presidents, Abraham Lincoln. Just elected, he had to go to Washington to take his "seat," did he not? Traveling east from his home state of Illinois, the country lawyer-turned-president was committed to a number of speaking engagements.

In the late winter of 1861, the country was in turmoil over the slavery-secession issue. Civil War loomed, and the rail route from Pennsylvania to Washington would take Lincoln straight through a hotbed town of Southern sympathy, Baltimore.

Was Lincoln himself concerned? Was there real danger? In Philadelphia, discussing the Jeffersonian commitment to equality in the Declaration of Independence, Lincoln interrupted his line of thought to offer this: "I was about to say I would rather be assassinated on the spot than surrender it [the equality provision]."

He made the remark at Independence Hall the morning of February 22, 1861, assassination obviously and unavoidably on his mind. Just the night before, he had refused entreaties to head for Washington right away, rather than to maintain his planned speaking engagements. Lincoln said no, he would appear both in Philadelphia and before the Pennsylvania legislature in Harrisburg prior to resuming his rambling trip.

He had been en route to Washington for days and days, actually, with well-advertised stops at a train conductor's litany of towns—Indianapolis, Cincinnati, Columbus, Steubenville, Pittsburgh, Cleveland, Buffalo, Albany, New York City. He had been traveling since his poignant farewell to his hometown of Springfield, Illinois, on February 11. After telling his neighbors he was leaving them "for how long I know not," Lincoln, his trademark beard only recently grown, stood in the rear door of the rear car as his train gathered head for the trip east. It was "his last view of Springfield," noted his law partner and biographer William Herndon. "The journey had been as well advertised as it had been carefully planned, and therefore, at every town along the route, and at every stop, great crowds were gathered to catch a glimpse of the President-elect," said Herndon also.

But that was in the North, and in the South Lincoln was a hated man. In the South, delegates from the Secessionist states already had met in Montgomery, Alabama, to form a provisional Confederate States of America. In the meantime, officials of the Philadelphia, Wilmington and Baltimore Railroad had been hearing rumors of sabotage and other threats to their railroad by Southern sympathizers hoping to cut off Washington, the Federal capital, from the North. The railroad hired detective Allan Pinkerton to investigate; Pinkerton and his operatives soon focused upon Baltimore, where even the police chief was known as a Rebel at heart.

In short order, posing as a broker—and Rebel sympathizer—from Charleston, South Carolina, Pinkerton visited Baltimore in person. He and his aides heard a Baltimore man drunkenly reveal the outlines of an advanced assassination plot. Lincoln would arrive by one train at the city's Calvert Street station. Then, as carriages took his party across town to the Baltimore and Ohio station for the train to Washington, the killers would strike. Said this source, "I am ready to do the deed and then will proudly announce my name and say, 'Gentlemen, arrest me. I am the man!'"

And there was even more evidence. As Lincoln worked his way toward Washington, thirty conspirators met in Baltimore the night of February 20. They were told to pull slips of paper from a hat in a dark room. Whoever emerged with the red ballot was the man to do the job, and no one else would ever know which one he was. Ominously for Lincoln, the leaders of this group had placed eight red ballots in the hat, rather than one. Since all thirty had taken an oath to carry out the killing, that would mean eight sworn killers on Lincoln's trail, rather than just one.

Still other details being reported to the Lincoln party pointed to the Havre de Grace ferry carrying the Lincoln train across the

Susquehanna River as an obvious place for an outright attack.

Informed of the growing conspiratorial atmosphere, Lincoln nonetheless insisted upon going through with his plans for February 22. Thus he made his appearance at Independence Hall in the morning, then journeyed to the state capital of Harrisburg for visits with both branches of the legislature and dinner with the governor of Pennsylvania, Andrew Curtin.

Lincoln was stubborn . . . but he wasn't foolhardy. He would go through with the Philadelphia and Harrisburg schedules, he told his lifetime friend and adviser Norman B. Judd, but, "After this, if you, Judd, think there is positive danger in my attempting to go through Baltimore openly according to the published program, I will place myself in your hands."

And so it was that instead of spending the night of February 22 at the Jones House hotel in Harrisburg, Lincoln was spirited out of town in a single-car train. He was in the very able company of Ward H. Lamon, a burly, heavily armed Virginia-born lawyer who was a close friend from the Illinois courts. Judd, in the meantime, had arranged to intercept all telegraph and railroad wires leading out of Harrisburg.

The secret passage by rail route first took Lincoln back to Philadelphia, where he boarded a sleeper on the regular Washington-bound express, but in disguise. Joined by Pinkerton and his operatives, Lincoln boarded the rear of the sleeping car posing as a sick man. He and his companions then rode through the rest of the night in three adjoining rooms, with Lincoln, Lamon, and Pinkerton seated together in the center one. Delays forced the train to lay over in Baltimore for a tense hour, but they passed through with no change in trains. Before that, the ferry crossing-point had been successfully negotiated. Pinkerton men were everywhere on the route south, flashing signal lanterns to show that all was in order immediately ahead.

Lincoln's enemies apparently never did guess that he was on the night train. He arrived in Washington at 6:30 A.M., February 23, hours ahead of the publicly announced schedule. And all the while, it seems, Lincoln had been regaling his tense companions with typically Lincolnesque homespun stories. Pinkerton later said, "I could not then, nor have I since been able to understand how anyone in like circumstances could have exhibited such composure."

History in time would reveal Baltimore as the place where

local hotheads did attack Union soldiers passing through town in April of 1861, killing several, and as the place where hostile men concocted and set in motion still another plot that indeed would result in Lincoln's assassination in a crowded theater just four years later.

In the meantime, though, at this journey's end in 1861, the famously imperturbable Lincoln rose from his sleeper-car seat and told his worn, somewhat frayed companions of the long night, "Well, boys, thank God this prayer-meeting is over." Two weeks later, Abraham Lincoln was inaugurated as president of the United States.

Transition in Dallas

BACK AT LOVE FIELD, AFTER the motorcade left for downtown Dallas, it had been a quiet, relaxed period for the crew and personnel of *Air Force One*. Some had gone into the airport terminal for lunch. Two press office secretaries were still on board the big jet making copies of press releases for use at a fundraising dinner that night in Austin. Pilot James Swindal, a U.S. Air Force colonel in rank, also had stayed aboard to make his preparations for the afternoon flight to the Texas capital.

In the Kennedys' bedroom suite, valet George Thomas was laying out a clean shirt and lightweight suit for JFK to wear at the Austin affair that evening.

Swindal had ordered a roast beef sandwich from the airplane galley, and while it wasn't really his job to monitor the radio traffic marking the motorcade's progress toward the Dallas Trade Mart, he was aware of the background chit-chat carried on the radio link between the airplane's communications center and the motorcade. Flowers, they were being showered with lots of flowers, he couldn't help but hear.

Suddenly, at 12:30 P.M., the routine tones changed. A shout caught his attention, quickly followed by two more. One cry definitely had been the voice of Roy Kellerman, the ranking Secret

Service agent in JFK's limousine. The radio next crackled with a terse order:*"Dagger* cover *Volunteer!"*

Then came an overlapping array of shouts impossible to sort out, followed by sudden silence.

What could it all mean? *Volunteer* was code for Vice President Lyndon B. Johnson, also in the motorcade. As a Texas native and political figure of note, Johnson was accompanying Kennedy on a joint swing through Texas, but as only the "Veep," traveling in *Air Force Two.*

As Colonel Swindal also knew, *Dagger* was Rufus Youngblood, LBJ's chief Secret Service protector in the motorcade. Did it all mean LBJ was in trouble?

Before Swindal could learn much more, a telephone call came through from Parkland Memorial Hospital. Brigadier General Godfrey McHugh, Kennedy's Air Force aide, ordered *Air Force One* refueled immediately. He also said to file a flight plan for a fast return to Washington. The Austin stop was out. No further explanation for the moment.

Swindal realized the change in plans for *Air Force One* meant that JFK, not LBJ, was the focal figure in whatever had gone wrong. Thoroughly alarmed by now, Swindal thought to check the television set in JFK's stateroom for a news outlet. There, he and others who had remained on the plane wouldn't have far to look. But Swindal in the meantime also alerted the flight engineer, USAF Chief Master Sergeant Joe Chappell, to have the big jet refueled, pronto. "Get ready to go!" he told the startled Chappell, who was out on the tarmac shooting the breeze with Douglas Moody, pilot for the Pan American jet chartered by the press for the presidential trip to Texas.

Seconds later, a stunned Colonel Swindal was back at the door to *Air Force One* with the latest TV bulletin on the mysterious goings on in Dallas. "Hey, you guys! I just heard it—the president's been shot!"

The dread news now was all over the television. First, the flash from United Press International that three shots had been fired at the motorcade. Next, from CBS, word that President Kennedy might have been seriously wounded. According to the detailed scenario pieced together by Jerry van terHorst and USAF Colonel Ralph Albertazzie for their book *The Flying White House: The Story of Air Force One,* the professional personnel attached to the president's official airplane were just as disbelieving and shocked as the rest of the nation, if not more so.

The two secretaries were "sobbing wildly" and valet George Thomas, his eyes brimming with tears, "wandered back to the bedroom and methodically began putting away Kennedy's clothes."

A short distance away, the co-pilot, USAF Lieutenant Colonel Lewis "Swede" Hanson, heard the news while visiting his wife's ailing mother. In minutes, he was rushing back to the airfield to rejoin Swindal and their crew.

"In the airport restaurant, others of the crew sensed a restlessness in the room, a strange and growing apprehension," added the terHorst-Albertazzie account. The waitresses and some of the diners seemed confused and concerned. Before the crew members could investigate, they heard the public address system blurt out orders for the personnel of both *Air Force One* and *Air Force Two* to report to their aircraft right away.

The grim facts no longer were seeping into the national consciousness, they were flooding, cascading. At 1:23 P.M. local time came the news that JFK had been given the last rites of the Catholic Church. At 1:35 came the news that JFK was dead.

Actually, President John F. Kennedy had been pronounced dead more than half an hour earlier. So why the delay at Parkland Memorial Hospital in announcing the final outcome? The fact is, the Secret Service agents on the scene were not alone in fearing a possible conspiracy that might call for an assassination attempt against Vice President Johnson as well. While the doctors tried to cope with JFK's massive gunshot wounds, the Secret Service kept LBJ and his wife, Lady Bird, out of sight in a guarded cubicle at the hospital. But it was LBJ himself, now president of the United States, who ordered the thirty-five-minute delay in announcing Kennedy's death—"to give himself time to get out to the plane."

Out at Love Field, meanwhile, President Kennedy's bloodied limousine—"now with its bulletproof top securely in place"—reappeared on the tarmac. It would be flown back to Washington aboard an Air Force C-130 cargo plane. "Furious Secret Service agents milled around the grim reminder of their failure to save the President, shouting that the back seat was too horrible to look at, hurling imprecations at the unknown assassin."

Inside *Air Force One,* the temperature was heating up fast. Told to prepare for fast departure, Swindal had ordered the plug pulled on the ground air-conditioning unit outside the plane.

Then, just before word of Kennedy's death was flashed around the world, here came a "motorcade" consisting of two unmarked police cars with motorcycle-police escorts. Lyndon Baines Johnson was back at Love Field, safe and sound . . . but of course shaken by the day's events.

The two cars and their escorts raced across the tarmac . . . not for LBJ's *Air Force Two,* but for *Air Force One,* the president's plane.

Agent Youngblood ("*Dagger* cover *Volunteer!*") was "physically shielding" Johnson in the lead car, reported terHorst and Albertazzie. As they also wrote, the Secret Service agent would always remember one of the most welcome sights he had ever seen—"the big gleaming blue-and-white jet, with UNITED STATES OF AMERICA painted along the fuselage above the long row of windows and the number 26000 tracing the tail rudder."

In minutes, after a welcoming salute from pilot Swindal, Johnson, Lady Bird, and their entourage of additional agents and Texas congressmen were safely aboard the big jet. Youngblood quickly ordered the window shades drawn—any snipers lurking nearby in hopes of shooting the new president at least wouldn't be able to see where he was aboard the airplane.

Not yet sworn in, President Johnson wasted no time taking charge, it seems. Passing the Kennedys' bedroom, he told Youngblood to keep it "strictly for the use of Mrs. Kennedy."

From the rear of the plane, where he had entered, he moved on forward, to the now-crowded president's stateroom and office—which he reached close to the moment that President Kennedy's death was announced on television. "As Johnson entered the stateroom, everyone stood up and fell silent, even his own staffers and longtime Texas friends," reported terHorst and Albertazzie. Suddenly, he no longer was "Lyndon," but "Mr. President," the authors noted.

Johnson himself later said, "It was at that moment that I realized nothing would ever be the same again. A wall—high, forbidding, historic—separated us now, a wall derived from the Office of the Presidency of the United States."

But . . . now what? It still was a moment of shock, grief, suspicion, and even torn loyalties for all concerned.

Before leaving the hospital, Johnson later said, he told Kennedy aide Kenneth O'Donnell that "we would board the plane and wait until Mrs. Kennedy and the President's body were brought aboard."

For flight engineer Chappell, that meant making fast arrangements aboard *Air Force One* to find an appropriate place for the slain President's nine-hundred-pound casket. It wouldn't do to place it in the cargo hold, he realized. He, Swindal, Hanson, and flight steward Joe Ayres hurriedly removed four seats from the passenger compartment to make room for the big coffin, finishing up, Chappell later said, "just moments before the hearse arrived."

Added the terHorst-Albertazzie account: "With sheer grit, the ponderous bronze casket was muscled up the narrow stairs into the tail compartment and pushed and tugged into its resting place, forward of the doorway and opposite the rear galley. It was an exhausting task."

Only now did various persons in the JFK entourage discover that LBJ was aboard "their" airplane . . . except that it wasn't the Kennedy presidential aircraft anymore, a bitter but perfectly logical and reasonable fact that some emotion-wracked JFK men found difficult to accept. As the *Flying White House* authors explained, "The fact is that Johnson and his Secret Service men never considered using any other aircraft once Kennedy was dead." It wouldn't have made good sense for LBJ to fly back to Washington in *Air Force Two* while *Air Force One* returned to the nation's capital simply as an airborne hearse. Only the year before, in 1962, *Air Force One*, a big Boeing 707 Intercontinental, had taken over from *Air Force Two* as the latest, best-equipped presidential jet, "and it contained superior communications equipment for keeping a Chief Executive in touch with Washington and the rest of the world."

Thus, in a national emergency such as the Kennedy assassination in Dallas that November day in 1963, it would have been "inconceivable that the new president would use a backup plane."

As another decision LBJ made in those tumultuous moments at Dallas, it would be both seemly and wise to be sworn in as president, even if there was no constitutional requirement to take that step on the spot, right away.

It could be done, or at least the wheels could be set in motion, while they were awaiting the arrival of Jackie Kennedy and her husband's body, Johnson apparently decided. "Johnson was President now, and he knew it, but he plainly did not believe he looked that way in the eyes of the world, least of all in the eyes of those who revered John Kennedy."

Technically unneeded, Johnson's decision nonetheless was "psychologically astute." As is well known, he indeed was sworn in aboard *Air Force One* at 2:28 P.M. by federal district judge Sarah T.

Hughes. The timing was such that the distraught Jackie had to wait about twenty uncomfortable minutes in the hot airplane for the ceremony to take place. She and others in the Kennedy party apparently were anxious and irritated over the delay in taking off because they didn't know about LBJ's swearing-in plan. While the Johnsons had sought to console Jackie upon her arrival with the casket, LBJ "had neglected to inform the young widow and her dead husband's chief aides of the ceremony about to take place in the presidential stateroom in the middle of the plane."

With the mix-ups gradually sorted out, Jackie was present for the oath-taking, along with nine others from the JFK entourage—all told, twenty-seven persons were stuffed into the stateroom for the somber ceremony, which consumed just twenty-eight seconds once it was started.

Then it was take-off time, and *Air Force One* lifted off the ground

Is there an American alive even today who has never seen White House photographer Cecil Stoughton's historic photo of Lyndon B. Johnson's swearing-in as president aboard Air Force One *in Dallas, Texas, on November 22, 1963? (LBJ Library Photo by Cecil Stoughton)*

at Love Field at 2:47 P.M. for the flight of two hours and twelve minutes to Andrews Air Force Base outside Washington. On the flight back the parties faithful to each of the two presidents aboard stayed with their own man for the most part—the Johnson group in the stateroom, and "the Kennedy people clustered protectively around the widow and the bronze box in the tail compartment."

Some of the feelings involved were now made evident. Jackie sent word to the two pool reporters on the plane that "she had spent the entire flight keeping vigil over her husband's body," wrote terHorst and Albertazzie. "She felt it was important that the world know she was at *his* side, not sitting with the Johnsons." One of the Kennedy aides personally approached pool reporter Charles Roberts of *Newsweek* and told him roughly the same thing. The JFK staff was sitting in the rear with Mrs. Kennedy, "not up here with them [the Johnsons]."

President Johnson in the meantime, making calls, checking on national security posts, and also touching base with the pool reporters, spent time with his aides composing his first remarks to the nation as president, to be uttered when they arrived at Andrews. In the short statement, he said, "We have suffered a loss that cannot be weighed." Calling the Kennedy assassination a "deep personal tragedy" for himself, he also said: "I know the world shares the sorrow that Mrs. Kennedy and her family bear. I will do my best. That is all I can do. I ask for your help—and God's."

As *Air Force One* flew down the Potomac River corridor and passed National Airport (now called Reagan National) on approach to nearby Andrews, flight engineer Chappell noticed something odd. It was going on six o'clock local time, "rush hour" at National, and yet where was all the usual air traffic? In an instant, he realized "pilots of incoming craft in the area were voluntarily holding their patterns, waiting until *Air Force One* was on the ground." This was no ordinary *Air Force One* flight sharing their air space. In recognition of that fact, quite obviously, they were holding off in salute to the slain JFK.

More muted but additional fact: due to the same tragic circumstances that made an airborne hearse of *Air Force One,* the big and majestic jet also was bringing Washington and the nation a brand-new president.

Additional note: The publicly released photograph of the LBJ oath-taking ceremony aboard *Air Force One* at Love Field was taken by White House photographer Cecil Stoughton, as one of sixteen shots he made in all. He had to climb on a sofa and ask everyone to move back in order to record the historical tableau involving so many people in such a small space as the stateroom. In fact, the photo that was released prompted some to think that none of JFK's staff aides were present, even though Jackie is clearly seen in the photo. The fact is, said terHorst and Albertazzie in their book, the other pictures show six male Kennedy aides in the background. Anyone who later said the Kennedy men refused to attend the ceremony was thus proven wrong.

Nor was LBJ able to swear on the traditional Bible for the occasion. Judge Hughes did not bring one, and a quick search of JFK's bedroom effects produced only a small leather-bound book still wrapped in cellophane—apparently a brand-new, never-opened Catholic missal. But that was the book used for the LBJ swearing-in ceremony . . . only to disappear from the historical record within minutes. Judge Hughes said she handed it to an "official-looking person" when she left the presidential jet, thinking he was a security man.

"Good to Be Home"

AWAKE AT 7:45 A.M., AND ahead a big day. . . Inauguration Day. Breakfast in the hotel suite with Pat. On to the prayer service in the State Department Auditorium. Next, on to the White House.

As our car slowly turned into the driveway, we could see the Johnsons waiting for us on the porch under the North Portico.

Into the Red Room for the now-traditional rolls and coffee, and light banter with Hubert Humphrey . . . who had lost the election. He responded in kind. *I remembered from 1961 how painful this ceremony could be for a man who had lost a close election, and I was touched by Humphrey's graceful show of good humor.*

And now on to the Capitol. Lyndon Johnson waved to the crowds. Conversation in the limo was friendly, lively.

At the swearing-in, two Milhous family Bibles. Pat held them. Inaugural speech focused upon a theme of peace. Then, back from the Capitol, on to the White House again, parade and all.

But not all was pleasant and cheerful.

When we were ready to begin the inaugural parade from the Capitol, back to the White House, I saw that the Secret Service had put the top on the presidential limousine. The agent in charge explained that there were several hundred demonstrators along the route and there already had been some skirmishes with the police and the other spectators.

For the first few blocks the cheering crowds were friendly. Around Twelfth Street I could see protest signs waving above a double line of police struggling to keep the crowd back. Suddenly a barrage of sticks, stones, beer cans, and what looked like fire-crackers began sailing through the air toward us. Some of them hit the side of the car and fell into the street. I could hear the pro-testers' shrill chant: "Ho, Ho, Ho Chi Minh, the NLF is going to win." A Vietcong flag was lifted, and there was a brief struggle as some in the crowd tried to tear it down. Seconds later we rounded the corner onto Fifteenth Street, and the atmosphere changed com-pletely. A loud cheer rose from the crowds on the sidewalks in front of the Washington Hotel and the Treasury Building. I was angered that a group of protesters carrying a Vietcong flag had made us captives inside the car. I told the driver to open the sun roof and let the other agents know that Pat and I were going to stand up so the people could see us.

That night, toward the end of the long day, four inaugural balls. Visits to each.

At 1:30 A.M., return, finally, to the White House. *Tricia and Julie found the refrigerator stocked with butter brickle ice cream and Dr. Pepper, left by the Johnson girls.*

Newly elected, newly installed President Richard Milhous Nixon sat down at the grand piano in the center hall of the second-floor family quarters. He played "Rustle of Spring" . . . *and a song I had composed for Pat before we were married.*

Then they all "gathered" on sofas in the West Hall. Pat sighed hap-pily. "It's good to be home."

Startling thought. Nixon would cite all the memorable

moments of his first Inauguration Day, January 20, 1969, in his book *The Memoirs of Richard Nixon,* published in 1978. And yes, an especially startling and memorable moment, that. "It's good to be home," Pat had said. *Everyone looked up. The White House was now our home.*

Public Housing

AT 7 A.M. THE DAY AFTER his swearing-in, wife Betty recorded in her diary, "The President of the United States, in baby-blue short pajamas, appears on his doorstep looking for the morning paper, then goes back inside to fix his orange juice and English muffin. Before leaving for his office, he signs autographs on his lawn."

It will be nine or ten days before they move into the White House. In the meantime, they'll continue to live in their suburban, just-us-folks house on Crown View Drive in Alexandria, Virginia, across the Potomac (and then some) from Washington.

Normal life will not resume, however. "At 10 A.M., an aide from the White House phones the wife of the President of the United States in

Betty Ford, wife of President Gerald Ford, photographed the year (1974) they moved into the White House. (American Memory Collections, Library of Congress)

Alexandria, and says, 'What are you going to do about the state dinner?'"

State dinner? Wha . . . who, when? Just a visiting king, it turns out, Jordan's King Hussein. And in six days.

Staggering thought . . . but then, hasn't it all been somewhat staggering? First the midterm appointment to vice president in October 1973, replacing a resigning Spiro T. Agnew. Then, before even moving into the official vice-presidential residence in town, Richard M. Nixon's sudden and unprecedented resignation from office on August 9, 1974. As a result, long-term congressman from Michigan (and House minority leader) Gerald Ford vaulted in just months from his suburban Alexandria neighborhood to the White House.

As new first lady Betty Ford recorded in her diary that tumultuous summer, it all happened so fast . . . and they wouldn't be moving into the White House until young David Eisenhower and his wife, Julie Nixon Eisenhower, could finish packing up the Nixon belongings. "They must have labored morning, noon and night," to get the job done in just ten days, wrote Betty Ford later, but they did it.

In the interim, she did play official hostess at the state dinner for King Hussein and his American-born queen. Betty Ford also toured the White House on August 13 and picked a second-floor bedroom for herself and Gerald Ford, while daughter Susan chose the third-floor bedroom, sitting room, and bath that David and Julie usually stayed in when visiting the Nixons. On moving day itself, August 19, President and Mrs. Ford flew to Chicago on *Air Force One* for his speech before the Veterans of Foreign Wars, then returned to Washington. "When we get to Andrews Air Force Base, a helicopter picks us up and takes us directly to the White House," adds her present-tense diary at this point. "It's the first time, and it's a very strange feeling."

In the meantime, there had been that fuss over Betty Ford's statement that "Jerry and I were not going to have separate bedrooms at the White House and that we were going to take our own bed with us." That caused "a good deal of whooping and hollering," she acknowledged in her later book, *The Times of My Life* (written with Chris Chase).

That night, the first night there, she and "Jerry" crawled into their controversial common bed "and Jerry looks around and laughs. 'It's the best public housing I've ever seen,' he says."

Born There

THEY WERE BORN IN THE White House itself.

- First of all, an unnamed slave child, during Thomas Jefferson's term, was born and died in January 1803, followed by slave babies in January 1805, December 1806, and October 1807, plus, in January 1806, a grandson to Jefferson, James Madison Randolph.

- Another presidential grandchild was Mary Louisa Adams, born December 2, 1828, to John Adams II, son of President John Quincy Adams (and grandson, himself, of a president, for whom he was named, John Adams).

- Soon after, during widower Andrew Jackson's term, four children were born in the White House to Jack and Emily Donelson, he a nephew of the late Rachel Jackson and secretary to the president; and she, his cousin Emily, a niece of Rachel and official hostess of the White House in her Aunt Rachel's place.

- Next, in March 1840, Martin Van Buren's daughter-in-law Angelica had a difficult delivery with infant daughter Rebecca. Angelica, a cousin to Dolley Madison, recovered, but the infant daughter died in the fall of 1840.

- During the Mexican War and the James K. Polk administration of the 1840s, presidential nephew and secretary James Knox Walker moved into the White House with his wife and two children; they soon had two more children while living at the White House.

- In the years after the Civil War, President U. S. Grant's son Fred and daughter-in-law Ida produced baby Julia in the White House.

- Soon after came an occasion never matched before or since, a president's child born in the White House! To Grover and Frances "Frank" Cleveland, little Esther was born September 9, 1893, and was so zealously protected from the public eye that no attempt was made to scotch the story that she was deformed.

• Another grandchild born in the White House was Francis B. Sayre Jr., born to Woodrow Wilson's daughter Jessie on January 17, 1915, half a year after her mother, Ellen Wilson, had died in the White House. Jessie Sayre at the time was living in New England, but she returned to the White House for her baby's birth. This was where she once had lived and where she was married to her attorney husband in an elaborate White House wedding in late 1913.

9/11

WIFE LAURA WAS IN THE Caucus Room of the Russell Senate Office Building, just off the U. S. Capitol itself. Parents George H. W. and Barbara ("Bar") were in Milwaukee, and their scheduled flight out of there was about to be grounded. Brother Marvin, close to the epicenter, was in a subway train beneath the streets of Manhattan itself.

Twin daughters Jenna and Barbara were safely stowed away at their two university haunts, Texas and Yale, respectively.

Dick Cheney was holding down the fort at the White House itself. Strictly routine.

And George W. himself was in a grade school classroom in Sarasota, Florida, indulging in elbow-rubbing with the public, albeit a very young public at the moment.

In New York moments before, the two towers of the World Trade Center in lower Manhattan had been teeming with their freshly arrived daily army of office workers, business executives, restaurant waiters, security personnel, elevator operators, and the others too numerous to categorize.

For thousands of them, however, terror and a horrifying death were approaching, literally on wings.

Approaching and then, exactly at 8:48 A.M., suddenly, unexpectedly, right there.

Just before going into the Florida classroom, President George W.

Bush, together with millions of Americans, learned that an aircraft of some type had flown straight into one of the giant towers in New York—the North Tower.

Tragic news, people were bound to have been hurt and even killed . . . but surely enough, an accident.

Not so. Just eighteen minutes later, with millions watching on television, the second fuel-heavy airliner plunged into the second tower—the South Tower.

At the Florida school, White House Chief of Staff Andrew Card approached in the classroom and whispered into the President's ear. "A second plane hit the second tower. America is under attack."

Up in Washington, as the news struck *everywhere,* Laura Bush had been about to testify before a Senate committee. "As she stood with Sen. Ted Kennedy, her face quickly turned ashen and tears welled up," Peter and Rochelle Schwiezer reported in their book *The Bushes: Portrait of a Dynasty.*

In Manhattan's warren of subway tunnels, Marvin Bush would be stuck underground until his subway car was evacuated. He then had to "walk across Manhattan through the soot and smoke of the towers in order to escape the catastrophe," wrote the Schweizers also.

But first, George W.'s reaction.

"A look of horror came across George W.'s face like none ever seen before."

His world, his nation, his presidency, had changed, right then. At first, however, he would carry on before the grade-schoolers sitting before him, carry on calmly, as if all was well. "Really good readers," he managed to say. "These must be *sixth*-graders."

Although he stayed "for the rest of the lesson," he escaped the classroom as quickly as possible. The world outside—and the nation—were waiting.

Up in Manhattan, a devil's cauldron of horror upon horror was spewing. "It kept getting worse," wrote N. R. Kleinfeld in the next morning's *New York Times.* "The horror arrived in episodic bursts of chilling disbelief, signified first by trembling floors, sharp eruptions, cracked windows. There was the actual and unfathomable realization of a gaping, flaming hole in first one of the tall towers, and then the same thing all over again in its twin. There was the merciless sight of bodies helplessly tumbling out, some of them in flames."

In Florida, the president received a briefing in a holding room at the school. Vice President Dick Cheney up in the White House reported he had seen the second airliner strike while watching the news on television. Wrote the Schweizers: "They briefly discussed how they would organize the national security team and how terrorists were likely behind the attack."

It was the attack of Tuesday, September 11, 2001, the very year that George W. had assumed the presidency of the United States.

Still at the school, he told aides Andrew Card, Karl Rove, and Ari Fleischer, "We're at war."

In the Russell Senate Office Building up in Washington, the Secret Service realized that Laura Bush might well be in danger. Senator Kennedy had sought to comfort her after they heard the shocking news, but the Secret Service interrupted and hustled the first lady away in an armored vehicle. Daughters Jenna and Barbara "were tracked down" at their respective college campuses and given added security.

The FAA was about to order all commercial aircraft grounded . . . but not before two more airliners were commandeered by Al Qaeda terrorists intent upon their own destructive suicide missions. At 9:40 A.M., one of those two aircraft plowed into the western wall of the Pentagon across the Potomac River from Washington itself, with more loss of life resulting. The fourth hijacked liner, its controls perhaps seized by its hostage passengers, crashed in the Pennsylvania countryside, killing all aboard.

In New York, the fate of the World Trade Center towers, their thousands of occupants and, by now, their hundreds of would-be rescuers had become even more stark. First one tower, then the other, collapsed.

"Finally," wrote Kleinfeld in the *Times,* "the mighty towers themselves were reduced to nothing. Dense plumes of smoke raced through the downtown avenues, coursing between the buildings, shaped like tornadoes on their sides."

People, running for their lives, didn't know which way to go. "Should they go north, south, east, west? Stay outside, go indoors? People hid beneath cars and each other."

From Emma E. Booker Elementary School in Sarasota, Florida, President Bush returned to the waiting *Air Force One,* at first thinking of flying back to Washington immediately, but the Secret Service, fearful of more attacks, ruled that out, the Schweizers wrote. Instead, *Air Force One* and its unique passenger went to Barksdale Air Force

Base in Louisiana. "It was here that President Bush made his first appearance to the American people on 9/11."

Unfortunately, it was not to be his best moment. Appearing in a conference room, "he stood and spoke with a halting voice, looking down at his notes and mispronouncing several words."

A still stunned American public might have wondered if its president "was up to the task."

He next winged west to Offutt Air Force Base outside Omaha, Nebraska.

He called his father, George H. W., on a cell phone and asked where he and "Bar" were. Told they were in Milwaukee, George W. asked, "What are you doing in Milwaukee?"

Wryly, his father, President Bush 41, said, "You grounded my plane."

Just three days later they would be together for a highly charged emotional moment—for all the Bushes and for the nation. This would be the solemn, widely televised national prayer service for the 9/11 victims and their families, held in the great nave just inside the soaring Gothic towers of the Episcopal Church's Washington National Cathedral, with President Bush the featured speaker.

If ever there was a moment for just the right mix of gravity, firmness, and leadership, here it was . . . no wavering, shakiness, or mumbling allowed.

But George W. already was a changed—or, perhaps, still a fast-changing—man, intimates and associates had noted. Just days after the horrifying events of 9/11, Franklin Graham, evangelist Billy Graham's son, had visited the new president, the Schweizers recalled in their book. "I have certainly seen a change in the man," Graham said. "There is a more somber seriousness in him. It's hard to describe. He knows what he has to do and he has the inner confidence to do it. He used to tell corny jokes a lot. He doesn't do that any more."

Or, another view, similar point: "People are saying George is rising to the challenge," said family member Elsie Walker Kilbourne, according to the Schweizers also. "[I]t isn't that George is rising to the challenge, it's just that it's given flower to what is already there in him."

However to define or explain the change, a new public persona of George W. Bush as a much tougher, more decisive leader would be quite evident the very day he spoke at the National Cathedral.

That Friday (September 14, 2001) after the unforgettable Tuesday would be a National Day of Prayer and Remembrance, by George W.' s own decision and declaration. The memorial service at the National Cathedral "would be his first opportunity to address the nation at length."

Both Presidents Bush tended to be sentimental men. In grief or joy, they teared up easily, as when Bush Senior for the first time saw Bush Junior, his son the president, standing alone in the Oval Office after the latter's inaugural in January 2001. Now, as presidential son George W. took the podium to speak—on the heels of several clergymen of various faiths—it seems that he didn't dare look his two parents square in the eye. "My biggest concern was looking at my parents," he said later. "If I looked down at my mother and dad, and they'd be weeping, then I'd weep."

Instead, he spoke firmly and resolutely. He set the prevailing tone with his very first statement: "We are in the middle hour of our grief. So many have suffered so great a loss, and today we express our nation's sorrow. We come before God to pray for the missing and the dead, and for those who loved them."

He called for national unity, he urged sympathy for the victims and their families, he spoke repeatedly of remembrance, of God and His love, all as befitted a memorial. But here and there the discerning listener would catch the hints of steel . . . of retaliation. "This nation is peaceful," he declared, "but fierce when stirred to anger."

And then the warning: "This conflict was begun on the timing and terms of others. It will end in a way and at an hour of our choosing."

That warning would be spelled out in harsh and steely detail just days later, on September 20, when Bush addressed a joint session of Congress to tell the Taliban regime of Afghanistan to hand over the terrorists harbored in that country "or share in their fate."

He declared war on terrorism everywhere with this warning for the nations of the world, "Either you are with us, or you are with the terrorists."

To the world also he said: "This is the world's fight. This is civilization's fight. This is the fight of all who believe in progress and pluralism, tolerance and freedom."

To the American military he said, "Be ready," and, "The hour is coming when America will act, and you will make us proud."

To the American people more generally, he pledged to direct

"every resource" at the government's command "to the destruction and to the defeat of the global terrorist network."

Americans, he said, "should not expect one battle, but a lengthy campaign unlike any other we have ever seen." The campaign "may include dramatic strikes visible on TV and covert operations secret even in success."

Indeed, in short order, an American-led military coalition deposed the Taliban and largely purged mountainous, landlocked Afghanistan—previously resistant to both the nineteenth-century British Empire and the twentieth-century Soviet Union—of its terrorist infestation, setting the stage for installation of a democratically elected government in place of the Taliban dictatorship.

More controversially, President Bush then led the nation into its war with Iraq, initially described as necessary to purge that country of weapons of mass destruction that dictator Saddam Hussein could turn against American interests and security. When no such weapons were found in the aftermath of quick military victory for American and, to lesser extent, British forces in 2003, the Bush Administration defended its war policy as a blow to global terrorism anyway. As the early military successes of 2003 bogged down into a counter-insurgency, counter-terrorism operation in 2004, with more than a thousand American soldiers killed, George W. Bush would not back away from his commitment to creating a free Iraq.

Even his mother apparently was surprised. "What has surprised you about George W.,?" *Time* magazine's Hugh Sidey asked her in an interview late in the year. "I think his steadfastness has," she replied, then added quickly, "I think that's a surprise—not a surprise, but it's something to be very proud of. Let me put it that way."

Apparently a majority of the American people felt much the same, since they gave George W. Bush a clear victory in the 2004 presidential election over the Democratic candidate, Senator John Kerry of Massachusetts, who was critical of the Iraq war.

By then, too, it was clear that the war on terrorism, begun on 9/11 by the terrorists themselves, would be the hallmark of the first four years of the George W. Bush presidency.

"Mr. President," Said Each

YET ANOTHER BEGINNING . . . AND A variegated tale to be found in its numbers. For this president's *second* inauguration, and the nation's *first* since the terrorist attacks on the World Trade Center on September 11, 2001, forevermore known as 9/11, some 13,000 troops and law enforcement personnel provided security, and yet 265,000 persons attended the swearing-in ceremony on the front steps of the U. S. Capitol.

While an estimated hundred square blocks in downtown Washington were closed to vehicular traffic, probably 150,000 persons filtered through on foot to reach historic Pennsylvania Avenue anyway. Here, they watched an inaugural parade cover the 1.7 miles from the Capitol to the reviewing stands in front of the White House. About fourteen arrests were made within the hundred-block area, "mostly for trespassing or clashing with law enforcement officers," the *Washington Post* reported. Unfortunately, this meant ten District of Columbia police officers suffered injuries "in incidents involving antiwar demonstrators and other protesters, and . . . several were hospitalized." In addition, thirty-three non-official persons were treated at hospitals, "mostly for exposure to the cold or for slip-and-fall injuries," while nearly three hundred others were treated at twenty-nine first aid stations.

More distantly, all boat traffic was barred along sixteen miles of waterways along the Potomac and Anacostia rivers in the District, the *Post* added. And further, small private aircraft were kept out of 3,000 square air miles over the Washington-Baltimore area, "a ban enforced by F-15 and F-16 fighter patrols and Army anti-aircraft missile units."

In the meantime, the man at the center of all this activity on January 20, 2005, was George Walker Bush, the 43rd president of the United States, son of George Herbert Walker Bush, the 41st president. Together, they constituted only the second father-son tandem to hold the exalted office in the entire history of the

Republic. John and John Quincy Adams of course were the first such duo.

The younger Bush may also claim a distant maternal tie to the nineteenth century's obscure President Franklin Pierce, thanks to the genealogical roots of former first lady Barbara *Pierce* Bush, George H. W.'s wife. The younger Bush may claim a really distant relationship, as well, to Queen Elizabeth, and even to his defeated rival in the 2004 presidential election, Senator John Kerry, Democrat of Massachusetts, according to *Time* magazine. No surprise then that nearly 150 Bush-Pierce extended-family members were in town for the inaugural events, although only twenty or so would "pile into vans" for the two-minute, three-block motorcade trip from the White House to St. John's Episcopal Church across Lafayette Square for a 9:00 A.M. worship service on January 20 with their man of the hour, according to the *Washington Times.*

Just before delivering an inaugural speech of twenty-one minutes at the Capitol, President Bush the 43rd took his oath of office from an obviously ailing Chief Justice William Rehnquist, and here a key number was the Bible's Isaiah 40:31, *The Washington Times* also reported. That was the passage Bush, a born-again Methodist, wanted the family Bible open to as he took the oath. "But they that wait upon the Lord shall renew their strength," the passage says; "they shall mount up with wings as eagles; they shall run, and not be weary; and they shall walk, and not faint."

Then, in his inaugural speech, Bush used the words *free, freedom,* or *liberty* forty-nine times, by the *Post*'s count. In addition, reported Julia Duin in the *Washington Times,* he "mixed images of the Almighty as a just ruler, as a judge, and as a freedom-loving deity in a speech that surpassed his 2001 inaugural address in references to God."

That night he and first lady Laura Bush would attend nine inaugural balls, spending roughly thirty minutes at each. In 2001, they had attended eight balls and danced for an average forty-eight seconds at each, reported Peter and Rochelle Schweizer in their 2004 book *The Bushes: Portrait of a Dynasty.*

All day on January 20, 2005, as was the case exactly four years earlier, Washington had been host to *two* President Bushes, one of them on occasion known to call his son "Quincy," in wry reference to John Quincy Adams, son of John Adams. In fact, the twenty-first century Bush pairing, unsurprisingly, has led to many

stories about the two and their relationship, some humorous . . .
some touching, too.

After the inaugural parade of 2001, for instance, a weary and
chilled George Bush 41 was relaxing in a hot tub at the White
House when a butler knocked on the door and said the "president" wished to see him in the Oval Office.

President?

"At first," reported *Time* magazine in December 2004, "a grog-
gy Bush was a bit confused about who this president was. Then,
of course, he realized it was his son. He considered saying no,
wanting to finish his soaking, but he thought better of it, and so
the wet former president sprang out of the tub, got dressed and,
with still damp hair, went over to the Oval Office to visit his
eldest child."

Then, four years later, came the triumphant election of 2004,
with a clear and decisive victory for George Bush 43—quite a
contrast to the narrow, disputed, and delayed Electoral College
victory he experienced in 2000. At 7 a.m. the day after the 2004
victory, a weary but thrilled George 41 once more was in the
bath—this time taking a shower—when his presidential son
dropped by the senior Bush's quarters and said to Barbara Bush,
"Mom, where's Dad?"

"He's in the shower," she replied.

"Well, tell him if he wants to come up to the Oval Office, I'd
love to have him over there."

According to Barbara Bush, narrator of the tale, "You never
saw a guy get out of the shower so fast in your life and get over
there."

Meanwhile, harkening back to that first inaugural for
George W., the Schweizers recalled in their book, there was
indeed a poignant moment for the two Presidents Bush at the
same Oval Office in the West Wing.

After George W.'s inauguration that time, it seems, after the
family repaired to the new-old White House, a contemplative and
sentimental George W. "slowly" stepped into the Oval Office for
the first time as president. Naturally, since his own father had
been president before him, he had been there before, "plenty of
times."

But this was different. At the center of the room, he looked up
at the presidential seal on the ceiling; he looked down "at the

same seal on the rug." He stepped behind the mahogany desk and stood there just a moment. Silent.

Then came approaching footsteps. It was his father, presumably still damp from that interrupted bath. "Chief of Staff Andrew Card watched as the former president stood at the door a moment and looked at his son. 'Mr. President,' he said with a crack in his voice.

'Mr. President,' responded W. Then both men began to cry."

Ronald Reagan always kept coat and tie on in the Oval Office as a mark of his respect for the presidency. Here he appears to be issuing the day's marching orders to members of his political inner sanctum. Michael Deaver is pictured at far left; David Gergen and Ed Meese can be seen at far end of Reagan's desk. (Courtesy Ronald Reagan Library)

II: Middles

The White House. The public has never understood this, but the White House is appreciated by its tenants, if at all, for the honor of living there, not for its luxury. The handsome rooms on the first floor—the ones the public sees on tours—are public rooms: showcase rooms for state occasions, otherwise a museum. Well and good. But the public, if it could see the private apartments on the second floor, might be dismayed to discover that the First Family lives in a suite of awkwardly connected rooms furnished chiefly with what they have brought from home. Only a half a dozen rooms are really private, and the family sitting room is actually a part of the west hallway.

—*The White House Pantry Murder*
by Elliott Roosevelt, son of a president

Joe and Edy Saga

FROM JOE FOSSETT'S POINT OF view, one hundred and twenty miles away, Edith, his woman, his love and future wife, simply was being held hostage in the President's House up there in the Federal City arising on the banks of the Potomac.

She certainly was not free to leave of her own volition. And he could not go to her.

Four years separated from each other?

When the boss came home one time, leaving Edith up there, Joe waited five days, then made his move. He shocked everybody in the mountaintop community. He took off. Ran away.

The boss sent a head carpenter in pursuit but soon realized the meaning of reports the young man had taken the road north to Washington. That's where "Edy" was—it dawned on the boss what was going on here. "He may possibly trump up some story to be taken care of at the President's House till he can make up his mind which way to go," wrote the boss in a letter on July 31, 1806, "or perhaps he may make himself known to Edy only, as he was formerly connected with her."

Odd word. *Connected.* But perhaps accurate.

Born at Monticello, Thomas Jefferson's mountaintop plantation, in 1780—born there, raised there from infancy—Joe Fossett, twenty-six in 1806, was a slave. So was Edith. She had gone to the Jefferson White House in 1802 at the age of fifteen to train as a cook under a French chef named Julien. With her in the official residence was another slave and cook-trainee named Fanny. Back at Monticello, Joe Fossett, a nail-maker as a teenager, was, by 1806, a young blacksmith for the Jefferson plantation.

It's possible that he had not seen Edith since she went to Washington with the president in 1802. When he ran off in July of 1806, as his master Jefferson apparently soon realized, young Joe was not really a runaway slave in the normal sense of the word—he was simply running to the President's House to see his love Edy, the future mother of his children.

"Fossett's desperate journey was evidently precipitated by something he heard from two hired slaves who had accompanied Jefferson from Washington," wrote Lucia Stanton in *Slavery at Monticello,* a monograph published by the Thomas Jefferson Memorial Foundation.

Joe's visit wasn't destined to be a long one. Joseph Dougherty, Jefferson's Irish coachman, spotted the runaway slave leaving the White House soon after his arrival. Jefferson's blacksmith then was placed in jail for another short period before his return to Monticello. "No record has survived of the reception the runaway met on his return," added the Stanton account. Pitifully, "he waited three more years for Edy to return with the retiring President."

At that point and after, happy to say, "they renewed their connection and raised eight children."

Some of the facts known to the Monticello researchers of today do *not* all point toward Joe as father of all eight of Edith's children. From 1802 to "Joe's sudden appearance in 1806," Stanton noted, Joe and Edy "may have seen each other very little, if at all." During that same period, however, two children were born to Edith in the Jefferson White House. She had a third child at the President's House in 1807, before returning to Monticello.

The specifics, as reported by Stanton: "Edy was at the President's House from at least the fall of 1802 until the spring of 1809. She bore three children in that period: an infant that did not survive in Jan. 1803; James, born Jan. 1805; and Maria, born Oct. 1807. . . . Edy, who was only fifteen when she went to Washington, may have been considered too young by her parents for formal marriage."

Nobody knows today if Jefferson gave her the option of staying behind at Monticello when he became president, if he was unaware of her "connection" with Joe the blacksmith, or if he knew and simply "chose to disregard it," according to Stanton also.

In any case, it appears that Edy's first baby was the first child ever born at the White House . . . and likely the first death in the White House as well. Jefferson's own grandson, James Madison Randolph, born in the President's House in January 1806, also was one of the very first "White House babies."

The rest of the Joe Fossett-Edith Fossett story resonates with images of better times combined with bitter heartache. In the years ahead, Edith became Jefferson's chief cook at Monticello, while Joe took charge of the plantation's blacksmithing and mechanical needs altogether. Joe in fact became head blacksmith by the end of 1807, less than two years after his runaway adventure. Both were favorites of the master.

Jefferson died in 1826, and his will freed Joe Fossett as of a year later, but that was only a mixed blessing for the couple and their children. The catch was Jefferson's indebtedness when he died—his "assets" to be liquidated included slaves, many slaves. Edith and five Fossett children and two grandchildren, among others, were sold off to help satisfy the Jefferson estate's debts.

By the time of Joe's freedom, the sales had taken place, the slaves had been dispersed. "Joe Fossett had watched his wife and children sold to at least four different bidders," wrote researcher Stanton. Joe's wife and their two youngest children went to one new master. Their son Peter, twelve at the time, went to another master. A fifteen-year-old daughter went to a third, and a seventeen-year-old daughter went to the fourth, a professor at the University of Virginia, founded by Jefferson. Fortunately, Edith and those five Fossett children went to homes located in the nearby area, but unknown today are the fates of the couple's three remaining children.

Fortunately, too, there would be a somewhat happier ending to the Joe-and-Edith story. As a free man, Joe Fossett practiced the blacksmithing trade for several years, perhaps still at Monticello. After the Jefferson estate was sold 1830, however, he bought a lot in nearby Charlottesville and operated his smithy there.

Meanwhile, "at some time before September 15, 1837," he had become "the owner of his wife, five of their children (two born subsequent to the sale), and four grandchildren," wrote Stanton. Joe Fossett apparently had the financial help of his mother, born Mary Hemings but by now Mary Hemings Bell. Mary, it seems, had been "leased" and then sold to Charlottesville merchant Thomas Bell back in the 1780s. She subsequently had children by her owner Bell and "shared in Bell's estate in 1800." Her daughter Sally later married Jesse Scott, a "free man of color, said to be part Indian." Their "combined resources" may have given Joe the $505 needed to buy back part of his family—"Edy and the two youngest children"—plus the funds needed to buy a third child.

The free Fossetts moved to Ohio "about 1840," but young Peter Fossett remained a slave in Virginia for two decades after Jefferson's will freed his father. Peter made "at least two attempts to run away" before, "by the combined efforts of members of an extended network of kin, he was able to purchase his freedom and join his family in Cincinnati." There he prospered as a caterer, became a prominent Baptist minister and an activist in the Underground Railroad providing an escape route for runaway slaves from the South. He was able to visit his childhood home of Monticello in the year 1900 as Thomas Jefferson's last known surviving slave.

Incidentally, Edy's fellow cook-trainee Fanny suffered a similar separation from her husband and fellow Jefferson slave Dave, who only saw his wife when delivering items to and from Washington two or three times a year. They fell into a "terrible quarrel," according to Edmund Bacon, a white overseer at Monticello. "Davy was jealous of his wife, and, I reckon, with good reason," said Bacon also.

The quarrel, though, was very nearly the end of their relationship with President Jefferson. According to researcher Stanton, "Bacon was summoned to take them to Alexandria to be sold." But they begged and pleaded so much, Jefferson relented and allowed them to remain in his extended "family" of relatives, white workers and surprisingly light-skinned slaves.

According to the extensive, two-volume White House history written by William Seale, Fanny also produced an ill-fated White House baby, probably in December of 1806. "Both Fanny and the child seemed to have done well at first, but beginning in the summer of 1808 a succession of nurses was employed to tend Fanny's baby," wrote Seale. "Shortly before its second birthday, the child died."

Jefferson's French steward Etienne Lemaire noted the construction of a small coffin for *"l'enfant de fany"* in his daybook entry for November 8, 1808.

Lemaire, Julien, and Dougherty were the white members of Jefferson's household staff, which grew from five to twelve persons in size during Jefferson's eight years as president, Seale also noted in his history. "All the other servants were slaves from Monticello," wrote Seale; "all were troublesome, probably because they did not like taking orders from the Frenchman [Lemaire, apparently]. At Monticello, Jefferson and his daughters dealt personally with the house servants. The French-chattering intermediary at the White House . . . must have weighed heavily on the country blacks."

Nor was Jefferson all that forgiving of their occasional transgressions. He didn't want any more of the Monticello slaves sent to him at the White House, he wrote in 1804. "I prefer white servants, who, when they misbehave, can be exchanged," he explained.

Additional note: The best-known of Thomas Jefferson's slaves, of course, was Sally Hemings, who, according to the scientific methodology of the late twentieth-century, bore him a son named Eston. DNA testing in the late 1990s seemed to establish Jefferson as the father of Eston, who took on the surname Jefferson, but the same DNA testing seemed to eliminate Jefferson as father of Eston's brother, Thomas Woodson. No DNA testing has been done in regards to Sally's remaining children.

Monticello says there is "no evidence" that Sally Hemings ever stayed at the White House with her master, President Thomas Jefferson.

The same Sally Hemings had six children in all, two girls and four boys, but only her four sons, Eston, Thomas, Beverly, and Madison, and one daughter, Harriet, survived their infancy.

Sally was a daughter of Betty Hemings. So was Mary Hemings Bell, mother of Joe Fossett. Thomas Jefferson acquired all three slave women and other Hemings family members from the estate of his father-in-law, English-born John Wayles.

If, as often alleged, Wayles was Sally's father, Sally then was a half-sister to Jefferson's own wife Martha (who died young). By the same theory, Sally would have been a half-aunt to Martha and Thomas Jefferson's two children. If Wayles also fathered Mary Hemings by Betty Hemings, then Joe Fossett was Martha's half-nephew, but the historical record has pointed to Wayles as the sire of others among Betty's children rather than Joe's mother Mary.

According to Monticello researcher Stanton's monograph, John Wayles's slave Betty Hemings herself was of mixed blood, since she was the daughter of an African slave woman and an English sea captain. Further, "at least seven of her [Betty's] children had white fathers."

Visitors and others, even the slave community itself, were struck by how white-looking the Jefferson slaves were. Jefferson himself called Joe a mulatto. The Duc de La Rochefoucauld-Liancourt, a

Frenchman visiting Monticello in the summer of 1796, noted "slaves who have neither in their color nor features a single trace of their origin, but they are the sons of slave mothers and consequently slaves." Another Frenchman visiting Monticello that same summer, the Comte de Volney, said he saw slave children "as white as I am."

Along the same lines, onetime Monticello slave Isaac Jefferson remembered two of Betty's sons as "bright mulattoes" and the famous Sally Hemings as "mighty near white."

To that account, researcher Stanton added the observation that "several and perhaps all of Betty Hemings' daughters formed relationships with white men." Indeed, "In at least one case, that of Sally Hemings, the children had seven-eighths white ancestry and thus were white by Virginia law."

Jefferson "freed" all of Sally's children, although not always openly, nor right away . . . nor even in his own lifetime. "He allowed Harriet and Beverly to 'run away,' providing Harriet money and stage fare to Philadelphia, and [he] gave Madison and Eston Hemings their freedom in his will," reported Stanton. According to her also, Jefferson's granddaughter Ellen Randolph Coolidge many years later said that Jefferson would "allow such of his slaves as were sufficiently white to pass for white men, to withdraw from the plantation [Monticello]; it was called running away, but they never were reclaimed."

The controversial story that Sally Hemings in effect was Thomas Jefferson's concubine first came to public light in an article by journalist James Thomas Callender that appeared in the Richmond *Recorder* in 1802. The controversy stirred by the Callender accusation dogged Jefferson and his legendary status as a Founding Father both before and after his death, then burst forth again in 1974 with the publication of Fawn Brodie's book *Thomas Jefferson: An Intimate Biography.*

Even without Callender's public attack, there apparently were rumors about the Jefferson-Sally Hemings "connection." According to researcher Stanton, white overseer Edmund Bacon once recalled that when Harriet was allowed to leave the slave community at Monticello, "people said he [Jefferson] freed her because she was his own daughter."

Still, only Eston has been connected to Jefferson by DNA testing. That analysis was based upon a study of the Y chromosome found in blood samples of nineteen men, among them known descendants of Jefferson's uncle, Field Jefferson, and of Sally Hemings's two sons Eston and Thomas. Since the Y chromosome usually passes down generation to generation with hardly any change, the DNA testing makes it seem likely that Jefferson was Eston's father (although not Thomas's). The evidence is not absolutely, one-hundred percent reliable, but it is close to that standard.

According to Jefferson's "hometown" newspaper, the Charlottesville *Daily Progress,* Dr. Eugene A. Foster, the pathologist who spearheaded the DNA study, summed up the Jefferson linkage this way: "I can't say it seals it, but it's very, very, very likely."

A Most Courageous Patient

WITH THE COUNTRY IN A financial panic, the stricken president's surgery should be carried out quickly and secretly, it was felt in the White House. And that is the way it was done—on a yacht cruising the East River in New York City, with the doctors on board ducking out of sight to avoid recognition by some sharp-eyed intern at Bellevue Hospital on the Manhattan side of the river.

The story begins on May 5, 1893, when President Grover Cleveland, fresh in a second White House term, first noticed an odd "rough spot" on the roof of his mouth. He didn't do anything about it at first, but by mid-June it was bothering him and he called in the White House physician, Dr. Robert M. O'Reilly.

What O'Reilly found was very serious indeed—a cancerous growth extending from Cleveland's upper teeth on the left side to nearly the center of his mouth. A surgeon called into the case, Dr. Joseph Bryant, urged fast action. "Were it in my mouth," he told the portly Cleveland, "I would have it removed at once." At the time, however, the country was gripped by economic crisis, the panic of 1893, a period of railroad failures, mortgage foreclosures, collapsing stocks, and dangerously low gold reserves. And then, on June 27, the New York Stock Market crashed. Cleveland called for a special session of Congress to deal with the crisis—but he had to delay the date until August 7 to allow time for the secret operation on his mouth.

Was such secrecy really necessary? According to Cleveland biographer Allan Nevins, "The knowledge that Cleveland's life was in danger would have precipitated a new and far greater panic." A strong, healthy, and confident Cleveland was needed for the fight against the Sherman Silver Purchase Act, seen as a major cause of the depleted gold reserves. "The whole strength of the assault upon the Sherman silver-purchase clauses lay, as everyone realized, in the grim determination of Cleveland's purpose. His weight of character could force enough members of the party [Democratic] into line, and nothing else could. Even temporary incapacitation might be fatal to his aims, while if any accident suddenly removed him from the scene, all would be lost; for Vice President Adlai E. Stevenson would infallibly bring the nation to the silver standard."

And so, the well-meaning conspirators laid their plans. Bryant lined up a medical team for the oral surgery to be performed upon the president: Dr. W. W. Keen of Philadelphia, an eminent surgeon; Dr. E. G. Janeway, general practitioner, and Dr. Ferdinand Hasbrouck, dentist, both of New York; along with Bryant's own assistant, Dr. John F. Erdmann. Bryant coordinated the details with the White House physician, Dr. O'Reilly, and Daniel Lamont, Cleveland's former private secretary and now the nation's secretary of war.

In the meantime, E. C. Benedict, close friend and New York City neighbor to Cleveland between his two presidential terms (1885–1889, 1893–1897), agreed to provide his yacht the *Oneida* for the surreptitious enterprise.

Lamont and his wife accompanied the presidential party to New York on June 30, traveling by private railroad car. The group boarded "Commodore" Benedict's yacht at Pier A—quite openly, since it would be no surprise for Cleveland to enjoy Benedict's seagoing hospitality. He had done so before. After all were aboard, including the various doctors and their equipage, the yacht remained anchored for the night in Bellevue Bay on the East River. It was here that Bryant "warned the medical staff to keep out of sight, lest they be recognized by the interns at Bellevue Hospital."

Cleveland was a good patient and apparently resigned to placing his fate in the hands of those aboard the yacht. He had asked earlier if he would look markedly different after his surgery; he was told the major sign of his secret operation would be a speech defect, but he

Grover Cleveland began his second presidential term at the age of fifty-one, as the only U.S. president to leave the White House and come back for resumed—that is to say, interrupted— tenure as the nation's chief executive. He also would be the only president to marry in the White House! (American Memory Collections, Library of Congress)

would not look abnormal. Any surgery under a general anesthetic of course carried risks, but with Cleveland the doctors were more than normally concerned about how he would react to the anesthetics involved—nitrous oxide and ether. He seemed to be strong and healthy, but at fifty-six he was "very corpulent . . . and of just the build and age for a stroke of apoplexy," to say nothing of the stress he had had to face since moving into the White House for a second time just four months earlier. Whatever fears Cleveland may have had personally, he sat in a deck chair and "chatted until nearly midnight" the evening of June 30, then slept in his berth without the help of sedatives, reported Nevins in his two-volume biography *Grover Cleveland: A Study in Courage.*

The next morning appeared to begin quite normally for a presidential sojourn aboard a friend's yacht: "newspapers were taken aboard and there was a leisurely breakfast." But soon the staff cleared out the salon to make room for the operation, and the yacht raised anchor. At half speed or so, it cruised up the East River. "The anxious Dr. Bryant told the captain, 'If you hit a rock, hit it good and hard, so that we'll all go to the bottom!'"

Cleveland, propped up in a chair against the mast, "went under the anesthetics after some innate resistance." After the dentist Hasbrouck removed two left upper bicuspid teeth, Bryant began the surgery on the roof of Cleveland's mouth. In thirty-one minutes, adds the Nevins account, "They removed the entire left upper jaw from the first bicuspid tooth to just beyond the last molar, and took out a part of the palate; this extensive operation being necessary, writes Dr. Keen, 'because we found that the antrum—the large hollow cavity in the upper jaw—was partly filled with a gelatinous mass, evidently a sarcoma.'" Actually, writes Nevins, "it was a carcinoma."

With no external incisions necessary nor any of the surgery affecting his eyeball, Cleveland would appear fairly normal, but he later would need an artificial jaw of vulcanized rubber to maintain normal appearance (and speech). The surgery ended at 1:55 P.M., and Cleveland was given a shot of morphine to help him rest comfortably in the immediate aftermath. "What a sigh of intense relief we surgeons breathed when the patient was once more safe in bed hardly can be imagined," wrote surgeon Keen later.

Two days later Cleveland was on his feet again while Benedict's yacht continued on its course for Buzzards Bay on Cape Cod, where Cleveland kept a summer retreat called Gray Gables. "And when on July 5 the *Oneida* after five days of cruising, dropped anchor in Buzzards Bay, he was able to walk from the launch to Gray Gables with little apparent effort. On July 17, there was a second brief operation to remove some suspicious tissue, from which Cleveland quickly recovered. Dr. Keen pronounced him the most docile and courageous patient he ever had the pleasure of attending."

A recovering Cleveland then did press his fight for repeal of the Silver Purchase Act . . . and won! The country nonetheless suffered four years of severe depression. In the meantime, the public "gradually learned something of the ordeal he [Cleveland] had been through."

Not for "almost a quarter century," however, would all the salient facts be known in what Nevins called "one of the dramatic minor episodes of American history."

Additional note: Dental technology consultant (and serious American history buff) Markus Ring of North Bethesda, Maryland, asserts that the actual operation on Cleveland's mouth probably did not take place in the all-too-turbulent East River. "While the *Oneida* may have anchored overnight in the East River in sight of Bellvue Hospital," says Ring, ". . . the operation was performed in a sheltered cove on the North Shore of Long Island where the water was calm. (Oyster Bay may well have been the location.) It is logical to assume that the operation did not take place in Bellvue Bay, as ships plying the East River would rock the *Oneida* with waves and swells."

Hardly Anyone Knew Her

THE CRIPPLED CHILD BROUGHT INTO the inner sanctum of the White House was obviously frightened by his strange surroundings and by all the strangers around him. He was there for a photo op with the first lady on behalf of a worthy cause.

She tried her best to ease his fears, but nothing seemed to work. The little boy remained stiff and tightlipped. Finally, though, he blurted out, "This isn't your house!"

"Why do you say that?" asked the first lady.

"Because I don't see your washing machine," he explained.

No problem, decided the first lady. She simply took him up to the third floor and gave him a long, reassuring look at the washing machines in the laundry rooms up there. "He returned to the first floor holding her hand, as contented and cheerful as if he were with his own mother," recalled the daughter of a president telling this story. "His awed parents said it was the first time he had ever been at ease with a stranger."

In the view of Margaret Truman, the little-known incident was typical of "the First Lady nobody knew." In fact, Harry S. Truman's daughter devoted an entire chapter to this little-appreciated, self-effacing first lady in the book *First Ladies: An Intimate Group Portrait of White House Wives.*

"Another unknown side" of this nearly invisible first lady was her attempt "to read every letter she received and send a personal answer." No easy task, since the volume of letters "swelled to over two thousand a day." Still, the first lady tried, perhaps answering more of the personal mail than any previous president's wife. "She came from a small town and knew what a letter from the White House could mean. 'It's shown to all the neighbors, and often published in the local paper,' she told reporters. 'It's important to people who receive it.'"

One time she responded more dramatically to a personal letter. It came from a young woman in the grip of drug addiction who threatened to commit suicide. The first lady picked up the telephone and "persuaded her to change her mind, and it [the personal call] was followed up by psychiatric help, which soon had her on the road to stability."

By Margaret Truman's reckoning also, this was the first first lady ever to visit American soldiers in a combat zone. Veering into only relatively safe Saigon as part of an official visit to Southeast Asia, she startled her handlers by turning down a proposed schedule of "having tea and shaking hands with the wives of Vietnamese officials." No, she said, "I want to see some wounded Americans."

Soon she was in a helicopter riding above jungle terrain "rife with potential Viet Cong sharpshooters," her destination an American evacuation hospital. Once at the field hospital, she brushed aside attempts to give her a formal briefing and said, "I want to see the boys." She then spent two hours "going from bed to bed, talking with each wounded man in tones too low for frustrated reporters to overhear," wrote Margaret Truman. "More than once she got down on her knees beside a man who could not sit up in bed."

Then, too, "like Eleanor Roosevelt three decades earlier," she took down names and addresses the wounded men provided—for a self-imposed follow-up task of writing their parents at home and "telling them she had seen their sons and how much she admired their sacrifice for their country."

Speaking of the widely protested U.S. attempt to stop the Communist takeover of South Vietnam, the same first lady couldn't really shake the haunting image of the Vietnam War back home in America—not with at least "forty thousand protests, bombings, and assorted acts of violence" greeting her husband's first year in office. As well known, too, there were major protests, marches and demonstrations right in Washington itself—more than 250,000 gathered there for Moratorium Day, October 15, 1969, while in the spring of 1971, 200,000 protesters "tried to shut down the federal government."

Said one of the first lady's staff about the violent 1971 confrontation: "It was like a war." Armed guards carrying tear gas stood behind the White House fence. The grounds themselves were blocked off by a cordon of buses as elsewhere in the capital city, not all that far away, marchers fought police and pelted motorists with rocks and other debris.

Through it all, though, this first lady stoically went ahead with her schedule, with her duty as she saw it. "We are not going to buckle to these people," she said.

"On one of the 1971 protest's worst days," added Margaret Truman's account, "she went ahead with a luncheon for congressional wives. On other days she maintained her full schedule."

Meanwhile, Jackie Kennedy Onassis was one of those who learned what a soft heart this unappreciated first lady kept hidden from the public. Jackie was invited to see the portraits of herself and her assassinated husband, John F. Kennedy, that had been hung at the White House. "Jackie responded that she could not face a public ceremony," wrote Margaret Truman. "She wanted to bring John Jr. and Caroline, but feared the visit would revive grisly memories—especially if the press were swirling around them, asking personal questions."

Once again, no problem. Not only did the first lady abandon all plans for a public ceremony, she deliberately didn't tell the press staff that Jackie would be dropping in with her children—a first visit for all three since JFK's assassination. Only four White House staffers of any kind were let in on the secret plan. No advance publicity was the goal.

Assured of privacy, Jackie made the trip to Washington with her two children. Personally greeting her in the second-floor family quarters at the White House were the first lady and her own two daughters. The small entourage then went down to the first floor and viewed the two portraits.

But that was only a first stop, it turned out. Rather than react with anguish at seeing their father's portrait by artist Aaron Shikler,

John Jr., ten, and Caroline, thirteen, said they wanted to see the rest of the White House—to them "a fabulous place ... which they had been told about many times but barely remembered." As a result, the first lady's two daughters took the Kennedy children on a tour of their own onetime home while the first lady showed Jackie the first-floor state rooms, all recently redecorated.

The memorable wind-up to the day was dinner with the president and informal visits to both the Oval Office in the West Wing and the Lincoln Bedroom on the second floor. There, incidentally, the President "sat John Jr. on the huge bed and told him if he made a wish, it was guaranteed to come true." This was a White House legend of course, but John Jr. later wrote in a thank-you letter that "he had had great luck the next day at school."

More important, in a thank-you note of her own, an appreciative Jackie said she would not soon forget the top-secret visit to the Richard M. Nixon White House. "The day I always dreaded turned out to be one of the most precious ones I have spent with my children," Jackie wrote to Pat Nixon, whom Margaret Truman called "The First Lady Nobody Knew."

Additional note: Reporters and others privately called Pat Nixon derogatory names such as "Plastic Pat" for her publicly frozen smile—almost a grimace—and seeming demeanor of painfully going through the paces expected of a first lady. She neither sought nor attained an attentive, warm press. For one thing, unlike many of her counterparts, she did not publicly adopt an exciting cause. "She felt that approach narrowed the first lady's role, excluding all sorts of people and organizations who could use her help."

Pat Nixon's way "left her free to visit the aged, the blind, the orphaned, the handicapped—to give as many people as possible the benefit of a First Lady's power to attract sympathy and help."

Nor was she afraid to be innovative in other ways as well. It was Mrs. Nixon, evidently, who inspired the Nixon White House's Sunday prayer service in the East Room, with government clerks sitting next to cabinet members or U.S. senators, and all receiving "a personal greeting and a warm handshake from the President and his First Lady." Pat Nixon also arranged tours of the White House gardens and ordered the splendid old mansion bathed in the glow of floodlights at night.

She was bold enough also to redecorate the public rooms of the mansion, an exercise that meant replacing or adding to Jackie Kennedy's widely ballyhooed redecorating and restoration efforts just a few years before. After millions of visitors passing through on tour and hundreds of social affairs in the interim, it was time in any case—the place had become shopworn at the edges. Even so, to undo the legendary Jackie's work could have been a disaster for someone lacking in refinement and taste. In Margaret Truman's view, however, Pat Nixon met the test and "was Jackie Kennedy's equal— some think her superior—in redecorating the White House."

Writing the Great Document

IN DECEMBER OF 1861 LINCOLN spoke a certain word to Senator Charles Sumner, Massachusetts abolitionist, but with the caution, "Don't say a word about that." And no wonder: in a country already badly rent by civil war it was an issue that could tear even more. He would have to creep up on its blind side, even though—and perhaps because—others already were tossing around that word. And fighting over it. Various senators in fact urged Lincoln to take his stand, make his move—even the Confederacy, it was feared, might take the dramatic step, if only to win recognition from England and France.

Always, even if not yet time, it was in Lincoln's mind. And finally, in the summer of 1862, when things were going dismally for the Union armies in the field, he wrote a draft. As he presented it to his cabinet, his thinking on the timing of the great event, he later said, was this:"Things had gone from bad to worse, until I felt that we had reached the end of our rope on the plan of operations we had been pursuing; that we had about played our last card, and must change our tactics, or lose the game . . . I now determined upon the adoption of the emancipation policy, and without consultation with or the knowledge of the Cabinet, I prepared the original draft of the proclamation, and after much anxious thought, called a Cabinet meeting upon the subject."

There was that word, almost hidden away in a small shrubbery of verbiage. *Emancipation!*

Rarely, though, had Lincoln been so wrong in his political instincts. And it was Secretary of State William Henry Seward who pointed out the problem. Such a moment, coming after a string of military defeats for the Union, was no time to attempt such a bold step. "His [Seward's] idea was that it would be considered our last shriek, on the retreat." Far better, argued Seward, to wait for military success, then issue the dramatic policy statement.

So Lincoln "put the draft of the proclamation aside." And thankfully so, since right after that John Pope lost the second Battle of Bull Run. But then, late in the summer, came the Battle of Antietam, a fearful slaughter also close outside of Washington, yet this time with a Northern tilt to the outcome. Lincoln was then staying at the Soldiers' Home three miles out of town, and there he finished writing a second draft. He invited his vice president, Hannibal Hamlin, for a supper at the Soldiers' Home one night after Antietam, then took Hamlin behind closed doors in the library and read him the document. "Now listen while I read this paper," said the recent circuit rider from Illinois. "We will correct it together as I go on." He did, they did, and the cabinet heard the results on September 22, 1862. (*Note:* For the moment, it would abolish slavery only in the Confederate states.)

At that meeting the course of the great document's development and issuance was determined, and that is the real-life story behind it ... except for one little detail—a man, an old friend, named Swett, Leonard Swett, attorney-at-law back home in Illinois.

Still in the throes of finding his path, the right path, some months before, Lincoln had sent to Bloomington, a two-day train trip away, for his old friend and fellow trial lawyer from a legal circuit so rustic they occasionally had been required to share the same bed when traveling to try cases. Told by Carl Sandburg in his *Abraham Lincoln: The War Years,* the tale is that the president took Swett into the Cabinet Room at the White House, talked for a moment or two about mutual friends, then got down to the business at hand—emancipation. Yes, that, and yet it wasn't much of a discussion, really. Or perhaps it was—but a one-sided discussion, in which Lincoln did all the talking.

He pulled out first one letter (pro-emancipation), read it aloud to Swett, then another (anti), and yet a third (also anti). Lincoln then "began a discussion of emancipation in all its phases." As Swett listened, Lincoln went on and on. "He turned it inside out and outside in," wrote Sandburg. "He reasoned as though he did not care about convincing Swett, but as though he needed to think out loud in the presence of an old-timer he knew and could trust."

After an hour or so, Lincoln stopped, wished Swett and their mutual friends back home well, and ended the interview. He never asked his friend for any comment, but it was only after this session that the Great Emancipator laid his historic decree before his cabinet, the country . . . the world: the Emancipation Proclamation.

End to an Affair

AS AMBASSADOR TO ENGLAND IN the 1850s, James Buchanan employed a colorful aide named Dan Sickles as secretary of the U.S. legation, a controversial choice since Sickles, among other indiscretions, once refused to rise for the entrance of Queen Victoria at a formal dinner.

In Washington just a few years later, "Old Buck" was president and the prickly Sickles was a House member from New York City. Married to a very young bride, and with little visible signs of support, Sickles indulged in a grand residence on Lafayette Square, across the street from his old boss, mentor, and friend Buchanan in the White House.

Few would have guessed, despite Sickles's many, many past indiscretions, that he one day would shoot a man almost at Buchanan's doorstep—and "Old Buck" would urge an eyewitness to the murder to leave town in a hurry. But it did happen that way.

After coming to Washington in 1857, Sickles, thirty-seven, plunged into politicking, and one of his first actions was to urge the reappointment of Philip Barton Key, a casual acquaintance, as U.S. attorney for the federal city of Washington. Even more casual was Sickles' innocent introduction of his wife, Teresa, to Key at

Buchanan's inaugural ball in 1857. As the pair danced, none among the onlookers thought any more of the chance meeting.

In the months ahead, life in the nation's capital was a whirlwind of activity, political and social, for the impetuous young congressman. His wife, Teresa, was more privy to the social entertainments than the political, and since her congressman-husband was often busy with more serious business, she often was escorted by the dashing U.S. attorney, son of Francis Scott Key. It was in the fall of that year, 1857, wanting to entertain on a more lavish style than his hotel quarters permitted, that Sickles leased the fine Stockton Mansion on Lafayette Square, that very upscale address across Pennsylvania Avenue from "Old Buck."

Sickles never hesitated to drop in on his friend the president, while also staffing, furnishing, and stocking his own fine home in a manner far beyond his obvious financial means. The Sickles couple entertained frequently in their new quarters, with Key a frequent guest.

Key's presence caused social comment, not because he was a handsome widower thrown in with the extraordinarily young wife of the busy congressman, but because he represented Southern aristocracy at a time when the grand house of the Union was developing cracks and fissures over the slavery and states' rights issues. It just seemed odd that such an intimate of so many Southerners in the capital would spend so much time in the company of a brash Yankee congressman of somewhat dubious reputation. Over the next two years, though, Key did spend time . . . more and more of it.

As Sickles won a second House term, the nation's political stew was close to boiling—and Sickles, himself, seemed closely aligned with the Southern bloc in the House.

At his own house in the square, however, other things were coming to a boil, and rumor to that effect brought a confrontation with Key and wounded denials. Sickles appeared fully assured. "I like Key," he told a confidant. "This thing shocked me when I first heard about it, and I am glad to have the scurrilous business cleared up."

But it wasn't. Only two blocks from the white-brick mansion in Lafayette Square was the intersection of K Street, Fifteenth Street, and Vermont Avenue, and on Fifteenth Street, in a rundown neighborhood near that corner, was an empty brick house, No. 383. The man renting the innocuous abode in the fall of 1858 was Key, and the furtive, shawl-wrapped woman who sometimes met him there was Teresa. Except for their clandestine meetings, the house remained empty.

The neighbors noticed, and one of them eventually found out that the woman was Mrs. Sickles. At Teresa's home, the servants also were becoming aware of the affair. Not only did Key visit or escort the lady of the house on social calls quite frequently, but he signalled her from points in the square with a white handkerchief.

"By midwinter," writes Sickles's biographer W. A. Swanberg (*Sickles the Incredible*), "the 'secret affair' was known, though perhaps not to its full extent, by almost everybody in Washington except for one person—Daniel Sickles."

An anonymous tipster took care of that omission with a note disclosing the existence—and purpose—of the house on Fifteenth Street. There came a night of confrontation in the mansion, accompanied by sobs and unearthly groans from Sickles. A servant and a visiting friend were called in to witness Teresa's full written confession.

The next morning, a Sunday, Sickles managed to shave, but he was "seized with paroxysms of sobbing." He sent for two friends and greeted them with bloodshot eyes.

He told them the facts, and all three debated what he should do, personally—and, of course, politically, since such scandal could be absolutely ruinous. Sickles, pacing the floor, stopped at a window and looked out, unthinkingly.

His two companions saw him pause, speechless. Across the way was Philip Barton Key himself, handsomely dressed as usual and waving his white handkerchief at the upper windows of the Sickles house.

For Key, it was incredibly bad timing.

"That villain," shouted Sickles, "is out there now, making signals!"

Sickles grabbed a pistol and dashed out. He accosted Key before more than a dozen witnesses. "Key, you scoundrel," yelled Sickles. "You have dishonored my bed—you must die!"

The wronged congressman took aim, fired, and missed. Key ducked behind a tree. "Don't shoot," he entreated. He hurled his opera glass at Sickles, to no avail.

The congressman fired again. Struck this time, Key tumbled into the gutter with a scream, begging for mercy. "Sickles fired again—some witnesses said twice again," reported Swanberg. "Then he walked up to the prostrate figure, aimed the weapon pointblank at

Key's head, and pulled the trigger. But the gun misfired, and suddenly several passersby came to their senses and stayed his hand." Samuel Butterworth, one of the two friends conferring with Sickles moments before, took the congressman by the arm to lead him away. But not before Sickles asked, "Is the damned scoundrel dead yet?"

A witness to the shooting was a White House page, J. H. W. Bonitz of Wilmington, North Carolina. "Old Buck's" first reaction, of course, was shock when the young man raced into the White House to tell him what had just happened in the square outside. But then Buchanan rallied and suggested that his page should leave town.

"He told young Bonitz that as an eyewitness he would be held in jail without bond unless he left Washington immediately. He presented Bonitz with a razor as a personal memento, and a sum of money for more practical purposes, and advised him to clear out of town. . . . Unacquainted with the law, he [Bonitz] did not know that he would not have been jailed, nor did it occur to him that Buchanan's motives might have been to remove a witness whose story could be damaging to Sickles."

Damaging? Hardly anything could have been more damaging to Sickles than his *own* actions and words before many other witnesses. And yet, in modern parlance, he "got off," fully acquitted of a killing he made no attempt to hide or to deny. It wasn't merely that the prosecution, deprived of its "first-string" in the form of the slain U.S. Attorney Key, had to rely upon a fumbling substitute. Nor was it entirely the embankment of eight "high-ranking" lawyers representing Sickles in his murder trial. What saved Sickles was not even having Edwin Stanton, the future secretary of war, among his many attorneys (although Stanton treated the often sobbing and emotional Sickles "with the greatest solicitude even as he heaped ridicule on the prosecution, browbeat the judge, and spoke with feeling of the sanctity of the home"). Rather, the successful defense in Sickles's case was a legal "first"—an early and apparently unprecedented use of temporary insanity as grounds for dismissal.

And so, the hot-tempered congressman was set free; Buchanan in 1861 gave way to Lincoln, and in the Civil War that followed, Sickles reappeared on the national scene as a minor Union general . . . but one quite honorably wounded at Gettysburg.

A Swim in the Potomac

THE U.S. NAVY, AT THE start of World War II, didn't have much use for the large but rather unseaworthy yacht it had bought from wealthy businessman Hugh Chisholm. She had no watertight compartments, was a bit unstable, and couldn't carry heavy guns. No surprise, then, that she was beached for the duration.

Even so, the *Williamsburg,* steadied considerably by the addition of pig iron in her bilges as ballast, would find glory of sorts in the postwar years, a bit inland and upstream from her lonely berth in Norfolk, Virginia.

She cruised and she cruised, in her element at last, up and down and across the Potomac River off Washington, D.C., for the most part. She now had a full crew, upright pianos, and a dining room with tables that could handle thirty persons. She had a lounge and two bedroom suites with bath, plus sitting room, and of course many lower-deck compartments for added passengers. Almost everywhere she went, she had an escorting "fleet" of two smaller yachts, the *Margery* and the *Lenore.* It was the *Lenore* that carried the Secret Service fellows, and of course the patron to whom the *Williamsburg* owed new life and fame was President Harry S. Truman.

"President Truman loved this yacht and used it to full advantage," recalled its former skipper, Rear Admiral Donald J. MacDonald, at that time a commander in rank. "He often told me, 'It's just wonderful. In ten minutes I'm away from everything.' Several times a week he'd call me—he had a direct line—and say he'd be coming to lunch."

If Truman didn't bring guests, he simply asked MacDonald to join him. The future admiral thus had a ringside seat for many of Truman's major decisions as president. One time, while debating what to do about headstrong General Douglas MacArthur's actions in Korea, Truman, obviously "bothered," asked MacDonald what he thought.

"Well, Mr. President," said the navy man, "you can't be boss in a military organization and have people not carry out the orders, or you lose control."

As events proved, Truman obviously came to the same conclusion—he fired MacArthur.

They also discussed Truman's tough wartime decision to use the atomic bomb against Japan. "He seemed a bit haunted by the power he'd unleashed, but it was just another one of those momentous decisions he had to make."

An army man all the way (he served in the U.S. Army field artillery in France during World War I), Truman thought Chief of Staff George Marshall, whom he made secretary of state, was great. "And he thought that since General Eisenhower was army, he must be great, too." As Truman neared the end of his second term, he had high hopes for Ike—hopes that he would run for president as a fellow Democrat. "He said he wanted to groom Eisenhower to follow him," and "it just about broke his heart when, all of a sudden, Eisenhower shifted to the Republican Party."

More generally, Truman repaired to his yacht as an escape from the pressures of the White House. He would rise early in the day, spend the morning at his work ashore at 1600 Pennsylvania Avenue, then arrive at the yacht at the Washington Navy Yard (then called the Naval Gun Factory) in time for lunch. Next came a nap on board. And afterward a rubdown by a navy pharmacist's mate who was a masseur. Finally, back to the White House about 4:30 P.M.

The *Williamsburg,* while seldom bracing the ocean itself, was not strictly a dockside yacht, it should be emphasized. There were the weekends. There were the poker games. And there were the weekend poker extravaganzas. "Sometimes he'd come down on Thursday. He'd have poker parties that night, still at the dock, and then about midnight some of the people would leave, and the rest of the players would continue on down the river with him." MacDonald would guide his craft and its coterie of Truman guests about the Potomac River, usually stopping off Quantico or Blakistone Island. A seaplane often zoomed in with papers and mail demanding fast presidential attention. Sometimes, the seaplane unloaded a fresh squad of poker players!

Truman, it seems, had essentially three sets of poker friends, and all three groups had their own kind of game. The "high-flyers," personages such as Chief Justice Fred Vinson or Agricultural Secretary Clint Anderson or George Allen, head of the Works Project

Administration, played high stakes—no limit. Secondarily, "There was a sort of $700-limit group." And lastly, "when no one else was available," Truman played with staff members, aides, and other old friends, with a $100 limit usually in force.

Whatever the case: "He loved to play and he often won. It relaxed him." Unbelievably, that was a period of such calm innocence that the president of the United States could pop into the Potomac and take a swim, undisturbed and usually uncontaminated by pollution.

"When we used to anchor off Blakistone Island and Mr. Truman wanted to go in for a swim, who'd be standing to watch him but me and my executive officer? The Secret Service would be standing up on the deck, but they wouldn't be in a position to go in and save him. Truman wore his glasses all the time that he was swimming. He'd keep his head up while he was paddling around."

As for the pollution possibility, "Before he went in I'd take samples of the water, because even then the pollution was drifting down the Potomac."

It was all so different, as MacDonald said in an interview years later for the U.S. Naval Institute's oral history program. "When he wasn't napping or playing cards, President Truman was often up on the bridge with us, or sitting on the deck. Boats would come alongside and wave to him, which he seemed to enjoy. The boaters were just thrilled to see him. It was a different time, and no one thought of taking a pot shot at him."

So very different . . .

Additional note: Still another Potomac swimmer while occupying the White House was Teddy Roosevelt. French ambassador Jean Jules Jusserand once recalled the many times he joined a small party headed by TR in exploring the Potomac marshes. One particularly hot day, recalled Jusserand in his book *What Me Befell,* the entire group of men shucked their clothes and leaped into the water to cool off. Jusserand, though, was still wearing his gloves. When TR pointed out he was still wearing his gloves, the Frenchman's quick reply was: "We might meet ladies."

Bachelor Status Ended

BUILT LIKE A WELL-FED SHOAT, the man who moved—all alone—into the White House in 1885 was a sitting duck for gossipmongers, snobs, and critics of all stripe. He was a middle-aged onetime sheriff, a reformer who had progressed up the political ladder from sheriff to mayor of Buffalo, New York, to governor of New York, to president. He was the first Democrat to occupy the White House since Lincoln was first elected in 1860. He followed six Republicans in a row.

A minister's son, he recently had been forced into public acknowledgement of an illegitimate child. A bachelor with little experience in "society," thick and brutish looking, he excited no great expectations in Washington, especially in the town's more exclusive social circles. After his inauguration, a Cleveland newsman found it interesting to write about how big a man the new president was, while Wisconsin's Senator Robert La Follette commented on the reformer's "coarse face, heavy, inert body."

With the bullyboy look came a brusque manner and a hard stare that alienated or even frightened some people. Others in 1885 were unhappy to know that he had no Civil War record of service.

How could such a man win over those who watched the occupants of the White House? How could this bachelor approaching fifty years of age even begin to gain the confidence and affections of his countrymen?

At first all they knew about him was that he was very businesslike; he did plunge into his new job as president, and he worked long hours at it. He also was scrupulously honest in just about everything he did. And he brought in his sister Rose to serve as acting White House hostess for him. She a spinster, he a bachelor, they held down a very quiet White House, except for the most obligatory social events.

All so dull, dull, dull. . . .

But Rose, a feminist, teacher, and writer of verse, soon won many a social lion's heart . . . even while her brother pursued his great secret.

As for that matter—that secret he carried in his heart—could any of the gossipmongers have anticipated this serious, all-business, unblinking man of forty-eight would have a secret love? Would be planning to wed while in the White House? Would wed a girl still in college and twenty-seven years his junior!

But that was Grover Cleveland's plan, his earnest intention, even if he himself was afraid of the ridicule, of the inevitable Beauty and the Beast thoughts that would cross the public mind.

The demure beauty was the daughter of his late law partner Oscar Folsom. He had known the young Frances since her infancy, literally, and when her father had died in a carriage accident in 1875, Grover Cleveland had been like a kindly, supportive uncle to the grieving child of twelve and to her mother.

Oddly, you might say, the illegitimate son he acknowledged, a boy just about the same age as Frances, carried the name Oscar Folsom Cleveland—after both law partners. His mother was a widow. As in the case of Frances, Grover Cleveland "was there" for the youngster in the way of financial support.

But back to the lonely Cleveland White House, where early in his

Grover Cleveland, no Adonis, not only braved serious oral surgery in secret, but the possible taunts of a nation titillated by his White House marriage to a winsome young lady just out of college. Say what you will, both the surgery and the wedding (depicted here) went quite smoothly, thank you. (Wood engraving by Thure de Thulstrup; American Memory Collections, Library of Congress)

term the new president would wake up at night "and rub my eyes and wonder if it was not all a dream."

In the meantime, he called the dark-haired Frances Folsom "Frank." She and her mother visited their friend Grover in the White House in the spring of 1885, then the young woman visited other times at the invitation of Miss Rose. The president and the college girl—for that's where she was, in college—also corresponded, with her mother's permission.

The young woman, a student at Wells College in upstate New York, was due to graduate in 1886, but she moved the date up to 1885. Cleveland was delighted but regretful that she next would spend months touring in Europe. Before she could leave, he asked her hand in a letter. Secretly, that is. She said yes, and they planned a small, circumspect wedding upon her return in nine months.

A news leak tabbed Mrs. Folsom as the lucky lady, but that soon was clarified . . . and the word was out. The news and gossip that initially sprung up just as quickly died down in the young woman's absence, however, and Cleveland had until June of 1886 to make his circumspect wedding plans, now turning to another sister, Mary Hoyt, for advice.

The White House would be the setting, it was decided, a scheme that at the least would keep the affair controlled and out-of-bounds to the press—the "dirty gang," as Cleveland called reporters.

Frances returned from Europe aboard ship on May 27, 1886, to be met by a tugboat in the New York harbor and whisked in secret to a hotel in the city. The next day, she and her betrothed communicated by telegraph, since they couldn't yet resort to long-distance telephone calls. And that night, their engagement was announced officially.

On May 29, the future bride's hotel was a mob scene. Cleveland was on his way to New York to review parades marking Memorial Day, the next day. He paid a call on his fiancée the evening of May 29, with more good-natured mobs cheering him on. He stayed the night at Navy Secretary William C. Whitney's home, and at the Manhattan parade the next day, he was on the reviewing stand and she was on her hotel balcony two blocks away. She waved her 'kerchief, and he saw and tipped his hat. The crowds and the nineteenth-century "newsies" loved it all.

For the wedding June 2, Frances traveled down to Washington by train that very morning (more crowds, more press), spent the day at the White House and married the President in a 7:00 P.M. ceremony held in the Blue Room, richly banked with flowers, flowers, and more flowers. There followed dinner in the State Dining Room. They spent their honeymoon, accompanied by unwelcome minions of the press, at a mountain resort in Maryland.

The newlyweds returned to Washington in timely fashion, but not simply to the White House. By now, Cleveland had bought the big rambling farm mansion near the National Cathedral they would call Oak View. This president, first to marry in the White House itself, would have at his disposal both a private residence in Washington and the all-too-public Executive Mansion.

All the Way With LBJ

TRAVELING WITH LBJ COULD BE entirely unpredictable.

The Australian prime minister, Harold Holt, had drowned. It was shortly before Christmas 1967, and LBJ decided he would attend the funeral. In Australia, naturally. He took along advisers McGeorge Bundy and Walt Rostow—obviously Vietnam could be a possible stop on the way back from that part of the world.

And that is what LBJ had in mind, yes. But there would be more to the unannounced and unplanned itinerary. Why not see the president of Pakistan, too? Why not visit the pope at the Vatican in Rome on the way back from the down-under funeral as well?

Why not indeed? *Air Force One* pilot James Cross was first alerted as the White House entourage hit Australia for stop one. "As we arrived at Canberra just a little after daylight," recalled Cross later, "the President came in the cockpit. He said, 'Cross, we'll leave here in about thirty-six hours. You make some plans to go maybe up to Vietnam.'"

Maybe Thailand, too, Johnson said. Maybe Ayub Khan . . . and maybe a little Christmas doings with the pope—the unsuspecting pope—in Rome, too.

"But now don't go telling anyone."

At the end of the thirty-six hours, the president of the United

States more or less had vanished from sight, so far as the world could tell. He now was on unannounced travel—first to visit American air force personnel in Thailand, then to spread Christmas cheer among the troops at Cam Ranh Bay in warring Vietnam itself. The next stop was Karachi, for the visit with Ayub Kahn.

In Rome, meanwhile, the crowds already were gathering for the annual solemn pageantry of Christmas. And Cross, still operating on the q.t., was doing his best to line up "fuel and ground communications, as well as ground transportation, so that we could go into Rome without tipping our hand that we were going." The idea of all the secrecy was to avoid a Communist demonstration, apparently, and indeed, "The Communists never realized we were there."

On *Air Force One* itself, in the meantime, LBJ kept denying his plans. He sat on his exercise bicycle, bigger than life as usual, and said: "I ain't going to Rome. I don't know what you're talking about." He sat on the exercise bike, which was bolted to the floor, and kept denying the plan, recalled *Time-Life* correspondent Hugh Sidey. "Only Johnson could conceive that on Christmas Eve [actually it was still December 23] he would drop in unannounced on the pope."

In the end, in Rome, Johnson did concede that was the plan. In the end, without telling his own American embassy, Johnson did whirl into the Eternal City, literally whirled by helicopter into the Vatican gardens, and did visit Pope Paul VI. One point was to ask papal help on behalf of the American POWs held by Hanoi, and another point, more generally, was to dramatize the U.S. desire for peace in Vietnam.

The onlooking reporters were bemused, and more, as Johnson and the pope exchanged gifts—the pope on short notice had been able to produce a Renaissance oil painting, while Johnson presented His Holiness with a large package wrapped in plain brown paper and tied with thick rope.

When the pope couldn't pull the rope loose, Johnson came up with a jackknife, Sidey also recalled. "He flicks open the blade, rips the package, excelsior springs out all over the Oriental rugs and everything else. The press is over in the corner and by this time we are in a state of shock."

In seconds, the Johnsonian Christmas present to the pope was out in full view—a bust of LBJ himself!

Johnson and his entourage were back in Washington—he, of

course, at the White House—well in time for Christmas Eve, 1967, after some four days of whirling, unannounced for the most part, around the globe.

Rebel in the House

UNREPENTANT AND UNRECONSTRUCTED WAS THE old Confederate-loving codger who lived in one corner of the White House, who regaled the press with his "inside" stories, who sat next to the president's wife at dinner, who even then could be scathing in his remarks and unawed by any company—especially that of the president, who in fact was his son-in-law.

Old "Colonel" Frederick Dent was not about to change his spots—or dispense with his mint juleps—just because he, a Democrat from Missouri, was moving into the White House within a decade of the Civil War with his daughter Julia and her Republican president-husband, Ulysses S. Grant, surely the most *Yankee* Yankee of them all.

He not only was a White House fixture after the Grants moved in, he accompanied them on family vacations and even on an occasional political foray.

He could say very embarrassing things regardless of who was present at the presidential dinner table, and one of his favorite victims apparently was the president's own father, Jesse Grant. Dent called him "that old gentleman" and once complained in the elder Grant's presence, "He is feeble and deaf as a post, and yet you permit him to wander all over Washington alone."

Ten years younger than the eighty-plus Rebel, and a bit sharp-tongued himself, the elder Grant heard and replied: "I hope I shall not live to become as old and infirm as Grandfather Dent."

Jesse Grant usually passed up a White House guest room and took a local hotel room instead, saying the presidential home held too many from "that tribe of Dents."

Indeed, the "Colonel" or "Judge," as he alternately was called, had a space all his own in the office suite on the second floor. It was here, indeed, that he often held forth for visitors from the gossip-hungry world of the press. (It was also at the dinner table, even at his beloved daughter's very elbow, that he sometimes espoused his more embarrassing opinions.)

He occupied a bedroom close to the North Portico. And there he died one night in his own bed. His coffin then rested for a time in the "Yankee" White House, the final stopping place for the ex-slaveowner from Missouri.

Poker Players, Do Your Duty

Winston Churchill's famous Iron Curtain speech took place in Fulton, Missouri, and thereby hangs a tale of presidential travel by train, really serious poker, and a factor in Anglo-American relations to be determined by the fall of the cards (or, more accurately, the kindly disposition of the card players).

The "factor," one to be handled with awe, reverence, respect, and kid gloves, was Winston Churchill himself, recently the political hero and stout leader of his country during World War II, but now displaced as prime minister by the British electorate, although due to serve again just short years ahead.

The presidential train left Union Station in Washington in the early afternoon of March 4, 1946, for the overnight trip that would place Churchill at the podium of Westminster College in Fulton, Missouri—Harry Truman's home state—the next evening. Traveling quite comfortably in Truman's private railroad car, sofas and easy chairs at their disposal, were not only Truman and Churchill, but Admiral William D. Leahy, General Harry Vaughan, Clark Clifford, and Charlie Ross, all Truman aides, confidants, and advisers, plus Colonel Wallace Graham, the president's physician.

Truman and Churchill already had settled the matter of calling each other by first names, had shared drinks (no ice in his Scotch for Winston) and were having dinner when the subject of poker came up. According to the late Clark Clifford's autobiography *Counsel to the President* (written with Richard Holbrooke), it was Churchill who broke the ice by saying, "Harry, I understand from the press that you like to play poker."

Truman allowed that such a report could be true, yes. "I have played a great deal of poker in my life," he acknowledged.

Churchill, claiming to have started his poker while covering the turn of the century Boer War as a newspaper correspondent, was just delighted. When he suggested they all get up a game, Truman acceded with a warning: "the fellows around you are all serious poker players."

Churchill hustled off to change into something more comfortable—"his famous World War II zippered blue siren suit." Truman took advantage of the visitor's absence to enjoin his troops. Just as Nelson at Trafalgar signaled his fleet that England expected every man to do his duty, Truman now told his American colleagues that they faced a serious challenge. "Men," he said, "we have an important task ahead of us. This man is cagey and is probably an excellent player. The reputation of American poker is at stake and I expect every man to do his duty."

In the game that ensued, it turned out that Churchill "was not very good at the game" after all. Perhaps a whiz at gin or bridge, he was to poker as a lamb is to wolves, it seems. In fact, in his present company, he was a lamb among wolves.

In an hour, he had lost about $300. Then, as Churchill excused himself for a moment, Truman had to back up and tell his associates they were not treating Winston very well. Vaughan snorted, "This guy's a pigeon" and said, "If you want us to give it our best, we'll have his underwear." But Truman delivered fresh marching orders: "I don't want him to think we are pushovers, but at the same time, let's not treat him badly."

And so, Churchill was allowed to win a few hands that evening. At one point, in a game of stud poker, Charlie Ross had an ace showing on the board and a second one facedown, "in the hole." Churchill had only a jack showing but kept on betting despite the one visible ace, clearly outranking his jack. "Then," wrote Clifford, "at the end, Churchill bet a substantial amount of money right into this ace. Charlie studied what he knew had to be a winning hand, looked over at the president, gave what I thought sounded like a sigh, and folded."

By evening's end, his American hosts pressing a bit harder, Churchill may have lost about $250 all told—and apparently was happy. "He had enjoyed himself thoroughly, but had dropped just enough money so that he could not go back to London and brag that he had beaten the Americans at poker."

He did, of course, impress his American "cousins" in Fulton the next day with his forty-five-minute speech that kept the audience riveted. He had worked on it during interludes on the train, and now a young Clark Clifford saw and heard the orator Churchill in full throat. "From the point of view of high rhetoric, I had never heard anything like it before. As a demonstration of the power of ideas, it was an astonishing tour de force."

The speech at Fulton, with Truman on the podium in black academic robe and Churchill in scarlet, was the past and future prime minister's famous Iron Curtain speech, the one in which he warned the world that across continental Europe, dividing the West from an East under Soviet domination, had descended an iron curtain—the same barrier, of course, that then lasted for another forty-five years.

Dancing in the Moonlight

DINNERTIME AT THE WHITE HOUSE and a visiting Will Rogers was at the table as a guest of the Coolidges, Calvin and Grace. But they were not alone, not by any means.

Occupying the floor were the Coolidge dogs, hungry dogs at that. "Well," related the pure-American humorist later, "they was feeding the dogs so much that at one time it looked to me like the dogs was getting more than I was. The Butler was so slow in bringing one course that I come pretty near getting down on my all fours and barking to see if business wouldn't pick up with me."

Will Rogers may have stretched a point or two, but it is a fact that White House pets have wielded a peculiar power all their own for more than two hundred years. For the onlooking public, they also have been a source of great and enduring fascination.

Creatures of some influence, do we suggest? Warren G. Harding, Coolidge's immediate predecessor, and Lyndon B. Johnson, four decades later, were known to take their dogs into cabinet meetings. Benjamin Harrison was led on a merry chase down the streets of Washington by His Whiskers, the pet goat he had given his grandchildren. The same ornery creature not long before had sent the White House coachman, Willis by name, scurrying up a fence to avoid its charge. Now the goat dashed through the White House gate with three Harrison grandchildren in tow aboard a goat cart. Hence the unseemly and undignified sight of a nineteenth-century president chasing the goat in his frock coat, with cane and top hat in hand.

Goat influence? Abe Lincoln's two goats, Nanny and Nanko, had the run of the house—Nanny once was found snoozing on son Tad's bed. On another occasion, Abe piled Tad and both goats into a carriage for a ride out to the Washington Soldiers' Home. Another Lincoln animal, incidentally, was a turkey named Jack. He once had been marked for the dinner table, but Tad spared Jack that fate by adopting him as a pet.

Such house privileges, of course, were not restricted to goats. Nor to the more commonplace dogs, cats and pet birds, either. As mentioned earlier, Teddy Roosevelt's pony "Algonquin" once rode the elevator to the family quarters to cheer TR's ailing son Quentin while he briefly was restricted to bed.

Additional family pets that enlivened the White House during the tenure of Teddy Roosevelt and his six children included guinea pigs, two kangaroo rats, a badger, a one-legged rooster, a pig, a hyena, a small bear, an owl, a lizard, Peter the rabbit, a flying squirrel, and a piebald rat that TR himself once depicted as crawling "all over everybody" and described as having "a most friendly and affectionate nature." Then, too, there were in the TR household Eli Yale the macaw and Alice's pet garter snake, Emily Spinach.

Speaking of snakes, a proud young Quentin one time burst into his father's office with four handsome wigglies just purchased at a pet store. Never mind that TR was a bit occupied with VIP visitors—Quentin simply dumped out the snakes on a tabletop. As Niall Kelly reported in the book *Presidential Pets,* "all hell broke loose." Everybody shrunk back, but the snakes paid little attention—they were busy fighting each other. In time, Quentin and TR managed to corral the creatures . . . for a fast return to the pet shop.

The same helpful source book also reported that Teddy's oldest child, Alice, was the proud owner of a black Pekingese named Manchu, a gift from the last empress of China. "Manchu lived with Alice for several years and she once claimed to have seen it dancing on its hind legs in the moonlight on the White House lawn."

Other White House pets over the years made their presence known in various ways. Ulysses S. Grant's gamecocks fought so much they had to be kept at opposite ends of the White House grounds, but then they woke the neighbors all the time by scream-ing—crowing, that is—insults at each other in the early hours of dawn.

Before acquiring his widely adored, gentle Scottie, Fala, FDR had to banish a dog named Major that tended to bite people. Fala, on the other hand, in one instance became a victim of his adoring public. Traveling to Hawaii with FDR on the U.S. Navy cruiser *Baltimore* in 1944, Fala temporarily wandered off, then reappeared with much of his hair mysteriously missing.

The mystery was solved when it turned out the sailors aboard had lured Fala below decks for a friendly visit, than plucked entire "tufts of his hair" as souvenirs.

Dogs, of course, have been ubiquitous and pampered as White House pets for years. The Washington Children's Museum, it may be recalled, hired an interior decorator to build Ronald Reagan's dog Rex a doghouse replete with small portraits of Ron and Nancy on the inner walls. As another kind of shaggy-dog story, Jerry Ford would signal his dog Liberty to run into the Oval Office as a dis-traction when it was time to end a visitor's visit. Let it be noted also that Richard M. Nixon's dog King Timahoe liked to shake hands with his visitors.

One dog, Warren G. Harding's Airedale, Laddie Boy, was destined to be immortalized by a statue built of melted-down pennies gath-ered by newsboys the nation over. This celebrated canine not only sat in at cabinet meetings, he sat on a chair all his own. He once was "interviewed" by the *Washington Star* and another time was central figure at a birthday party—his own, of course, with neighborhood dogs as guests. After former newspaperman Harding's sudden death in San Francisco, the newsboys began their penny drive—one coin asked of each boy. The 19,134 pennies they collected were molded into a statue of Laddie Boy that wound up in the Smithsonian.

Among the nation's earliest presidents, horses were favorite and

Widely forgotten today, Warren G. Harding did have his day in the White House sun. So did his pet dog Laddie. Scandal would taint the obviously inept Harding's tenure, and yet when he suddenly died in San Francisco, he was greatly—and even widely—mourned. (National Photo Company, American Memory Collections, Library of Congress)

sometimes famous pets. Former general Zachary Taylor's Mexican War mount Old Whitey was allowed to graze on the White House lawns, where tourists loved to pluck hairs from his tail. Less than two years after Taylor's 1849 inauguration, however, Old Whitey was the symbolic riderless horse in his master's funeral cortege.

Another famous horse was President John Tyler's General, later buried at his master's Sherwood Forest plantation home in Virginia.

It wasn't always horses back in those days, either—at least three presidents shared their White House experience with cows. William Henry Harrison boasted a bovine named Sukey; Andrew Johnson brought along one or more such creatures; while William Howard Taft obtained household milk from a cow named Mooly Wooly and then from a more productive Holstein named Pauline Wayne, the last known cow at the White House.

A handful of other White House pets generated history of a sort. The Rutherford Hayeses, for instance, go down in history for introducing the Siamese cat to America . . . but through no initiative of their own. David Sickles, the American consul in Siam, had read that first lady Lucy Rutherford loved cats, so he sent her a Siamese kitten. "I am informed that this is the first attempt ever made to send a Siamese cat to America," he wrote to Mrs. Hayes.

Surviving travel first to Hong Kong, then to San Francisco by ship, then to Washington, the kitten arrived safely and became a member of the president's household, only to sicken and die a year later. Speaking of pets dying an untimely death, President Grant took drastic action after several of his son Jesse's dogs mysteriously died, one after the other. When Jesse acquired still another dog, Faithful, President Grant warned the entire White House staff that they all would be fired if anything happened to the new dog. Nothing did, and Faithful lived on.

Dolley Madison not only rescued the famous Gilbert Stuart portrait of George Washington before the British burned down the White House during the War of 1812, but also a family pet: their parrot, which then outlived her husband, James Madison.

One of the very first White House occupants to own a bird was Thomas Jefferson. His feathered companion was a mockingbird named Dick. According to the Niall Kelly book: "Dick's cage hung among the roses and geraniums in a window recess at the White House. Whenever the President was alone he opened the cage and gave Dick the freedom of the room. The bird would sit at the table and sing or would perch on the President's shoulder and take food from his lips."

More publicly, for a while Jefferson was host to grizzly bears sent back to Washington by the Lewis and Clark expedition. They stayed in a cage on the White House grounds, sometimes then called "The President's Bear Garden."

Another exotic animal briefly in residence at the White House was an alligator on loan, more or less, to John Quincy Adams by the Marquis de Lafayette while the Frenchman toured the United States in 1824 and 1825, many years after his contributions to the American Revolution. Lafayette reclaimed his alligator before returning home to France. The animal had spent its White House stay in the East Room.

Dwight D. Eisenhower was one president eager to get rid of some animals—not pets, exactly, but squirrels that kept digging holes in his pristine putting green. First, his staff created a similar sward of smooth grass for the pesky critters and covered it with alluring nuts. But the animals simply used both patches of grass.

Next, the squirrels were trapped and removed to the area of the Lincoln Memorial, but some then wandered back to their old White House haunts. Finally, the squirrels were trapped again and moved to a park several miles away, this time gone for good.

Additional note: Among a few more pets seen in the presidential home over its two-hundred-year history were the John F. Kennedy pony Macaroni; John Adams's horse Cleopatra; more mockingbirds; William McKinley's parrot named Washington Post; Lyndon Johnson's two beagles Him and Her; George and Barbara Bush's dog, the "author" named Millie; a mule or two; a donkey; and the Coolidge family's Rebecca the raccoon.

Still more presidential pets ranged from opossums, to sheep, an antelope, a bobcat, several fish, even elephants and two tiger cubs. The more exotic creatures, such as Martin van Buren's tiger cubs or James Buchanan's elephants, gifts from abroad, were turned over to the nearest friendly zoo. It was Buchanan, however, who owned that quintessential symbol of America, the bald eagle. Actually, he owned a pair of eagles but instead of bringing them to the White House, he kept them at his private home, Wheatland, in Lancaster, Pennsylvania.

Daily Mission Accomplished

Issuing forth from the great house morning after morning was a determined young man on a mission for the president and his household. It would be embarrassing if he failed . . . and a culinary delight when he succeeded.

In his search, he prowled pathways destined to become today's streets, alleys, and avenues. Back then, in 1801, they were woodland paths across open fields or perhaps muddy roads meandering through shrub. And the young man, soon to establish himself as one of the all-time great explorers, was Thomas Jefferson's protégé and private secretary, Meriwether Lewis, who hailed from Albemarle County, where Jefferson had built his beloved Monticello.

Lewis arrived at the unfinished White House soon after Jefferson's inauguration on March 4, 1801, and took up his duties in his employer's absence. Jefferson had retreated to Monticello for about thirty days when Captain Lewis of the U.S. Army led his pack horses overland from Detroit to take up his posting with the third president. The White House was so far from finished even after John Adams's four-year term that Jefferson stayed on at his boarding house in Washington for fifteen days after his inauguration, then left for his month-long stay at Monticello. Further work on the White House was to be completed by the time he returned. One thing he wanted done as quickly as possible was the removal of the outdoor privy the Adamses had installed, and its replacement with a pair of more private and seemly water closets installed inside the President's House.

Lewis, though, would "rough it" as a White House aide, confidant, messenger, and secretary to Jefferson. He would be given space screened off in the large public room later known as the East Room. There, makeshift partitions provided a small bed chamber and a small office space for the young man. Jefferson's own office would be at the opposite end of the house, at the west end of the long transverse hall.

In 1804, Lewis, with William Clark, would set off on a three-year exploratory journey across the continent that opened up the West as no other single event. The famed Lewis and Clark expedition, instigated by President Jefferson, proved the feasibility of overland travel all the way to the West Coast.

Young Lewis already was an outdoors type before his sojourn in the White House—he had hunted 'coon and 'possum alone in the Virginia woods at night at the age of eight. And now, even in such a sophisticated setting as the President's House, he kept up his outdoorsman skills through his daily mission. Leaving the White House in the early-morning mists, he hunted and killed game for the household dinner table, hunting on land today covered with brick and tar and concrete, in the teeming city surrounding the same white-hued President's House of a simpler day.

Three Days of Oratory

THE LIFESTYLE OF A PRESIDENT, the gold-plated spoons he found in use at the White House, and his own "pretty, tapering, soft, white lily fingers" were the subject of a famous and scathing congressional speech in the early-nineteenth century.

The butt of Whig congressman William Ogle's "Gold Spoon" speech was Martin Van Buren, a widowed father of four sons who indeed had brought an effete and elegant air to the presidential mansion in comparison with his more plebeian predecessor, Andrew Jackson. And it was Van Buren's unfortunate lot, politically, to preside over the nation's first real depression.

He first "cleaned house" by auctioning off the more worn or gaudy of the Jackson furnishings, though Jackson had been his political ally and mentor. He next refurbished or installed new rugs, chinaware, upholstery, and the like. Ironically, though, the gold-plated spoons that Ogle would soon castigate him about were a legacy from President James Monroe and not Van Buren's own affectation.

But Van Buren definitely did create a more aristocratic, less democratic atmosphere at the White House. He favored a Continental menu for his elegant little dinner parties. He didn't balk at attending the widely ballyhooed wedding of the aging Russian minister to Washington, Count Bodisco, to a Georgetown school girl, all of fourteen years in age. But then, neither did most of Washington society.

Dolley Madison, meanwhile, returned to her beloved Washington in 1837 and took up residence across Lafayette Square from her old abode. She then set out to find for Van Buren an official White House hostess, since he and his four sons were not quite that, no matter how hard they might try.

The happy result was the Dolley-maneuvered introduction of her own distant relative, Angelica Singleton of South Carolina, to Van Buren's oldest son, Abraham, who was his father's private secretary. In short order, they fell in love, married in South Carolina, and moved into the White House. There, in proper time, Angelica gave birth to a baby girl, but the infant died soon after.

More happily, Angelica was a lively success in her role as hostess of the White House. Her first social affair, on New Year's Day 1839, set off a Washington tradition that would last for many years. After visiting the White House New Year's reception, the social lions of the capital would move on to Dolley Madison's house across the famous square.

One who had dined at the Van Buren White House often enough himself was the famed Pennsylvania orator William Ogle; but with the presidential election of 1840 looming, that did not stop him from castigating Van Buren for a long list of White House frills, many of which were not of Van Buren's doing.

The presidential home, Ogle said, "glitters with all imaginable luxuries and gaudy ornaments." How could the citizenry support "their chief servant in a Palace as splendid as that of the Caesars and as richly adorned as the proudest Asiatic mansion?"

Finger bowls, *pâté de fois gras,* golden knives and forks, silver plates and a silver soup tureen, foreign-cut wine coolers, and "golden chains to hang golden labels around the necks of barrel-shaped flute decanters with cone stoppers"—all came under Ogle's attack. The food served at Van Buren's White House, of course, would never do either, offerings such as "*dinde dessosse* and *salade a la volille.*" "Where, oh where," admonished Ogle, were good old "fried meat and gravy, or hog and hominy?"

Fastidious, dapper, and small, Van Buren really was not so extravagant, but a time of shaky national economy was no time for indulgences that might be misconstrued, no matter how reasonable. Such as new curtains for the Blue Room ($1,307.50 for three). Such as foreign-made carpeting. Overall, though, Van Buren had only cleaned and scrubbed, upholstered, papered and painted. Later White House historian William Seale wrote, "Van Buren actually spent less than half of what Andrew Jackson had put out on the house, approximately the same amount of the second Adams [John Quincy], and not half as much as the first Adams."

Two steps that Van Buren did take were well worth the effort, if not the expense—he added shower baths and copper bathtubs to the bathing facilities of the East Wing (but no running water for the second floor), and he replaced and improved upon the heating system installed by Madison that had been destroyed by the British in 1814. Van Buren implemented a hot-air heating system for the first floor and the great hall upstairs. The upstairs rooms still would be heated strictly by individual fireplaces tended by "fireman" servants.

Van Buren's mistake was to allow appearances that made him vulnerable to charges of elitism and antipathy to truly democratic thought. His coach, with its silver trim and matching four, was the "finest seen in the capital since General Washington's," wrote Seale in his two-volume history, *The President's House.* His son John, after visiting Queen Victoria, acquired the nickname "Prince John." That being the case, Van Buren's daughter-in-law Angelica as White House hostess might have thought better than to receive guests while seated on a platform . . . somewhat like a queen!

Unable to fix the nation's economy, unwilling to mend his small affectations, Van Buren was a tempting target for political bullies, and Ogle was so glad to play the part that he kept up his "Gold Spoon" speech for three days while the entire House sat as a committee of the whole and the crowds in the galleries grew ever larger and more gleeful.

Ogle's exaggerations were typical of the year's "Log Cabin" campaign that elected William Henry Harrison in Van Buren's stead. Harrison was an old Indian fighter, an Ohio resident, a colorful and heroic figure who might have spent some time at frontier log cabins in the past, but he also was the scion of an aristocratic Virginia family, and he had lived in grand homes in both the Indiana territory and in Ohio.

If Van Buren held the election outcome against Harrison in any way, he hid his feelings quite well. When the president-elect visited Washington a month before his inauguration on March 4, 1841, he visited Van Buren at the White House, and Van Buren visited him at Gadsby's Hotel. The outgoing president even invited Harrison to move into the White House before the inaugural activities for a bit of rest and to get away from harassing job-seekers.

Harrison instead visited his daughter in Virginia, but thanks to Martin Van Buren, a well-heated White House could have been his before he became president . . . before he caught a cold at his inauguration that led to his death in a month's time.

Additional note: As if he needed another tussle with Congress, Van Buren had one anyway—this one over a pair of tiger cubs sent as a present to the president of the United States by the Sultan of Oman,

Kabul al Said. "Before Van Buren could decide how to accommodate these new pets in his household," wrote Niall Kelly in his book *Presidential Pets,* "Congress stepped in, insisting that the ship had embarked while [Andrew] Jackson was president and that therefore the cubs were the property of the people of the United States." Van Buren countered that if they were sent to the president, he was now president and they should be his. In the end, after debate over the issue "raged back and forth," it was Congress that prevailed—"the cubs were confiscated and sent to the zoo."

Press Conference Tactics

WHEN JFK REPLACED IKE IN the White House, the minions of the press had to change press conference tactics to suit the new man's personality and style. For reporters, the name of the game was to be noticed by the president, and, of course, to have a pithy question at the ready for the moment the presidential lightning struck. Might strike, that is.

The stalwarts of the *New York Times* had it pretty well doped out back in the early '60s.

Dwight David Eisenhower, a more elderly man than his successor, John F. Kennedy, had tended to start on one side of the press conference site and stay there.

The first question, therefore, very nearly decided which side of the room would get in all the questions. Purely a random guess in advance. At the same time, there was a protocol that granted some favors—to the "wires," for instance, since the Associated Press, United Press, Reuter, and so on, provided nearly instant access to an audience of millions. They had White House respect.

Beyond the lopsided room ploy, Ike had three other quirks worth noting, each often dictating journalistic strategy:

1. He didn't recognize too many reporters by name, so he would give the nod to "you with the glasses there" or "that man with the bald head."

2. His mangled syntax was notorious, almost as well known as Casey Stengal's "Stengalese." Not known for their reverence, the postwar reporters covering Ike had a cruel jibe for him (and/or his speechwriters) on the occasion of a globe-circling presidential trip—"Around the World in Eighty Platitudes."

3. No sympathetic tears were shed when poor Ike ran afoul of Sarah McClendon. Here, far from the battlefields of Europe, was a challenge utterly foreign to Ike. Neither West Point nor the Crusade in Europe had quite prepared him. Wrote *Times* reporter W. E. Kenworthy in the book *The Working Press: Special to the* New York Times (edited by Ruth Adler):

> There was one sure way of getting in a question with Eisenhower. That was to wait until Sarah McClendon asked one of her outrageous questions. Amidst the ensuing laughter, Eisenhower, red-faced and suffocating with exasperation, would practically embrace the reporter who at that moment rescued him by jumping up and saying, "Mr. President."

With the advent of the JFK years, the *Times*'s Washington bureau adopted new tactics to suit the new man's style.

For one thing, his eye roved across both sides of the room, which meant dispersing the troops. Tom Wicker, the paper's White House beat man, had an automatic seat front and center, first row. He was "certain to be recognized," along with the wires, also up front. Kennedy could be expected to rove up and down the first three or four rows—but how, even then, to catch his eye? "With Kennedy," wrote Kenworthy, "it's strictly a matter of timing—you must begin to rise as his finger begins to fall, and just as it is wagging his afterthought you must come in fast and he will say, 'Yes?' "

The typical JFK press conference called for careful planning, especially late in the day and close to the morning paper's early-evening deadline. For the *Times* reporters, longtime columnist and political savant James "Scotty" Reston in those days was "presiding inquisitor" in the strategy huddle held in his Washington bureau office.

The strategy was to eschew the obvious and most basic questions, since they quickly would be disposed of by the news-agency reps. What the *Times*men instead must pose were the follow-ups, the less obvious issues. They developed a list of perhaps six or more questions. They even calculated the right wording "to entice or force a responsive answer." (With Ike, but no longer with JFK, it had been necessary to set the stage for the question with background information as a reminder.)

The questions assigned in advance, the *Times* crew of five to seven reporters would arrive in a large black limousine for the JFK press conference, usually held in the State Department auditorium before at least 250 reporters. With JFK's arrival after his own staff briefing session, the questions would fly fast and furious. Then, it was off to meet the deadline. First, though, a copy boy had obtained the first few pages of the official White House transcript of the press conference—the rest of the session's every utterance to be ready in less than thirty minutes from the closing "Thank You, Mr. President." Armed with these first pages (the copy boy staying behind to retrieve the rest) and their own notes, the *Times* reporters flew back to the bureau offices in the same limo, usually all together, still in a pack.

The man to write the lead had been selected, and the early transcript pages were his meat, especially if the lead stemmed from a presidential announcement. In the seven-minute run back to the bureau, the *Times*men divided their spoils, their news editor up front in the limo and facing the passengers in the rear.

"He flips through his notes, conferring with Scotty," wrote Kenworthy. "The lead is obvious—nuclear test ban. 'John, you take that. Tom, politics. Tony, civil rights. Max, Laos and wrap the rest of the foreign stuff with paramarks. Jack, McClellan and the TFX.' So it goes. By the time the car reaches the office, the conference is cut up." And so, making history . . . another presidential press conference, far different, not only from Ike's but also from the onetime gatherings of a few familiars at the presidential desk in the Oval Office.

"This Damned Old House"

THE WHITE HOUSE THAT ABRAHAM Lincoln took over in 1861 was in many ways like a state capitol in a state capital. For one thing, inconceivable now, people thronged its hallways, it was a public building open to the public. And filled with the public.

To "go home" to his private quarters for lunch, Lincoln had to push his way through the crowds jamming the hallways.

His normal routine was to rise at 7 A.M. and work for about two quiet hours, then have breakfast with his family in the private quarters allotted to the president at the west end of the second floor.

Then he "went to work," to his office at the east end, same floor, a room that also doubled as the Cabinet Room. He kept a large desk with pigeonholes containing various papers, but he did his paperwork at a table nearby. In the winter he would be warmed by a fire beneath a marble mantel. An oil portrait of an earlier frontiersman looked on silently—Andrew Jackson. Other decorations were sparse, unless you count the maps pinned to the walls or lying on the lengthy cabinet table.

The cabinet met at noon on Tuesdays and Fridays, but even without that complication, Lincoln soon found that as president he could not maintain his original idea of having unlimited visiting hours. So he fixed those times as 10 A.M. to 1 P.M., Monday, Wednesday, and Thursday. During these hours, even unannounced, ordinary citizens could see him if they were willing to wait long enough.

A guard kept order in the jammed hall outside his office and took visitors' cards. A private secretary, John G. Nicolay, did screen the most pressing visitors. Lincoln accomplished his office work with the help of three secretaries through most of the Civil War period. The daily staff in the "business" section of the White House also included a doorman.

By 1864 new interior modeling would permit Lincoln access to his family quarters without pushing through the awaiting throngs.

His routine also called for a daily outing in a carriage with Mrs. Lincoln, usually at 4 P.M., and walks. Since the White House had no telegraph of its own in those days, Lincoln had to go to the nearby War Department every night to see the day's Civil War dispatches. It wasn't until late in 1864 that a Washington police officer, in plainclothes but armed, was assigned to accompany Lincoln on such outings on foot.

Dinner was usually served at 6 P.M., but state dinners began a bit later—at 7:30 P.M. In time, the Lincolns held public receptions on Tuesday evenings and Saturday afternoons. It is said that souvenir hunters constantly snatched away bits of drapery and carpet.

Since the place did look tattered when they moved in, Mary Todd Lincoln was given a $20,000 congressional appropriation to spruce up the presidential home. She spent the money in no time on carpets, draperies, furniture, chinaware (666 pieces of Limoges!) and in fact ran up a deficit of another $6,000. Her husband was mortified, and in perhaps their best-known domestic tiff, later complained to Benjamin Brown, commissioner of public buildings, that "it would stink in the nostrils of the American people to have it said that the President of the United States had approved a bill overrunning an appropriation of $20,000 for flub dubs, for this damned old house, when the soldiers cannot have blankets."

The president's own salary, meanwhile was an annual $25,000, and, amazingly, he apparently was able to put much of that sum aside for a rainy day. He entered the White House worth $15,000, and when he was assassinated four years later, his estate had grown to $85,000. He kept his money at the Riggs Bank in Washington.

Certainly earning his salary, he on most days in the White House went back to work in his office after dinner. He would quit his labors at about 11 P.M.

The Lincolns did not enjoy a very active social life in their new city of Washington, traditionally and still dominated by a southern social elite and hostile in mood to all that Lincoln represented. There were fears, when he first arrived as president-elect, of plots to seize the Capitol—still lacking its dome—and he had been inaugurated with Federal cavalry spotted at key points in the city and with riflemen on the rooftops.

No surprise, then, that the Lincolns seldom went "out," except to the opera and the theater.

They did entertain, however, holding Friday evening "levees" or dances, during which Mary Todd Lincoln would stand slightly behind her husband in the receiving line rather than shake every hand. Their son Willie's death from a fever early in 1862 took her from the social scene for at least a year. Lincoln's assassination in 1865 ended it all for the Lincolns . . . except for the grief and the memories of an unbalanced Mary Todd Lincoln and her two surviving boys.

Anger in Stages

IN HIS DAYS AT THE White House as a top aide to President William Jefferson Clinton, George Stephanopoulos learned to deal with, even to categorize, anger—not his, but that of his boss, Bill Clinton.

"The most common and least virulent strain of Clinton's anger was the morning roar," wrote Stephanopoulos in his 1999 book *All Too Human: A Political Education.* "He's not a morning person. He wakes up cranky and moves slowly. The morning roar was a way of clearing his throat before breakfast, like a rooster greeting the dawn, but with an edge. It rarely signified any deep seething, just irritation at an outside event that he couldn't control, like an overcrowded schedule, a speech draft he didn't like, or almost any story in the morning paper."

The Roar usually came with Clinton seated at his desk in that room Stephanopoulos called "the Oval." Typically, Clinton had emptied piles of notes from his overnight briefcase on the desk, and now he thrust out the irritating article. "He'd push the paper toward me, his voice rising in staccato bursts to emphasize his point: 'This . . . is . . . just . . . wrong. . . . It's just not honest. . . . I don't . . . have time . . . to think. . . . I try . . . and try . . . and try . . . to tell you . . . but they never . . . get it . . . right!'"

Sounds bad to the uninitiated, but no real problem for those used to Clinton's outbursts, it seems. "As long as Clinton stayed seated at his desk, there wasn't much to worry about. I'd promise to fix the problem, explain the reasoning behind the day's events one more time, sympathize with him on the press bias, and change the subject."

Another category, "a close cousin" to the Roar, was the "nightcap." Stephanopoulos rarely witnessed this phenom in person. He usually was exposed to it in a nighttime phone call, "but I could imagine him in jeans and a sweatshirt at the kitchen counter, surrounded by his ubiquitous piles, with the television on in the background."

Again, no really big deal. "The trigger event was usually a conversation with Hillary, a phone call from a friend in Arkansas about some new right-wing outrage, or a critical Senate floor speech that he had just seen replayed on C-Span. Like the morning roar, it usually wasn't too serious. Again, a promise to fix it in the morning , coupled with some reassuring words, or a tidbit of gossip, usually worked like a glass of warm milk."

But watch out if the Nightcap "didn't fade with a good night's sleep." That likely meant "more serious trouble was brewing."

So did the "slow boil." *Especially* the Slow Boil. Building in a single meeting, in the course of a couple of days, or over a period of weeks, this was "the eruption of a resentment that had been churning inside him, and every external event became new evidence that the underlying condition wasn't being addressed."

The onetime Clinton aide made the Slow Boil sound positively volcanic. "The slow boil built like a baroque concerto, with intricate variations on a theme, repeated and repeated at increasing volume until the crescendo ended in a crash of exhaustion. Slow boils were the product of deep-seated structural problems, not trivial matters. Although the outbursts were unpleasant, they were usually justified."

Moving on, Stephanopoulos next listed the Show and the Last Gasp. The first "was Clinton's way of making himself mad for the benefit of someone else in the room, usually Hillary." She, the first lady, carried the ball during the first Clinton term in the struggle for congressional action authorizing some sort of national health insurance program, a crusade that ended in failure. During that "health care fight," Stephanopoulos explained, Clinton "often exploded in legislative strategy meetings as a way of protecting Hillary and telling us to take her seriously."

And the Last Gasp? This was the weapon of choice when Clinton "suspected he had made a mistake but didn't want to admit it." This approach could feature "elements of counterattack and a little preemptive blame laying." For instance: "I'll do this if you want me to, but I have to say, I think it's *wrong!*"

Finally, there was the Silent Scream, apparently the worst Clinton anger of all. "No yelling, no finger in your face, nothing. Just silence. I would walk into the office, and he wouldn't look up; the slightly formal 'Hello, George' would sound more like an irritating obligation than a greeting. He wouldn't automatically turn to me to gauge my reaction to his new idea or his proposed answer in a press conference. He wouldn't stop by. He wouldn't call. And worst of all, he wouldn't mention what had made him so mad—because it was me."

What did make Clinton *silently* furious with Stephanopoulos one time was the publication of *Washington Post* reporter Robert Woodward's book *The Agenda* halfway through Clinton's first term. Stephanopoulos had given Woodward "broad access" to White House staff and functions and now was being blamed for unflattering quotes that others gave Woodward.

For instance, the book reported that Stephanopoulos told others that Clinton was like a kaleidoscope because he tended to show the onlooker just one of many facets at a time. Another reference said Clinton was slow to make decisions and quoted Stephanopoulos as saying (not to Woodward, but to someone else again), "The worst thing about him is that he never makes a decision."

It was during the Clinton trip to Normandy for the fiftieth anniversary of D-Day in June 1994 that Stephanopoulos found out just how angry Clinton was over the then-new book. "Toward the end of the D-Day trip, I knew Clinton was raging about Woodward— he had to be. But he didn't discuss *The Agenda* in my presence. The only inkling I got of how angry he was came below the decks of the USS *George Washington*. As we walked toward a makeshift television studio for the president's interview with NBC's Tom Brokaw, I warned Clinton about a new *Newsweek* poll that rated Colin Powell [former chairman of the Joint Chiefs of Staff] and Bob Dole [then Senate Majority leader and later the Republican nominee in the 1996 presidential campaign against Clinton himself] ahead of him as 'role models' for America's young people. Both were potential rivals, and if Brokaw blindsided Clinton with the news, it could make for a petulant interview."

Clinton, usually glad to be forewarned of such unpleasant tidings, this time was not particularly appreciative of his close aide's information. "Clinton seized up and stared straight down at me, his clear blue eyes clouded with suppressed rage. 'I didn't need that now, George. I didn't need you to bring me down.' I perceived the rebuke as an outburst, but he wasn't yelling at all. He was all control, and his words had a metallic tone. It was the first manifestation of a resentment that would last for weeks."

Nor was Hillary happy with the Woodward book's impact. "Hillary didn't mask her anger. Over the next several weeks, *The*

Agenda became her single-bullet theory for our summer troubles. 'The whole problem with this administration is the Woodward book,' she said at one July strategy session. 'It's hurting us overseas, and it's the reason all our [poll] numbers are down. There are people who go out there with no loyalty to the President, no loyalty to the work we have to do for the country, just seeking to aggrandize themselves. And I hope they're *satisfied!*' "

After serving in the White House for four tough years, Stephanopoulos left the Clinton administration to become a visiting professor at Columbia University and a political analyst for ABC News. He was frank to say in his book that the pressures of working in the White House gave him sleepless nights and even a skin condition that he tried to cover by growing a beard.

Bungee Jump With No Rope

EVER HEARD OF THE JUDSON Welliver Society? Unless you're a former speechwriter for the White House, probably not. Especially since Mr. Welliver is widely forgotten today, despite a historic stint as "literary clerk" to President Calvin Coolidge. As recalled by former White House aide George Stephanopoulos, though, Welliver qualifies as the first White House speechwriter ever, and his namesake "society" in the 1990s was "a group of former White House scribes of both [political] parties who met periodically at the home of William Safire, the Nixon speechwriter and *New York Times* columnist."

When invited to speak to the group early in President Bill Clinton's first term, newcomer Stephanopoulos found arrayed before him "speechwriters from every president since Eisenhower—Stephen Hess, Ted Sorensen, Jack Valenti, Pat Buchanan, Jim Fallows, David Gergen, Peggy Noonan, and several more."

Stephanopoulos, senior adviser to Clinton at the time, didn't arrive until after 10 P.M., and when he did, he was "still flustered from the day's events." Appropriately enough, a major flustering factor had been a presidential speech.

Two days before delivering his first formal State of the Union address on February 17, 1993, Clinton had decided to go on the air to announce bad news on taxes. "The economic plan we finally developed . . . seemed disappointing at first to a liberal like me," explained Stephanopoulos in *All Too Human.* "We had to drop the middle-class tax cut and drastically reduce the human capital investments proposed in the campaign. But we were hamstrung by the size of the deficit and the demands of the bond market."

Even so, some campaign promises could be fulfilled. Clinton and staff were "still fiddling with the numbers" on Monday, February 15, "the day Clinton was set to give an Oval Office address designed to break the bad news on taxes before he outlined the popular agenda items in the State of the Union two days later." This meant a speech—close work, many last minute changes on an *important* speech. "All day long Clinton scrawled over the text in black felt marker, ignoring the clock. I gave up on getting an advance copy to the press. At 8:48, the text was loaded into the TelePrompTer, and Clinton raced through a single practice before the [television] networks went live at nine."

Clinton, Stephanopoulos, and company in the White House thought the presidential speech had gone well, considering the circumstances. Not so the savants of the speechwriters' society, however. "The verdict from the jury sequestered in Safire's basement was not so favorable; they thought the 'class warfare' rhetoric was too hot and the delivery too hurried."

Stephanopoulos admittedly was "deflated a bit by their reviews," but he nonetheless "felt protected in that room, as if I were being inducted into an exclusive club where I wasn't just Clinton's guy anymore but part of the community of people who would always know they had written for a president."

Stephanopoulos spoke informally to his fellow scribes about the speech-writing process as then practiced in the Clinton White House, as practiced earlier that very day. "As I recounted the chaotic details, the members began to stare, their jaws dropping in disbelief. Pat Buchanan finally broke the spell. 'You mean, you mean,' he faltered, 'he didn't practice for the first time until ten minutes before *nine*?' Incredulous murmurs swept over the tables. I hung in for a few more minutes, until Bush speechwriter Tony Snow finally exclaimed, 'George, you guys are bungee jumping without a rope.'"

Stephanopoulos wrote that he "just didn't know it at the time," but Tony Snow was absolutely correct. "It's hard to develop a sense of perspective from the cramped quarters of the West Wing, which is at once the most intimate and transparent corner of the government, where you're bombarded hourly with more information, advice, and attacks than you can possibly absorb, where snap decisions may shape history and thoughtful deliberations can lead to nothing, where the mundane details of daily life mingle with majesty and mystery."

Before the evening ended, White House veteran Safire took the young Clinton tyro aside and advised him occasionally to stop and smell the roses in the Rose Garden. Avoid getting all caught up in the details of life at the pressure-cooker White House, Safire warned. Sound and simple advice, Stephanopoulos agreed, but "difficult to follow."

On Saturdays, however, the somewhat slower pace did allow time to "take my newspapers and coffee to the steps leading from the Oval Office to the Rose Garen savoring the feeling of being the first one up in a quiet house that happened to feel like the center of world."

One Saturday, however, the grim realities of life in that world struck home unexpectedly. Stephanopoulos had ventured out to a tree on the South Lawn. He leaned against it and began reading. Suddenly, three uniformed guards were standing over him. "The trees were wired, and alarms were ringing all over the White House grounds."

Another South Lawn shock, far more serious, came on September 12, 1994. That was the day a small airplane appeared out of nowhere and made a beeline for the south walls of the White House in the dark of night. An ancient magnolia tree planted in Andrew Jackson's tenure proved to be "Bill Clinton's last line of defense" in the incident, wrote Stephanopoulos. Flown by "a depressed veteran," the plane "skidded across the [South] Lawn, hurtled through a holly hedge, and winged the branches of the old magnolia before slamming into the wall two floors below Clinton's bedroom."

It wasn't clear whether the dead pilot, identified as Frank Corder, meant to endanger the president and do him real harm, or merely intended to prove he could land the plane on the South

Lawn. Friends said he had boasted he could do it, but they had "brushed it off as beer talk." Either way, the Secret Service and others concerned with White House security were not amused.

Harry Homebody

THROUGHOUT HIS CAREER IN PUBLIC office—even as senator, vice president, and president—Harry S. Truman was one to keep in close touch with family and old friends back home. He wrote to his elderly mother every three or four days, often with pithy comments on the great issues or towering public figures of the day, and he kept up old ties in other ways, too.

The April evening he unexpectedly became president, due to Franklin Roosevelt's sudden death, Vice President Truman had planned to play poker with his old World War I artillery compatriot Eddie McKim and others in a Washington hotel. Just three months later, though, *President* Truman's informal activities before and during the Potsdam Conference with Stalin and Churchill were still typical of the man.

Crossing the Atlantic aboard the U.S. cruiser *Augusta,* he soon found a distant relative among the crew—"Lawrence Truman from Owensboro, Kentucky, who was the great-grandson of Grandfather Truman's brother," reported daughter Margaret in her biography simply titled *Harry S. Truman.* But that brief encounter would not be the full extent of her presidential father's extracurricular interests at Potsdam, it seems.

Using a scrambler phone, he called Margaret and her mother, Bess, in their hometown of Independence, Missouri, almost every one of the seventeen days he spent with Stalin, Churchill, and Churchill's successor as British prime minister, Clement Atlee. "He never mentioned affairs of state. It was just family chit-chat. Even when he was trying to settle the problems of the world, he kept in touch with his family in Missouri," wrote Margaret years later.

At Potsdam also, Truman issued a presidential order stopping

U.S. Army Sgt. Harry Truman—the president's nephew—from boarding a troopship on his way home from war-devastated Europe. The same order "whisked him to Potsdam for several days of high-style relaxation."

Truman also was able to visit his cousin Ralph's son Louis—Col. Louis Truman. By family "networking," he then found himself a White House doctor. "He heard that Wallace Graham, son of his old family doctor of the same name, was stationed near Potsdam, and invited him over for a visit," wrote daughter Margaret.

Truman was so impressed with the young man, he asked him forthwith to be the White House physician. But the "intensely idealistic" Graham tried to demur. "I want to take care of as many people as possible, not just one man."

"Even if that one man is the president of your country?"

"I've got a hospital full of men who've shed their blood for their country. I can't leave them."

In the end, they worked out a Missouri compromise. Doctor Graham stayed with his army hospital unit until all his wounded patients had left for stateside wards or had recovered. He later reported to his new White House post, but only with Truman's agreement that the doctor could keep up his surgical duties at Walter Reed Army Hospital in Washington.

Potsdam, Truman's first big international conference as president, was occasion for "instant" friendship kindled between Truman and Churchill but tough confrontation and disillusionment with wartime ally Stalin. Serious issues, such as prosecution of the war with Japan and the fate of postwar Europe, were on the table, but still there were light moments to break the tension—one of them supplied by another old Truman pal.

Back in Washington earlier, Treasury Secretary Henry Morgenthau had resigned his post because Truman refused to include him in the Potsdam entourage for various political reasons. The party that did go, of course, was studded with many others of high rank, but it also included "an old Missouri follower, Fred Canfil."

Who was Fred Canfil? Stalin's aides and even the KGB most likely searched their dossiers on American officialdom long and hard in a futile effort to find this obviously very important American's pedigree. Who was he, then? "Fred had been a county courthouse employee when Dad was elected county judge, and he attached himself to Harry Truman with total devotion and loyalty," wrote

Margaret. "Built like a bull," the old courthouse retainer from Missouri "had a voice which could shatter glass at a hundred paces."

For Canfil, the trip to Potsdam in such exalted company no doubt was the thrill of a lifetime, especially the moment when old friend Harry Truman called Canfil over to meet Stalin himself. "Marshal Stalin,'" said Truman, "I want you to meet Marshal Canfil."

Due to a certain President's recent appointive action, Fred Canfil indeed was a "marshal," not the all-important Soviet-style marshal, but a U.S. Federal Marshal. Truman, of course, saw no reason to explain it all to Stalin and his entourage. "From that moment forward," said Margaret, "the Russian delegation treated Fred with enormous respect."

White House Honeymoon

AND THEN THERE WAS THE time a young lady living in the White House broke off her engagement to an earlier resident of the presidential home in order to marry a another member of the president's household, the first young man's own brother. Whom she then married— the second young man, that is. In the Blue Room. And the president in question, John Quincy Adams, danced at their wedding. By his own account, he danced "a Virginia reel with great spirit."

Not that everybody in the family was so pleased with the union of presidential son John Adams II and his bride, Mary Catherine Hellen. In fact, neither of John's two brothers attended the wedding on February 25, 1828.

The White House triangle among cousins began with the death of Nancy Hellen, eldest sister of the president's wife, Louisa Catherine Johnson Adams. The first family that resided in the White House in the latter 1820s thus included Nancy's three orphaned children, Mary Catherine, Thomas, and Johnson, in addition to the three Adams boys—Charles, George, and John II. And Mary Catherine soon was a tempting apple in the eye of one Adams brother after another. Charles, for one, willingly or not, escaped her net with a sour comment in his diary labeling her "one of the most capricious women" of a "capricious race."

Also falling under her spell was George Adams, who became engaged to the wily young woman as early as 1823—the Hellen children had moved in with the Adamses in 1817 and simply went on to the White House with John Quincy in 1825. George had studied at Harvard and was pursuing his career as a lawyer in Boston. He became a Massachusetts state legislator in 1826. It was his plan to be well launched on his professional career before taking the engagement to its final point of marriage. Four, five, six years, apparently seemed a reasonable waiting period to him.

But not to his prospective bride, who rarely saw her proper young man from Boston, and who did see another young man practically every day at the White House. That was young John, who had been tossed out of the Harvard ranks in 1823 and who now served his father as private secretary.

In the meantime, Charles, the third Adams brother, already had noticed the storm signals. Also a budding lawyer in Massachusetts, he recorded after one visit to Washington that his brother George's winsome fiancée "has some alluring ways which are apt to make every man forget himself."

Poor George. He would be "in a perfect fever and sickness if he was to imagine that she had encouraged me in the least," wrote Charles.

George, it must be said, did not exactly press his long-distance courtship, so busy was he up there in Boston.

On another visit, Charles discovered that John apparently had fallen "victim of her arts." The young woman was "behaving unworthily" of George, and the family obviously was upset—"My Mother [Louisa Adams] is half inclined to the marriage [with George] and half opposed, my Father tacitly opposed." And Charles was "sorry for" John, caught in her alleged snares.

In the end, predictably, Mary Catherine broke her engagement with George (he was distraught, despite the lukewarm nature of their romance) and married John, whose mother, Louisa, then wrote to Charles: "I shall . . . only announce to you the fact that the wedding is over, that Madame is cool, easy, and indifferent as ever and that John looks already as if he had had all the cares of the world upon his shoulders and my heart tells me that there is much to fear."

The honeymoon, no great change for the newlyweds themselves, was nonetheless a rarity—it was spent at the White House. And their first child, Mary Louisa Adams, completed the cycle by her birth at the White House, on December 2, 1828.

As for Louisa Adams's "much to fear," it is sad but true that both Adams sons who were seriously involved with Mary Catherine, John and George, had many problems, became heavy drinkers, and died young. That is not to say their shared fate was the fault of Mary Catherine, who later in life provided comfort and care to her infirm mother-in-law, Louisa, through the latter's final years as a widow, until her death in Washington in 1852.

Fishing Was His Passion

HARRY TRUMAN HAD HIS LITTLE White House in Key West, Florida; FDR had *his* Little White House at Warm Springs, Georgia; Nixon had San Clemente and Reagan his ranch, both retreats located back in California. As an alternate choice, presidents since World War II have had Camp David, located near Washington in Maryland, as an official presidential retreat.

And then there was Camp Rapidan.

Camp who?

Nowadays a National Historic Landmark and undergoing a six-year, $240,000 plan of restoration, Herbert Hoover's mountain retreat by a trout stream preceded Camp David as a summer White House or weekend retreat. Located at the headwaters of the Rapidan River in Virginia's Blue Ridge mountains, Camp Hoover, as it now is called, didn't cost the federal government very much—Hoover and his wife Lou bought the 164-acre site personally and reached into their own pockets to pay for the lumber used to build a complex of thirteen cabins and supporting structures set on a smaller eight-acre site at the core of the isolated acreage. The United States Marines did the construction work.

At the start, the mountain slope was a strictly unimproved site in Virginia's Madison County about 2.5 miles below the Big

Meadows stopping point on the Skyline Drive . . . and yet above the 2,500-foot line considered necessary to avoid mosquitoes. It also was within one hundred miles of the White House in Washington.

According to Reed Engle, a cultural-resource specialist with the National Park Service, Mrs. Hoover designed the complex, hired the architects, laid out its gardens, and even did much of the planting herself. Hoover himself either did his presidential work—up to eighteen hours a day—or *fished.*

Yes, the passion that brought President Hoover to the site was, in fact, trout fishing.

"One would assume that the President selected a site with a spectacular view," says Albert Highsmith of nearby Charlottesville, Virginia, a Hoover associate as a young man. "But the view from Camp Hoover is anything but spectacular. Camp Hoover is far down from the summits of the mountains. Its view, with only a glimpse of the mountains above it, is of the forest and, most important to Herbert Hoover, of a trout stream."

In a talk at the White-Burkett Miller Center for Public Affairs at the University of Virginia, Highsmith recalled a Hoover thought or two on fishing. "Hoover once wrote: 'Fishing is a constant reminder of the democracy of life—for all men are equal before

Harry S. Truman also had a favorite vacation retreat—the "Little White House" in Key West, Florida, now converted into a museum. He liked it so much, he once wrote his wife Bess, "I've a notion to move the capital to Key West and just stay." (Courtesy Harry S. Truman Little White House Museum)

fishes.' He titled a short book he wrote, *Fishing for Fun and to Wash One's Soul.*"

As for the non-fishing aspects of life at the Camp Rapidan of Hoover's day, the *Baltimore Sun* reported in 1998: "Charles and Anne Morrow Lindbergh were frequent guests. British Prime Minister J. Ramsay MacDonald and Hoover talked around the campfire about reducing world armaments."

Camp Rapidan was a factor in Hoover's presidential order to build the Skyline Drive itself. The entire area—mountaintops and slopes for miles on either side—in the 1930s became a part of the Shenandoah National Park. The Hoovers by then had deeded over their land purchase for public usage.

So isolated was the retreat that an airplane dropped mail and presidential papers on the nearby village of Criglersville, reported the Baltimore newspaper. "A phone line to the White House kept busy. The troubles of the 15 million Depression unemployed prompted such headlines as 'Problems Pursue Hoover to Rapidan.'"

The Hoover retreat only could be reached on foot, by horseback or by mule. Even so, it became "so busy," reported the *Baltimore Sun,* "that two more camps were built within a mile downstream— one of seven cabins for Cabinet officers and one of 15 barracks for a Marine guard."

By 1998, only three of the original cabins at the core site remained standing. They were, said the newspaper, "The President's," also known as the "Brown House;" "The Prime Minister's" and a third log cabin called "The Creel," a fishing term. The newspaper account by Ernest F. Imhoff also explained, "They sit on a wooded wedge-shaped area bordered by two modest streams, Mill Prong and Laurel Prong, that merge to form the Rapidan river, which flows into the Rappahannock."

In the years, and then decades, after the Hoover presidency (ended in 1933), various officials briefly visited the largely forgotten, still-remote site, among them Hoover's successors, Franklin Delano Roosevelt and Jimmy Carter, plus Vice President Al Gore. For a time, Camp Rapidan-Hoover was used as a camp site for Washington area Boy Scouts. For years also, hikers from the Appalachian Trail or the Big Meadows stop on the Skyline Drive were its most frequent visitors.

In addition, "Once a year, on a Sunday in August nearest Hoover's Aug. 10 birthday," said the Imhoff article, "buses carry visitors from . . . Big Meadows down the usually closed Rapidan Road to tour the remaining three buildings."

After the six-year restoration of Camp Hoover is completed, however, it may be opened to a daily bus tour or two. And it once more will be called Camp Rapidan.

Righteous Crusade Sabotaged

RATS, RATS, RATS! WITH THE basement kitchen area and adjoining store rooms serving as vast dining halls for the large population of rats and mice, Andrew Johnson's daughter Martha Patterson went on the warpath.

She was a strong-willed young woman, as evidenced by the fact that she emerged as the primary White House hostess and domestic supervisor after her father the vice president succeeded the assassinated Abraham Lincoln in 1865. Altogether, ten Johnson family members had moved in, including the new president's wife, Eliza. But she was ill, nearly an invalid, and reclusive. At first their daughters, Mary and Martha, both served as hostesses, but it was Martha, wife of David Trotter Patterson, a U.S. senator from their home state of Tennessee, who gradually took over the social stewardship of the White House. (It was certainly a rarity in the history of the White House for a U.S. senator to live in the presidential quarters.)

As one of her crusades to spruce up the hotel-like Executive Mansion, Martha declared war against the vermin infesting the venerable and historic walls.

Little did she know, it seems, that her every effort was being foiled by another resident of the self-same house, by sabotage at the hands of another family member—her own father, the president himself!

Not that he cared for rats, one may suppose. But for mice he apparently did have a soft spot. The story is that while daughter Martha strenuously imported cats, scattered poisons, and placed traps down in the White House bowels, Andrew Johnson was busy two floors above feeding the mice with white flour ground at his own farm in Tennessee.

It seems that he had noticed the nibble marks on a flour package, then he actually saw a mouse in his bedroom—not the traditional presidential bedroom on the south wall, incidentally, but a room on the north side. After espying the mouse, Johnson placed the flour packet on the bedroom hearth to allow the mice to "get their fill."

As a result, he told an aide that he had won the confidence of "the little fellows" and not only would supply them more flour, but also "some water that they may quench their thirst."

He may have gone to a newly equipped bathroom by his bedroom for the water—it previously had held bath tubs but no real plumbing. Johnson had changed that by converting it into a full-fledged bathroom, complete with a barber's chair.

Daughter Martha, in the meantime, proceeded not only with her war on vermin but also with a clean-up of the entire White House, top to bottom, even the attic, along with redecorating and remodeling. Her efforts included complete removal of the low-lying East Wing and its replacement by a single-story colonnade that gave the famous East Room a pleasant balcony on the roof of the new structure.

Collaborators

ONE OR BOTH OF THE two young men in the White House called their boss "the Tycoon." One liked "the Ancient" a bit better. The same, John Milton Hay, called the president's wife "Hell Cat." And one or both thought that Robert E. Lee deserved to be shot.

Abraham Lincoln's secretaries, John George Nicolay and John Hay, were young, still undistinguished men, as they began interwoven careers in the White House of the Lincoln administration. Both were, or would be, writers. Both would be diplomats. Both began their tenure with Lincoln as secretaries answering the mail, screening the visitors, even preparing a daily news summary.

Both worked long, hard hours and both slept in the White House.

Both, in future years, would spend more than fifteen years collaborating on a ten-volume biography of their boss, Lincoln, that is still considered an absolutely vital source on the history of the period, on the Lincoln administration, and on Lincoln himself.

Before they came together in Washington again to work on the gigantic biography, Nicolay had spent a few years as the U.S. consul resident in Paris. After they delivered their monumental work to the reading public (five thousand sets quickly sold), John Hay moved on to serve as secretary of state under Presidents William McKinley and Theodore Roosevelt. Nicolay, for his part, much earlier had accepted a sinecure as marshal of the U.S. Supreme Court.

The biographical work the two men composed has defied analysts in their attempts to determine which one wrote which sections, since each could write well, and each certainly knew the subject matter from first-hand observation. Not content with mere observation, however, they enlisted the aid—and the papers and the authorization—of Lincoln's oldest son, Robert Todd Lincoln. They researched meticulously and were wary of accepting interviews as totally reliable source material. One further aid to their labors was a somewhat erratic diary that Hay had kept while serving as one of Lincoln's three White House secretaries. Both also had various notes and letters of their own to fall back upon, along with full knowledge of the whereabouts of other documentation.

The two had met in Illinois shortly before Lincoln became president. Nicolay, born in Bavaria in 1832 and most recently a newspaper editor-publisher, was a clerk in the office of the Illinois secretary of state, Ozias M. Hatch, in Springfield, when Lincoln ran for president. Hay, born in Indiana in 1838, first encountered Nicolay while attending school in Pittsfield, Illinois, in 1851. Hay then spent his college years at a school in Springfield and at Brown University. He became reacquainted with Nicolay when he returned to Springfield in 1858 to work in an uncle's law office.

Nicolay, meanwhile, had met presidential nominee Lincoln and soon became his secretary. Later, when the mail volume of the president-elect shot past fifty letters a day, he prevailed upon Lincoln to hire Hay as well.

Both men accompanied Lincoln to Washington for his first inauguration in 1861, and both stayed.

More than desk-bound secretaries, they ran political errands for Lincoln and went on out-of-town trouble-shooting trips for him on occasion. Obviously, he trusted in their honesty and their discretion to the utmost.

Nicolay, disliked by Mrs. Lincoln, had spent his free time in the White House studying French, and he was on his way to the consul post in Paris when Lincoln was assassinated. Hay, who disliked Mrs. Lincoln, had also wrangled an appointment to Paris—as secretary of the U.S. legation there. He too would have been gone, but he lingered to break in a new office staff at the White House. He rushed to the Lincoln bedside the fateful night of April 14–15 and was at the side of the beloved "Ancient" when he died the morning of April 15.

Nicolay and Hay began their biographical collaboration in Washington in the 1870s, with Robert Todd Lincoln's okay. Hay found time also to publish a novel and serve as assistant secretary of state. Nicolay labored through family problems—an infant son's death in 1878 and his wife's death in 1885. In that year, too, the pair agreed to allow *Century* magazine to begin publishing their *Abraham Lincoln: A History* in serial format for $50,000. Their ten-volume work then appeared in 1890, with half of the series already run in the magazine.

Hay soon was off to serve as American ambassador to England, but he and his partner still were able to collaborate on a two-volume production of Lincoln's own writings. Soon after that, Nicolay hoped to turn out a greatly shortened single-volume version of their *Lincoln History* but, in 1901, death came first. His name would live on in fresh form, however, after his daughter Helen produced a biography of Nicolay himself—*Lincoln's Secretary: A Biography of John G. Nicolay.*

Hay, meanwhile, was now fully devoted to public service. As for his view of the "Tycoon" or "Ancient" they both had served, Hay one time told another biographer, William Herndon, that Lincoln had his blind spots ("absurd to call him a modest man," and so forth), but, "as Republicanism is the sole hope of a sick world, so Lincoln with all his foibles, is the greatest character since Christ."

Controversy Over Dinner

WHEN PIONEER BLACK EDUCATOR BOOKER T. Washington, born into slavery, was invited to sup at the White House with Teddy Roosevelt, there was instant furor. "Probably the First Negro Ever Entertained at the White House," headlined the *Atlanta Constitution*. Other papers in the South wailed, too.

Teddy Roosevelt defended his action as a perfectly innocuous attempt "to show some respect to a man whom I cordially esteem as a good citizen and a good American." But even Teddy eventually had to admit that politically, in the South especially, it had been a mistake.

The fact is, furor aside, other blacks had made appearances at the White House before that dinner in 1901. The freed slave and abolitionist Sojourner Truth once visited Lincoln, while another famous ex-slave, Frederick Douglass, played a presiding role over black performers appearing in concerts at the Rutherford B. Hayes White House. Such appearances, of course, were exceptions, were a bow to "celebrities" of one kind or another, and most blacks seen at the White House at any time during the latter nineteenth century, Civil War and Reconstruction notwithstanding, were servants. "From all indications," wrote White House historian William Seale, "no Negro received a social invitation to the White House before Booker T. Washington in 1901, nor did many thereafter for many years."

This is not to say that the dinner with Teddy Roosevelt was Booker T. Washington's first White House visit. On the contrary, the black educator had achieved auspicious results in a visit to the Executive Mansion just three years earlier when he went there, unbidden, in hopes of gaining an audience with Roosevelt's predecessor, William McKinley.

That was in 1898, and Washington, chief founder and still head of the Tuskeegee Institute in Alabama, had just learned that President McKinley would be traveling to nearby Atlanta to attend a "Peace Jubilee" marking the end of the Spanish-American War. Here was a chance, a heaven-sent opportunity, to persuade a president of the predominately white nation to visit its preeminent black school of the day, Washington realized. He wasted no time traveling to Washington. A letter request would not do—he had to see the president in person.

But how could he quickly arrange such an all-important audience? By his own account (in *Up from Slavery*), he went to the White House unannounced. "When I got there, I found the waiting rooms full of people, and my heart began to sink for I feared there would not be much chance of my seeing the President that day, if at all."

But Washington managed to gain presidential secretary J. Addison Porter's ear, and the Booker T. Washington calling card then wafted into the inner sanctum of McKinley's own office. "[A]nd in a few minutes word came from Mr. McKinley that he would see me."

After that, no problem. Plans for the Atlanta trip were still flexible, and McKinley was receptive after Washington argued the visit "would not only encourage our students and teachers, but would help the entire race." McKinley couldn't yet promise, but after a second visit by Booker T. Washington the next month, McKinley—the last veteran of the Civil War to serve in the White House—agreed to go. In between the two visits by the black educator, it so happened, several race riots had erupted in the South. "As soon as I saw the President [the second time], I perceived that his heart was greatly burdened by reason of these race disturbances," wrote Washington later.

McKinley said he wanted to show his "faith in the race," according to Washington, and Washington for his part said hardly any gesture would "go farther in giving hope and encouragement" to his fellow blacks "than the fact that the President of the Nation would be willing to travel 140 miles out of his way to spend a day at a Negro institution."

When the day came, December 10, 1898, not only blacks but many white citizens and leaders crowded into the "little city of Tuskegee" for the rare presidential visit. Drawn to the spot were "a host" of newspaper correspondents, the Alabama state legislature and governor, along with McKinley's own cabinet.

The entire student body of the school paraded before the eminent visitors—float after float along with farm animals and equipment, or students carrying stalks of sugar cane, often with a single cotton boll attached to one end. Speeches, of course, were made, including McKinley's own, and even an oration by the postmaster general.

It may have been navy secretary John D. Long who really put his finger on what was happening, whose sentiments, if felt more widely, might have avoided the furor that greeted Booker T. Washington's social visit with Teddy Roosevelt just three years later.

The dramatic picture rendered at Tuskegee that December day in 1898, Long said, was of the nation's president sharing the platform with the governor of a former Confederate state on the one hand and a black leader, Booker T. Washington, on the other. This, said Long, was a "trinity," this was "a picture which the press of the country should spread over the land." This was a picture, he said, which should be "transmitted to future time and generations."

"Royal Pup" Chastised

ALEXANDER HAMILTON WAS KILLED IN 1804. Naval hero Stephen Decatur in 1820. And, in that day and age, so were many others—victims, one and all, of the vicious social convention called dueling. Over offended feelings of honor, over a matter of insult, perceived or real, "gentlemen" settled affairs by killing, maiming, or merely pinking the offender in a ritual that allowed each to take shots at the other.

It was a time when a chip on the shoulder could be dangerous. And so the president's son, the son of John Quincy Adams, set all the grim ritualistic wheels in motion one day when he publicly insulted a visitor to the White House.

The incident took place in the East Room during a reception on April 2, 1828, a time when young John Adams II—a newlywed—lived at the White House with his bride and served his father as private secretary.

The second son of John Quincy Adams had not sailed an entirely smooth course as a young man about town—as, indeed, the son of a very circumspect president. He had been given the boot at Harvard, and two months before, he had married a cousin and fellow White House resident who had broken her engagement to his own brother George.

Now, at the reception in April, John bridled at the sight of journalist Russell Jarvis of the *United States Telegraph,* who had just entered the East Room with his wife, her parents, and two additional women. They already had been formally received by John's mother, Louisa, with no problem.

Nor would there have been any problem, except that John recognized Jarvis as a critic of his father (as was the newspaper's editor, Duff Green). A companion asked John about one of the women, and he, in reply, loudly and unmistakably said the woman was the journalist's wife—and there, with her, "is a man who, if he had any idea of propriety in the conduct of a gentleman, ought not to show his face in this house."

The offending group promptly turned and left, but as the town plunged into the inevitable gossip, the first repercussion was not long in coming. Sent by mail, it was a challenge to duel. Young Adams did not respond. Nor did he hide. As private secretary to his father, he continued to deliver presidential messages to Congress at the Capitol, which was still under construction.

Denied his gentleman's "satisfaction," Jarvis waited one day—April 15, it was—in the Capitol's rotunda for the president's son. When John Adams appeared on his usual rounds, Jarvis accosted him in no uncertain terms. He pulled the young man's nose and slapped him in the face, insults to make anybody pale, and more than enough for a duel under the unspoken rules of the day.

The president, himself an opponent of dueling, complained in a message to Congress that son John had been "waylaid and assaulted" in the legislature's own house. He called for legislation to guarantee the safety of couriers between Congress and the White House. And who knows what he said to his "courier" son?

In any case, Congress investigated with an eye to censure, calling forth both men to testify, and newspapers, pro-Adams and anti-Adams, reported and trumpeted over the unhappy matter. In the end, no duel ever took place. Congress refused to censure Jarvis. His newspaper, the *Telegraph* could stick by its language calling the pulling of the prince's nose "a signal" chastisement for the "Royal puppy."

Early Social Doings

PRESIDENT AND MRS. JAMES MONROE thought it best, socially speaking, to have people in rather than to go out—at least not to private homes. And so they missed the major party of the season in January of 1824, a ball given by John Quincy Adams for the Hero of New Orleans, General Andrew Jackson. A thousand men and women attended— everybody who was anybody in Washington of the day (except the sitting president and his wife).

Adams, who would succeed Monroe at the White House, thought to install additional pillars to hold up the lower floors under the expected crush in the Adams home on F Street. He was Monroe's secretary of state at the time, and Jackson, also a future president, was a newly elected senator. More pointedly, in 1824, both men would be presidential contenders. Against each other.

Coming in an election year, the party obviously had political undertones, overtones, in-between tones—the gamut, politically. In the end, although Jackson won the popular vote of 1824 for president, no single one of the four presidential candidates had gained a majority of the electoral votes. That development threw the final vote into the House of Representatives. It, after considerable political tumult and name-calling, selected Adams as the nation's sixth president.

His then was a difficult presidency, fraught with political and personal problems. But the stiff New Englander and his wife, Louisa, nonetheless did have an active, if not flamboyant, social life. Like the Monroes, they would stay in rather than go out. While in, they staged an annual New Year's reception that would attract several thousand. Their biweekly levees, receptions also, were popular as well.

A recent Harvard graduate attending a White House dinner under the Adamses found that twenty congressmen and twenty "gentlemen from different parts of the country" made up the guest list. The table was lit by "an enormous gilt waiter, with many vases, temples, and female figures in different attitudes holding candles." Dinner lasted from 6 to 10 P.M., and in the interim the guests had supped upon "every variety of fish, flesh, and fowl." Included was a boned and finely sliced canvasback duck that struck the young visitor as "cake." He also recalled the meal included macaroni, and for drink there had been "every drinkable under the sun—porter, cider, claret, sherry, Burgundy, champagne, Tokay, and the choicest madeira that ever passed my larynx."

Alone, the Adamses could turn to themselves and family members for quiet eveningtide entertainments. Louisa Adams or her sons could take a turn at the harp or pianoforte. The mistress of the mansion also wrote both verse and drama, and it is thought that household members acted out Louisa Adams's scripts such as *The Wag,* or *Just from College: A Farce in Three Acts,* or a more serious but melodramatic piece supporting independence for Greece.

There were those who found the scholarly Adams, son of a president, veteran diplomat, cultured and urbane, a bit dull, while others found him to be quite eloquent. Both words were used by White House guests.

Whatever the case, he and his family either entertained or politically fought some astounding historical figures—Henry Clay, secretary of state under Adams; Daniel Webster; John C. Calhoun, vice president during Adams's term of office; and of course Andrew Jackson, who in 1828 handily defeated Adams in a heated and scathing campaign for president.

Still destined to serve honorably and well as a House member, Adams left the White House the day before Jackson's famously rowdy inaugural festivities in March 1829. The Adamses moved to a house beyond the capital city, on Meridian Hill. Jackson did not make the customary courtesy call on the outgoing president, and Adams did not attend the Jackson inauguration, so bitter were their respective feelings. That day, alone, Adams rode his horse along F Street, where he had lived just before entering the White House himself.

Busy, Busy, Too Busy

A WORKAHOLIC FROM HIS FIRST days in the White House, this wartime president rarely took a break. He did his business with a staff of one, a private secretary whose salary he paid himself.

Calling the job of president "no bed of roses," he usually was up and at 'em early in the day. He took a morning walk, then repaired to his office and made himself available to visitors from just about any station in life.

And they did pile in: outright beggars and kooks mixed with spokesmen for legitimate political interests or charitable causes. It could be wearing—he once joked he would like to "clear" his office area with a Colt revolver and thus spend more time attending to "public duties."

In most cases his visitors apparently were unaware of the frustration their own presence had caused. "Generally he was gentle, courteous and firm in explaining that he had neither jobs nor alms to give," wrote Frank B. Williams Jr., a historian from this president's home state. "Privately, he sarcastically referred to able and patriotic men who wanted to serve their country by holding government sinecures."

He stopped work to have dinner about four in the afternoon, took another walk, "then returned to his cluttered 'table,' which he seldom cleared before retiring."

His first lady wife, meanwhile, received callers twice a week, on Tuesday and Friday evenings, wrote historian Williams. "Not infrequently she dragged her protesting husband from his office to circulate among the guests."

This was a socially active White House. "She entertained thirty or forty of her husband's dinner guests once or twice a week—although the president generally took credit for them when he confided to his diary, 'I had a dining party on yesterday.'"

His choice of the same woman as his wife may not have been exactly to his credit, either. Eager to go into politics, the story goes, he asked his state's ranking political figure, also destined to serve as president, how to go about it. Well, for one thing, said the mentor, quit your womanizing and get married. The political tyro then asked his mentor whom he should marry. Pick a woman who would be no trouble, was the reply. In fact, the novice politico could hardly do better than a certain young woman well known to them both for her excellent qualifications in the areas of family, education, wealth, and health.

The future president's marriage to that very woman, by this possibly apocryphal story, came about soon after.

Twenty years later, they both were in the White House, where the husband put in his long, long hours. He did take off Sundays, but he worked at least one Christmas Day to clear out "a mass of business which had accumulated," by his own account.

At first he was so closely bound to his "table" that he ventured outside the District of Columbia only twice in his first seventeen months as president. His first travel was to George Washington's Mount Vernon estate on the Potomac. For his third outing (the second was a personal visit, also just outside Washington), he spent four days at Fortress Monroe overlooking the great and scenic Hampton Roads harbor in Virginia. A fourth sojourn—to Chapel Hill, North Carolina, for a commencement address at his alma mater, the University of North Carolina—was accomplished by a combination of steamboat, train, and carriage. Down and back, plus stay-over, took nine days.

By now loosening up his travel itinerary, he next spent two weeks in New England, followed a year later by ten days at Bedford Springs, Pennsylvania, with a stop at another recreational watering hole on his return trip to Washington.

In the unpopular war he prosecuted, two generals stood out, but he was notably tight-fisted in providing them men and supplies. He wanted them to be victorious, but not too much so, since one or the other then could become a political rival possibly able to succeed him as president.

One of them, "Old Rough and Ready"—General Zachary Taylor—did succeed him as president in 1849. By then, though, James Knox Polk had won his Mexican War, thereby adding the future states of Arizona, New Mexico, California, Utah, and Nevada and parts of Colorado, Wyoming, and Texas to the United States. On top of the potential wealth represented by this gigantic chunk of land, gold was discovered in California just months after the

Mexican War was concluded—the California Gold Rush of 1849 was on.

Before James K. Polk and his wife, Sara Childress Polk, turned for home in Tennessee and possible rest, the outgoing president crossed one final bridge—he met General Taylor, the president-elect, for the first time when Old Rough and Ready paid a preinaugural courtesy call at the White House. Taylor was invited back for dinner several days later with about forty other guests, among them the incoming vice president, Millard Fillmore, also destined to be president, and Jefferson Davis, future president of the future Confederate States of America.

"On Saturday, March 3, 1849, Polk cleared his 'table' for the last time and left the White House," wrote historian Williams in his 1981 book *Tennessee's Presidents.* The normal inauguration day of March 4 that year fell on Sunday, but in deference to the Sabbath, the official ceremony investing Zachary Taylor as Polk's successor was postponed until Monday the fifth.

On that day, they rode together to the inauguration at the Capitol.

With the former president saying he was happy to leave behind his "incessant labor, . . . anxiety . . . and great responsibility," the Polks left for home, but made many (too many?) stops. Steamboats, ships, trains, and carriages conveyed them to Richmond and Petersburg, Virginia; Wilmington, North Carolina; Charleston, South Carolina; Savannah, Macon, and Columbus, Georgia;, Opelika and Mobile, Alabama; New Orleans, Louisiana; Memphis, Tennessee; "and many places in between," noted Williams. The fetes and ceremonies encountered were many also. Cholera was met in New Orleans and on their steamboat moving up the Mississippi River, but it didn't strike either Polk as they rounded the last turn on the road to home in Nashville, Tennessee.

He soon, however, would be brought down by *something,* perhaps exhaustion, perhaps a severe bout of the intestinal troubles, the diarrhea, that had plagued him on and off for years. At Nashville, the newly refurbished Polk Place awaited the retired president and his wife. And thus, still more work to do . . . the work of unpacking, settling in, arranging books, papers . . . receiving visitors. His fatigue, his old indisposition and illness dragged him down. Under other circumstances, he could have enjoyed a status as the state's most illustrious citizen, because Tennessee's first U.S. president, the colorful

Andrew Jackson, had died four years earlier. But soon after arriving in his new home, in June 1849, James Knox Polk, only in his mid-fifties, joined Jackson in death . . . reunited, you might say, with the old friend and political mentor who allegedly had helped the younger, politically untutored Polk find himself a wife.

Additional note: The third and last of Tennessee's presidents was the tailor-turned-politician Andrew Johnson, who would become best known historically for his impeachment by the House of Representatives and his acquittal in the Senate by a margin of one vote. Another hard worker, scrupulously honest, Vice President Andrew Johnson came to the White House by virtue of Abraham Lincoln's assassination in 1865.

Johnson previously had served in both the House and the Senate . . . he stayed in his Senate seat even after Tennessee seceded and officially joined the Confederacy. The Union loyalist later was appointed military governor of Tennessee by Lincoln, then was on the successful Union-Republican national ticket headed by Lincoln for the presidential election of 1864.

With the onetime penniless tailor's vault to the presidency in April 1865, his stubborn adherence to principle as he saw it underwent stern test. In the absence of a recessed Congress, the new president moved quickly to begin his own version of a post-Civil War reconstruction program in the defeated South. (He viewed Reconstruction as more an executive responsibility than a congressional one.) His program allowed pardons for all taking an oath of allegiance to the United States, but also called for presidential approval of pardons sought by community leaders. Slavery was abolished, but "black codes" imposed on newly freed blacks in the South struck Johnson's critics as overly restrictive on the freedoms presumed granted to former slaves.

When Congress reconvened, the Radical Republicans wasted no time in challenging Johnson's reconstruction program, often with the support of more moderate northerners who considered Johnson too lenient on the South and its white wartime leadership. The Radicals wouldn't seat Senate and House members sent to Washington from former Confederate states and at one point led

Congress in over-riding a Johnson veto, the first such action in American history. Congress soon passed the Civil Rights Act of 1866, which prohibited discrimination against blacks and granted them U.S. citizenship. Next, Congress sent the states the Fourteenth Amendment to the U.S. Constitution, which promises "due process" under the law for all citizens. (Among the former Confederate states, only Tennessee went along with ratification of the amendment.)

Strengthened by the congressional elections of 1866, the Radicals next wrote their own program of reconstruction, one that reimposed military rule over the former Confederate states. Congress also passed its Tenure of Office Act, which Johnson then "violated" by firing Lincoln's fire-eating secretary of war, Edwin Stanton. Although the Supreme Court would invalidate the Tenure Act years later, the Stanton dismissal was the final straw that prompted the House action impeaching President Johnson, another "first" in U.S. history.

Battered but unbowed after his House impeachment and narrow Senate acquittal, Johnson returned home to Greeneville, Tennessee, in 1869, after completing his one term as president, only to reappear on the political stage in 1875 as a newly elected Senate member. He died, however, in the first year of his latest Senate term.

Final note: None of Tennessee's three presidents actually was a native. Instead, all three—Andrew Jackson, James K. Polk, and Andrew Johnson—were born in the Carolinas.

Unfit for a Queen

EVERY FIVE MINUTES THEY VACUUMED the red carpet covering the asphalt drive at the South Portico. The queen was coming, the queen was coming.

And at what a time in the nation's history!

It was the American Bicentennial, two hundred years since the dramatic events of the American Revolution, and the queen of England was coming to the Gerald Ford White House for a state din-

It was the American bicentennial year of 1976, just three days after the Fourth of July, when President Gerald Ford danced with his guest of honor that evening, Queen Elizabeth II of England. (Courtesy Gerald R. Ford Library)

ner, one of the most elaborate ever held in the presidential mansion. "The evening was magic," wrote White House social aide Stephen M. Bauer later.

Guests sat at twenty-four tables under a colorful tent erected in the Rose Garden. Rain and a thunderstorm had threatened to disrupt the dinner on July 7, 1976, for Her Majesty, Queen Elizabeth II, until the last moment, with lightning reportedly striking trees on the nearby south grounds. But no rain dared sully the freshly vacuumed carpet this night.

"She wore a spectacular diamond necklace, diamond earrings and a fabulous diamond tiara," said Bauer in his book *At Ease in the White House: The Uninhibited Memoirs of a Presidential Social Aide,* written with Frances Spatz Leighton. In addition to administration officials and leaders of the Washington diplomatic corps, those hobnobbing with the queen and Prince Philip included celebrities Cary Grant, Barbara Walters, Julie Harris, Telly Savalas, Texas governor John Connally, and baseball star Willie Mays.

For all the elaborate planning, however, for all the historic grandeur intended, the queen of England on this bicentennial occasion at the president's house had to endure pop music with lyrics that some would consider banal, tasteless ("the Queen's face unfortunately showed she caught every syllable all too clearly.")

Next, she sat through British-born comedian Bob Hope's stand-up appearance, which included a comment about her diamond tiara: "In this country when we see a crown we think of margarine."

Finally, after all had moved into the State Dining Room, came the sight of President Ford dutifully taking the visiting queen's hand to lead off the gala's dancing—unfortunately to the strains of "The Lady Is a Tramp."

Skinny-Dipper

VERY EARLY ONE DAY IN the 1820s, a gentleman from New York was in the vicinity of Tiber Creek, at its conjunction with the Potomac River, a thoroughly bucolic setting behind the new President's House. The sun had not yet risen when along came another gentleman, dressed (for the moment) in pantaloons and blue pea jacket.

He was walking "rapidly" from the White House, as indeed the President's House already was being called, and he clearly was hurrying to the river. The summer morning's encounter would have been close to today's Washington Monument, near the foot of Seventeenth Street.

Having recognized the man in pantaloons and pea jacket as President John Quincy Adams, the onlooking Thurlow Weed withdrew a discreet distance and watched as Adams began to shed his clothing even before he reached "a tree on the brink of the river."

Seconds later, bereft of all clothing, Adams was enjoying his frequent early-morning swim in the Potomac behind the presidential mansion. "[He] struck out 15 or 20 rods, swimming rapidly and turning occasionally upon his back, seeming as much at ease in the element as on terra firma." Since all good things must end, Adams in a short while returned to shore and dried himself off "with napkins, which he had brought for the purpose in his hand."

Others in the early days of the capital occasionally espied Adams taking his watery constitutional, but the historians of today tend to dismiss the story that a zealous female reporter once nailed down an interview with the austere president—and son of a president—by sitting on his discarded clothes.

The fact is, though, that in those seemingly innocent beginnings of its life as the first family's home, the White House could not boast of any plumbing or running water! More like a country estate, it faced a dirt road running west to Georgetown. To the east a mile or so was the Capitol, and Adams—as part of his physical regime—liked to walk there and back. He started out by completing the round trip in an hour and fifteen minutes; he eventually knocked the time down to an hour flat. He also rode horseback in his rural setting. The White House during his term as the nation's sixth president had a stable for eight horses.

The vista from behind, down to the river, was of a farm, really. To the west beyond Sixteenth Street, the view was of open country. From the south porch, the occupants could see past their gardens of flowers and shrubs to pasture ground for both cows and sheep all the way to the river, a stretch of several hundred yards. This was where Tiber Creek came in from the east. And as it joined the Potomac after crossing the line of Fifteenth Street, there were islands and some marshlands.

Back at the great house, there were low-lying sheds, a dairy, a vegetable garden. The North Portico had not yet been built.

Looking a bit bare by our image today, the presidential home still lacked tall, grand trees to soften the outline and keep its grandiose scale in proportion.

The nation almost lost its sixth president to his fondness for the Potomac. It seems that one day he, his son John, and a servant named Antoine set off from the riverbank on the White House side in a leaky canoe. The younger Adams was swimming. His father, partially disrobed, was in the small craft, along with Antoine, who was already naked and ready for the water.

In mid-river, the leaking boat foundered completely, leaving all three in the water. The president began swimming for the opposite shore, their goal from the outset, but he was weighted down by the long sleeves of his shirt as they filled with water. Describing the sleeves as two "56-pound weights upon my arms," Adams later wrote, he was left "struggling for life and gasping for breath."

Fortunately, he did reach the far shore, as did John and Antoine.

Assembling clothing from what they had left among them, Antoine had to walk back into town to find a carriage. They were six hours late returning to the White House. It is said they weren't even missed.

Dinner With Old Hickory

COMING INTO OFFICE ON THE heels of the cultured and urbane John Quincy Adams, the frontier hero Andrew Jackson—Old Hickory to his countrymen—might have been expected to serve his dinner guests far more simple fare. For the plebian, somewhat populist Jackson, perhaps a slab of smoked venison would have been appropriate and symbolic.

But not so . . . not always, at any rate.

Attending an informal White House dinner with the widower Jackson and several guests in 1834, a Pennsylvania lawyer found a table "very splendidly laid and illuminated." He noticed a chandelier above that held thirty-two candles, and other candles on various surfaces about the room.

He and his fellow guests sat down with their host at 6:30 P.M., and then came one sophisticated course after another. "The first course was soup in the French style; then beef bouille, next wild turkey boned and dressed with brains; after that fish; then chicken cold and dressed white, interlaided with slices of tongue and garnished with dressed salad; then canvasback ducks and celery; afterward partridges with sweet breads and last pheasants and old Virginia ham."

All was accompanied by select wines—sherry and port for the soups and first meats, Madeira for the turkey and fish, champagne for the later fowl courses. Then came desserts—jelly and small tarts, followed by "blanche mode and kisses with dryed fruits in them." Then preserves, followed by ice cream and grapes and oranges. With the desserts came claret.

Here, clearly, was a meal for anybody to remember for some time. And the only way to possibly enjoy so many foods was by the methodology imposed by Jackson's "French servants," that is, to move the courses on and off the table quickly, thus affording the diners mere tastings of each offering.

The meal took until 9:00 P.M., the Pennsylvania lawyer later recalled, and afterward the party retired to a drawing room, where the guests sipped coffee and then a liqueur while the ladies played the piano and sang. The party ended at 9:30 P.M.

Lavish as it was, wrote Jackson biographer Marquis James, the dinner was, for the Jackson White House, only an "an informal affair, a degree removed from a family dinner." The added fact is, "General Jackson's state entertainments were marked by a richness and a dignity devoid of stiffness [and were] unequalled since Washington's day."

Persistent Bodyguard

ON ELECTION NIGHT OF 1864, when things had been running hot and close for Abraham Lincoln in his bid for a second presidential term, a burly, Virginia-born lawyer set himself up outside Lincoln's White House door with pistols and knives.

Born in the Old Dominion but later an attorney on the eighth judicial circuit in Illinois with Attorney Lincoln, Ward Hill Lamon was a devoted disciple, it certainly did appear.

More or less appointing himself as a bodyguard, he had accompanied the president-elect in his secret dash by nighttime train through Rebel-infested Baltimore for the first Lincoln inauguration in Washington. The new president rewarded his old friend and circuit-riding colleague by appointing him marshal of the District of Columbia. The post, much like that of an old-time sheriff, was suitable enough for the man who had accompanied Lincoln on the train with protection gear that included brass knuckles, pistols, a knife, and the like. Now, "Hill," as he was called, could preside at special ceremonies and run the local prison.

He found Virginia troops to follow his banner early in the Civil

War—as Union men, of course. Later, when Lincoln spoke at Gettysburg, Lamon was marshal-in-chief for the ceremonial parade into the cemetery that was being dedicated. He later introduced a speaker—his old colleague Lincoln.

Still, times were rough and he worried over Lincoln's safety. The president at least once had been shot at in public (a hole apparently was shot in his hat one day when he journeyed the four miles from the real White House downtown to the "summer White House" at the Soldier's Home).

Lamon kept warning Lincoln of possible betrayers right in the White House, suggesting a screening system for anyone asking to see the president. He once proposed the arrest of a seditious-sounding congressman and during the heated campaign of 1864 began spending the night at the White House to keep Lincoln safe. He warned Lincoln repeatedly to be more careful in public, and even after the election, he was terribly upset to hear that Lincoln went to the theater one night with a foreign diplomat and Senator Charles Sumner of Massachusetts . . . and no one else. Neither of Lincoln's companions on that outing, asserted Lamon, "could defend themselves against an assault from any able-bodied woman in this City."

He begged Lincoln's secretary and aide John G. Nicolay to make sure that Lincoln never left the White House alone, "either in the day or night time."

One night in April 1865, of course, Lincoln attended the theater again—Ford's Theatre. He wasn't alone, he was under guard, but he was shot and fatally wounded anyway. One has to wonder what might have been the result if Lincoln himself had not sent Lamon to Richmond, the fallen capital of the fallen Confederacy, just three days before to report on conditions in Virginia and the prospects for reconstruction. Now Lamon came hurrying back to become marshal of the state funeral for his old friend.

One has to wonder also why Lamon, seven years later, lent his name to a biography of Lincoln that was perceived at the time as being overly critical and "vulgar." Lincoln's parents never married, it seemed to hint, and Lincoln himself wasn't really so pious, and he liked dirty jokes. The book apparently was written by Chauncy Black, son of a Lamon law partner, and was largely based on Lamon's recollections and notes from onetime Lincoln law partner William Herndon. In happier days, one has to recall, Lincoln had called Lamon "my particular friend."

Alice's Bad Idol

FOR A WHITE HOUSE GATHERING, it apparently was an uneasy and dreary dinner party on this night before an inauguration, when the Teddy
Roosevelts had in the William Howard Tafts as a friendly gesture, one
set of Republicans to another.

Although Teddy Roosevelt had hand-picked his successor rather
than run in 1908, his usually ebullient daughter Alice Roosevelt
Longworth was not at all happy with such a turn of events—even
among political friends. Indeed, who was entirely happy? The
Roosevelts were sad at leaving, the Tafts fidgeting and anxious to
move in the next day.

Already, word had seeped through official Washington that Taft,
far from overcome by gratitude, was planning to give many of
Teddy's political appointees the boot, from cabinet on down. Alice
was also annoyed that she was offered a ticket to Taft's White House
reception following the next day's inauguration. Imagine! A ticket to
get in! And never mind that it was Taft's kindly wife, Nellie, who
made the offer. Alice was not yet ready to relinquish her claims to
the White House. "I! I, who had wandered in and out for eight happy
years!" she later anguished.

How truly distraught Alice may have been at the thought of her
family leaving the White House is difficult to judge now. After all, she
by this time was a married woman whose husband, U.S.
Representative Nicholas Longworth, had his own career in politics
(he one day would be Speaker of the House), and in 1909 she no
longer lived at the White House.

But . . . who knows? After all, it was a fully grown-up Alice who
slipped into the garden that evening and buried "a bad little idol"
there in the dirt. And with dire incantations, it is said, with a girlish,
flippant curse on future occupants of the grand old structure.

The next day, a howling storm of rain, sleet, and snow drove the
inaugural ceremony indoors—into the Senate chamber of the
Capitol, the floor and galleries filled with onlookers standing elbow
to elbow. Nellie Taft broke tradition by riding next to her president-

husband in his horse-drawn carriage—the first time a first lady had ridden in the inaugural parade down Pennsylvania Avenue from the Capitol. "After getting 'Will' to pressure Congress to appropriate money for four autos, she felt she had earned a place on the seat next to him," wrote Alice's biographer Howard Teichman. And that night they traveled to the inaugural ball by motorcar.

In the meantime, the weather was so bad that in the outdoor festivities the band players found their brass mouthpieces frozen . . . "valves closed, reeds split."

At this point, too, newly installed President Taft himself now apparently changed . . . or revealed his true self. He came in from the day's festivities, dumped his gloves, silk hat, and greatcoat and "threw himself" on a sofa with the announcement: "I'm president now and I'm tired of being kicked around! "

Until that very moment, "Mr. Taft had been the jolliest, friendliest visitor the Roosevelts ever had entertained," said Teichman. "With that statement, his speech and his attitudes toward the servants and staff members changed radically. He snapped, he scowled, he snarled."

In another change, the very corpulent Taft ordered a new bathtub. At more than three hundred pounds, it seems he could hardly squeeze into the tub that had served so many other presidents for decades.

Taft's wife, Helen (nicknamed "Nellie") contributed other changes, too. Nearly all the Teddy Roosevelt servants and staff were replaced. The new first lady hired a housekeeper and a chef—"entertainment grew lavish." She also was a confidante and adviser to her

This replica of William Howard Taft's enormous bathtub is on display at the Taft Museum. (Photo by Mindy Bryant)

husband on political and policy matters, it seems, more openly so than many of her predecessors. She even attended his political meetings. And then, just ten weeks or so into their presidential term, she suffered a stroke. "Will spent the rest of the days of his Presidency teaching his wife how to speak and walk again."

Still another unhappy experience for Taft was the ghost. True or untrue, the story is that an aide pecked at his office door one day and reported a that kitchen worker was quitting suddenly. Worse, other White House domestics were considering the same drastic action.

"But why?" Taft wanted to know, his ire on the rise.

"Well, Sir, it seems they are afraid of the ghost."

"Ghost!?"

The bearer of this unfortunate news explained that more than one maid and houseman had seen a gossamer figure or felt a frigid hand on their shoulders. A couple of the maids couldn't keep from screaming. Sometimes they left their tasks, burst into sobs, and ran for more populated areas such as the kitchen.

Taft immediately saw the obvious danger here—the story would leak out to the newspapers! "I won't have it," he warned direly. "I forbid anyone who works in this house ever to mention the subject to me or anyone else again."

But then he thought of the obvious question: *Whose* ghost?

"Abraham Lincoln's youngest son," was the sad answer.

"Tell them it's nonsense, and never again do I want that story repeated."

But somebody did repeat it, and Alice heard it and commented, "There are worse things than ghosts—bad Presidents in the White House are worse than apparitions."

Slaves in the Attic

OTHERS HAD DONE IT BEFORE him, but "Old Zach" had his doubts, what with the country already arguing over the slavery issue. Others, Southern presidents before him, had brought slaves into the White

House . . . but now, at the halfway point of the nineteenth century, this was an issue aboil, and perhaps discretion should be the order of the day.

Taylor, former general and hero of the recently concluded Mexican War, moved up to Washington and its White House from Louisiana. He owned slaves.

As he and Mrs. Taylor settled in, the White House staff they kept or assembled consisted of outgoing president James K. Polk's old steward, Henry Bowman, followed in the same post by German immigrant Ignatius Ruppert; one Swedish and two Irish housemaids; a butler, Charles Beale of Virginia; the perennial doorkeeper and messenger; and. . . fifteen Zachary Taylor "house slaves" brought up to Washington from Louisiana.

Taylor worried over having highly visible slaves tending to White House chores, even if the practice did save money and help the family budget. So he kept them "invisible." They were steered away from the public rooms on the first floor and told to do their work upstairs in the private family territory. According to pre-eminent White House historian William Seale: "They must have slept in the eight attic rooms." And it is his suggestion that Taylor was acutely aware that allowing them to move about their duties in full view of the "hundreds" passing through the public rooms every week "might have invited incident." By 1850, Seale notes, "Northerners in Washington were increasingly uncomfortable about the presence of slaves."

After all, in Taylor's day, the major debate in Congress was over the slavery-fostered Compromise of 1850. And the Civil War itself was only about ten years away.

As a Southerner, native of Virginia, Taylor was not unique in bringing slaves to the White House—indeed, his immediate predecessor, President Polk, had fired paid White House servants and replaced them with his slaves. Unbelievable as it may sound today, Polk not only imported his own slaves from his home base in Tennessee, he actually bought slaves while serving as president and then housed them all in the basement servant quarters of the White House.

Slaves also were a "normal" fixture at the White House under Thomas Jefferson, James Madison, John Tyler, and Andrew Jackson. A Madison slave, in fact, once returned to the White House several of its silver items—urns, trays, candelabra—after the mansion was looted and burned during the British occupation of Washington in the War of 1812. Another Madison slave, Paul Jennings, would produce the first known insider memoir from the White House.

His own slaves notwithstanding, it also should be noted that President Zachary Taylor was a stalwart defender of the Union, and did not want the country to be split asunder by the action of rebellious states. When three Southern congressmen sought his support one day during the raging Compromise debate, they made the mistake of saying that if California were admitted to the Union as a free state, the Southern states might seize New Mexico as added slavery territory.

Taylor, shouting and raging, practically chased the trio from his second-floor office and down the White House stairs.

He was found moments later, it is said, "rushing around like a caged lion" and calling the departed congressmen "those damned traitors."

Public Audience Room

AH, YES, IF THESE OLD walls could only speak . . . or did they when Lincoln dreamed that he himself was lying in state in the East Room—and then there he was in reality, just a few weeks later.

What volumes these walls could speak! And not only of the seven presidents who have lain in state here, but also of the joyous times, the frivolous moments, the incidental and unimportant yet captivating moments.

Here is where the first White House occupants hung their laundry to dry. Where Thomas Jefferson threw up partitions to provide living quarters for his private secretary Meriwether Lewis, future cocaptain of the Lewis and Clark expedition. Where the ceiling fell in during the Jeffersonian term. Where, one hundred years later, Teddy Roosevelt's children allegedly roller-skated. Where, no doubt about it, his daughter Alice was married to Nicolas Longworth, the congressman and future Speaker of the House for whom today's Longworth House Office Building is named.

Here, too, were married Ulysses S. Grant's daughter Nellie and Lyndon B. Johnson's daughter Lynda (to future Virginia governor and

U.S. senator Charles S. Robb). Here Lincoln gave a reception early in 1864 for his new master of the Union armies, the same U. S. Grant.

The East Room in the beginning was conceived as the "Public Audience Room." White House architect James Hoban envisioned the large, airy chamber at the east end of the White House as the Executive Mansion's primary reception room, the site of social gatherings and major sit-down dinners.

The large space remained an unfinished cavern for nearly twenty years after the John Adamses first occupied the White House in 1800.

Little is known of its earlier furnishings—or day-to-day uses under the first few presidents. John and Abigail Adams could not make much use of the room in its largely unfinished state in 1800. Jefferson, the nation's third president, not only housed Lewis in the room—until the waterlogged ceiling came down—but may also have used it as a pantry and storage room. His inventory of 1809 mentions a table and kettle used for washing "tumblers" and says that thirty-four chairs were kept in the "Large Unfinished Room."

James Madison held cabinet meetings in one part of that room, at its south end. And speaking of Madison, hanging in the East Room in more recent years has been the famous Gilbert Stuart portrait of George Washington that Dolley Madison is so often credited with rescuing from the British in the War of 1812.

Remember? As the British swooped down upon Washington and the government fled, she found that the portrait was screwed to the wall. So, she ordered the frame broken and the canvas itself pried out and given into "the hands of two gentlemen from New York, for safekeeping." (Former Madison slave Paul Jennings said, however, that rather than Dolley, it was two White House workers who did the rescuing.)

After the British had left town and reconstruction of the White House took place, the East Room underwent finishing touches—and even received some furnishings. But the four sofas and two dozen chairs placed in the grand chamber had not been upholstered when John Quincy Adams, son of the mansion's first occupant, used the room for his New Year's Day receptions. Following Adams, Andrew Jackson the frontiersman added some fancy furnishings that began to do the "Public Audience Room" justice. He installed wallpaper (yellow), carpeting (red-bordered), cut-glass chandeliers, black mar-

Judging by the artist's aquatint of 1814, a view from northeast of the White House, the exterior walls still stood intact after its burning by the British. The fact is, the walls were only a shell hiding the full extent of damage inside. George Munger (1781–1825) was the artist. (American Memory Collections, Library of Congress)

ble fireplace mantels, gilt-framed mirrors, and various lighting fixtures of the nonelectrical sort. Under Jackson, too, there appeared curtains in white, blue and yellow pastels and upholstery that one visitor described as "light-blue satin-silk."

All this was a far cry from the busy, baroque tastes of the Victorian Age, which found U. S. Grant adding phony beams above gilded columns and Chester Arthur apparently happy with New York designer Louis Tiffany's lining for the ceiling—silver paper!

In the interim, of course, from the time of Jackson to that of Grant and Arthur, the East Room had other, more serious, uses. The first Union officer killed in the Civil War, Ephraim Ellsworth, was brought here to lie in state in the home of his good friend Abe Lincoln. Lincoln's own son Willie passed through the room in a coffin after he died of fever at age twelve. Union troops were briefly quartered in the room, and of course Lincoln's body was placed here, in state, as the nation absorbed the shock of its first presidential assassination.

On happier days, however, it was here that the Teddy Roosevelts held a memorable Day-After-Christmas Party for Washington-area children—memorable because 550 children, accompanied by mothers, nannies or nurses, responded to the invitations; the entertainment schedule ran out and the children, for a brief period, ran wild.

It was here, too, under another Roosevelt—FDR—that England's visiting King George VI received the Washington diplomatic corps one summer's day in 1939, just before the eruption of World War II in Europe. And immediately after the war, Harry S. Truman, FDR's successor, held a reception in the East Room honoring the chief architect of the victory in Europe, General Dwight D. Eisenhower. Only a short time before, FDR himself had passed through the East Room in a coffin; but in accordance with his own prior instruction, he had not actually lain in state in the chamber. Less than twenty years later, a still-young WWII veteran, John F. Kennedy, would lie in state in the "Public Audience Room."

The East Room—like the White House itself, restored in the latter twentieth century to its early look of classic yet simple elegance—has seen them all . . . every president and entourage but one, George Washington. And that only because the White House was not yet built and Washington, D.C., was not yet the nation's capital city. Seen them all come and go . . . funerals, weddings, entertainments . . . if walls could only speak, what tales, what memories, what volumes!

Doing Nothing

CHILDREN DON'T MAKE HIGH POLICY or run for reelection, but children nonetheless have been a part of the White House since it first became a home. They have provided some of its happiest and liveliest moments. One such child, hardly recalled today, was known throughout the land as "Baby McKee." This was Benjamin Harrison's grandchild—Benjamin also—who was among the four generations of Harrisons living at the White House between the two Grover Cleveland terms of the late-nineteenth century.

As mentioned earlier, Baby McKee liked to hitch up his goat cart to the pet goat named Old Whiskers, and one time the animal raced onto Pennsylvania Avenue in front of the North Portico, with President Harrison himself giving chase in formal frock coat and top hat.

Even the ill-fated Lincolns had their happy, proud, and poignant moments with their sons. For instance, when Tad, age seven, began wearing a Union officer's uniform cut down to fit his frame,

Secretary of War Edwin Stanton gave him a "commission" as a colonel.

The Ulysses S. Grants in the 1870s passed a happy time in the White House with three sons and a daughter, ages eleven to eighteen when the family moved in. Young Fred and his brother "Buck" served their father as confidential secretaries during a second term, and their sister Nellie was married in the White House. After Fred married elsewhere in 1874, he and his bride, Ida, lived at the White House, and their daughter Julia, named for the first lady, was born in the White House.

The Teddy Roosevelts descended, one might say, on the White House with five young children, three to fourteen in age, plus half-sister Alice, seventeen, in 1900. "A nervous person had no business around the White House in those days," said Chief Usher Ike Hoover years later. The White House that had just seen William McKinley die of an assassin's bullets now rang with "howls and laughter," and "nothing was too sacred for their amusement and no place too good for a playroom." Even TR played in the attic (with the children, of course). One time a child turned off the lights while his father was chasing another of the wild crowd, and bang! Theodore Roosevelt, president of the United States, ran into a post in the dark.

Two decades later, the nation was saddened by the slow death of Calvin Coolidge's son Calvin Jr., infected with blood poisoning from a blister on his foot. But happier days came again with the sights and sounds of Franklin Roosevelt's ever-growing crowd of grandchildren—a rare gathering of all thirteen for his fourth inauguration in early 1945 was the largest gathering of presidential grandchildren ever assembled at any one moment in the White House.

One of the most romantic stories to come from family life at the White House has to be the meeting of two children, both age eight, at Dwight D. Eisenhower's second inauguration, one a boy, the other a girl, and both—in the photographs—showing buck teeth. That was in 1953, and neither child then lived in the White House. Later, however, the young lady did . . . and later, they were married, the climax of a happy, storybook romance. They, of course, were "Ike's" grandson David and Richard M. Nixon's daughter Julie, the later Mr. and Mrs. David Eisenhower.

After FDR died and Harry S. Truman gave way to Ike, and Eisenhower in turn bowed to John F. Kennedy as White House occupant, a series of teenaged girls lived at the White House. They were the Lyndon B. Johnson daughters, Luci and Lynda Byrd, the Nixon daughters, Julie and Tricia, Gerald Ford's daughter Susan, and Jimmy Carter's daughter Amy.

Just before that hair-dryer parade, the Kennedys had moved into the White House with daughter Caroline, all of three years of age, and infant son John Jr. ("John-John"), two and one half months. If for no other reason, Caroline may go down in history for her answer when asked one day what her father the president was doing just then. "Oh," she said, "he's upstairs with his shoes and socks off, not doing anything."

Fit for Clerks or Queens

KINGS AND QUEENS, A FAMOUS prime minister, and even a sour-visaged Soviet foreign minister have slept here. An artist of some note slept and worked by the northern light here. Presidential secretaries traditionally worked in this room. At one time six clerks used it for their office. Another time, with the door locked, it may have been the setting for a key bit of political sleuthing by Abe Lincoln. Peel away the historical layers of the Queen's Bedroom, or Rose Guest Room, at the eastern end of the second floor, and the geological strata of American history appear, one by one.

Here, in Andrew Jackson's day, lived his friend and longtime houseguest, artist Ralph E. W. Earl. The widower of the late Rachel Jackson's niece, Earl both slept and worked in the bedroom above the East Room on the north side of the great house. He previously had stayed for long periods at Jackson's Tennessee mansion called the Hermitage, and his portrait of Rachel now was hanging in the bereaved Andrew Jackson's own bedroom.

Later it became traditional for presidential secretaries to live in this northeast room; Lincoln's two secretaries both slept in the bedroom and one, John Hay, used the small corner room next to it as his office. The smaller room, eventually a dressing room, saw different uses over the White House eras—as office, as storage, as bedroom. And across the hall from both were once the president's own offices.

In between was the very public hallway where visitors waited in hopes of gaining access to the man inside those offices. Oilcloth covered the floor as some protection against its rough usage, and spittoons were a common sight in the hallway. It was like that, with crowds lining the hallway and the nearby "business stairs" in effort to see the president, when Lincoln first took the reins of government. When he officially took office in March 1861, the Civil War was not yet a fact. Could it somehow be averted?

In Charleston Harbor that April, Fort Sumter was isolated, under threat . . . if Lincoln did nothing, the Secessionists might regard that as weakness. To do something, on the other hand, would mean sending supplies by U.S. Navy vessels, an action possibly to be misread as an affront and challenge. Virginia had not yet seceded but was teetering when Lincoln received a loyalist Virginian behind locked doors in a second-floor bedroom of the White House—probably in the Rose Guest Room, historians say.

From this agent's report on events in Richmond, Lincoln deduced that the Unionist cause in Virginia was weak, probably doomed. After his informant John Baldwin left, Lincoln ordered the supply expedition to sail for Fort Sumter. If Virginia would not hold, what had he to lose? He also sent courteous word to the governor of South Carolina on April 8. On April 12, Fort Sumter came under Confederate fire and the Civil War had begun. Two days later, Fort Sumter surrendered . . . the rest, as they say, is history.

When the smoke had cleared four years later, Lincoln himself was one of the many victims and his successor, Andrew Johnson of Tennessee, had moved into the White House, where the former bedroom for the presidential secretaries became an office for six clerks. Still later, in 1881, when assassin's victim James Garfield lay dying in his bedroom at the west end of the second floor, the future Queen's Bedroom was for a time converted for use as an emergency telegraph office.

As the White House moved into the twentieth century, the Teddy Roosevelts made sweeping changes. The eastern hall no longer housed spittoons or even offices, and Edith Kermit Roosevelt insisted upon rose as the bedroom's color. By the time of Herbert Hoover, the large, comfortable Rose Room and its dressing room in the corner were fixtures—probably the favorite guest room suite in the house. It now contained a four-poster canopied bed known as the Andrew Jackson Bed. And maybe it was.

Later still, at the advent of World War II, Winston Churchill slept in the Rose Room—and during the war, so did Stalin's unsmiling foreign minister V. M. Molotov (as in Molotov cocktail).

By late in the twentieth century, the venerable room had welcomed guests ranging from those two major figures of the world stage to a number of queens, among them Elizabeth of England; Wilhelmina and Juliana of the Netherlands; and Frederika of Greece. And so it is, and has been since the 1960s, "The Queen's Bedroom."

Hanging on one rose-hued wall in recent years has been an apt painting, a portrait of Emily Donelson, Andrew Jackson's niece who acted as a surrogate first lady for the widowed president. And the artist? Ralph E. W. Earl, the same artist and friend of Jackson who once occupied the very same room.

Man Reclining on Bed

A DAY IN THE LIFE of the nation's only crippled president usually began about 8 A.M., with breakfast carried to his bedroom on a tray. While partaking of his meal, he would breeze through half a dozen newspapers, seated half-dressed in a sweater or cape. He liked, his wife once said, no conversation during this initial hour of the day's activities.

Still not quite ready for the outside world, he would receive his chief staff aides—press secretary Steve Early, other confidants, or military aide Edwin M. Watson. Staying roughly from 9:00 to 9:30 A.M. they would brief him on the day's schedule, and then they left the field to Franklin Delano Roosevelt's personal valet, Irvin McDuffie (whose wife, Lizzie, was a White House maid).

It was time for dressing and shaving. He had to be wheeled into the bathroom, but once there he shaved himself. His interior secretary, Harold Ickes, recalled conferring with him there one day. "There he was, sitting before a mirror in front of the washstand, shaving. He invited me to sit on the toilet seat while we talked."

Next, back into the bedroom and Ickes, struck by the scene before him, watched as FDR "reclined on his bed while his valet proceeded to help him dress." What struck the onlooker at this intimate—and yet apparently commonplace moment—was "the unaffected simplicity and personal charm of the man."

Said Ickes also: "He was the President of the United States but he was also a plain human being, talking over with a friend matters of mutual interest while he shaved and dressed with the help of his valet. His disability didn't seem to concern him in the slightest degree or to disturb his urbanity."

By 10:30 A.M., FDR ordinarily would be ready to face his more public schedule for the day. That meant, first, being pushed in his wheelchair to the office suite in the West Wing, built by another Roosevelt—cousin Teddy. The way for polio-victim FDR was eased by newly constructed ramps.

Roosevelt, like many presidents before and after, would spend most of the working day in his Oval Office (he created a new one in 1934), but this was also the spot where he had his lunch. He first would run through appointments of about fifteen minutes each with people he should see, for a total of about two hours.

The former assistant secretary of the navy had embellished the room with ship models on the mantel and engravings of river settings with more watercraft by Currier and Ives on the walls. Since he was a grandfather, wrote historian Arthur M. Schlesinger Jr. *(The Coming of the New Deal),* the presidential desk bore an oddly mixed combination of government papers, books, and his grandchildren's toy pigs or donkeys, and nearby, but inconspicuous, were the presidential flag and the Great Seal in the ceiling. "Behind the President, light streamed softly in through great glass windows running down to the floor, and to the east, briefly glimpsed, were the quiet rose garden and the porticoes and magnolia trees."

Compared to the Washington world immediately outside, said the historian, "this bright and open room had an astonishing serenity." Another visitor and close observer, Swiss biographer Emil Ludwig, said, "You would think you were in the summer residence of the general manager of a steamship company, who has surrounded himself with mementoes of the days when he was captain."

Similarly, the bedroom FDR had left earlier in the day was most informal—more ship prints on the wall, and on the mantel there, more toy animals, plus family photos and various knickknacks. The bed itself was of white iron, and next to it was a white table. The room, in its entirety, Schlesinger found, was old-fashioned, thrown together indiscriminately, cluttered, and "ugly and comfortable."

Now it was time for lunch—in the Oval Office, and served at the desk straight from a hotel-like portable warmer. It very well could be ham with a poached egg.

Afterward came a few more appointments, followed by one to two hours of dictation to secretary Grace Tully.

Next, at five o'clock, came the famous "children's hour" of FDR's White House tenure. Gathering in the office staff, it was "an interlude of relaxation and gossip," explained historian Schlesinger.

At 5:30 P.M., FDR repaired to his new White House swimming pool, financed by a fund-raising campaign started by the *New York Daily News*. Then, after a twenty-minute swim, came cocktail time— a martini or old-fashioned before dinner.

Dinner itself was followed by more office work in the private FDR study; located in the second-floor private quarters, it was one of the three oval rooms in the White House proper. He might deal with papers here, dictate, or have more meetings.

And finally, into bed before the witching hour. In just five minutes, usually, the president of the United States was sound asleep.

One thing, though. Unlike some others, this crippled occupant of the White House had a stern rule for the Secret Service. They were never, said Schlesinger, "never allowed . . . to lock the doors of his room at night."

Sentimental Evenings

STRIKE UP THE UNITED STATES Marine Band in the Eisenhower White House and what do we hear? On this particular occasion, it was the Wedding March from *Lohengrin*. And entering the East Room at measured pace, veiled in white, was no nervous young bride, but Mamie Eisenhower!

And following her this evening in 1959 were two more middle-aged women, dressed in white also. Close friends, in fact—Mrs. Neil McElroy, wife of the secretary of defense, and Mrs. Leonard Heaton, whose husband, a general, was commander of Walter Reed Army Medical Center in Washington.

All walking this measured tread. And at the center of the room met by their respective husbands. And a slight readjustment, as now the Marine Band played a waltz, and the couples glided and bowed around the room before onlooking friends.

And after that, all three couples assembled in front of a clergyman, who led them in repeating their marriage vows. "There were audible sobs from some of the guests," reported Lester and Irene David in their book *Ike and Mamie.*

The reason for the unusual White House "wedding"? An anniversary—the forty-third anniversary for Ike and Mamie. It also marked anniversaries for their old friends the McElroys and the Heatons. So realistic was the planning for the mock wedding that the women carried bridal bouquets.

But this was not the first such sentimental occasion noted in the Eisenhower White House. In 1954, Ike and Mamie celebrated their thirty-eighth anniversary by inviting one hundred members of his 1915 West Point class (and a few widows) to dinner at the White House, with both the Marine Band and the Air Force Symphony Orchestra playing for the president and his guests. After Ike on that evening squired Mamie through "The Anniversary Waltz," he told a friend it was their first dance in sixteen years—the first since before he had gone off to war in World War II!

During the same evening, the Marine Band had played popular songs of the 1915 era, and Ike had "distributed West Point song books and led the guests in a community sing." Apparently, on both evenings, a good, sentimental time was had by all!

JFK Misses Lunch

FOR SOPHISTICATED DIPLOMATS, GRIZZLED OLD pols, and teary-eyed senti-
mentalists alike, there was one hallmark of the Kennedy White
House that was special and unforgettable—children.

There were, on the one hand, two very young Kennedys, John
and Caroline, always much in evidence despite the size and official
function of the presidential home. "Every morning, like the merriest
of tinkling chandeliers, the house resounded with the laughter of
the children and their friends," recalled White House social secretary
Letitia Baldridge years later.

Further, their childish accoutrements had become a part of the
landscape. On the south lawns, a tree house, swings, a jungle gym.
Or the sight might be Caroline riding her pony, Macaroni. Or, upon
an accommodating snowy day, "Mrs. Kennedy driving the children
around the snow in an old-fashioned horse-drawn sleigh."

On most mornings, Caroline walked her "daddy" from the
second-floor family apartment to his office . . . his Oval Office in
another part of the house. The children's accoutrements did not
confine themselves to the south lawns or the private quarters
upstairs, it also seems. "No matter how stern or unbending a foreign
official and his wife might be," wrote Tish Baldridge, "as I was escorting them through the Mansion, I loved to watch their faces change
from sternness to enthusiasm, from seriousness to laughter, at the
sight of one roller skate peeking timidly out from under a historic
damask drapery—or a tricycle dumped momentarily against the
marble pedestal holding Abraham Lincoln's bronze bust."

In addition to the impact of the Kennedys' own children, there
was the concerted and deliberate stress on youth that was a hallmark of the Kennedy White House—concerts, performances, tours,
and like extravaganzas by young people, for young people. The first
in a series of youthful outdoor concerts on the White House lawn
was given by the Greater Boston Youth Symphony and the
Breckinridge Boys' Choir from Breckinridge, Texas—the unexpectedly chilly April day forced a change in the day's drink menu from

cool lemonade to hot chocolate. The concert established a little-known Kennedy "tradition," too. President John F. Kennedy briefly appeared to welcome the young White House guests and to encourage their musical calling. "He apologized for not being able to stay through the concert, but promised to leave the door of his office open, so he could hear everything. The children kept looking back, and sure enough, the French doors of the Presidential office were kept open throughout, as they were for every children's concert thereafter." Kennedy, in fact, always took pains to greet young visitors whenever he could—one day, an eleven-year-old who had been eating chocolate cake found himself shaking JFK's hand. JFK, in turn, found his hand covered with sticky icing. Unperturbed, he licked his palm and told his young onlookers: "Mumm, good! I'll have to have a piece of that, too."

On another occasion, the visiting Korean Orphans' Choir, escorted by Ms. Baldridge, "bumped into Caroline and her nursery school classmates." Without prompting, the Korean tykes lined up in two rows "and burst into song right in the hallway." Caroline and her playmates stood and listened, then applauded at the end . . . the admittedly sentimental Social Secretary hurriedly reaching, at the same time, for her handkerchief. Typically, too, the Korean orphans left with White House presents—PT-boat tie clips for the boys and "little link bracelets with the PT-boat charm" for the girls. "Each child had an enormous lollipop in his hand—and, of course, the precious memory of having sung for Caroline Kennedy."

Another occasion for tears was the day the Interlochen Music Camp National High School Symphony Orchestra and Ballet Corps appeared before an audience of handicapped and orphaned children, the Interlochen children dressed in uniforms and "looking like an army of scrubbed angels." At one point, JFK strode forth to deliver his greeting. The children broke into a choral rendition of "Hail to the Chief." And among the onlookers, the tears really flowed ("it was heartening to notice that even some of the Social Aides were flicking tears away from the corners of their eyes.").

Still to come, though, was the bright, sunshiny day when Tish Baldridge and her cohorts led "a wheel-chair brigade" of disabled children into the Rose Garden as part of a special private tour for the terribly afflicted youngsters. It was not expected that they would see the president, or he, them. "The President, we knew, would be upstairs having lunch, prior to rushing to the State Department Auditorium for a televised press conference." The Rose

Garden had been chosen as a stopping point to avoid disturbing the wartime commander of PT-109.

But, lo, here came a man quite suddenly, "through a French door onto the terrace." And it was. . . it was JFK, running late, but insistent on briefly visiting with each child. Visiting meant a snatch of conversation with each, a shake of the afflicted hands or a touch on the cheek. Meanwhile, the clock was ticking, recalled Baldridge in her book, *Of Diamonds and Diplomats: An Autobiography of a Happy Life*. No time now for a presidential lunch. Unlike everyone else, Kennedy seemed to comprehend when the spasm-tortured children talked to him. "Their speech had been so affected by their affliction, I could not understand one word," recalled social secretary Baldridge.

Kennedy reached one child in particular, a boy. He knelt down to hear him. "Then he dashed back into his office, returned with an old PT-boat skipper's hat he had used in the war, and plopped it down on the boy's head."

The president of course missed his lunch that day and was late for his nationally broadcast press conference. Did it really matter? Tish Baldridge would forever remember the child's reaction. "The child's face radiated a joy totally impossible to describe. I will never forget the look in his eyes."

Somehow, as JFK knelt by his side, the boy had been able to explain . . . to tell about his father. As JFK himself later explained the exact situation: "His father was in PT boats, too. His father is dead."

Two-Stepping at the White House

IT WAS A DREAM COME true. There they were, this California couple, Richard and Christina, dancing to the strains of "Shall We Dance?" Dancing nearly alone, with only one other couple on the floor with them—the hosts, George and Barbara.

It was just after 11 P.M., and all the other guests had left, including the guest of honor, one Boris Yeltsin, recently named president of the new post-Soviet Russian Federation; including the chairman

President George Bush. (White House Photo by David Valdez, Library of Congress)

of the Joint Chiefs of Staff; including the chief justice of the United States; including two cabinet members, assorted diplomats, Congress members, other politicians and bureaucrats, various celebrities, business leaders—136 guests in all.

Even for the White House, the state dinner in honor of visiting Russian leader Yeltsin had been a major, major production. Staffed by seventy personnel, the State Department's Office of Protocol (established by Calvin Coolidge) had planned and worked for six weeks orchestrating the Yeltsin appearance in Washington, the twenty-third such state visit to mark George Bush's term in office (1989–1993). Among other decorous touches, the National Park Service showed up the afternoon before the state dinner with four hundred geraniums in pots, plus eighteen potted delphiniums and ten baskets bursting with maidenhair ferns, all to be scattered throughout the main-floor state rooms of the White House.

The guests began arriving at 7:00 P.M., but they would be on their own for a short time. At 7:30 P.M. the Bushes would be standing at the North Portico, ready to receive the Russian leader and his wife. Upon their arrival, the two couples retired upstairs, to the Yellow Oval Room, for a few private moments of conversational exchanges—and an exchange of gifts.

What to present the first non-Communist state visitor since the nineteenth-century days of

Mrs. Barbara Bush. (White House Photo by David Valdez, Library of Congress)

Rutherford B. Hayes? Well, little-known fact: the twentieth-century leader was a tennis nut, wasn't he? Why not simply give him . . . no, not a tennis racquet, but one of those machines that spit out one tennis ball after another at up to eighty-five miles per hour! Battery-powered at that. Startled perhaps, but Yeltsin was, it is said, quite pleased.

Downstairs, meanwhile, fourteen dishes of Russian caviar and a meal of Roast Loin of Veal Ambassadeur awaited—140 finger bowls of crystal glass, too. Plus the guests.

At 7:50, the two official couples began their descent of the Grand Staircase to initiate the next phase of the formal dinner, George in his tux, Boris in dark suit and tie. This phase would be a joint receiving line.

Soon after would come the sit-down itself, in the elegant State Dining Room. Then the official toasts. Dinner over, the guests would leave demurely, without undue lingering. By 11 P.M., the Bushes had said their goodbyes to the Russian couple, who would be spending the night just across the street (across Pennsylvania Avenue, that is) in Blair House, the U.S. government's official guest house for visiting dignitaries. Scrawled in the diplomatic guest book for a curious posterity and any other onlookers would be the Yeltsin signature, thin lines, a fancy loop on the first letter, in the middle a sudden, upsurging, EKG-sort of line, followed by a nearly straight line for the rest of the historic signature.

Meanwhile, what of Richard and Christina Snyder, still inside the august presidential home? *Life* magazine told their story in 1992. Rich Snyder, president of the California fast-food chain In-N-Out Burgers, "had dreamed for years of attending a state dinner, mingling with people he'd seen on TV, in a house he'd seen in history books."

How or why had the little-known California couple been invited? Said *Life*: "perhaps because of the $25,000 he'd raised for Bush's 1988 campaign."

In any case, dream of dreams, the Bushes returned to the Entrance Hall from their goodbyes to Russia's first couple, they slid into a dance, the about-to-depart Snyders watching, and Bush beckoned them to join in.

According to *Life*'s account, Christina murmured, "I don't think we should." But her husband, Rich, took another view entirely. "Hey, when the President of the United States tells you to do something, you do it."

So it was, shortly after 11 P.M., the staff beginning to clean up, that the two couples, the Snyders and the Bushes, "were alone on the floor, two-stepping in the White House." A dream come true.

Additional note: Speaking of entertaining at the modern White House, the Clintons—Bill and Hillary—could have done without the day in early 1995 when overnight guests, a king and his queen, appeared at the diplomatic entrance . . . and no one was there to greet them.

Red carpet, yes, but no one to step forward, welcoming hand outstretched, as King Harald of Norway and Queen Sonja alighted from their sleek limousine.

The report is that the royal couple, expected for dinner and an overnight visit, stood around uneasily for several minutes. Inside the great mansion, life proceeded as normal when such visitors were expected—but not for another fifteen minutes. The king and queen, it seems, were a wee bit early. Not the fault of the Clinton White House.

Eventually, an official greeter rushed out and guided the visitors into the Diplomatic Reception Room. After a few minutes, first lady Hillary Rodham Clinton appeared, followed after another short interval by the president himself.

Then, it was out to the red carpet area again for an official picture of the two couples together . . . finally, the dinner-overnight visit by the two royals was underway.

Jackie to the Rescue

AFTER GLAMOROUS, SOPHISTICATED JACKIE KENNEDY "conquered" Paris in 1961, there came an all-important summit pitting her young American president-husband from Boston against an "old pol" of the Bolshevik school, Soviet premier Nikita Khrushchev. Typically, when Austria greeted the two heads of state with a black-tie dinner on the first night of summitry in Vienna, Khrushchev appeared with his standard bag-of-wheat suit. At a ballet performance in the historic Schönbrunn Palace that evening, White House staffers further noticed that the Soviet premier did not always watch the graceful dancers on stage. Instead, he was seen "ogling" first lady Jackie Kennedy, who of course was beautifully dressed for such an occasion.

While his more-than-just-plump wife, Nina, looked "schoolmarmish and self-conscious" in her "plainest of dark dresses," Jackie made a startling contrast, recalled social secretary Letitia Baldridge.

Nonetheless, the White House staffers working on summitry protocol and social arrangements behind the scenes "immediately liked" Nina Khrushchev. "She was sweet and gracious whenever we talked to her." By contrast, her husband was "diffident and difficult." Perhaps Khrushchev was conscious that in Vienna in 1961 he was "being publicly compared to the glamorous young President in a city that frankly loathed anything Soviet." In any case, his smiles that first evening were reserved for the glamorous Mrs. Kennedy. "Interpreters were, naturally, used all the time, but one could tell he enjoyed the extra time just to gaze at her."

Vienna's complete disenchantment with the Soviet visitor was obvious when the official motorcades took to the streets with their high-ranking passengers. The Soviets evoked "sullen silence" from the Austrian onlookers, while the Kennedy motorcade "instigated near-riots of joyous, screaming Viennese."

Meanwhile, as the husbands met officially during the second day of summitry, first lady Jackie was all diplomat—and kindhearted human being—when a minor crisis arose at a luncheon for the visiting ladies. The hostess was the Austrian president's daughter, and the luncheon was held in the Palais Pallavacini, with "an exact balance" of Austrian, Soviet, and American guests.

The meal over, the party had moved to the living room for coffee. Meanwhile, a crowd of three thousand or so onlookers had gathered in the square outside the palace. Now they began chanting—chanting Jackie's name. "In every country, the rhythm had been the same," wrote Baldridge in *Of Diamonds and Diplomats*. The crowds would chant "Jac-kie!" over and over.

Here, though, there was an embarrassing complication. The

crowd outside showed no recognition of that other first lady—Nina Khrushchev. Conversation among the luncheon guests faltered as Nina sat there, "gazing sadly down at her feet, saying nothing." The atmosphere in the room was tense, with the Austrian hostess obviously wondering how to salvage the situation. Instead of the hostess, however, it was Jackie Kennedy to the rescue.

"She went to the open window to appease the impatient crowd, smiled and waved at them. The volume of noise became an ear-splitting symphony of cheering and applause. After about one minute, she took Mme. Khrushchev gently by the arm, and led her back to the window. She held up Mme. Khrushchev's hand for a second, and then the Russian began to wave on her own."

That did it! The crowd fell into step right away. Now the roaring chant was: "Jac-kie! Nin-a! Jac-kie! Nin-a!"

Old Compatriot's Visit

THERE WAS REAL WAR TALK in the air when an old fighting compatriot arrived in Andrew Jackson's capital, talk of force to make the states' righters in the South fall into line behind the federal government's lead . . . talk of armed conflict, secession, and nullification. Specifically, South Carolina had nullified the 1828 and 1832 federal tariffs, and Jackson wanted to use federal troops to push South Carolina into line.

It was a bitter debate, with Jackson's own vice president, John C. Calhoun of South Carolina, openly opposing the president, even resigning to join the battle in the Senate. So it was that Martin Van Buren ran with Jackson in 1832. And after Jackson won reelection with New Yorker Van Buren by his side, South Carolina withdrew its original nullification, only to "nullify" a congressional action authorizing use of federal forces against the state—a denial never tested per se. There was no satisfactory resolution to the growing schism between North and South, which would erupt thirty years later in the Civil War.

Caught up in the hot political battle shortly after his reelection, Jackson heard his old "Sergeant," Sam Dale, was in town. A compatriot of Jackson's in the war against the Creek Indians and again against the British at New Orleans, Dale in the years since 1815 had advanced to the rank of general in the Mississippi militia. Still, he was "too modest" to seek an audience with Jackson. And so, Jackson sent for him, using a willing U.S. senator as the messenger.

Dale arrived at the White House to find Jackson closeted in the upstairs study in a strategy session on the nullification issue. Among the six or seven gentlemen present was the Jackson ally Senator Thomas Hart Benton of Missouri. But Jackson obviously didn't want his old comrade-in-arms to feel awed. He pointedly included Dale in the conversation, saying: "General Dale, if this thing goes on, our country will be like a bag of meal with both ends open. Pick it up and it will run out."

Later, with the political associates gone, the president took out a decanter of whiskey for his old friend and they talked. Jackson opined that Dale, true to his country all these years, was now advancing in age and paying the price of solitude for having remained a bachelor.

Apparently this reference brought Jackson to the painful subject of his late wife, Rachel, since he paced the room with his eyes suddenly full of tears. Then, their discussion came back to the nullification issue. "Dale," said Jackson, the Mississippian's former commander on the field of battle, "they are trying me here; you will witness it; but, by the God in Heaven, I will uphold the laws."

Dale, of course, responded he hoped all would "go right."

"They SHALL go right, sir!" Jackson slammed his hand on a table "so hard that he broke one of his pipes," wrote his twentieth-century biographer Marquis James. Meanwhile, before the nullification storm ran its course, Jackson sent fighting ships to Charleston Harbor in South Carolina, denounced any state's right to nullify or secede, and issued his Proclamation on Nullification (December 10, 1832).

Dale soon passed from history's sight, but not the nullification edict troubling his old comrade-in-arms. Meanwhile, one who closely read the ban against such threats to the Union was an unknown country lawyer in Illinois. Abraham Lincoln would consult it again when composing his inaugural address of 1861—one month before the start of the Civil War.

Minor Embarrassment

YOU CAN'T BE IN TWO places at once. This old saw was almost refuted by an episode in the life of a president—and that of a private secretary. Grover Cleveland's second-term secretary, Henry T. Thurber, otherwise sober and well-suited in every way to his job, pulled up short in judgment one day when the boss was away from the office. In fact, that was part of the problem—the boss was away for the unannounced and slightly frivolous purpose of fishing.

Unfortunately, a major public figure chose that very moment to die, and White House comment would be appropriate. As the reporters gathered, Thurber was on the spot. They wanted a comment, but the boss had said to keep his fishing trip quiet. No disclosure!

Next best choice for a loyal secretary?

Thurber was nothing if not creative, and he simply ... well, created.

Receiving the newshawks, he told them to wait. He then ostentatiously entered Cleveland's executive office, the inner sanctum, and stayed for a few moments.

That done, he emerged and briefed the reporters in solemn tones. Yes, the president was sorrowful; yes, the nation had suffered a great loss, and in fact, he, Thurber, hardly had ever seen the president quite so moved!

All this came out the next day ... but unfortunately so did news that Cleveland had just passed through Virginia on his way back to the White House in Washington, where he had NOT been the day before.

"Mrs. Presidentress"

IN THE ANTEROOM, AMONG THOSE awaiting an audience with the president, was one fellow who was "oval-faced" and "bilious looking." This same specimen was distinguished by the fact that he "sucked the head of a thick stick, and from time to time took it out of his mouth, to see how it was getting on."

Also in the waiting room were "a Kentucky farmer, six-feet-six in height" and "a tall wiry, muscular old man, from the West." So observed English novelist Charles Dickens when visiting the John Tyler White House in 1842, the year before Dickens would create perhaps his best-known tale, *A Christmas Carol.*

Dickens tended to concoct caricatures of people he'd observed, so it shouldn't be too surprising that he would seize upon the spitting of the American favor-seekers awaiting their turn in the White House. "Indeed, all these gentlemen were so very persevering and energetic in this latter particular [spitting] and bestowed their favors so abundantly upon the carpet, that I take it for granted the presidential housemaids have high wages," wrote the Englishman.

Dickens returned soon to England and to deserved literary fame, much of it based upon novels first printed in installments in British and American periodicals. He could have looked to the Tyler White House for just such a serial story.

Tyler, a Virginian who had been a state lawmaker, U.S. representative, governor, and U.S. senator, was vice president when Virginia-born William Henry Harrison of the Ohio "frontier" died just a month into his presidency. Tyler, who was far more experienced in politics than his predecessor, at first was called "His Accidency." True, he was the first vice president to succeed so suddenly to office upon the death of a sitting president.

Even so, Tyler insisted upon being a president rather than simply a caretaker. That was in the spring of 1841, when he entered the White House as husband to the gracious Letitia Christian Tyler and as the father of their five living children.

But his wife, a stroke victim, was an invalid, and once settled into the family quarters on the second floor, she came downstairs only rarely. One such occasion was the wedding of their daughter Elizabeth ("Lizzie") in the East Room in January 1842. For the most part, though, their daughter-in-law Priscilla Cooper Tyler (Mrs. Robert Tyler) acted as White House hostess.

All that changed not long after Letitia Tyler's death on September 10, 1842. Priscilla, a stage actress before she married Tyler's son (and secretary), wrote that after the death of her widely loved mother-in-law, "Nothing can exceed the loneliness of this large and gloomy mansion."

As months passed, Priscilla continued as acting hostess, becoming a genuine hit with Washington society. She was ably advised by the grand dame in her seventies who lived across today's Lafayette Square, Dolley Madison. During this period, Tyler children and slaves from the family homestead in Virginia lived at the White House. The president was not wealthy, and his salary was only $25,000 a year. The Whigs in Congress, angered by Tyler's political independence, would not provide the public monies needed to keep up the downstairs public rooms of the Executive Mansion, and they became so rundown that the press began calling the White House the "Public Shabby House." Tyler, a brave man politically but until now most conservative personally, struggled on—even though he was so unpopular that the Whig press called an outbreak of influenza the "Tyler Grippe."

Enter now a plump, rosy-checked young woman the age of Tyler's older children—one Julia Gardiner, socially prominent daughter of former New York state senator David Gardiner.

It was the winter social season of 1843, a few months after Letitia Tyler's death, and suddenly John Tyler, age fifty-three, was falling in love with Julia, age twenty-three. But . . . no, no, she allegedly said to his earnest entreaties at first, even though she admired "the incomparable grace of his bearing," the elegance of his conversation, the "silvery sweetness" of his voice. No, no, marriage would be unthinkable, despite the mutual attraction and his loneliness.

Even so, the busy social activities continued, and one February night in 1844 she gladly joined many others at a White House ball, anticipating a Potomac River cruise the next day, a gay champagne outing aboard the U.S. Navy's new frigate, the *Princeton*. On board were the president, Julia, her father, the secretary of the navy, members of the cabinet, various military officers, and even the redoubtable

Dolley Madison. They had boarded at Alexandria, across the Potomac shoreline from the District of Columbia, on the morning of February 28, 1844—350 distinguished guests and a crew of 178.

The *Princeton* shoved off and shortly after, the new twelve-inch bow gun, called the Peacemaker, was fired—a success! This iron gun represented a major new development in ordnance.

Near Mount Vernon, where the frigate turned about for the return leg of the day's extravaganza, a second shot thrilled the festive onlookers anew. They then were treated to dinner below decks, followed by singing. Around four o'clock, the guests were told another shot would soon be fired. Since Julia Gardiner had just told Tyler that their favorite song was coming, he declined to go above. Her father, though, went topside with others in the party to watch the final shot from the new cannon.

That was when the breech burst and on the gun's left side all seven men standing by, including two of the ship's crew, were killed. The slain visitors included the Secretary of State Abel Upshur; Navy Secretary Thomas Walker Gilmer; and . . . Julia's father, David Gardiner.

Below, they heard the shouts: "The secretary of state is dead!" Julia was distraught: "Let me go to my father," she cried. And later she wrote: "Someone told me that there had been an accident, the gun had exploded . . . that drove me frantic." A woman, noting Julia's distress, told her, "My dear child, you can do no good. Your father is in heaven."

Would Dickens have written this sequel to such events? For it wasn't long before Tyler's daughter-in-law Priscilla left the mansion, and Julia took over as first lady, the first to be married to a president already in office. Not everybody quite understood. John Quincy Adams, by now seventy-seven, confided to his diary that Tyler and his new wife were the laughingstock of official Washington.

Be that as it may, Julia Tyler put on a brave show—so "brave" that she became noted for her queenly reign at social functions, for sitting on a dais in the Blue Room to receive guests while ostentatiously flanked by twelve "maids of honor." She obviously loved her role as queen of the White House and did not at all resent it when Daniel Webster or John C. Calhoun presented toasts to "Mrs. Presidentress." The conservative president, meanwhile, welcomed the waltz at White House soirees, even though he once had condemned the dance as "vulgar."

A realist in gauging his popularity, Tyler declined to seek reelection and took his new wife home to Virginia and his Sherwood Forest plantation house.

Power Dive Underway

OH, OH, COMING STRAIGHT AT the White House out of the sky one spring day in 1946 was a large, large, ever-LARGER airplane . . . looming bigger and bigger every fraction of a second. Aboard the four-engine job, his face pressed against a window, waving, laughing all the while, was the passenger who had ordered the pilot to break all the rules, who had told him to "dive" on the White House. To make "like a jet fighter," because, "I've always wanted to try something like that."

And so . . . first leveling off at 3,000 feet in the forbidden zone above the Capitol and White House . . . and then down to 2,000 feet, throttle up to full power, and then down some more, to 1,500 feet. And here, said the pilot later, "Our angle was still steep and our noise was deafening."

On the roof of the White House, the Truman White House of the 1940s, people were watching warily . . . "stiffly" goes the story. At 1,000 feet, "the flat, white target looked big, filling our whole world."

At the cockpit window was the chortling, middle-aged, bespectacled passenger who had ordered the power drive.

And 1,000 feet was nothing yet for the roaring big plane, named the *Sacred Cow.* Nothing, that is, to 500 feet instead. Which is where the plane was next, in mini-seconds. "At 500 feet," said the pilot (and Air Force Colonel) Hank Myers later, "I had the *Cow* leveled and we roared over the White House roof wide open. I caught a split-second glimpse. Everyone there was frozen with fear and wonder."

And the man in command, face pressed against the cockpit window? He knew Margaret and Bess Truman were on that roof.

Nor were the fiends in the airplane through yet!

"We climbed up to 3,000 feet again, swooped, circled, and fell into another dive. Everybody was watching us. But this time

Margaret and her mother were jumping and waving. We shot past them, at little below 500 feet and roared back upstairs once more."

The president's wife and daughter, of course, had recognized the plane by now—the president's own official aircraft. It now turned quickly out of the forbidden air space and headed for Independence, Missouri, where the bespectacled man in the cockpit planned to visit his mother that Sunday, May 19, 1946.

Things were a bit looser in those days. Harry Truman, according to Seth Kantor's magazine story later, had just buzzed the White House.

Violent Reaction

ONE HAS TO WONDER. WHO was the more surprised? The president or his assailant?

Taking a Potomac River steamer downriver on the way to Fredericksburg, Virginia, to lay a cornerstone for a monument honoring George Washington's mother one day in 1831, Andrew Jackson merely looked up and apologized when a nicely dressed, clean-cut looking young man approached him during the steamer's stop at Alexandria, Virginia.

Jackson thought the young man was there to proffer a friendly greeting. And Jackson was discomfited because he was caught in a chair "wedged" between a berth and a table. "Excuse my rising, sir," said the president.

It then seemed the intruder was taking off his glove to shake hands.

Still polite, Jackson said, "Never mind your glove, sir," and offered his own hand.

Looking on, among others, were Jackson's recent secretary of state, Edward Livingston, his new secretary of state, Louis McLane, and the famous writer Washington Irving. Looking on . . . as, totally by surprise, the young man "thrust his fist violently into Jackson's face as if to pull his nose."

Jackson, not known, no matter how polite, to abide by such an affront, reacted violently. "What, sir! What, sir!" he exclaimed as, with a crash, he kicked the table out of his way and jumped to his feet. In seconds, the room was in tumult. "McLane, Livingston and Washington Irving grappled the intruder, who threw them off and darted through a door with Jackson after him, cane upraised," related Jackson biographer Marquis James.

At the door, in fact, friends quickly decided the wisest course at the moment would be to stop the enraged Jackson, his health known to be delicate. While the president's assailant disappeared beyond, they shut the door. Jackson was left to pound on it, to shout that they had better open it up, or he would break it down.

Eventually, a cooler president was allowed to proceed to the deck. There, he was told the intruder had fled down the landing dock and into the town of Alexandria. He had escaped, but only for the moment, since he had been recognized "as Robert B. Randolph, a former lieutenant of the navy dismissed for attempted theft of funds belonging to the late John D. Timberlake, whom he had succeeded as purser of the frigate *Constitution*," wrote James.

Told all of this, Jackson was sufficiently calm to turn down a Virginia man's offer to chase Randolph and kill him within fifteen minutes.

"No sir," said Jackson, "I want no man to stand between me and my assailants, and none to take revenge on my account."

More privately, Jackson was still sputtering in fiercer terms—announcing that had he known what Randolph was up to, the young man "never would have moved with life from the tracks he stood in."

After a bit more time, though, Jackson was willing to forgive. Given a chance to testify against Randolph after leaving the presidency, Jackson not only declined, but asked that any sentence or fine imposed upon the former naval officer should be suspended. "I have to this age," explained Old Hickory, "complied with my mother's advice to indict no man for assault or sue him for slander."

High-Toned Ball

COME ONE, COME ALL (ALMOST) . . . to the Chandelier Ball! "I went first when I was a girl of 18," said one ball-goer years after the fact. "The Chandelier Ball was the finest dance in town, and the food was fabulous, though my mother would not let me go up to the dining room because of the wine."

To be invited was a high honor. "Everything was done just like at the White House," added Lillian Rogers Parks, who was a seamstress in the by-now-venerable presidential residence and who later wrote the book *My Thirty Years Backstairs at the White House.* "The palms were from the greenhouse, the little gilt chairs, I guess the white damask tablecloths and napkins, and even the coat racks from the coatrooms." Also more or less borrowed for the festive annual occasion was another White House fixture, the Marine Band.

White House dignitaries were invited—and expected to attend. But not the president and his wife. The hosts were all male and all black—and all employees of the White House. Their ball, probably started around 1910, according to White House historian William Seale, was named for the chandeliers in the East Room, itself the scene of many an entertainment and dance. There, too, many of the black employees spent time serving and cleaning up. They were an indispensable support at White House social functions.

So why not have a ball of their own? At first it was held annually at the Oddfellows Hall in Washington, Sixteenth and M Streets— dinner on the second floor (where the wine was located) and dancing on the first floor.

According to historian Seale, "The prestige of the Chandelier Ball generated a kind of rivalry among the white employers of the blacks who attended." Mrs. William Howard Taft, for instance, went out of her way to provide maid Annie Anderson a silk gown with train, adorned with silk chiffon roses. And Ellen Wilson's social secretary Belle Hagner gave cook Alice Green an evening dress with pearl beads and a net veil.

Alice Green had had to wait until 1914 before she finally was invited to the exclusive affair, "having been passed over before as not being of sufficient rank." Afterwards, she pronounced it "very high toned." All too short-lived, however, the Chandelier Ball tradition came to a halt with the advent of World War I during the same Woodrow Wilson tenure. Alice Green had done her dancing just in time.

Locked Out

FOR LADY BIRD JOHNSON, ONE of the "funniest little moments" spent in the White House came the night she found herself—in her robe and slippers—locked out of the family quarters with no one to hear her gentle knocks or calls for help. "I thought about all those funny ads—I went to the Opera in my Maidenform Bra—and I thought how awful it would be if I walked through the main entrance hall of the White House at about 1:30, in my dressing gown, and met a dozen or so of the departing guests."

Earlier the same evening, she and her husband, Lyndon B. Johnson, had been entertaining Danish prime minister Jens Otto Krag and his wife, Helle. It was not uncommon for a president and his lady to retire to the family quarters upstairs before all the guests left the premises. And after the guests, of course, there still were the staff cleaning up downstairs.

Late that night Lady Bird had thought everyone had left. But about the time she was preparing for bed, she noticed the lights in the upstairs hall outside the bedroom were still on. She went out and started turning out one hall light after another, until she reached "the staircase that leads down to the State floor." At that point, she heard "clattering feet below disappearing in the distance," and she saw "a great blaze of light going down the steps."

To complete her mission of turning off the lights—now a main set of lights—she would have to step "out into the hall only a few feet." But would the door at that end of the hall then swing shut behind her . . . and lock?

It would. It did. Cautious at first, she tried leaning and reaching while holding open the door with one foot. No good. So . . . "Some giddy instinct of daring led me to just let the door close gently and to walk over and turn out the lights. Then I went back and turned the knob—sure enough the door was locked!"

That was when she began gently knocking, "hoping maybe the guests in the Queen's Room would hear me." And thinking about the Maidenform ads.

Below, no more sounds, but still a few lights on. What to do?

There wasn't any real choice, short of loudly banging on the locked door itself. There was nothing for it but to be bold, assume "a very assured look," and head on downstairs for the little elevator that would carry her back to the inside of the family's second-floor quarters. Girding herself, she demurely walked on down the stairs. She walked through the first-floor hall and met "only" two or three people, departing musicians and staffers. Met them and, what else to do? "Smiled as if the whole thing were a matter of course." And, minutes later, so to bed … after a brief recording stint with her diary. No great harm done.

Additional note: Jerry Ford, too, was locked out of the family quarters of the White House late one night, it seems. According to the book *Presidential Pets* by Niall Kelly, President Ford's nocturnal adventure began with the first family's golden retriever Liberty at three o'clock one morning.

Normally Liberty lived in a kennel outside, so her bathroom needs were no issue. On this occasion, however, she was about to have pups and she had been moved indoors to "be near her trainer." But the trainer on this particular night was away.

Gerald Ford was awakened by the wet muzzle of Liberty pushing into his face. Time for a walk, it seems. So the president put on robe and slippers and escorted Liberty outside through a downstairs door.

"When she had finished her business, they returned to the house." And that's when the trouble began.

They were able to enter the first floor again, but when Ford tried the small elevator to the second-floor family quarters, "nothing happened." No problem, he thought. He and Liberty simply could go up the nearby stairs, but at the top he found a locked door barring his way. Shades of Lady Bird's predicament not long before … if only he had known!

Worse, the door to the third floor also was locked. Ford, growing more impatient by the minute, marched up and down the stairs a few times, then "started pounding on the walls." That did the trick. "The White House sprang alive, lights came on everywhere, and the Secret Service rushed to the scene to let the president back into his own house."

Ugly Fellow Encountered

WALKING ONE TIME BETWEEN THE White House and the War Department building was a worn, weathered man. The site at the time was a small park. Along came a crippled soldier cussing and swearing and complaining about the government, president and all. And then he encountered this tall, lanky stranger who asked what the problem was. The young Union private, recently released from the Confederacy's Libby Prison in Richmond, said he couldn't seem to collect his pay from the War Department, despite his good and faithful service.

Well, said the tall stranger, he once had been a lawyer and if he could look at the soldier's papers, perhaps he could provide friendly advice. They sat down under a tree to go over the documents. The soldier's friendly benefactor then wrote something brief on the back of the papers and told him to see "Mr. Potts," who was the chief clerk in the War Department.

They parted, each going his own way, the story goes, but a pair of unnoticed onlookers, bemused, stopped the young soldier and asked if he knew the identity of the helpful stranger.

The soldier obviously had not been all that impressed. "Some ugly fellow who pretends to be a lawyer," said the crippled soldier, perhaps made a bit bitter by his recent POW experiences. But he showed the two onlookers where the stranger had written the line: "Mr. Potts— Attend to this man's case at once and see that he gets his pay."

By the end of that day, the young man who had been heard cussing the president received both his discharge and his pay, in full.

Small Talk Among World Leaders

WHEN FOREIGN STATESMEN VISIT THE White House, the American public doesn't always know what goes on behind the protocol, the formal dinner table, the receiving line, or perhaps the photos of couples dancing. Once in a while, though, from behind the facade of smiles, perhaps years later, may emerge a glimpse of the real life—the small talk, that is—among the world leaders.

The substance (or lack thereof) may sometimes be a bit startling.

When Indonesian President Sukarno visited the Eisenhower White House in the 1950s, for instance, the small talk went very badly. When he "conferred" with Ike, Sukarno later wrote, "We had an immediate nonmeeting of the minds."

In his book *Sukarno: An Autobiography* (as told to Cindy Adams), the Indonesian leader said, "At the White House he [Eisenhower] could manage only to discuss our mutual love for motion pictures."

According to the Sukarno-Adams reconstruction, the "exact conversation" with Ike went this way:

He: I hear you like movies, President Sukarno. Tell me, how often do you see them?

I: Three times a week in the palace.

He: Can you guess how many times I see them?

I: No. How many times do you see them, President Eisenhower?

He: Every single night. What kind of film is your favorite, President Sukarno?

I: Adventure stories, history, and biographies.

He: Is that so? Well, I like only Westerns. And I bet you'll never guess who my favorite star is.

I: No. Who?

He: Randolph Scott.

To be sure, Sukarno also wrote (with Adams) that he slipped in a few pointed comments about more serious matters. He told

Eisenhower, for instance, "Your government's present attitude fails to comprehend the Asian mind. Asia is in a euphoria of independence. The entire continent is in ecstasy about freedom. Please . . . please . . . tell your America she must understand if all their lives a people have endured pain, curses and threats for independence, they cannot give it up once they have attained it."

His point seemed to be summed up in his plea, "America should counsel us, yes. But meddle in our affairs, no."

Still lecturing Ike, the visiting Sukarno added, "We saw capitalism and Western democracy in action through the Dutch [former colonial masters of Indonesia]. We have no wish to maintain that system."

Indonesia, the former anti-Dutch revolutionary leader explained further in his book, could never adopt Western-style democracy and its notion of majority rule, "where 51 percent wins and 49 percent ends up with a grudge." Sukarno didn't report Ike's side of their more serious conversation.

Visiting John F. Kennedy in the White House a few years later, though, Sukarno was much happier with his reception at the hands of JFK. He was very pleased that Kennedy took him for a ride on a helicopter, then proceeded to present him with a complimentary chopper to take home to Indonesia.

What was their small talk about? Women, it seems, young women, girls . . . and freedom of the press.

"Kennedy was very warm and friendly to me," said the Sukarno book. "He took me upstairs to his private bedroom, and there we had our talk."

The Indonesian, known as a bit of a ladies man, was upset with an American "girlie magazine" that recently ran a patched-together picture showing Sukarno in full military dress standing next to a half-naked stripteaser. Sukarno complained to JFK, "Look here, are you aware that while you personally might be cementing a friendship, you can often spoil relations with foreign countries by ridiculing, lampooning, or permitting constant criticism of their leaders in your press?"

Added Sukarno: "Sometimes we may be inclined to act or react more strongly because we are hurt or angered."

To which Kennedy replied, in an obvious attempt to sooth: "I agree with you, President Sukarno. I, too, have had difficulties with our newspapermen. But fortunately or unfortunately, freedom of the press is part of the American heritage."

Sukarno wasn't quite ready to let the issue go. He noted that no newspaper in his country ran photos of American vice president Alben Barkley being kissed—while visiting Indonesia—"by a swarm of beautiful young girls."

Said a "chuckling" Kennedy, "I'm quite sure Vice President Barkley must have enjoyed himself immensely."

Barkley was such a "jolly man" said Sukarno at this point, that he perhaps wouldn't have minded if the papers had printed photos of the kissing episode. "But that is not the issue. The point is, we believe in protecting world leaders [from embarrassment] in our country."

What could JFK say at this point? He and Sukarno obviously came from two different belief systems. "Kennedy sympathized with this greatly and confided to me, 'You are perfectly right, but what can I do? Even I am cursed in my own country.'"

Even after this, Sukarno (by his book's version) got in a parting shot. "So I said, 'Well, that is your system. If you are cursed at home, I cannot help it. But I don't think I should suffer the same indignities in your country that its own chief of state must suffer. Your *Time* and *Life* have been particularly nasty to me. Look here, *Time* said, 'Sukarno can't see a skirt without getting sexy.' Always they say bad things. Never the good things I've done."

Final complaint—even though he and JFK had what Sukarno considered "a meeting of the minds," this "small circle of agreement never widened to the American press," which continued "day after day" to "picture me as a Don Juan."

Ironically, the same press, back in the 1960s, didn't report on any wide basis that JFK apparently was quite a Don Juan himself.

Chippewa Revenge

TSHUSICK WAS THE VISITOR'S NAME, and Louisa Adams, wife of John Quincy Adams, hung closely upon her words because Tshusick, a Chippewa Indian woman, talked often of Louisa's sister, Harriet Boyd, out there on the frontier. Harriet was married to George Boyd, an Indian agent in the Detroit area, Michigan Territory.

Tshusick had appeared out of the gloom one winter's night in 1827, to knock on a Georgetown tinsmith's door and ask to warm herself by his forge. Her story was that she had walked all the way to Washington to find Mrs. Boyd's sister, "who lived in the White House of the Great Father."

That would be Mrs. Adams, the first lady of the land, of course, and it wasn't long before helpful hands brought them together.

More of the Indian woman's story was that she began her trek after her husband died, and she persevered in her quest to reach the White House despite snow, rain, ice, sleet—you name it.

But why? Why had she come? It apparently had something to do with her husband's death. Her account was that she made a vow after he died to find Mrs. Boyd's sister, who as the wife of the Great Father would help her to become a Christian.

Louisa Adams was more than happy to give her blessings, social and otherwise, to the Indian woman who could speak French so well, sew and design dresses so well, and just in general comport herself so well. And such a virtuous goal Tshusick had set for herself! With the president's wife as her sponsor, says James D. Horan's book *The McKenney-Hall Portrait Gallery of American Indians,* "Tshusick was soon one of the most talked about women in Washington."

For Louisa Adams, cut off from her sister on the remote frontier, it was incredibly fascinating to hear the enchanting Indian woman's stories about Harriet Boyd's "life in the wilderness, her husband, their daily chores, the Indians, and how Harriet kept house in a log cabin."

Even the president was taken by the visitor's charms—he gave her a silver medal. And arrangements indeed were made to have Tshusick christened at Christ Church in Georgetown. She took the name Lucy Cornelia Barbour, borrowing the first two names from the appropriately touched wife and daughter of the secretary of war. The new Ms. Barbour found an attentive escort about the capital city in the person of the U.S. Army's next general in chief, Major General Alexander Macomb.

Clearly, Washington officialdom was agog over the comely visitor from the West, but Colonel Thomas McKenney, head of the federal government's Bureau of Indian Affairs, had become just a mite suspicious that all the appearances were too good to be true. He had written for information from the governor of the Michigan Territory,

Lewis Cass—another name that Tshusick-Barbour often cited with proprietary abandon.

Informed of McKenney's supposedly casual note to his friend Cass, the Indian woman suddenly announced that she must return to her people back West. As a result, Horan's book reports, "So many presents from disappointed admirers who begged her to stay poured into the White House that President Adams told his wife to buy Tshusick a trunk."

The first lady and family also loaded her up with gifts for the Boyds in their wilderness cabin, and the White House itself "arranged for the Chippewa to travel to the end of the stagecoach line, then buy a horse to continue her journey to Detroit."

Before she left, her constant escort, General Macomb, personally fastened about her waist a money belt "stuffed with currency." On the way west, Tshusick arranged to stay, free, at Barnum's Hotel in Baltimore for several days as the owner's guest.

Long after the Indian woman had passed from sight, it seems, came the reply to McKenney's letter from Governor Cass. Its news was somewhat deflating. In the first place, the woman's husband was alive and well. He happened to be a short, fat Frenchman employed as a "scullion" in Harriet Boyd's kitchen.

Next, Tshusick was known far and wide in the western territories as a "superb confidence woman." She had "duped the great and the near-great" throughout "the whole length of the Canadas, from Montreal to St. Louis and from Quebeck to the Falls of St. Anthony and many times in the interior."

Now, she also had conned Washington, the White House included! Call it Chippewa revenge.

Wedded There

THEY WERE MARRIED IN THE White House, one president and several presidential progeny:

- John Quincy Adams's son John Adams II and his brother

George's onetime fiancée Mary Catherine in 1828. They then spent their honeymoon in the White House as well!

- Lynda Byrd Johnson and Charles S. Robb in December 1967. Like many another young wife, Lynda Byrd then had to watch her Marine Corps officer-husband go off to war—the Vietnam War that ended her own father's dreams of a second elected term as president. Lynda returned from seeing off "Chuck" in late March 1968 looking "like a ghost—pale, tall and drooping," said her mother. Robb, once assigned to the White House as a social aide, came back unscathed from Vietnam and acquired a law degree from the University of Virginia, won election as lieutenant governor and governor of Virginia, then as a U.S. senator from Virginia.

- Richard Nixon's daughter Tricia and Edward Cox, who set a new precedent in June 1971 as the first couple to be married at the White House but *outside* the White House—in the Rose Garden. Only four hundred guests and onlookers could squeeze into the garden confines, and flamboyant Martha Mitchell's "orange sherbert" garden party dress and parasol were not the only news to come out of the affair, as reported later by UPI's veteran White House reporter Helen Thomas. The big news was the rain, which delayed things for "a few hours." In the end, Tricia Nixon made the decision to brave the elements and proceed, as planned, in the Rose Garden. She was "petite and exquisite in white lace as she came down the aisle on her father's arm." Wet chairs, but no more rain, it seems.

- A guest at Tricia's wedding was Alice Roosevelt Longworth, Theodore Roosevelt's daughter, herself one of the few persons ever married in the White House. Was her wedding of 1906 comparable? Not a bit, she exclaimed, "I was married twenty years before Hollywood. This wedding was quite a production." Actually, hers also was quite a production—it took place in the East Room, the service conducted by a bishop, the altar area adorned with gold cloth, and all decorated with Easter lilies. Looking on were diplomats and members of her father's cabinet, along with the socially prominent, family members, and friends. One high point (of sorts) came when the irrepressible Alice borrowed an officer's dress uniform sword to cut her wedding cake. Which she then did with stroke after stroke from the saber. The groom was Nicholas Longworth, already a member of Congress and later destined to become Speaker of the House.

- Another president's daughter married in the East Room was Ulysses S. Grant's winsome Nellie, united with her Englishman fiancé Algernon Sartoris in 1874 beneath a huge bell of flowers, set off by orange blossoms imported from the South, to decorate the large room. Slices of this wedding cake were "put up in little white boxes about six inches long and three inches wide," recalled White House doorkeeper Thomas Pendel later. It was his job to pass out the wedding cake to the ladies in the nearby Red Parlor.

- Only one presidential family saw *two* daughters married within the White House confines—the Woodrow Wilsons. One of their weddings was a grand affair with thousands of guests, and the other, just a few months later, a more intimate, family-*cum*-friends wedding. The first Wilson daughter to make White House nuptials history was young Jessie, married the evening of November 25, 1913, to Francis B. Sayre, an assistant district attorney in New York City. Their vows were exchanged in the East Room. The throngs of guests were received afterward in the Blue Room and then offered refreshments in the State Dining Room. Next came sister Nell, who surprised all by falling in love with a widowed member of her father's cabinet, Treasury Secretary William McAdoo, twenty-six years older than she. Nell's wedding took place in the Blue Room on May 7, 1914, and during the ceremony, McAdoo's oldest daughter, Nona, became hysterical and had to be led away. Later, Nell and her new husband dodged reporters by leaving from the South Portico in the fifth car to pass through the gates. By then, the awaiting reporters had all gone after the wrong cars.

As Nell left, she looked back and saw her mother and father standing hand in hand, and, she later said, "I horrified my husband by dissolving into tears in the darkness of the car." The next time she saw her mother, Ellen Wilson, was in late May, after Ellen had taken a fall and become ill. In bed when Nell returned from her honeymoon, "She [Ellen Wilson] had changed—she looked very small and white, and all her lovely color was gone." The daughter's "heart sank" at the sight. And all too soon Ellen Wilson died—in early August of the same year—of tuberculosis of the kidneys.

- As for the one and only president's wedding to take place in the White House, the hour was seven o'clock in the evening, the day June 2, the year 1886. The groom was Grover Cleveland, the bride, Frances "Frank" Folsom, his late law partner's daughter, a recent college graduate he had known since her infancy. Eight marriages had preceded Cleveland's within the White House, but none, of course, featured a president. Cleveland himself walked the bride down the grand stair to Mendelssohn's "Wedding March," along the transverse hall on the first floor and into the Blue Parlor of that era. He wore black evening clothes, with a white lawn necktie and a white rose in his lapel. Her wedding gown, with a four-yard train, was decorated with orange blossoms.

  The ceremony in the Blue Parlor was followed by a wedding supper served in the East Room, where the chief decoration was a "full-rigged ship" composed of flowers—roses, pansies, pinks—and set on a mirror in the center of the main table as the ship's "sea". Guests received their slice of historic wedding cake in small white satin boxes also containing a card autographed by the happy couple the night before. Since the White House was really theirs, they could have honeymooned on the spot, like young John Adams in 1828, but they chose not to. They slipped away that very evening to a special train that sped them to a hideaway in the Alleghenies.

Additional note: Since Dolley Madison's sister was married in the White House in 1812 (before the British burned it), one president (Cleveland); one presidential son (John Quincy Adams II); eight presidential daughters; and one presidential aide (Harry Hopkins of the FDR era) have made their wedding vows at the White House, by *Life* magazine's count. By that same accounting, two divorces eventually resulted. For the record also, seven of the nuptials took place in the East Room, seven in the Blue Room, one outdoors, and one—that of Harry Hopkins—in FDR's second-floor study. (Hopkins and his wife then simply stayed on for quite a while, as temporary residents of the White House.)

Progress Report

PROGRESS AT THE WHITE HOUSE . . . electrician Ike Hoover came to the venerable mansion in 1891 on behalf of the Edison Company, which had been engaged to install the first electric lights in the grand old structure. He was on the job for four months, installing both the electric-light wiring and an electric call-bell system.

The official White House occupants, the Benjamin Harrisons, were hopelessly inept in dealing with such wonders of modern science. They were afraid to turn a light on or off "for fear of getting a shock," Hoover later recalled. For a long time, the president's family simply wouldn't use the lights now at their disposal in the upstairs family quarters. Hoover himself had to turn on the lights in the halls and parlors. They would burn all night long, "until I returned the next morning to extinguish them."

As for the electric call bells . . . perish the thought! Hoover recollected, "The family were even timid about pushing the electric bell buttons to call the servants! There was a family conference almost every time this had to be done."

Ike Hoover was so helpful that he stayed on . . . and on, soon joining the ushers' staff and finally becoming a famous chief White House usher and author of the well-known book *Forty-two Years in the White House.*

Progress, progress . . . the John Adamses' outdoor privy was replaced by Thomas Jefferson's indoor water closet. Iron stoves were installed in 1809 (Jefferson also), and Martin Van Buren added a rudimentary central heating system in the 1830s.

Progress . . . Teddy Roosevelt built the enclosed West Wing containing the Oval Office and did away with the old greenhouses next to the nineteenth-century White House.

Calvin Coolidge moved out, to be out of the way while the shaky attic and roof were replaced with an entire, fully livable third floor, complete with sky parlor, or sun room, above the South Portico—a quiet retreat ever since for presidential folk, its view of Washington vistas considered magnificent. Coolidge also shook things up when he shucked the traditional morning coat in favor of a dark business-man's suit for normal workdays in the Oval Office.

Progress . . . Andrew Johnson installed a barber's chair in the 1860s.

Under Andrew Jackson, a running water project was initiated. And what an intricate job that was! Until then, the White House had relied upon two wells, situated between the main structure and the low side wings that Jefferson had added.

During Jackson's tenure, engineer Robert Leckie devised and built the complex water-delivery system that, with the help of gravity, would supply water to the White House and nearby public buildings such as the Treasury and the State Department or War Department. By this plan water was sent coursing through iron pipes from a spring at Franklin Square to three brick-lined, sand-bottomed reservoirs—holding ponds, really. Here, the piping surfaced to spew out the water as fountains that served to keep the reservoirs properly stirred up, the water treated. Gravity had carried the water downhill to this point, but when the water moved from the reservoirs into the nearby buildings, it took constant hand-pumping by an attendant at the "ponds" to achieve the pressure necessary to push the water "uphill" through the internal piping.

The job took about a year to reach completion, but the result was real luxury for that era. Moreover, it wasn't long before Jackson then installed a "bathing room" in the ground-level East Wing, with hot and cold baths and a shower (the water heated by coal fires under boilers).

Jackson also installed a fine brick-and-stucco stable southeast of the house to replace a jerry-built arrangement long occupying Jefferson's West Wing.

Progress, progress . . . there would be other improvements, many, many of them, as history moved on, so much that we take for granted today. Freezers. Cars. Telephones. The latest, always, in communications equipment, even a hot line to Moscow. And the items we just might have forgotten . . . like the bomb shelters dug under the lawn during World War II.

Workers All

THEY WORKED AT THE WHITE House . . . all these, and so many more:

- William Henry Crook came to the Lincoln White House as one of four plainclothes guards assigned to the president and served through five administrations before he retired. "Colonel" Crook by then, he served in many capacities—as doorman for the U. S. Grants, as executive clerk and disbursing agent for Rutherford B. Hayes, as chief disbursement officer under Grover Cleveland and William McKinley. He saw, and later said, a lot. He said it was he who brought the news of Andrew Johnson's Senate acquittal from impeachment to the Executive Mansion. Crook couldn't believe it when William McKinley was fatally wounded by a shooter in Buffalo, New York—"Good God!" he thought. "First Lincoln—then Garfield—and now McKinley!" He claimed another Lincoln guard, John F. Parker, had left his post outside the Lincoln box at the Ford Theatre to watch the play himself, leaving the way clear for John Wilkes Booth to enter and shoot Lincoln in the back of the head. By the time of McKinley's arrival, Crook had been at the White House longer than anyone else, except possibly usher Tommy Pendel, who had been a doorman and guard in the Lincoln era himself. Crook had little hair on his head but a bush growing from his chin instead.
- John Ousley began his stint as a gardener under John Quincy Adams and stuck for more than twenty years, his home being a small cottage on the White House grounds. Always faithful to his job, never adequately paid, he grew the flowers and the vegetables in oasis-like beds to the sides of the long White House sweeps, placed the shrubbery stands more visibly, and used a heavy roller to flatten the grass, often after it had been nibbled close to the ground by cattle and sheep. The effect was a clean, closely cropped vista of green like a golf course tee. He watered with the big wooden vat on wheels that Andrew Jackson provided. Then, in 1852, Millard Fillmore and his advisers wanted something much fancier. Ousley, an old man by now, received a

notice from the commissioner of public buildings: "Your services as gardener or laborer on the President's Square will not be required after the end of the present month." As White House historian William Seale has put it, "Ousley and his wife passed through the gates; . . . within two brief years, both vanished from the written record."

- Arthur Brooks, first joined government service as a War Department janitor, but he quickly saw that the White House offered good opportunity for a determined and ambitious African-American man like himself. He had reached the status of messenger at the War Department by the time he joined the William Howard Tafts as a valet in title, but he soon was a domestic confidant and aide to a succession of presidents, until his death in 1926 as a member of the Calvin Coolidge entourage. In the meantime, the "beloved" Brooks wielded considerable influence within the White House—and he always seemed to know what was happening. He is credited with persuading Woodrow Wilson to loosen up and begin wearing his now well-known straw boater, blazer, and white flannel trousers. For many years too, he was in charge of the White House silver. "Arthur Brooks's title was Major—a shortened version of major-domo, his position in the White House," says dental technology consultant Markus King of North Bethesda, Maryland. "I knew him quite well. He brought the president's shoes to my father to be repaired, and I delivered them back to his office in the White House basement."

- A romantic little tale is the story of Antoine Michel Giusta and his wife, steward and housekeeper under John Quincy Adams. Adams found and hired Antoine Michel as his valet in Belgium in 1814, not long after he had deserted Napoleon's French army (before Waterloo). The new valet then married Mrs. Adams's maid in London. As husband and wife, they worked for the Adams couple when they were a private family and then as first family. They stayed on in the White House after the Adamses left, but they did not care for the hot-tempered presidential successor, Andrew Jackson, and his entourage. They left his employment in about 1834, to open a highly successful oyster bar in the federal city. In six years, they were able to retire to a farm and live out their lives without any further domestic service.

- A man for all seasons, but ill-fated, was a White House favorite under Teddy Roosevelt and William Howard Taft—Major Archibald Wilingham Butt, military aide, chief ceremonial and protocol expert, riding companion to Teddy, confidant to his wife, Edith, and the only White House staffer to go down with the *Titanic*. Exhausted by his pace at work and the busy social schedule he and his housemate Frank Millet kept up among the city's elite, Butt went off for a long-planned vacation in Europe early in 1912, "with gifts and slaps on the back," reported historian Seale. "Everyone loved Archie Butt." He and fellow bachelor Millet, an artist, decided to return early, however, because they then could sail aboard the fabulous and "unsinkable" new ocean liner, the *Titanic*. When the ship hit the iceberg, Butt, typically, was attending a small dinner party in the first-class smoking room on the A Deck. In the confusion and tumult that followed, there were other glimpses of him—with Millet and two other men, he calmly remained at a table in the smoking room for a time. Later, a departing wife, Mrs. Walter D. Douglas, begged her husband to "get off with Major Butt and. . . [another man]," since "they are big, strong fellows and will surely make it." Butt even later was seen, still calm, near the boat deck rail as others panicked or even fought to get off. How he (and Millet) died is not exactly known. "In the stories told later," wrote Walter Lord in his *A Night to Remember,* "Archie Butt had a dozen different endings—all gallant, none verified." In Washington, President Taft at first was told most passengers survived, but when informed that wasn't true after all, he wired for news of Butt and Millet. It was a full day before he found they were not among the survivors. Taft was distraught. "He was like a member of my family, and I feel as if he had been a younger brother," he wrote afterward.

- She was found through an "exclusive" New York employment agency. She had her own second-floor suite in the White House overlooking the North Portico. One room would be her office, the other (with bath), her bedroom and living quarters. Elizabeth Jaffray, an army officer's wife who was widowed young, came to the William Howard Taft White House as the first housekeeper in decades. Aloof and severe, she joined twenty-five fulltime servants and was regarded by many as a real terror. Some, like Arthur Brooks, were unawed and wise enough to work with her, although she admitted to a revolt when she decreed that the black servants, "regardless of rank or position," must take their meals separately from the whites. The revolt dissipated when she threatened firings for backtalk or resistance. Under the Woodrow Wilsons, she issued another decree. The kitchen workers had been arguing and even resorting to brawls over the new war in Europe. Mrs. Jaffray, surprising one kitchen fray, ordered no more discussion of the Great War. She served on through the Warren G. Hardings, but then encountered Calvin Coolidge, who called her "Queenie"... and who replaced her, for reasons not totally known. Except that word? *Queenie.*

- Another, later housekeeper was Eleanor Roosevelt's import from Hyde Park, Henrietta Nesbitt, who was notorious for overturning Mrs. Jeffray's notorious racial edict by firing all the white servants in the household staff and replacing them with blacks. Her reasoning, apparently backed by the Roosevelts, was that "a staff solid in any one color works in better understanding and maintains a smoother-running establishment." Her simplistic menu, meanwhile, soon gave the FDR White House the reputation of having the worst food in official Washington, said historian Seale. Indeed, FDR himself insisted upon having his meals prepared by his mother's longtime cook, Mary Campbell, in a newly installed diet kitchen on the third floor. Nesbitt's food and attitude were still an issue when the Harry Trumans suddenly took over the mansion, daughter Margaret has recorded. "Her taste in food was atrocious and her attitude toward the Trumans was openly condescending," wrote Margaret Truman. Then came the great "Brussels Sprouts Flap." Margaret's father hated them. So informed by Margaret after she served them one night, Mrs. Nesbitt wouldn't stop there but served them again for the next two nights. That did it—just weeks later, Mrs. Nesbitt was gone. "Retired," was the word, and by the Trumans, not a moment missed.

Silver Jubilee

No one who saw it, or shared it, could possibly forget. From the rooftop, kept straight and unfurled by hidden fans, floodlit and spectacular, a huge American flag was extended. And all over the grounds were thousands of electric lights, all colors, some of them long strings of lights borrowed from U.S. Navy ships at Norfolk and Annapolis and hurriedly shipped to Washington by freight car.

Not only the White House's own shrubs and trees were displayed in this extravaganza of light, but so were banks upon banks of tropical plants and trees borrowed from florists and greenhouses all over the Washington area. The weather on this June night was just right, described as "balmy," and when the eight o'clock arrival hour came, it appeared that nearly all eight-thousand-plus invitees were

President and Mrs. William Howard Taft and family took time from the Taft couple's extraordinary silver jubilee affair to pose for a twenty-fifth wedding anniversary photograph. (Courtesy William Howard Taft Museum)

standing at the gates ready to rush in. Indeed, thousands of onlookers had gathered also to watch, to ohh and ahh, at the spectacle of
President and Mrs. William Howard Taft's silver wedding anniversary
party at their White House in 1911.

"On the south grounds, night was to be turned into day by
means of multicolored electric lights," noted historian William Seale.
Taft, himself, was so excited and caught up in the plans that on the
day before he "paced the flat platform atop the roof of the White
House, issuing orders for more strands, more spotlights, more paper
lanterns." By then, electricians had been working for four days to
prepare for the gigantic garden party and "illumination."

The guests were given an hour to wander the grounds and take
it all in before the Tafts, to the crescendos of "The Star-Spangled
Banner," made their deliberate way down the grand staircase inside,
along the first floor transverse hall, through the Red Room, and out
onto the South Portico.

Alternating that evening were the Marine Band and the
Engineers Band, and it was the Engineers' turn for the presidential
couple's appearance. "A great cheer rose from the several thousand
people by then on the lawn, and the cheering spread to the estimated 15,000 outside the fences. The President smiled, took his
wife's hand, and nodded to the band; and as the band played the
Wedding March, the Tafts walked down the stair to the lawn, Mrs.
Taft in white satin embroidered with silver roses and carnations."

They then received guests under the trees for hours. Buffet supper was served at 11 P.M.—in the State Dining Room and East Room
and in tents outside, in "groves flanking the south lawn." Mrs. Taft had
to retire at midnight, quite exhausted, but her portly husband told
the bands to keep playing and stayed with his guests until the music
finally stopped at 2 A.M. Even then, he sat in the dark on the South
Portico "until the last guest had gone."

It had been a real spectacle; no one could say the party had
failed in any way . . . or ever could be forgotten. In fact, Taft liked it
so well, he ordered that the lights should stay where they were, the
bands should again be at their respective stands . . . and the very next
night, the grounds would be reopened, not merely to his guests this
time, but to the general public as well.

Horses

OLD HICKORY LOVED HIS HORSES, and thereby hangs a tale or two from his presidential stewardship during 1829–37. In 1832, although about to seek reelection, Andrew Jackson insisted upon keeping racehorses in the White House stable. He raced them at nearby tracks under the name of his young ward and secretary Andrew Jackson Donelson (relative of his late wife, Rachel), "but it was no secret to whom they actually belonged," noted Jackson biographer Marquis James.

In April of that year, a close Jackson associate, quite well meaning, stopped Jackson's Hermitage overseer from sending three horses and three black jockeys to join the stable entourage at the White House. "With a campaign coming on, further display of the President's sporting proclivities would be inadvisable; and to run the horses under Donelson's name would deceive no one," was the point that this old friend, former secretary of war John Henry Eaton, earnestly hoped to impress upon the man in the White House.

Old Hickory took it all in stride . . . and again sent for the horses and their handlers anyway. On arrival, they were installed in a "show place carriage house and stable, with stalls for ten horses." And he was indeed elected for a second term.

Not long after, Andrew Jackson could boast of three "promising" fillies in his White House environs, Emily, Lady Nashville, and Bolivia by name. Indeed, "The stable, with its complement of colored jockeys, was as much a part of the White House establishments as the East Room, and as frequently honored by eminence and fashion."

One spring day in 1834, Jackson, his vice president, Martin Van Buren, and several other close associates and "devotees of the turf" were at the National Jockey Club "to watch a trial of the White House horses."

All three fillies were there, plus a brute of a stallion named Busirus, property of a Jackson friend. The stallion was to be ridden by a White House jockey named Jesse. Two stout fellows held the high-spirited animal for the rider, who promptly lost control . . . and the onlookers scattered in a hurry. As the horse dashed against a fence and others panicked, the Hero of New Orleans was clearly heard to offer protection to his vice president: "Get behind me, Mr. Van Buren! They will run over you, sir."

Then, when it appeared the onlookers were safe enough, the president admonished the still-clinging jockey: "Hold him, Jesse! Don't let him break down that fence."

And to the stallion's trainer, one Balie Peyton, Jackson said: "Why don't you break him of those tricks? I could do it in an hour." To which Peyton muttered, out of Jackson's hearing, that "he would like to see any man break Busirus of those tricks in a week."

On the way home that day, Jackson related another racehorse tale, although in this case the White House stable was not involved. Years before, after a race at Jackson's own Clover Bottom track in Tennessee, an angry crowd of disappointed bettors confronted a horseman friend of Jackson's beside the stable. Jackson happened along and, seeing the crowd's ugly mood, first offered to have his friend meet any one of them in a duel, then said he would himself meet any such champion in a duel.

When no one accepted but the unruly crowd showed no signs of desisting either, Jackson realized that he was in a dangerous situation and he also realized that the evening dusk was fast thickening.

This was in 1811, and telling the story on the way back to the White House in 1834, Jackson related that he pulled a tin tobacco box from his coat pocket and told the mob, "I will shoot dead the first man who attempts to cross that stile." One of the crowd did step forward, as yet undeterred.

And so Jackson played out his bluff. "I raised my arm and closed the [tobacco] box with a click very like the cocking of a pistol. It was so dark they could not distinguish what I had in my hand—and, sir, they scampered like a flock of deer!"

It might be, added Jackson, that in the crowd there would have been individuals quite willing to "meet" Jackson or any other man "on a one-to-one basis." And now Jackson came to the moral of the story for his vice president. "But, Mr. Van Buren, no man is willing to take a chance of being killed by an accidental shot in the dark." It is not recorded if Van Buren ever had occasion to take Jackson's homily to heart.

Boy With Message

A GOOD OLD BOY OF the old school was Starling of the White House. Secret Service Agent Edmund W. Starling, that is, for many years and four presidents a member of the White House detail. Quite a gentleman . . . quite an old boy with old-fashioned, all-American values and a no-nonsense attitude.

Meeting Teddy Roosevelt for the first time, Starling liked the fact that Teddy appeared "a strong man with a good, courageous eye." Starling tended to look a man in the eye and measure the other fellow that way. And he was very direct at times, even if most of the time he had to be fairly circumspect.

One of those "direct" exceptions came the day that Woodrow Wilson was in the Palace of Versailles outside of Paris to sign the famous Versailles Treaty of 1919 officially ending World War I. Great was the excitement throughout the world, and very exacting— indeed circumspect, you might say—was the protocol laid on for the great event among the nations.

In the Hall of Mirrors, the French, the British, and the Americans, led by Wilson, were ranged at the center of a long, long table. At a far, far end, sat the defeated Germans. Starling, of course, was concerned with the security of his ward, and he wasn't too happy with the deterioration of Wilson's health—nor with what he viewed as condescending treatment of his president and entourage by various of the Europeans.

When Starling chose on his own to stand directly behind Wilson, a Frenchman in a cutaway came over and seemed—in French, of course—to be telling Starling to move on. Starling wasn't about to do any such thing. Giving vent to pent-up fury, he told the Frenchman that it was his job to guard the president, and no "sniveling little pipsqueak in a hired suit" was going to interfere with him.

The direct approach. The Frenchman, whom Starling knew to be superintendent of Versailles, did the moving on.

Then there was the time Starling, a young railroad detective in those years, helped the Secret Service guard Teddy Roosevelt on a trip in the South in October 1905, including a stop to visit the fair-grounds at Birmingham, Alabama. The presidential carriage followed a pathway between ropes, with Starling and a colleague walking on either side and two Secret Service agents in the carriage. One of them, Frank Tyree, was perched on a high seat in front.

Starling was startled at one point to see a man jump the rope barrier and start running alongside, "crowding close to the carriage." From his high perch, Agent Tyree yelled: "Get him outside the ropes and keep him out." Starling complied by "hustling" the intruder out of harm's way.

In seconds, however, he was back. Starling again chased him off.

Once more the stranger darted into the roped-off area and crowded too close

That was enough. "I picked him up and threw him over the rope and into the crowd like a sack of corn meal."

Direct approach. That was Starling; that sometimes had to be his job. But there was more. He also was a compassionate, understanding, likeable, and sometimes funny man who really loved his presidents; who taught Calvin Coolidge to hunt and fish; who tried to look the other way—or at least dawdle way behind—when Woodrow Wilson was courting his future second wife; who insisted the doctors immediately get together and sign a death certificate at the time of Warren Harding's sudden death on the West Coast (cerebral hemorrhage, they said); who actually cried when Wilson was taken ill while promoting the League of Nations across the country; who did his best to comfort Calvin Coolidge when young Calvin Junior died of blood poisoning. One day he saw a boy, sad face pressed against the iron railings outside the White House, and asked him what he wanted. To see the president, was the reply. "I wanted to tell him how sorry I am that his little boy died."

Starling of the White House, Colonel Starling by now, brought them together and, since the boy then was overcome with emotion, delivered his message for him. Coolidge also couldn't speak for a moment, but afterward he said: "Colonel, whenever a boy wants to see me always bring him in. Never turn one away or make him wait."

Starling was the sort who never would.

Alice's "Majicks"

HARKENING BACK TO ALICE ROOSEVELT Longworth's buried idol in the White House garden, she—seriously or not—wished bad luck on Woodrow Wilson the day he returned to the White House from his long stay in Europe that produced the Versailles Treaty of 1919 officially ending World War I.

Democrat Wilson in 1912 had won his first term as president over incumbent William Howard Taft, the regular Republican nominee, and break-away Republican Teddy Roosevelt of the short-lived Bull Moose Party. Former President Roosevelt, Alice's father, was deceased by the year 1919.

Wilson had lost his wife, Ellen, in his first White House years; he now was married to the former Edith Galt. On his return from Europe, he hoped to win Senate approval for his dream of a League of Nations. But the proposal was not popular at home, as Wilson soon found out

He probably never knew Alice Roosevelt's vehement reaction to his return that summer day in 1919. With a friend, she checked out the crowd (very small it seems) awaiting Wilson's train at Union Station. Outside the White House itself, only two hundred to three hundred onlookers were waiting there. Again Alice was watching . . . watching . . . and more than simply watching!

When the Wilsons approached, Alice stood on her car's running board and resorted to her childhood trick of "magicks," but her incantation calling for a plague on Wilson was not so childish-sounding. "A murrain [plague or disease] on him, a murrain on him," she chanted.

Her companion, afraid of the Secret Service, told her to stop and get back into the car. Alice objected: "Who are you afraid for? Me or Wilson?"

It must be entirely coincidental, and it is no secret in any case, that Wilson's plea for Senate ratification was defeated—the United States never did join the League of Nations, which soon was viewed worldwide as a paper tiger despite its noble aims. And Wilson soon suffered a major stroke ending his political career and leaving him an invalid in the White House.

Looted, Burned . . . Gone

THE BRITS WERE SLOW AND they were methodical about the job. First, with Washington now empty of defenders, the officers marched their 150 seamen down Pennsylvania Avenue from the Capitol, already set afire. Fourteenth day of August 1814 and 7:30 in the evening, it was. Still quite light out. But a thunderstorm threatened as they wound their way down our historic mile—two by two, it is said.

They rounded up a local citizen, a bookstore proprietor named Roger Weightman, and made him an unwilling witness-participant in the sport to come.

They found the home empty, broke in and rummaged through. Others, citizens, had already been inside, themselves rummaging as looters.

Forbidden to steal and pilfer in earnest, the British sailors and their officers were allowed to take little things. For example, Rear Admiral George Cockburn took an old hat and a chair cushion. As their men made ready for the burning, the officers appreciated the well-spread dinner table, indulging themselves below the empty frame that had held George Washington's portrait just a short while before.

As the officers enjoyed themselves among the dinner plates— and the decanters holding several kinds of wine—the triumphant Admiral Cockburn forced citizen Weightman to make a mocking toast to the departed President James Madison.

The British sailors, in the meantime, had been busy methodically smashing windows throughout and piling up the furniture for an indoor bonfire. The officers then assembled—organized, that is— fifty men in a ring around the building, each holding an oil-soaked ball of rags on the end of a long pole. The rest of the company—and a few wary citizens—watched from nearby as the rag-balls were fired up until all were lighted, and then, in concert, by a single order, all were hurled through the windows from all sides of the stricken house at once. In an instant, said one onlooker, "The whole building was wrapt in flames and smoke."

The same witness said the spectators looked on in "awful silence," and "the city was lighted and the heavens redden'd with the blaze." The thunderstorm finally came and went, and by morning, only a shell was left—the outer walls. It looked better than it really was, because those very walls hid the complete gutting that had taken place inside the outer shell.

Indeed, the White House of old, the original, was gone. Not only would James and Dolley Madison have to live elsewhere for now (in Washington's landmark Octagon House), but when the job of restoration began in 1815, considerable portions of even those outer walls would have to be shored up or totally rebuilt . . . a fact not immediately and fully revealed to the public, to avoid admission that the White House had to be so completely reconstructed.

Herbert the Modern

EFFICIENCY WOULD BE THE BYWORD in Herbert Hoover's White House. Efficiency and new ways. It would be a thoroughly modern outlook befitting this brilliant mining engineer with an unequaled résumé as a humanitarian and public servant. He, after all, had been the relief organizer who "fed" a prostrate Belgium during the World War I era, who did the same for famine-stricken Russia, Bolshevik Russia at that, in the early 1920s.

The former secretary of commerce paraded through Washington on his inauguration day in 1929 with Army biplanes and even a dirigible overhead. He drew the largest inaugural visitation in Washington history to date, an estimated two hundred thousand persons. His was the first inauguration filmed for the "talkie" motion pictures, the first carried by radio nationwide.

The "perfect" president was no robot—he could react emotionally to things. He just didn't, usually. Or visibly. He did tip his top hat that inauguration day when a boy yelled from the onlooking fringes, "Oh you Herbie!"

The day before, though, a Sunday, while going to church publicly, he frowned when well-wishers at his church shouted too loudly.

In the White House he soon developed the reputation of being the workingest president. That may be opinion, but he definitely was the first president to install a telephone on his desk. Those who came before had used the device, to be sure, but they repaired to another room for that purpose. Hoover also installed five fulltime secretaries, to his immediate predecessors' one, and he installed buzzers that would bring them hurrying to his side.

Not interested in play, he retired the presidential yacht of the day and shut down the White House stables. Issues, actions, subjects of all kinds, were to be documented. Organized, all was to be organized.

At the Hoover campaign headquarters in California on election night the previous fall, reporter Thomas Stokes noticed that even then the victorious Hoover "showed no outward emotion."

As president, however, he was not afraid to break the rules. Reporters couldn't quote a president directly? Forget that tradition. Instead, let's have news conferences. But . . . with categories. One kind will be for direct quotes, one will be for remarks by an unnamed but White House–level source, and one will be strictly background information, non-attributable.

Then came the Crash, the 1929 stock market crash. Hoover would not panic. He immediately brought a series of corporate, labor, and farm leaders to the White House for conferences, and he made brave and encouraging pronouncements.

Then came the Great Depression. For the next round of agonized conferences, he often left the White House to see the financial magnates of the country in secret, rather than have the public worry over the sight of them arriving at the White House. He couldn't persuade them or Congress to take the restorative steps he thought best. He wasn't able to fire up the country with a strong, positive message. He felt, he knew, that so much of it simply was a matter of psychology—the nation's psychology.

He called writer Christopher Morley to the White House and asked him to write an uplifting poem. He once asked Rudy Vallee for a brave song—Hoover's own psychology needed the same boost, the same injection of new confidence.

To the world outside, however, it seemed that the nonsmiling Hoover was becoming more and more invisible. Many felt he was simply uncaring, callous.

Even now, he dressed formally for dinner every night, company or no company—probably the last president to do so.

He didn't like to see the White House servants at all, and little bells would warn them he was on his way to their individual sectors, reported Gene Smith in his book *The Shattered Dream: Herbert Hoover and the Great Depression.* "And so they hid ... footmen holding trays high in the air as they scurried into hall closets already crowded with maids."

Remote and sad, Hoover only once spoke to his wife's personal maid—to ask where his wife, Lou, was. "By the fall of 1930, Hoover while dining would sit in complete silence, sunk in concentration."

Then came the Bonus Army, World War I veterans desperate for jobs, setting up tent cities in Washington's parks, lobbying and pleading for help. Hoover had to call out the real army.

In the White House, Lou Hoover unfortunately had developed an uninspiring and severe image all her own. Everything was so precise—butlers and footmen all the same height, meals exactly on time, no talk in the pantry, no clink of silver against china while clearing the table, and for the butlers, tuxedos in daytime and tails in the evening.

Mrs. Hoover had a signals system like that of a baseball-team manager for her servants. "Her hand touching her hair meant dinner should be announced; her hand touching her glasses meant that the table should be cleared."

And always Herbert Hoover worked, totally, foolishly, unbending while hurting inside. "There was never a good morning or even a nod of the head," said head usher Ike Hoover. "Never a Merry Christmas or Happy New Year. All days were alike to him. Sunday was no exception, for he worked just as hard on that day if not harder than on any of the others."

In time, Hoover was working eighteen hours a day, sleeping three, trying to end the economic crisis gripping his country. "He worked those about him until they could hardly drag one foot after

the other," said press secretary Theodore Joslin later. Fresh workers
came and soon were burned out. Hoover, his hands trembling, kept
up the pace anyway. "My men are dropping around me," he once
admitted to Joslin. "Fighting this Depression is becoming more and
more like waging a war." His only exercise was to toss around a medicine ball in the mornings with male aides or friends.

Then came the election of 1932. Hoover versus Roosevelt,
Franklin Delano Roosevelt. Hoover regalvanized himself and
plunged into a fresh eruption of work. Mrs. Hoover had reconstructed the furniture and appurtenances of the Lincoln study, and
here Hoover relaxed, now sometimes smiling, full of fresh energy;
here he received his advisers and wrote his speeches and planned
his campaign stumping. For one speech, there was a draft of seven-
ty-one pages, but fifteen rewrites produced a more workable length.

Then came the vote, and Hoover lost to FDR in a landslide.

On FDR's inauguration day, they rode together to the Capitol, the
city grim, the crowds subdued, and Hoover unresponsive to FDR's
attempts at conversation.

And at the Capitol, when Hoover, ahead of the president-elect,
came out on top of the steps, in view of the crowd in the plaza,
silence, reported Gene Smith. Just silence. That afternoon, Eleanor
Roosevelt said she had been struck by the very solemnity of the
onlookers in the Capitol plaza. That night, her husband, the new
president, sat with friend and aide Louis Howe while others in the
family attended the inaugural ball.

The polio-crippled president sat in the Lincoln study that Mrs.
Hoover had so painstakingly refurbished for her husband, the most
modern president yet.

Thirteen years later, newly installed President Harry Truman
called Hoover to the White House one day to ask his services as
head of a new program providing food relief for war-devastated
Europe, a job somewhat familiar to Hoover. The presidential summons was the first time anyone in the White House had been in
touch with Hoover since the day he turned the mansion over to
FDR. Truman was startled to see Hoover was in tears, unable for a
minute or two to speak.

"Get That Father Out of Jail!"

HERBERT HOOVER MAY HAVE BEEN the most self-effacing president ever to occupy the White House. "A 'press agent' would say that he overlooks a million chances no politician should overlook," wrote biographer Earl Reeves in his 1928 book *This Man Hoover.*

Few who ever knew Hoover would contradict the observation. Consider the time cabinet-member Herbert Hoover appeared before the National League of Women Voters simply to convey President Warren G. Harding's greetings. Before he could leave, a public compliment by Lady Nancy Astor turned him into pure jelly. Recalling his relief work in Europe after World War I, she said all Europe looked upon him "as a sort of savior of mankind."

As her female audience burst into applause, even cheers, wrote Eugene Lyons in another Hoover biography, "The Hoover moon face blushed crimson; he was so palpably embarrassed that the demonstration was mixed with laughter."

Undeterred by his obvious discomfort, the ebullient Lady Astor raced on. "Look at him! He is not an ideal politician. He lacks the glad hand and perpetual smile, thank goodness."

Was she close to defining the real Hoover, the real inner man? Two incidents cited by Lyons in his *Herbert Hoover: A Biography* would seem to provide an answer in the affirmative. Traveling back in time to 1900, the year of the Boxer Rebellion in China, Lyons recalled that young American engineer Hoover rescued a Chinese child caught in the line of fire at Tientsin. When Hoover entered politics some years later, "his backers prepared for newspaper release a dramatic account of Hoover's exploits in the siege of Tientsin," including his rescue of the child.

His would-be press agents then showed Hoover the release. That was "a tactical mistake." Saying "you can't make a Teddy Roosevelt out of me," he tore it "into tiny fragments."

Another *child-rescue* story again revealed the kindly, if somewhat stiff, Hoover's avoidance of glory. Installed at the White House as president by now, Hoover was startled one day in the depression year of 1932 to hear that three children had arrived outside after hitchhiking all the way from Detroit. Distraught because their father was in jail for auto theft, they had come "in childlike faith that the President could and would restore their father, Charles Feagan, to the family."

Told that Feagan's thirteen-year-old daughter and two even-younger sons had mounted such an impossible mission, Hoover never hesitated. "Three children resourceful enough to manage to get to Washington to see me are going to see me," Hoover told his aides.

Before Hoover met with the youngsters in his study, his press secretary Theodore Joslin called Detroit, rounded up the pertinent facts, and presented them to his boss. Feagan had stolen a car while seeking work, it seemed, not a federal offense but still a violation of state law.

Hoover took a chance anyway and promised the youngsters he would use his office of president to free their father. "I know there must be good in a man whose children are so well behaved and who show such devotion and loyalty to him," he told the Feagan children. Their father would be waiting when they got home, he promised.

As soon as they left, Hoover called in Joslin, who "found him standing by a window, his back to the room."

Said Hoover, his voice thick with emotion, "Get that father out of jail immediately!"

Joslin, more than happy to comply, still was a press secretary—he wanted to pass along every juicy detail to the White House press corps of the day. But Hoover "would agree only to the barest announcement," wrote Lyons. "'Let's not argue about it,' he said. 'That will be enough. That is all I will say about it. Now we'll get back to work.'"

As Lyons also wrote, "It is easy to imagine what another kind of President would have made of the incident."

Bookends

BETWEEN ELECTION DAY OF 1928 and his inauguration the following year, Herbert Hoover spent six weeks on a goodwill tour of Central and South America. He traveled on two battleships provided by out-going President Calvin Coolidge, the *Maryland* on the southern leg of Hoover's trip and the *Utah* on the northbound. It was the *Maryland* that was struck by a violent storm off the Mexican coast—it smashed lifeboats and poured tons of seawater into the president-elect's stateroom through an open porthole. "Mountainous waves broke over the ship and there was a touch of panic in the air," wrote Eugene Lyons in his book *Herbert Hoover: A Biography*.

And where was Herbert Hoover during all the tumult?

Looking up at another swabbie's shout, young sailor William Vance found out:

> Mr. Hoover [Vance wrote many years later] was standing up above us, on the edge of the boat deck. He had on a sea-drenched overcoat and his pajamas were visible below the coat. He had his face turned to the sky and he was bareheaded. In the intermittent flashes of lightning and the light of the cargo flood, it was plain to every one of us that he was enjoying the storm! No one said anything, we just watched him . . . Hoover was still up there when we went below.

When Hoover was inaugurated just weeks later, he and his wife, Lou, rode from the Capitol to the White House in an open car, to allow the onlooking crowds unfettered gawking. The Hoovers rode stoically in a drenching downpour.

Just four years later, Herbert Hoover was on the way out of the White House, with the stock market crash of 1929, the depression, the Bonus Army march on Washington, and a bitter defeat by Franklin Delano Roosevelt behind him. In March 1933, it now was FDR's inauguration day, and Hoover, said Lyons, was denied the courtesy of Secret Service protection traditionally accorded an outgoing president. "The thirty-first President of the United States was not treated as a Chief Executive who had laid down heavy burdens but a felon driven from the scene of his misdoings," added Lyons.

As one result, railroad police took over the job of protecting Hoover as he prepared to entrain to New York, to his new life and residency there. And in New York, the chief of police, "having been informed of the curious state of affairs, showed up personally to greet the ex-president and to inform him that adequate police forces had been assigned to his safety," wrote Lyons.

If it was any comfort to the bedraggled Hoover, thousands did gather to say farewell as he boarded his train in Washington, then he gratefully acknowledged their presence from the observation platform of his private car.

Discovery Corps

OVER A TWO-YEAR PERIOD together at the White House, Thomas Jefferson had noticed at times that his young private secretary, Meriwether Lewis, exhibited "sensible depressions of mind." But Jefferson ascribed the younger man's "hypochondriac affections" to an inherited family trait and asserted later, "They had not . . . been so strong as to give uneasiness to his family."

Later still, Jefferson had to revise his opinion and blame the great explorer's mental state for his mysterious death in Tennessee at the conclusion of the famous Lewis and Clark expedition. Jefferson wrote that Lewis must have taken his own life, although others wondered if he were not murdered.

Jefferson had known the future explorer as a child in Albemarle County, Jefferson's own home. And long before becoming president, Jefferson had been convinced that Americans—rather than British or French subjects—should explore the American West, find a route to the Rockies, push on to the Pacific. He had British interests to fear on the one hand, and Napoleon's possible designs on the Spanish lands to the south and southwest to fend off on the other hand.

It was imperative to know more about the great unexplored landmass stretching westward from Atlantic to Pacific . . . but several proposed expeditions fell by the wayside in the years before Jefferson became president. When he took office in 1801, however, he recalled his youthful Albemarle neighbor who, as a boy, had volunteered for one of the aborted expeditions.

And so it was that a fairly untutored army officer—he couldn't spell or stake any claim to good grammar—found himself installed in the White House as private secretary to perhaps the most erudite of all American presidents. Not only that, Meriwether Lewis spent about two years in the job, working alone with Jefferson most of the time. And much of their time was spent in discussing and planning the expedition that Lewis (together with fellow army officer William Clark) would lead into the uncharted West.

Congress appropriated a few thousand dollars for the effort, and in May 1804 the so-called "Corps of Discovery" set off from St. Louis. In the months ahead, the party of whites, one black, one Indian, and one "half-breed" would travel to the West Coast and back to St. Louis, mapping, observing, and making note of various discoveries and geographic features all the way.

They went so far and were so isolated from all normal channels of communication that an anxious President Jefferson had to content himself with mere rumors of their progress or well-being, rumors passed along through Indian tribes and frontiersmen, and often altered or distorted in the process. By the summer of 1806, the explorers had been written off by many as irretrievably lost. Dead. But not by Jefferson. He kept faith in their return with the information—as did happen—that would help to open up the West to American settlement and development.

In retrospect, he might not have approved of the leadership style the two explorers adopted for their expedition, but he certainly would have found it interesting. He clearly intended his well-coached Meriwether Lewis to command, but the awkward fact was that Clark, younger brother of General George Rogers Clark of Revolutionary fame, had previously been Meriwether's company commander but was only a second lieutenant, while Lewis was an army captain. They arrived at their own private arrangement to share command, brickbats, or laurels equally, even in the land grants that Congress wished to bestow upon them afterward. With Lewis calling Clark "Captain on an expedition for North Western

Discovery," the army soldiers on the trip with them never knew that one really outranked the other.

They returned to St. Louis in September 1806, then turned to writing up their notes and observations. With a book in the offing three years later, Lewis left St. Louis for a visit to Washington (not for the first time since the expedition ended, however). He stopped, alone, at an inn on the Natchez Trace in Tennessee. Before this, a companion thought he showed "some symptoms of a derangement of mind," wrote Jefferson later. And Lewis fretted and worried over the possibility he might lose the papers and expense vouchers he was carrying.

Jefferson related more of the story: "He stopped at the house of a Mr. Grinder, who not being at home, his wife, alarmed at the symptoms of derangement she discovered, gave him up the house and retired to rest herself in an outhouse. At three o'clock in the night, he did the deed which plunged his friends into affliction, and deprived his country of one of her most valued citizens."

He died of a gunshot wound—apparently self-inflicted.

White Lodge Visited

AFTER VISITING RAW YOUNG AMERICA in the early 1820s, an astonished Englishman wrote that in front of the White House he had witnessed Indians dancing a war dance—Indians "in a state of perfect nudity, except a piece of red flannel around the waist and passing between the legs."

The dancers, he also wrote, were "men of large stature, very muscular, having fine countenances, with the real Roman nose, dignified in their manners and peaceful and quiet in their habits."

Actually, they weren't all men—those he saw performing war dances for some six thousand spectators were men from the Pawnee, Missouri, Omaha, and Kansas tribes, true, but their delegation visiting Washington and the White House of President James Monroe also included the eighteen-year-old wife of an Oto chief.

Eagle of Delight by name, she captivated all who encountered her.

Nor was the delegation of seventeen Native Americans who met with the president and attended his New Year's reception of 1821 at the White House unusual, historically speaking. It was one of the first Indian delegations to visit the White House, true again, but not the first and certainly not the last, since in the course of the nineteenth century, hundreds of Indians visited the "Great Father" in his White House abode.

Some didn't survive the capital pilgrimages—two Indians visiting George Washington in Philadelphia years before had died, their deaths rightly or wrongly blamed on rich food and drink. Later, in Washington, D.C., a chief died in a local hotel from "the croup," and another Indian stepped off a cliff to his death.

A delegation of Osage Indians who started out for Washington from the wilds of the West wound up on exhibit in Europe, thanks to an unscrupulous French promoter who told them the cross-Atlantic trip to Europe was the way they had to go to reach Washington. Years later, divided into two groups, they set sail for home. One group landed in Norfolk, Virginia, and found shelter in Rachel Anderson's boarding house while city officials sought federal help in directing them to their next stop. Two of the Osage Indians had died of smallpox on board their ship. All were penniless and confused. They were in a pitiful state.

In time, the Indians were brought to Washington, but not until weeks had passed and the boardinghouse bill had mounted up. And when the Osage did arrive in Washington, it turned out that Mrs. Anderson was holding one of their chiefs back in Norfolk as sort of a hostage, pending payment of her bill. The government paid, and the Osage did see the president—Andrew Jackson then was in office. He apologized for the treatment they had suffered, but at French, not American, hands, he pointed out. Meanwhile, the second Osage group later turned up marooned at a waterfront den in New York, also stranded without money or friends.

Still another time, a Mandan chief named Big White visited Thomas Jefferson in Washington and became so enamored of the *white* way of life that he wanted to live among whites. He was unhappy, extremely unhappy, when he returned West, he told a white friend. He allegedly complained of the insecurity of Indian life, the ferocious manners, and the ignorance of his fellow Indians. They, in turn, didn't believe his reports of white society and decided he was under the spell of a white witch. While that was not exactly the case, Big White was present for a truly historic White House event—the dinner that Thomas Jefferson gave in early 1807 for explorers Meriwether Lewis and William Clark in honor of their three-year exploratory expedition in the West. Indeed, the explorers themselves had been responsible for sending some Indian visitors on their way east to meet with the Great Father in Washington.

Later, the Indians visiting Monroe in the winter of 1820–21 appeared at his day-long New Year's reception fully decked out in colorful native dress. Eagle of Delight was a major focus, with the president's other guests crowding close to see, even to reach out and touch, these strangers from the western frontier and beyond. Wrote a local reporter: "The music and hilarity of the scene occasionally relaxed the muscles of their stern countenances and in the place of pensive gravity, a heartfelt joy beamed in the eye of the sullen Indian warrior."

As "sullen" might suggest, the Indians who visited Washington and its White House over the years were both a stereotype and a curiosity to most onlookers. When it came to sitting next to them at a hotel dinner table, some whites balked. Likewise, some hotels were not anxious to have them as guests. Unfortunately, the visiting Indians sometimes drank too much and broke up hotel furniture and glassware. But their reputation sometimes suffered more from their very strangeness to whites than from any fault of their own. A newspaper reported in the late 1830s that a Washington "gentleman" looked out the window of his carriage, saw an Indian's painted face in front of him, and fainted from the shock. But the Indian only wished to ask for money.

The Indian chiefs were often brought to Washington to discuss treaties, to mollify their outrage about the wave of settlement engulfing their ancient lands . . . to avoid hostilities on the frontier. But another purpose was to let them see the power of the white establishment that had taken firm root on the eastern seaboard. Thus, when Eagle of Delight and her companions visited the White House of James Monroe, the dances and sightseeing stopped one day for serious business at the White House.

As the local *Intelligencer* reported, someone had persuaded the Indians to trade their usual native dress for "completely Americanized" outfits—military-style clothing presented to them by government agents. Thus, "They were dressed in blue surtouts, red cuffs and capes, blue pantaloons and shiny black boots." They did wear paint on their faces, but "in less fantastic style than usual."

Monroe received them in company with his own chiefs—cabinet members, congressmen, Supreme Court justices, and the like. He spoke to his "Red Children" of peace, but also made careful note of the white man's military strength. In response, the leading Pawnee present, Chief Sharitarish by most accounts, said that, true, the white man could make clothing, guns, and furniture and feed on the flesh of domesticated animals. The red man, on the other hand, had to hunt for his skins and his meat.

But what did such differences matter? After all, "the Great Spirit intended that there should be both white men and red men, and he looks down and regards them as both his children." Unfortunately, some of the *children* have not always looked at it the same way.

Guests From the Street

RARELY HAS THE WHITE HOUSE been so stuffed to the rafters as it was during the Roosevelt era: the time of Franklin, Eleanor, their five children, their various relatives, their friends, their aides, their official state visitors, their servants, their mere acquaintances.

The FDR White House, wrote retired Chief Usher J. B. West, "was like a Grand Hotel." Eleanor Roosevelt found some guests who would stay for months—and some "she'd just picked up on the street." She sometimes forgot who her guests were, and it was not unknown for her to go to bed at night not really aware of "who was sleeping down the hall."

The visitors, often left to their own devices, "used the White House like a hotel, meandering in and out at will, sometimes stopping by the usher's office for help in scheduling their day in Washington."

If visiting themselves, the grown Roosevelt children "were accorded no special privileges," wrote West. He recalled the time

one of FDR's sons had to shift to "his third bedroom of the week," to
make room for an incoming guest.

In addition to staff, such as housekeeper Henrietta Nesbitt,
whose notorious menu FDR detested, or Eleanor's personal maid
Mabel Webster, the house residents included FDR aide Harry
Hopkins, a widower who not only made his own home in the White
House, but brought along his eight-year-old daughter Diana. He lived
in the Lincoln suite on the second or "family" floor, and Diana lived
in a room on the third floor. In time, Hopkins remarried and moved
his bride, Louise Macy Hopkins, into his own small apartment, a
development that provoked a long letter from Eleanor laying down
a few rules for the newcomer: "I hope you will feel entirely free to
have anyone there [the Monroe Sitting Room] for tea or cocktails at
any time you wish to be alone" was one thought; another was, "I
would suggest that you talk to Mrs. Nesbitt about some regular
arrangements for your wash, so that you will know on what days it
must be sent and when it will be returned to you, and what it costs."

Typically, West also wrote, Eleanor hosted breakfast in the West
Sitting Hall, "where she presided over a table of assorted house-
guests, business appointments, or just friends." Next came lunch. If
not traveling or invited out herself, she always had guests for
lunch—a formal sitdown in the Private Dining Room "for at least
twelve." Dinner, again in the Private Dining Room, would be a black-
tie affair, often for more people working in the areas of Eleanor's
many interests and public causes. And Sunday would be culture
night—"authors, artists, actresses, playwrights, sculptors, dancers,
world travelers, old friends," plus a mixed grill of diplomats and
administration figures. Since Eleanor served scrambled eggs that she
cooked at the table in a silver chafing dish, the staff called her
Sunday menu "scrambled eggs with brains."

A major feature of the Roosevelt "hotel" was its frequent VIP visitors—the kings and queens, the potentates of all stripe and variety
who came avisiting over a remarkable twelve-year period. Not only
the storied Winston Churchill, or the sour-faced Soviet foreign minister V. M. Molotov, but by private secretary Grace Tully's account,
those "favorite wartime royal visitors in Washington," Crown
Princess Marthe of Norway and her three children, one of them the
future King Harald.

And then there was Madame Chiang Kai-shek, the Chinese generalissimo's dynamic wife, described by Tully as "one of the most

spectacular of the Roosevelt guests," and described by West as "not so democratic as her publicity had us believe." Tully recalled hearing Madame's peremptory clapping of hands for service one day on the second floor and asked an usher, Wilson Searles, what was going on. He said the "Chinese crowd" had the staff running ragged and complained further, "They think they're in China calling the coolies."

For his part, West recalled "an entourage of forty, many of whom were stashed away on the third floor, the others at the Chinese Embassy." Sheets became a trial, he noted. Madame Chiang insisted her silk sheets had to be laundered by hand every day, then "stitched back inside the heavy quilted sleeping bag she had brought along from China."

Quartered on the second floor with the visiting "Mrs. Generalissimo" were her maid and her "closest aides," two individuals at first taken for nephews—until the valets sent to help them unpack discovered, to everyone's embarrassment, that one "nephew" really was a niece. Even after that staff discovery, a hospitable FDR at dinner kept calling her "my boy."

During all the comings and goings at the Roosevelt White House, West also wrote later, "We never saw Eleanor and Franklin Roosevelt in the same room alone together." They "met" in the evenings and discussed papers, ideas, issues, programs . . . all sorts of things. Eleanor "was perhaps his [FDR's] most trusted observer." But: "They had the most separate relationship I have ever seen between man and wife. And the most equal."

More of Progress

GAS LIGHTING CAME TO THE White House in 1848, under James K. Polk, and the story is that Mrs. Polk insisted upon keeping her favorite chandelier unconverted. It was in the Blue Room and she saw that it kept its wax candles. Then, the night of the first gaslight entertainment in the White House, the gas company inadvertently cut off the supply at 9 P.M. One light remained—Mrs. Polk's candle-powered chandelier in the Blue Room.

Progress . . . it never stops. Even at the White House.

Thomas Jefferson it was who in 1801 provided a sixteen-foot-deep outside "icehouse"—a wine cellar, in reality.

A primitive central heating system that James Madison had installed went the way of all other things when the British burned out the interior of the President's House, and no real hot air mechanics would replace it until 1840. Until then, the rooms were heated by fireplaces (four in the East Room, but only one in most nonpublic rooms).

In 1840, as Martin Van Buren's term was drawing to a close, the oval-shaped servants' waiting room in the basement was turned into a furnace room equipped with a coal-eating firebox that sent hot air coursing, more or less, through new plaster ducts up to the first-floor public rooms, a feat accomplished by the well-known principle that hot air rises.

Van Buren, meanwhile, could thank his predecessor, Andrew Jackson, for the fire engine–like water machine that kept the White House lawns and plants properly dampened. (A vat on wheels, actually.)

And if Jackson also had provided the bathing room in the East Wing with two copper bathtubs, Van Buren added several more, plus screening walls for added privacy. Upstairs, tin tubs in the bedrooms, filled by hand rather than running water, remained the vogue,

Franklin Pierce brought fairly dramatic change in the 1850s in the areas of heating, bathing, and toilet arrangements. More modern central heating improved upon Van Buren's gravity hot-air system, upon James K. Polk's two added furnaces, and upon Millard Fillmore's extended hot air ducts that reached all over the house. The improvement now was a gravity hot-air system in which the coal fires of the three furnaces heated water in copper coils, and the coils heated the air wafting upstairs through the duct system to registers in the rooms above. Less stale air and much greater efficiency, reported White House historian William Seale.

The plumbing advances accomplished under Pierce included the first "bathing room" on the second floor, a new amenity situated in the same southwest closet that had housed Thomas Jefferson's water closet all these years. Both hot and cold water now reached the new presidential bathroom. No more portable tin tubs here! No more trips to the East Wing shower-bath facility of many years' standing.

On the first floor, installed or improved under Pierce also, was a water closet handily placed near the private dining room. Much better for the White House guests.

The servants of the 1850s, however, still had to make do with the old rather than the modern—they bathed in portable tin tubs, and they still had only privies at their disposal, just outside the big house.

Some years later, after the Civil War, the bearded teetotaler Rutherford B. Hayes installed speaking tubes for internal communications, plus a typewriter, and a telephone for outside communication. He didn't use the telephone very much, perhaps because the Washington of the 1880s didn't have many other telephones to call. The mansion's first telegraph room, it should be noted, too, had been installed much earlier, in 1866, under Lincoln's successor, Andrew Johnson.

It was the ill-fated James Garfield who ordered the first White House elevator—but he was shot and grievously wounded shortly into his term as president, and so the difficult installation of the hydraulic lift had to await his successor, Chester A. Arthur. The job then took two months and resulted in "endless trouble," according to historian William Seale. "The hydraulic system included a large water tank on the roof made of wooden staves," he wrote. "Being extremely heavy, it caused serious damage to the timber framing in the attic." Its hot-air engine activating a hydraulic pump in the basement "was so undependable that it was eventually replaced by a steam engine," added the historian. Nevertheless, a pleased Arthur had the interior of the elevator upholstered "in tufted plush."

That was only the beginning of the small elevator's saga, which included the time, in 1902, when a Senate aide, Charles Moore, was caught between floors in the uncooperative contraption . . . until Teddy Roosevelt's usher Ike Hoover got it moving again.

The same Roosevelt era was the last in which the first family relied upon the foot or horse for local transportation. From then on, presidents—like everyone else—have used "motorcars" for getting around. The telephone, of course, also became ubiquitous, with the first transcontinental line installed in Woodrow Wilson's Oval Office in 1915.

Soon after, Herbert Hoover, as a most modern and successful engineer, not only added to the number of telephones, but also brought thirteen radios to the White House. Even the electrician-turned-usher Ike Hoover (no relation) was astounded. Thirteen!

Meanwhile, Herbert Hoover was the first president to place a telephone right on his desk.

The indoor swimming pool so famously favored by polio-victim Franklin Delano Roosevelt was built in 1933, thanks largely to the fundraising campaign launched by the *New York Daily News*. It was built in a thoroughly gutted west wing, its walls still containing lunette windows of Jefferson's original design. Once, too, this had been the site of James Monroe's stable.

Air conditioning came to the second-floor rooms in 1933 as another innovation of the FDR era with electrically controlled central air—and heat—units still to be installed in new subbasements created by Harry Truman.

It was the same Truman, of course, who—like the British fire—completely gutted the old White House and "installed" a new one inside the old shell, a complete reconstruction of the White House interior that was finished in 1952, complete with the "Truman Balcony" over the South Portico.

Visiting Mothers

AS ITS GUESTS, THE WHITE House of twentieth-century America has seen a veritable parade of historic, public, or celebrity figures come crowding through its doors. A few though, may not appear in the standard reference works.

Under Harry Truman, the first weekend guest was his own mother, then ninety years old. And no Lincoln bed for her! "I'll sleep on the floor first," said the elderly Southern belle. She would not sleep in the Queen's Room, either. "Too fancy for me," was her rejection of that one.

She wound up in the adjoining sitting room and placed daughter Mary in the Queen's bedroom.

Then Mrs. Truman tripped on some steps left bare by the removal of FDR's wheelchair ramp, but she didn't tell anyone she had hurt herself. A minor injury, but at her age, irksome, to say the least.

In the meantime, Bess Truman's mother, Margaret Gates Wallace, also rather elderly, actually lived in the White House. She stayed in her room most of the time, but daughter Bess spent time with her every day and often read the newspapers to her.

Even under the same roof, Mrs. Wallace always called her son-in-law "Mr. Truman."

She died in her room at the White House on December 5, 1952, four days after suffering what had appeared to be a mild stroke. It was just a month after Dwight D. Eisenhower's first presidential election victory over Adlai Stevenson. On December 4, the night before Mrs. Wallace's death, the Trumans held a farewell dinner for his cabinet. Stevenson, Ike's recently vanquished Democratic opponent, spent the night—his only overnight stay at the presidential mansion ever, even though he would run against Ike again in 1956.

The Eisenhowers, too, had a mother as their White House residential guest—Mamie's mother, Mrs. John S. Doud. She often ate dinner on tray-tables in the West Sitting Hall with the Eisenhowers as they all watched the evening news on television. She enjoyed playing her harmonica in her room, and Mamie frequently would accompany her on a small electric organ. Ike, for his part, teased her constantly and called her "Min," for a character in the Andy Gump comic strip.

Like her daughter Mamie, Mrs. Doud loved to stay in bed late in the morning, propped up against the pillows while planning and organizing her day. In fact, they often picked up the telephones beside their beds on the opposite sides of the second-floor corridor and talked back and forth, from one bed to the other, two women, mother and daughter, so comfy in the twentieth-century White House . . . talking, talking, talking on the telephone.

Happy Days Afloat

WILLIAM HOWARD TAFT'S WIFE, HELEN, took ill on one, Woodrow Wilson did his early courting of Edith Galt on another, Harry Truman enjoyed his poker binges and his swims in the Potomac, Calvin Coolidge enjoyed weekends on the river replete with guests, a string quartet, and other Marine Corps musicians. The Wilsons, for that matter, once they were married, enjoyed weekend river outings just as much.

"We both liked studying the charts to see if we could find some little tributary of the river to explore," wrote wife Edith later.

Yachts . . . presidential yachts were the means and conveyance for such pleasurable, relaxing excursions for many a White House occupant, although that was not the case the evening the Tafts embarked upon the U.S. Navy yacht *Sylph* in May of 1909. They were entertaining friends after a long day for the first lady, whose son Charles was in the hospital after surgery to remove his adenoids.

Suddenly still, unresponsive to conversation, shortly after the boat slipped its mooring, Helen Taft had suffered a stroke. President Taft was so distraught, said aide Archie Butt, that he "looked like a great stricken animal." And with good reason, since it would be more than a year before she recovered her strength. Her face, in the meantime, was partially paralyzed and she hated to be seen in public—so much so that she sometimes "attended" her husband's state dinners sitting alone in a small dining room next to the State Dining Room and, still alone, sharing the dinner viands being served to the president's guests on the other side of the wall.

On happier occasions, the Tafts used the larger yacht at their disposal, the *Mayflower,* for more serious seagoing trips, as did other presidential couples. The Tafts, for instance, would cruise to their summer place in Massachusetts.

Woodrow Wilson and his second wife, Edith, had nothing but pleasant memories of the *Mayflower,* where early in their courting days Wilson often entertained Edith at dinner. This large steam-powered craft offered a private suite and guest compartments, dining room, and salon, among its ample spaces, and all the crew, of course, courtesy of the U.S. Navy.

The Calvin Coolidges also enjoyed the *Mayflower*'s facilities, which included a fully equipped office for the president's use. They, too, cruised to Massachusetts for a bit of relaxed summering, while on more limited outings in the Potomac, say for a weekend, they often took along a pianist, that string quartet or other members of the Marine Band to help while away the hours for themselves and their guests.

Then came Herbert Hoover. The old steam-powered yacht no longer suited. Hoover decommissioned the venerable *Mayflower,* in use by American presidents since Teddy Roosevelt's day in 1901. Franklin Roosevelt, occupying the White House during World War II, then had to consign his yacht *Potomac* to combat duty. He often used U.S. Navy warships, both for official travel or for a bit of relaxation. The size of his "yachts," therefore, was on the order of cruiser or even battleship.

In the postwar years, Harry Truman rediscovered the joys his predecessors had found on the Potomac waters, often cruising with his poker cronies and—has any president dared to emulate him since?—even swimming in the Potomac.

Telephonitis in the White House

IF HERBERT HOOVER WAS THE first president to permit a telephone on his office desk in the White House, Lyndon Johnson must have been the first chief executive to treat the instrument as very nearly a physical appendage—perhaps as an emotional crutch, too.

Even before he reached the Executive Mansion, the onetime Senate majority leader spawned a "telephone story." It seems that Everett Dirksen, as the Senate's Republican minority leader, at last rated a government limousine complete with driver—and telephone.

Dirksen couldn't wait to call Democrat Johnson on his limo tele-

*President Lyndon
Johnson talks on the
telephone—a favorite
pastime that often
involved more than
one phone conversa-
tion at a time. (LBJ
Library Photo by
Yoichi R. Okamoto)*

phone, proudly pointing out that he at last had a telephone in his limousine, too. Just like LBJ!

Without missing a beat, it is alleged, Johnson said, "Just a minute Ev,
my other telephone is ringing."

As president, clearly, Johnson had greater need of the instrument
than ever. Often engaged with more than one call at a time, he used
telephones not only to communicate simple fact or instruction, but
also to cajole, scold, commiserate, gossip, persuade, threaten . . . whatever the occasion and/or his mood seemed to demand.

Horace Busby, longtime friend and a special assistant to LBJ in
the White House, recalled the time he came up to Johnson at Love
Field in Dallas and found him before a bank of public phones. "Then
I noticed that the receivers were off all six hooks and you could
hear the voices of the operators trying to complete all six calls."

Others close to Johnson told their telephone tales, too.

"We had all these little white phones leading directly from the

White House," explained cabinet member Robert C. Weaver one time, "and he would call at any hour, any time."

One time, recalled staff assistant Will Sparks, LBJ was in the midst of telling a "funny story" to various members of the staff assembled in the Oval Office "when one of his several telephones buzzed." Johnson picked it up and when he realized who was calling, delivered what Sparks described as "one of the worst tongue-lashings I've ever heard in my life." Said Sparks, "That guy at the other end of the phone must have been on the verge of a heart attack to be talked to like that by the President of the United States."

The conversation over, Johnson "slammed" the phone down and pushed it out of sight in a desk drawer. He then, totally unperturbed, turned back to his listeners. "Well, now, as I was saying . . ."

More often, it was LBJ doing the calling. "He was an inveterate user of Alexander Graham Bell's instrument," recalled Senate staffer William Jorden, "and it didn't take very much to prompt him to pick it up; so if he read something in the paper, or if he read something in the briefing memos or staff papers, etcetera, that interested him, he'd get on the telephone and call the guy involved and say, 'What the hell are they doing to us here?' and 'What does this mean, etcetera,' and he didn't just pick up the telephone; he grabbed the telephone."

In fact, Jorden added: "Secretaries say that he just grabbed the phone away from them while they were talking, cut off their conversation and dialed his number. And they would just be in tears."

He also loved to call folks early in the morning, said speechwriter Erv Duggan. Awakening them and pointing out he was up and at 'em "was a way of being in control."

White House staf-fers, of course, always had to be available at the end of that long wire from the Johnsonian Oval Office—whether in or out.

You had to leave word at all times with the White House operator, said special counsel Larry Temple, "if you went to the bathroom, or decided to scratch your nose or something. . . ."

Or a nice lunch out, added Peace Corps official Coates Redmon one time: "If you were having lunch—no matter what restaurant it was—the waiter would come with a message there was a telephone call. It would always be the President wanting to know what you were doing, what you were eating—'Now, have you salted and peppered it?, etcetera?'"

LBJ's little game at such moments was to pretend his listener was eating in one of the fanciest Georgetown restaurants going, although the White House operator knew the actual eating place and had dialed the number for him.

Was there something pathetic here? By Redmon's account, LBJ's often aimless chitchat with a staffer reached at some restaurant would end with: "Well, you enjoy your lunch—but hurry back—I need you."

And Jorden later would opine on this compulsive telephone business—on this compulsiveness, period: "I think it was the thing that almost did him in, trying to look at three television stations at once and trying to talk over two or three telephones at the same time."

Rose Garden Created

YOU'VE HEARD OF IT . . . THE Rose Garden, created for JFK by Mrs. Paul "Bunny" Mellon after his trip to Paris and Vienna for the Khrushchev summit in 1961. "The President had noted that the White House had no garden equal in quality or attractiveness to the gardens he had seen and in which he had been entertained in Europe," wrote Bunny Mellon. So at a picnic on Cape Cod later, he asked her to design a nice garden in "the area near his office at the west end of the White House, already known as the Rose Garden." Visiting soon after, she was struck by the disproportions that must have been bothering him. "The White House proper seemed exceptionally tall where it joined the long, low colonnade that linked it to the Oval Office and Cabinet Room," she recalled. Worse, no trees—none by the wing holding the Oval Office nor any at the corner formed with the west end of the White House. Only Andrew Jackson's "tall, dark Magnolia grandiflora near the South Portico."

The garden then greeting her had four rows of privet hedges interspersed with Tom Thumb roses "and occasional standard roses."

What was needed, she could see, was some "harmonious and

uncomplicated" way to unite "the tall central block of the White House in one corner and the West Wing, with its two low colonnades forming boundaries west and north." But, what harmonious way?

Further, JFK wanted a center lawn of fifty by one hundred feet that could hold a thousand persons and/or a festive tent.

Part of the answer came to Mellon when she visited New York that fall and noticed that the three magnolia trees in front of the Frick Museum looked especially attractive even without their summer foliage. "Their pale silvery branches with heavy twigs seemed to retain the light of summer," she thought. "I knew their pattern of growth would continue to give form in winter and would catch rain drops as well as tufts of falling snow." Now she knew what to do! "I felt I could now design the President's garden!"

Thus, she had found the anchors to her overall scheme, but she still had to find trees of the right size to plant right away, and preferably from public land. And she did—four magnolias taken from unkempt ground behind old Navy "tempos" (temporary wooden structures built during World War II) near the Tidal Basin that later were torn down.

Planted in the four "bare" corners of the Rose Garden, the magnolias "changed the entire character of this empty space." They were joined over the spring and summer of 1962 by borders of Katherine crab apple trees in sectioned flower beds . . . by roses, boxwood, perennials, annuals, herbs, and yet more roses.

"A large diamond-shaped outline of santolina would surround each crab-apple tree," she also wrote. Each diamond would be set in a larger outline: a small clipped English boxwood hedge and, next to the lawn, a low growing hybrid boxwood called Greenpillow, developed by Henry Hohman in Kingsville, Maryland."

In the process of developing the garden, designer Mellon "discovered" Irvin Williams, head horticulturist at the Kenilworth Aquatic Gardens in Washington—she was so taken with his knowledge and interest that she suggested he move to the White House. As a result, he did . . . he became the head White House gardener and could claim credit for "much of the beauty of the White House landscape" for years after, as well as the quality of the Rose Garden and the entirely separate Jacqueline Kennedy Garden that greets visitors beginning their tour of the public rooms of the White House as they enter the eastern end of the building.

The areas in which the Mellon-Williams team dug out and replaced topsoil to a depth of four feet for the new garden had its own historic background. It once held the original White House stable yard, it yielded even in 1962 "Civil War horseshoes." It once held U.S. Grant's vegetable garden and the huge greenhouses that had housed plantings as large as fruit trees and palms in the Victorian era. Teddy Roosevelt's wife Edith later planted a "Colonial Garden" on the same site, but only after she and her husband removed the greenhouses (thus making way for the West Wing). In the colonnade flanking the garden, noted Bunny Mellon, there had been "a milk house, icehouse, workshops, servants' dwelling rooms, and numbers of other small, thick-walled chambers called, in the earliest times, household 'offices.'"

As one minor problem in the 1962 digging, "We cut into a mysterious cable buried in the corner of the garden." Somewhat "hastily installed" during World War II, it was "the hot line that set off the Nation's military alert." The future garden space suddenly was "alive" with security personnel.

Another time that the revamped Rose Garden was "alive" with visitors was during a Boys' Nation appearance by select young men from each state of the Union. Shaking JFK's hand in the Rose Garden was a bright young lad from Arkansas—Bill Clinton by name.

Pluses and Minuses of *Un*impeachment

WHAT DOES A PRESIDENT DO while the U.S. Senate is in the process of voting on his impeachment?

In the case of presidential bad boy William Jefferson Clinton, only the second U.S. President ever to be impeached, it was to indulge in peripatetic-sounding activity, according to his aides. On the one hand, he was portrayed as doing his exercises in the White House gym, the Associated Press reported that the aides reported. On the other hand, according to the AP report on the reports by said aides, he was working on his postacquittal statement of contrition, which he pronounced standing alone in the Rose Garden shortly after the Senate vote.

All the while, it appears too, he was digesting reports from White House chief of staff John Podesta on the votes on the two articles of impeachment by the one hundred members of the Senate. Perhaps he really didn't choose to watch the proceedings that Friday, February 12, 1999 (Lincoln's birthday) on television, but with a minute-by-minute rundown on the vote being reported to him, it's obvious where his attention really was directed. And understandably so, considering his uncomfortable situation.

In the end, as is well known, Clinton had survived yet another crisis in a lifetime of political and personal cliffhangers.

It was about an hour after the Senate vote was completed that he left the Oval Office in the West Wing to respond publicly to his acquittal. "With the wind whipping his hair," said the AP account, "he gravely delivered the brief speech aides said he himself had written."

Clinton stood alone at a lectern beneath a blue sky with a ring of reporters and camera people before him, but several yards distant.

His brief statement was humble pie: "I want to say again to the American people how profoundly sorry I am for what I said and did to trigger these events and the great burden they have imposed on the Congress and the American people."

Clinton also thanked those who had rallied to his support during the impeachment crisis of 1998-1999. He urged Americans in general—and those in Washington in particular—to "rededicate" themselves to "the work of serving our nation and building our future together."

Said Clinton also, "This can be and this must be a time of reconciliation and renewal for America."

But at the end, there also came a "flash of defiance," in the AP's words.

"He had turned away from the microphones when a reporter shouted, 'In your heart, sir, can you forgive and forget?'

"Clinton went back to the lectern and said firmly, 'I believe any person who asks for forgiveness has to be prepared to give it.' Then he walked up a few stairs, along the portico and back to the Oval Office."

While Clinton, halfway through his second term, had escaped conviction and removal from office that day, it was not exactly a moment of triumph. After all, one half of the Senate membership (fifty members) had voted to convict Clinton on the impeachment article charging him with obstruction of justice. Then, too, well over a third of the membership (forty-five members, specifically) had voted to convict on the other impeachment article, which charged the president with perjury. Neither vote, of course, met the constitutional requirement of a two-thirds majority (sixty-seven members) in order to convict and remove a president from office.

As a result, Clinton had saved a final two years in office, he had avoided a damning and historic decision marking him as the first president ever to be removed from office, and he also had salvaged a helpful financial underpinning for his future after leaving the White House.

Clinton haters will hate to hear this, but Clinton as an ex-president need not lift one finger in order to receive an annual, taxpayer-paid pension of $150,950. Plus a private office, plus a small staff, plus Secret Service protection, plus travel expenses.

In addition, reported the Scripps-Howard News Service, "At least one expert said Clinton's Senate acquittal could entitle him to recover from taxpayers some of his huge legal fees—those accrued while he defended himself against impeachment proceedings."

Removal by the Senate would have cost Clinton both that recompense and the standard pension-office benefits routinely provided by the Former Presidents Act. While ouster from office would have deprived Clinton of those financial underpinnings for life, "now he gets them even if he is ultimately convicted of similar charges [similar to the impeachment articles] in a criminal court."

Both Bill Clinton and his wife, Hillary, certainly could improve their base annual income by many thousands (possibly even millions) more dollars as high-priced lawyers, lecturers, professors, and/or book authors; but as their months in the White House waned, they also faced huge legal bills that remained inescapable, regardless of the Former Presidents Act. As the postacquittal Scripps-Howard report noted, Clinton's "legal woes could drag on for years."

As stated in the same account, it could take years for the Clintons, many of their friends, and various White House aides who were interrogated before grand juries "to dig out from the financial toll stemming from half a decade of investigations of his public and private activities."

The Clintons alone owed close to $10 million in legal fees stemming from the many investigations and Clinton's costly defense and settlement of the Paula Jones sexual harassment suit, the Scripps-Howard account added. "Numerous others" caught up and questioned in the various investigations, no matter how innocent themselves, faced "six figure attorneys' tabs" as well.

Impeachment in late 1998 by the House of Representatives, the most damning of all Clinton's troubles, stemmed from moments of sexual dalliance with a young female intern, Monica Lewinsky, in the White House complex itself . . . in the modern, expanded mode of the original President's House.

Unofficial Annex

"This hotel, in fact, may be much more justly called the center of Washington and the Union than either the Capitol, the White House, or the State Department." So said, in harsh Civil War times, that politically attuned literary lion Nathaniel Hawthorne. The hotel he was talking about still is a hostelry of note today—not necessarily the center of the universe, but certainly a key landmark just two blocks from the White House, a major bustling modern-day attraction for lodger, diner, and tourist alike—and a symbol of haunting historical memories. And ah, yes, the stories, the stories the Willard could tell if hotels could only speak. . . .

Of the time, for instance, that delegates from twenty-one states (there were only thirty-four at the time) convened here in a desperate peace convention intended as a last-ditch effort to avert secession and Civil War. Right in the Willard, February 4 to February 27, 1861. And arriving secretly one dawn even before they left town, spirited during the night past rebelliously seething Baltimore, one Abraham Lincoln, who then stayed on until his inauguration March 4.

"Lincoln held staff meetings in the lobby and borrowed slippers belonging to the Willard family during his stay," says a Willard-produced history. And on inaugural day itself, he returned from events and ceremony at the Capitol to watch the traditional parade from the Willard, which fronted, as it does now, on Pennsylvania Avenue just before it runs up against the U.S. Treasury Building. A little later, "When Lincoln received his first paycheck as President, he paid his Willard bill of $773.75," adds the Willard historical account.

Stories, stories . . . more of the Civil War era. The famous and the infamous, in and out all the time. Troops once quartered here—Union, of course. In 1861 also, Julia Ward Howe, a registered guest, wrote "The Battle Hymn of the Republic" here.

But not all the Willard's remarkable history is Civil War history, not by any means. Take U. S. Grant. Not the Civil War Grant we all know so well, but the one in later metamorphosis as President Grant.

He liked the Willard. He liked the lobby. He enjoyed getting away from the White House, just on the far side of the Treasury. And so he would walk over and spend some time relaxing in the Willard lobby. He enjoyed his cigar and brandy here. In time, of course, people noticed . . . in time people hoping for presidential favor began to seek him out in the Willard lobby. Says the Willard history, "He called these people 'lobbyists.'"

Less happily, this is where a departing president's wife, Abigail Fillmore, wife of Millard, died in her bed from pneumonia just a month after they left the antebellum White House to Franklin Pierce—who also had been a Willard guest while awaiting his turn in the presidential mansion.

Here, too, in the wartime year of 1916, Woodrow Wilson addressed the League to Enforce Peace, a progenitor of the League of Nations that was born after the end of World War I.

More happily than wartime tidings, and much earlier in history, the Willard played host in 1860, during James Buchanan's term, to the first Japanese delegation ever to reach Washington for an official visit—three ambassadors with an entourage of seventy-four.

Less weighty but a gem as trivia is the fact that a U.S. vice president (Woodrow Wilson's Thomas Marshall) was so annoyed with the price of the cigars at the Willard newsstand that he then and there uttered those immortal words: "What this country needs is a good five-cent cigar."

The grand old structure now seen at 1401 Pennsylvania Avenue was built in the period 1901–1904, and don't be surprised if it seems reminiscent of the Plaza in New York City. Same architect—Henry Janeway Hardenbergh. The ground underneath has been the site of one hostelry or another since 1816. It passed into Henry Willard's hands in 1850 and it would be almost one hundred years—in 1946, specifically—before the family sold its interest in the hotel. It shut down in 1968, but sprang back to life in 1986 after a painstaking restoration job, new funding, and construction of an adjoining office building and retail shopping complex. The hotel then became the Willard Inter-Continental (Inter-Continental Hotels Corporation).

A magnet for today's visiting statesmen, jet-setters, politicos, beautiful people, moviemakers (the remakers of *Born Yesterday,* for instance), even an occasional corn-ripened tourist, the Willard is still the Willard . . . that place where Henry Clay allegedly mixed his first mint julep in Washington; where visited such luminaries of the not-so-distant past as Mark Twain, Walt Whitman, Houdini, the duke of Windsor, Jenny Lind, and even Tom Thumb. Even where one president made his official residence for nearly a month. For here it was that Calvin Coolidge, hastily sworn in as the deceased Warren G. Harding's successor in 1923, patiently waited for Mrs. Harding's departure from the official residence down the street, at 1600 Pennsylvania Avenue.

Secret Service Agent Edmund Starling later recalled the first time he reported for duty at the new president's side. He arrived outside the door of the third-floor Coolidge suite at 5:45 A.M. and had to wait half an hour for his first glimpse of Coolidge. When the glimpse came, at 6:15 A.M., "He stepped out, dressed to go for a walk."

After that walk and another one in the afternoon, a third one the next morning, and then a few more, Coolidge one day paused in front of the Willard and said: "You ought to move in here. It's a good place."

Starling did exactly that, he later noted in his book *Starling of the White House.* He stayed at the Willard even after the Coolidges finally moved into the nearby White House. As Starling related, he remained throughout Coolidge's two terms, "eventually getting a private telephone wire installed between my room and the White House."

Honest Man at Gettysburg

WHEN LINCOLN DELIVERED HIS NOW-FAMOUS Gettysburg Address, there was a totally honest man among his listeners, the real thing for any Diogenes.

He was there, at the dedication ceremony for the battlefield and its cemetery, as the main speaker of the day. He had already spoken for two hours while Lincoln waited. And he had kept Lincoln and a crowd of fifteen thousand waiting for half an hour for his arrival.

The president had taken a train to Gettysburg the night before, a ride from Washington of one hour and ten minutes.

The featured speaker, a former president of Harvard, had been invited six weeks before the dedication planned for November 19, 1863, just months after the battle that took place in early July. Lincoln was invited—an afterthought—on November 2.

But he said yes.

> Four score and seven years ago our fathers brought forth on this continent a new nation. . . .

He wrote a draft in ink on White House stationery, headed, in the style of the day, Executive Mansion. Not a mistake, not a single correction or change in the first, mighty paragraph.

> . . . conceived in liberty, and dedicated to the proposition that all men are created equal.

It isn't until the beginning of the third paragraph that one finds new wording written in, over a phrase crossed out by a single slash.

The draft converts to pencil near the end of the first page and continues in pencil through the second and last page. It is thought that Lincoln began writing it at the White House, put it aside for the train trip north from Washington—no jiggled words or letters are evident—then finished it at the Gettysburg home of David Willis, the local citizen who had taken the lead in establishment of the memorial grounds under official Pennsylvania aegis.

The morning of the nineteenth, a Thursday, Lincoln took part in the parade that proceeded along Baltimore Street in Gettysburg to the cemetery and battlefield grounds.

Then, together with the onlookers, he settled down to await the arrival of the "real" orator of the day, former Harvard president Edward Everett.

After appearing at last, Everett waxed long and dramatic with his silver tongue, and then came Lincoln—his two minutes of speech-making come and gone so quick, many in the crowd did not realize he had even begun.

Everybody by now knows of Lincoln's Gettysburg Address, and just about everybody is under the impression that it was not immediately appreciated for what it really was . . . that its full beauty and value were not immediately grasped by those initially exposed.

That is largely true, but there were some who immediately recognized the short speech for its grandeur. Henry Wadsworth Longfellow, no slouch with words himself, that same day told the editor of *Harper's Weekly* that it was "admirable." Others also were quick to praise, and before two years were out, the great savant of New England, Ralph Waldo Emerson, was willing to say it "will not easily be surpassed by words on any recorded occasion."

Lincoln himself, though, is said to have considered his second inaugural address as his best effort in the speech department.

The "honest" man present, however, a listener who put his reaction in writing the next day, was the ceremony's featured speaker, Edward Everett. Writing directly to Lincoln, Everett said, "I should be glad, if I could flatter myself that I came as near the central idea of the occasion, in two hours, as you did in two minutes."

"Only a Poor Indian"

LIKE ANY PRESIDENT, GROVER CLEVELAND usually had plenty to do, but one time he stopped his normal work to look—minutely at that—into the case of an American Indian facing execution by hanging for killing another Indian in a drunken brawl. It wasn't the usual fare for a president, or even the lawyer-politician from Buffalo, New York, which is what Cleveland was when he wasn't serving two separated terms as president.

The presidential examination of the facts in the case took some doing, too. "The record was an elaborate one," recalled White House aide Alexander Boteler later, "even as we had prepared [summarized] it, but it was still insufficient to satisfy the President and his scruples."

With little time to investigate further, Cleveland ordered a stay in the execution date and "called for the full shorthand report of the trial."

But even that didn't satisfy him. He also ordered up letters from the district attorney (the killing took place on federal Indian territory), from the judges in the case, even the jurors. "When these were submitted, he went all over them with the most elaborate and painstaking care."

Having digested the entire record, assembled for the unusual, strictly voluntary perusal by a president in the White House, Cleveland finally ended the legal matter with a short presidential memo. He ordered the death penalty commuted—the Indian would not be executed.

And what was Grover Cleveland's burning interest in the case? He told Boteler that he couldn't have slept nights if the defendant had been hanged simply because he, Cleveland, failed to take an interest and look into the man's case. Said Cleveland, "He is only a poor Indian, but I cannot forget that he had nobody else in the world to look after him and see that his rights are fully preserved."

Dolley's Black Benefactor

"WHEN MR. MADISON WAS CHOSEN President, we came on and moved into the White House; the east room was not finished, and Pennsylvania Avenue was not paved, but was always in awful condition from either mud or dust. The city was a dreary place."

So wrote Paul Jennings, born a slave at James Madison's Montpelier estate outside Orange, Virginia, later the man who prepared the White House dinner consumed by the British interlopers who burned the presidential mansion in the War of 1812, still later a free man working for Daniel Webster as a "body servant."

Often forgotten today is the fact that the federal city awaiting Madison and Jennings in 1809 was a major slave trading center, that it was situated between two slave states, Maryland and Virginia, that coastal vessels brought in slaves to be held in slave pens like the one just off Lafayette Square in front of the White House, that both public and private construction work here often was done by hired slave labor.

And yet, the city also was a mecca for free blacks—123 in 1800; 1,796 by 1820; 3,129 by 1830; 8,158 by 1850; and 9,200 by 1860, the year before the Civil War broke out.

To be free as a black, however, was not quite the same as to be free, period.

By law in Washington in 1808, no black, free or slave, could walk around alone after ten o'clock at night. Four years later, free blacks had to register with the city government and always carry a "freedom certificate" showing they were not runaway slaves.

Later still, free black families had to post $500 bonds backed by two whites (male, that is). And Congress went so far as to ban blacks from the Capitol and its grounds unless they could show that some legitimate "business" took them there.

Even so, blacks from 1800 to the time of the Civil War made up one-fourth to one-third of the city's population, (60,000 total in 1860), with the number of free blacks overtaking the number of slaves as early as 1830.

Some of the free blacks were homeowners, a few were professionals or business owners, but most blacks were laborers or servants. By and large, blacks and whites tended to live in separate black or white neighborhoods.

But not always without tension. . . . Virginia's Nat Turner Rebellion of 1831 resulted in new restrictions on the federal city's black population, and ugly vigilantism appeared after a slave allegedly attacked a prominent white woman. White mobs attacked schools, churches, and tenement houses, their actions known as the "Snow Riot" because they broke into the black-owned Beverly Snow restaurant and destroyed its furnishings. A spate of new laws forbade black ownership of restaurants, but these eased shortly afterward; another black entrepreneur reopened the smashed-up Snow establishment and ran it for twenty more years.

President Madison's body servant and slave Paul Jennings, meanwhile, stayed with Madison long past their White House years, until Madison's death at Montpelier in 1836. It apparently was a happy association. "Mr. Madison, I think, was one of the best men that ever lived," wrote Jennings later. "I never saw him in a passion, and never knew him to strike a slave, although he had over one hundred."

After Madison's death, Jennings remained with an ever-poorer Dolley Madison when she moved back to Washington to live on Lafayette Square. He was still a slave then, but arrangements were made to have an insurance man buy him for $200 and later sell him to Daniel Webster for $120. Webster then freed Jennings on the understanding that Jennings would work for him and pay off the $120 at the rate of $8 a month.

With Dolley "in a state of absolute poverty," wrote Jennings, he often took her a market basket of provisions at Webster's instigation, and he sometimes gave her "small sums of money from my own pocket."

The freed black Jennings later was one of the chief plotters organizing a mass escape of slaves from forty-one owners in Washington, Georgetown, and Alexandria by means of the Potomac River schooner *Pearl.* Unfortunately, the *Pearl* was becalmed downriver at Point Lookout the next morning, even as the shocked slaveowners gathered a posse back in Washington.

The posse gave chase in a steamer, after a black informer told them where the missing slaves had gone. The recaptured fugitives (and some free blacks with them) were severely punished. Northerners were shocked—Harriet Beecher Stowe, author of *Uncle Tom's Cabin,* among them. In 1850, meanwhile, slave trading finally was abolished in Washington by law.

Jennings almost was a victim of the *Pearl* fiasco himself. Planning to go with the schooner and its escaping passengers, he had left his benefactor Daniel Webster a note apologizing for leaving "with so little ceremony"—in secret, that is. But he felt so bad that he returned to Webster's house before the *Pearl* sailed and took back his note before Webster ever saw it.

Jennings, incidentally, is credited with writing the first insider memoir to come out of the White House. He says it wasn't Dolley Madison who rescued the Gilbert Stuart portrait of George Washington from the British in 1814, but rather it was the White House gardener and doorkeeper who did the rescuing . . . perhaps at her order?

Presidential Spy Plane

HERE WAS THE PLAN: SINCE the high-flying U-2 spy plane wasn't getting real close-up photos of Soviet military and missile installations, let's outfit the official presidential jet with spy cameras, too. After all, President Dwight D. Eisenhower will be flying into Moscow for an unprecedented presidential visit to the USSR right after his Big Powers summit meeting in Paris with Nikita Khrushchev, right?

That, in the spring of 1960, really was the plan. That really was the explanation for the Central Intelligence Agency's technicians swarming around Ike's recently delivered Boeing 707 in a hangar out at Andrews Air Force Base and, in the utmost secrecy, installing the cameras.

That potentially explosive possibility really was the CIA scheme until, irony of ironies, the world was stunned to learn the Russians had shot down an American U-2 spy plane flying over the USSR itself. The shoot-down and capture of pilot Francis Gary Powers came just when President Eisenhower was preparing for the crucial summit meeting in Paris, to be followed by the flight to Moscow. And all at the height of the Cold War.

With the various agencies of the Eisenhower administration offering up clumsy cover stories to offset the Soviet U-2 claim, many onlookers at first didn't believe it was true. Others, ignoring the Soviet Union's own systematic program of espionage, were quick to condemn the spy effort. Still others were simply amazed to learn the highly secret, high-flying U-2 had been overflying Soviet territory with apparent impunity for the past four years.

As one outcome, Khrushchev, sputtering and angry, walked out of the Paris summit. A disappointed Ike had to turn for home in his presidential jet—perhaps himself unaware of its secret load of reconnaissance cameras. The Moscow visit, of course, had been scrubbed . . . and just as well at that.

Just as well, because of the possible ramifications had an accident or other means of disclosure somehow revealed that the traveling president's official plane was equipped with high-resolution cameras and that the cameras were busily filming the ground below as Ike's big jet flew over the Soviet countryside and into the cities on his itinerary. Hadn't the inflammable Khrushchev already warned of possible war if the U-2 overflights were continued?

He had, with Eisenhower firmly retorting that the Soviet leader's reaction to the "unarmed, nonmilitary" U-2 "can only reflect a fetish of secrecy."

While the U-2 incident fueled headlines around the world, the CIA's additional plan to convert Ike's own aircraft into a spy plane initially remained under wraps. The cameras were removed with the advent of the Kennedy Administration in 1961, according to the 1979 book *The Flying White House: The Story of Air Force One* by J. E. terHorst and a former presidential pilot, Air Force Colonel Ralph Albertazzie.

Their account recalls the assignment of the big and then-new 707 jet in 1959 as the American president's official airplane, replacing the Lockheed four-engine Super Constellation *Columbine II* that had succeeded Harry Truman's DC-6 the *Independence,* which in turn had taken the place of FDR's prop-driven, Douglas-built *Sacred Cow.* The upshot here is that Ike became the first U.S. president to fly by jet airplane . . . and he loved it!

As he later wrote in his memoir *Waging Peace,* "Both in size and speed the new airplane completely dwarfed the *Columbine,* the Super Constellation that we had long considered the last word in luxurious transportation."

Mamie Eisenhower wasn't so easily impressed. As her presidential husband explained, "[N]o airplane ever looked attractive to Mamie." But Ike found his first jet-powered flight aboard the Boeing 707 "an exhilarating experience . . . with its silent, effortless acceleration and its rapid rate of climb."

Naturally, too, the faster, more efficient presidential airplane had immediate impact upon presidential air travel inclinations. Citing a study by Air Force Major Robert Mikesh, the terHorst-Albertazzie book said: "Using conventional piston-driven airplanes, Eisenhower had averaged approximately 120 hours of flying time a year, covering about 30,000 air miles. But with the use of jet aircraft in his last year in office—1960—Ike's air time increased by 62 percent (193 hours) and his air mileage rose by 262 percent (78,677 miles)!"

Meanwhile, another American advance in air travel had been taking place—in secret to the American public. That was the development of the superlight U-2, an aircraft able to fly immense distances at eighty-thousand feet or more.

Carrying high-resolution cameras that could show the lines of the spaces in an ordinary parking lot from its high altitude, the U-2 had been cruising above the Soviet Union on a regular basis since 1956—with Ike's full knowledge and approval. The post-World War II Soviet Union was, after all, an increasingly aggressive dictatorship newly armed with the stolen secrets of the American atomic bomb, with new-found missile capability and who-knows-what hostile ambitions. The same Cold War adversary had subjugated Eastern Europe, forced the West into supplying an isolated West Berlin by means of the extraordinary Berlin Airlift (1949), and had supported the North Koreans in their reckless adventure against South Korea (1950–1953).

By 1960, moreover, Russian satellites were whirring above American territory several times a day, while on the ground all kinds of spies did their silent work on behalf of Moscow. A recruit once told FBI interrogators that he was ordered to a city street corner in the Midwest one day to report if a truck carrying a U. S. missile passed that corner at a certain time. It did.

So it was that affable Ike, more of a realist than his critics would have guessed, not only approved the start of the U-2 flights but often went over a given mission's flight plan in person. "Before each flight," wrote Eisenhower biographer Stephen Ambrose, an intelligence adviser "would draw up on a map the proposed flight plan and spread it out on the president's desk." In the discussion that followed, Ike would say things like, "Well, you can go there, but I want you to leave out that leg and go straight that way. I want you to go from B to D because it looks to me like you might be getting a little exposed over here."

Actually, "exposed" was not a major worry since the U-2 flew above the range of Soviet fighter planes and, U. S. planners thought, above the range of surface-to-air missiles and ground-radar units. Thus, the Eisenhower administration's inner circle was startled soon after the overflights began to receive a private complaint from the Russians—their radar apparently *did* allow them to see the high-flying U-2 after all. Still, they couldn't shoot it down, and the overflights continued despite the protest—until the day that Francis Gary Powers was shot down in 1960, by a missile.

The CIA, in the meantime, had viewed Ike's planned trip to the

USSR as a prime opportunity to supplement the high-altitude U-2 photos with close-in shots taken as the presidential jet winged its way to Moscow and possibly Leningrad, along with stops in the Black Sea area or other points of interest to the intelligence experts. "It would be extremely valuable if the President's aircraft could photograph Soviet antimissile defense installations around the cities he would visit," wrote the authors of *Flying White House.* "Indeed, even aerial photos of bridges, road networks, rail lines, and the physical layout of Moscow and other cities would be valuable to the CIA and the Defense Department."

Moving Ike's Boeing 707 into a special hangar, a CIA team fell to work preparing the sleek jet for the surreptitious Operation Lida Rose, a name "borrowed from a hit song in the Broadway show *The Music Man*—a tune, ironically, that Ike liked."

The CIA workers installed the high-resolution cameras and their electronic controls in a secret compartment in the belly of the plane. An innocent-looking "fresh air valve" accessible to the occupant of the co-pilot's seat in the cockpit would "open and activate the big cameras hidden in the belly compartment below."

Further, a sequence of pinhead lights installed on the copilot's side of the plane's magnetic compass would signify how the camera equipment was working.

"By watching the sequence lights on the compass as he adjusted the fresh air valve, the co-pilot was able to determine—in one, two, three fashion—that the camera compartment doors were open, that the camera was in position, and that it was functioning," said the *Flying White House* book. "When the co-pilot decided he had shot sufficient film, he again adjusted the fresh air valve. . . . When the last light winked out, he knew the compartment doors had closed, the cameras were safely hidden from view, and everything was back to normal again."

As stated, the president's "spy mission" never did take place. U-2 pilot Powers was shot down May 1, 1960. An embarrassed and angry Eisenhower did go to the Paris Big Powers summit meeting anyway, only to see Khrushchev explode and walk out May 15.

"The summit was over before it started, all hopes for detente and disarmament gone with it," wrote Ambrose in his biography, *Eisenhower.* "Eisenhower, with only eight months to serve, would not have another chance to force progress toward genuine peace." At the same time, he canceled any further U-2 flights over the Soviet

Union for the remainder of his term as president, but that was not a complete loss, since American reconnaissance satellites appeared in the skies over the Soviet Union in August 1960.

Ironically, noted *Flying White House* authors terHorst and Albertazzie, the Russians were suspected of routinely using the same sort of hidden cameras in the Soviet aircraft ferrying their personnel to the United Nations in New York—and most likely in the big TU-114 that carried Khrushchev to the United States for a lengthy visit in 1959.

As one further irony, when the Soviets later released captured U-2 pilot Powers it was in exchange for a captured Soviet spy, Colonel Rudolf Abel.

Newspaper artists A. Berghaus and C. Upham combined efforts to produce this depiction of the pandemonium that broke out at the Baltimore and Ohio railroad depot in Washington, D.C., seconds after an assassin shot and fatally wounded President James A. Garfield in 1881. (Leslie's Illustrated, July 16, 1881. *American Memory Collections, Library of Congress)*

III: Ends

"... a fantastic discovery. We were free—as only private citizens in a democratic nation can be free!"

—Dwight D. Eisenhower in his book, *Waging Peace*

Leavetakings

LEAVETAKINGS. ALWAYS SO HARD FOR almost anyone. Sentimental at the least. Ronald Reagan left a note for George Bush in the top desk drawer in the Oval Office. Prayers and thoughts. Then went back the morning of Inauguration Day 1989 for a last look. He placed both hands on the desk and bowed his head, then he walked out the door leading to the Rose Garden.

At the door, pause, a last look back.

Gerald Ford, giving way to Jimmy Carter, heard the latter's inaugural speech and then flew to California, where he was hitting golf balls before day's end. He played in the Bing Crosby Pro-Am Tournament at Pebble Beach the very next day. Arnie Palmer was his partner.

Didn't matter all that much?

Well . . . before leaving Washington, he directed his helicopter pilot "to make one last swing over the White House and the Capitol," reported Henry F. Rosenthal for the Associated Press in 1989.

Harry Truman, the same story recalled, took the train home to Independence, Missouri, and began the chores of carrying the luggage or fetching the newspaper from his front yard himself. A concession to Secret Service concerns about protection was the addition of a fence in front of the unpretentious Truman home at 219 North Delaware Street.

Dwight Eisenhower was chauffeur-driven to the farm in Gettysburg and "a couple of days later" was off shooting quail in Georgia.

Iran's release—at last!—of the American hostages it had held so long in the latter half of Jimmy Carter's one-term presidency came five minutes into Ronald Reagan's presidency, and presumably Carter didn't have to do anything at all about them. No longer his problem.

But he flew off to Germany to greet the newly released hostages anyway, despite the exhaustion and badly needed sleep it cost him.

In an earlier day, an ever-so-courteous Martin Van Buren walked

along Pennsylvania Avenue to the Capitol in 1841 to attend successor William Henry Harrison's inauguration, and a bitter, cold day it
was, too. Among the first to shake his triumphant opponent's hand,
Van Buren then watched the exultant crowds from a friend's house
and, later, took a train home, back to New York State.

Harrison had planned to run again, but in a month he died of
pneumonia blamed on the weather on Inauguration Day. John Tyler
moved up to president, but the Democrats next time nominated neither him nor Van Buren, but rather James K. Polk.

After his one term in office, he and Mrs. Polk spent the night
before Zachary Taylor's 1849 inauguration at the nearby Willard
Hotel. Busy until the last minute signing papers and legislative bills,
Polk strolled through the empty White House the day before Taylor's
advent, happy at the thought of being "free from all public cares."

After Taylor suddenly died in office in 1850, Millard Fillmore
took over. In short order he gladly attended the fetes honoring his
successor, Franklin Pierce, on the latter's Inauguration Day in 1853.
In another antebellum leavetaking, Pierce gave way to James
Buchanan and with fond nostalgia said goodbye inaugural morning
to a cabinet that included Pierce's good friend the future president
of the Confederacy, Jefferson Davis. When Buchanan, slowed by illness, didn't appear at the White House, Pierce hopped into his own
carriage, proceeded to Buchanan's National Hotel lodgings and conveyed Buchanan to the Capitol for his inauguration.

It was Buchanan, of course, who then turned over the White
House in 1861 to perhaps its most towering occupant ever,
Abraham Lincoln. And Buchanan did the amenities to the end, even
with civil war brewing. Buchanan stood by as Lincoln delivered his
first inaugural speech at the Capitol in a cold wind. Buchanan then
returned to the White House with the newly sworn president. Just
inside the door, before they reached the public rooms and the waiting crowds, Buchanan halted. He said his goodbye to Lincoln and
left the gaunt, black-suited figure to his—and the nation's—destiny.

Much earlier, the nation's only father-and-son presidents each
managed, not entirely by accident, to skip the inaugural events
attending the ascension of a successor. John Adams, who had complained to Thomas Jefferson, "You have put me out!" rose in the
early-morning blackness of Jefferson's Inauguration Day in 1801 in
order to leave the White House and the still primitive capital city.
Traveling by horse-drawn coach, he took twelve days to reach home

in Quincy, Massachusetts. Later, his son John Quincy Adams moved out of the White House the night before Andrew Jackson's inauguration in 1829. Taking up residence in a private home on Meridian Hill in Washington, John Quincy went horseback riding the next day, while exultant mobs trampled the White House grounds, even its interior rooms, in celebration of Old Hickory's ascent to power.

More than a century later, Richard M. Nixon would be the first president to resign from office. As he spent his last night in the White House, family, staff, and the American public all were fully aware of his announced resignation because of the Watergate scandal, which had left him under threat of impeachment. The next day, before Vice President Gerald Ford's midday swearing-in as the new president, Nixon said his good-byes to tearful staff and administration figures. The Fords would not actually move in, though, until David Eisenhower and his wife, Julie Nixon Eisenhower, grandson and daughter of presidents, could finish packing up the Nixon belongings and memorabilia. For now, August 9, 1974, Jerry and Betty Ford walked to the White House helicopter pad with the downhearted Pat and Richard Nixon, the two wives behind the men, arm in arm, and Pat Nixon said: "My heavens, they've even rolled out the red carpet for us, isn't that something?"

But then she thought and said to her successor as first lady: "Well, Betty, you'll see many of these red carpets, and you'll get so you'll hate 'em."

The Nixon chopper took off from the White House grounds at eleven o'clock that Friday morning.

Shortly afterwards, as determined by the protocol experts orchestrating the unprecedented scenario, Nixon's formal written resignation was presented to the secretary of state, Henry Kissinger. And at noon, Ford, accompanied by his wife, Betty, followed Chief Justice Warren Burger into the East Room of the White House to be sworn in as America's thirty-eighth president.

Nixon Resigns

There was no talk. There were no tears left. I leaned my head back against the seat and closed my eyes. I heard Pat saying to no one in particular, "It's so sad. It's so sad."

They were in *Marine One,* the presidential helicopter, and they were leaving the White House that had been their home for more than five years.

Roll back a couple of minutes. Framed by the chopper doorway behind. *I raised my arms in final salute. I smiled. I waved goodbye. I turned into the helicopter, the door was closed, the red carpet was rolled up. The engines started. The blades began to turn. The noise grew until it almost blotted out thought.*

In seconds they were rising. *The people on the ground below were waving. Then we turned. The White House was behind us now. We were flying low next to the Washington Monument. Another swing and the Tidal Basin was beneath us and the Jefferson Memorial.*

What sharp, painful memories, frozen in place forever, he would write in *The Memoirs of Richard Nixon,* images such as *the red carpet, the green lawn, the white house, the leaden sky. The starched uniforms and polished shoes of the honor guard. The new President and his First Lady. Julie. David. Rose. So many friends. The crowd, covering the lawn, spilling out onto the balconies, leaning out of the windows. Silent, waving, crying. The elegant curve of the South Portico: balcony above balcony. Someone waving a white handkerchief from the window of the Lincoln Bedroom. The flag on top of the House, hanging limp in the windless, cheerless morning.*

It was a hot August day in 1974. Pat, Tricia, and her husband, Edward Cox, were already inside the chopper. Just seconds before, the Nixons, Pat and Dick, followed by Julie and husband David Eisenhower, accompanied by Gerald and Betty Ford, had walked the red carpet to the helicopter that would whisk Richard

Milhous Nixon away from his presidency, the only man ever to resign from it.

Roll back now, to the night before. Virtually certain to be impeached by the House of Representatives in the wake of the Watergate scandal, Nixon had gone on national television to announce his decision to resign. *Two minutes before nine o'clock I went into the Oval Office. I sat in my chair behind the desk while the technicians adjusted the lighting and made their voice check.*

At forty-five seconds after nine, the red light on the camera facing my desk went on—it was time to speak to America and the world.

Framed by the doorway of Marine One, this was the dramatic tableau as the Richard M. Nixons left the White House to the Gerald R. Fords in August, 1974, as climax to the Watergate affair that drove Nixon from office. (Courtesy Richard M. Nixon Library)

The family would be watching on the television sets in the family quarters . . . *they wanted to be in the Oval Office when I delivered the speech so that the whole world could see they were with me. I said it was simply out of the question, because I would not be able to get through the speech without breaking up if they were even nearby.*

Rose, that's presidential personal secretary Rose Mary Woods, said they had anticipated this and would be happy just to be next door, in an adjoining room. *I asked her to explain that this was something I would have to do alone, and, as a favor to me, to ask them to stay in the Residence and watch the speech from there.*

She then reported that a leader among the POWs from the Vietnam War had called—in tears—to argue against resigning. *I had not given up on them, he had said, and they would not give up on me.*

Rough day, all day. August 8, 1974, the last full day as president. *As on other mornings of my presidency, I walked through the colonnade that had been designed by Thomas Jefferson, through the Rose Garden, and into the Oval Office.* Vice President Gerald Ford had paid a late-morning visit in the Oval Office. He knew the score. Gray suit, somber. Sat down next to the big desk. Silence for a moment. Then they talked. Nixon thought Jerry Ford would measure up. He even said, "Jerry, I know you'll do a good job." *We talked about the problems he would face as soon as he became president in almost exactly twenty-four hours.*

At noon, Ford rose to go. They walked to the office door together. Oh, where would the swearing in take place? Interesting question. *He said that he had decided not to go to the Capitol because his former colleagues there might turn the occasion into some kind of celebration. I said that I planned to be gone by noon; if he liked, he could be sworn-in in the White House, as Truman had been.*

At the door, Nixon recalled Dwight Eisenhower's statement the night of Nixon's first election that henceforward "Dick" Nixon, once Eisenhower's vice president, would be "Mr. President," even to Eisenhower himself. And now Nixon was telling Jerry Ford the same thing. Jerry would be "Mr. President," even to Nixon. *Ford's eyes filled with tears—and mine did as well—as we lingered a moment at the door. I thanked him for his loyal support over the last painful weeks and months. I said that he would have my prayers in the days and years ahead.*

It was to be a day of many tears, many struggles to hold back the flood. After working on the resignation speech during the afternoon, it was time to visit the second-floor family residence, to prepare, change clothes. *Packing boxes lined the halls of the Family Quarters. I shaved and showered and then picked out the suit and tie that I had worn in Moscow in 1972 when I delivered my speech on television to the Soviet people. It was slate blue, light in texture, and consequently cool under the hot television lights.*

Not only the speech lay ahead, but final meetings with the cabinet and the Democrat-dominated congressional leadership. Republican Richard M. Nixon met with the leadership first, at 7:30 P.M. Not in the Oval Office, but in the study-like office he had maintained as a quiet retreat in the Executive Office Building (EOB) next to the White House. Mixed reactions—some of the leaders cordial, fairly sympathetic, others noncommittal, diffident.

Right afterward came the session with cabinet members, deputies, aides, in the Cabinet Room close to the Oval Office itself . . . a far different atmosphere prevailing. *Forty-six men were crowded around the table and in the chairs along the walls. Forty-six friends and colleagues in countless causes over three decades. Some of these men had already been in the House for years before I arrived as a freshman from Whittier; some of them had arrived with me in 1947, full of hopes and dreams and plans for America. Together over the past five and a half years we had worked together time and again to form a slim but sturdy coalition that repeatedly beat back the Goliath of liberal Democrats and liberal Republicans in the Senate and the House.*

This was a tough meeting. Diffidence had almost been better. Nixon talked about their shared "great moments," about the issues they fought for, the policy initiatives they had forged together. He said he would stay and fight the impeachment juggernaut, but "a six-month trial in the Senate was too long for the country." The presidency was more important than his own political fate. They should now give Jerry Ford all their allegiance, affection, support, and prayer.

A tough meeting all right. *The emotional level in the room was almost unbearable. I could see that many were crying. I looked at my watch. It was approaching 8:30. I had been talking for almost half an hour. When I heard Les Arends, one of my closest and dearest friends, sobbing with grief, I could no longer control my own emotions, and I broke into tears.*

One last thought. *"I just hope that I haven't let you down," I said, as I tried to stand up. Everyone was jammed together so tightly that my chair would not move, and Bill Timmons had to pull it back for me. I left the room.*

Then came the resignation speech, live and on national television. Secretary of State Henry Kissinger walked Nixon back to the

White House proper from the Oval Office in the West Wing, passing the now-dark Rose Garden. They had been close, very close. His voice in praise of the speech was "low and sad."

Nixon left him and proceeded through a still and darkened hallway to the elevator that would carry him up to the Family Quarters. *When the doors opened on the second floor, the family was all waiting there to meet me. I walked over to them. Pat put her arms around me. Tricia, Julie. Ed. David. Slowly, instinctively, we embraced in a tender huddle, drawn together by love and faith.*

As they all sat talking a few minutes later, Nixon suddenly began to "shake violently." Tricia, quickly holding him close, said he was soaked with perspiration ..."coming clear through your coat!" *I told them not to worry. I had perspired heavily during the speech, and I must have caught a chill walking over from the office. In a minute it passed.*

They talked on. For the most part, they talked about the media reactions to the resignation announcement. At first mostly favorable, but "within a few hours came the second thoughts, negative and critical." Outside, on Pennsylvania Avenue, a crowd chanted, "Jail to the Chief."

Nixon ordered some bacon and eggs, which he ate in the Lincoln Sitting Room. He was up until 1:30 A.M. making phone calls to friends and supporters around the country.

After a short sleep, he was up again before 6 A.M. It now was August 9, 1974, his last day in the White House ... this one not even a full day. He indulged in a favorite breakfast—poached eggs and corned beef hash. Again in the Lincoln Sitting Room.

He took a yellow pad and tried to write down some thoughts for his next farewell, this one to administration officials, White House staff and, once again, cabinet members, all to be gathered in the spacious East Room at 9:30 A.M. First, though, White House Chief of Staff Alexander Haig intruded on a difficult errand. "This is something that will have to be done, Mr. President," he said, "and I thought you would rather do it now." He offered a single sheet of paper. It bore a single sentence. Nixon signed it: "I hereby resign the Office of President of the United States." *It would be delivered in a few hours, at 11:35 a.m. on the 2,027th day of my presidency.*

Next came the farewell to the residence staff, up there on the second floor, the family gathered 'round, too—Pat in a dress of pale pink and white. *She was wearing dark glasses to hide the signs of the two sleepless nights of preparations and the tears that Julie said had finally come that morning. I knew how much courage she had needed to carry her through the days and nights of preparations for this abrupt departure. Now she would not receive any of the praise she deserved. There would be no round of farewell parties by congressional wives, no testimonials, no tributes. She had been a dignified, compassionate First Lady. She had given so much to the nation and so much to the world. Now she would have to share my exile. She deserved so much more.*

Like the crowded cabinet meeting the evening before, the farewell in the East Room the morning of departure was a highly emotional moment. In contrast to his "formal speech for history" the night before, Nixon tried to make his remarks in the East Room setting personal and intimate "to these people who had worked so hard for me and whom I had let down so badly."

What an ending. *This was the nightmare end of a long dream. I had come so far from the little house in Yorba Linda to this great house in Washington. I thought about my parents and tried to tell these people about them.* Humble, decent folk, too.

Battling a "floodtide of emotions," Richard Nixon tried to find words that could inspire his saddened listeners. He hoped to avoid any platitudes. He urged them to look to the future beyond the painful moment. He quoted a young Teddy Roosevelt's thought that the "light" in his life had gone out with the death of his first wife after childbirth. TR, of course, went on, to find a new wife, to have new children, to become president, even to assume legendary historical stature.

Finally, the East Room farewell was over. *We stepped down from the platform. People were clapping and crying as we went by.*

Next, the end clearly in sight, on to the ground-floor Diplomatic Reception Room. Jerry and Betty Ford were there. Waiting. Ready to take over from Dick and Pat Nixon. The two men shook hands. Again Nixon told Ford he would do just fine as president, the country would be in "good hands."

Marine One was waiting out on the South Lawn. *We walked out under the canopy and started down the long red carpet that led to the steps of* Marine One.... *Then we were there, quickly shaking hands with Jerry—Pat embracing Betty—kissing Julie—saying goodbye to David.* (David and Julie Nixon Eisenhower were staying behind to pack up the Nixon belongings and make room for the incoming Fords.)

Suddenly, Nixon was alone, framed by the chopper doorway, Pat, Ed and Tricia already inside. There he was, at the top of the steps, standing, looking back one last time.

That was the scene frozen in his memory forever. Red carpet, white house . . . green lawn, leaden sky. And the uniformed honor guard, the people, the crowd, the last goodbyes at the foot of the steps. The faces in the White House windows. "Silent, waving, crying." Who could it have been waving that white handkerchief from the window in the Lincoln Bedroom?

Raised arms in final salute, then into the helicopter cabin. In moments, up and away. No talk, no tears. Eyes closed and head pressed back against the seat. Pat saying it's so sad, it's so sad. All those landmarks left behind with every swing of the flying machine.

Another swing, and we were on course for Andrews, where Air Force One *was waiting for the flight home to California.*

Ford Theatre Aftermath

WHAT WOULD HAPPEN, SAY YOU, the moment after Abraham Lincoln was shot by his assassin? The chronicler in this case is Walt Whitman, and he first makes note that it was in a momentary stop of the stage business that the muffled shot was heard. First, as he says, there was that pause on stage at Ford's Theatre. A sort of hush. "At this period came the murder of Abraham Lincoln. Great as that was, with all its manifold train, circling around it, and stretching into the future for many a century, in the politics, history, art, of the New World, in point of fact the main thing, the actual murder, transpired with the quiet and simplicity of any commonest occurrence—the bursting of a bud or pod in the growth of vegetation, for instance. Through the general hum following the stage pause, with the change of positions [on stage], came the muted sound of a pistol shot, which not one hundredth part of the audience heard at the time—and yet a moment's hush—somehow, surely a vague startled thrill—and then, through the ornamented, draperied, starred and striped space-way of the President's box. . . ."

Appeared and leaped to the stage, fifteen feet below, while also spraining his ankle . . . John Wilkes Booth, of course. Who then faced the audience and mouthed his words attempting to justify the insane intent for himself, *Sic semper tyrannis.* And then, he is gone, into history. . . .

But in the theater, among those left behind, stunned, uncomprehending, what of them? What then? With the grievously wounded Lincoln slumped over but still living?

By Walt Whitman's account, there was the startling appearance of Booth and still another moment's hush . . . perhaps even the same one now twice punctuated—by the shot and by Booth's leaping flight. And now came the reaction! Mary Todd Lincoln's piercing cry, "Murder!" And, "He has killed the President!" Her cry and her leaning from the box and pointing to the departing Booth.

And next, confusion . . . pandemonium in Ford's Theatre. A storm of noise—"the people burst through chairs and railings, and break them up." In the turmoil also, women faint, the feeble are trampled underfoot. And there is a rush to the stage, quickly filled, many of the actors and actresses mixed with the howling mob and terrified, while some pass water up from the stage to the stricken man's box, and others try to climb up there, too.

A crowd of soldiers—Whitman calls them the president's guard—now burst and storm into the theater, two hundred strong and in absolute fury, charging the audience "with fixed bayonets, muskets and pistols, shouting Clear out! Clear out! You sons of. . . ."

And outside, with the chase beginning in earnest for Booth and his co-conspirators, the infuriated crowds are looking, too, on their own, wild with fury, and ready to punish on the spot. They "come near to committing murder several times on innocent individuals," wrote Whitman. In one case, the police must rescue a man being dragged to his own hanging from a nearby lamppost. They keep him in custody all night long at a station house for his own protection.

All night, too, in the Peterson residence across the street, the stricken president hovers between life and death . . . until death ends his struggle. RIP.

"You Yellow Rat!"

WARREN G. HARDING MAY HAVE "looked like a President," as his own attorney general once said, but as president, this twentieth-century occupant of the White House ran up a remarkable scorecard of scandals, albeit not all of his own doing.

He alone, of course, would be the one responsible for his extramarital affair with Nan Britton, but most, if not all, of the monetary conniving associated with his administration was done by others. One such case, the Teapot Dome scandal, is probably better known today than is Harding himself. It's just that Harding, generally described as genial (and unthinking) in the extreme, was not very astute in his choice of associates, such as cabinet members. He picked a one-time army deserter to be head of the Veterans Bureau, while for secretary of the interior, he chose an oil and land speculator. The same supposed protector, Albert Fall, was the very man who secretly leased government lands to oil speculators in the Teapot Dome scandal.

Naive or gullible he might have been about his associates, but Harding himself contributed to a certain White House and administration "atmosphere." About twice a week an early dinner at the White House was followed by a lively poker game. While poker itself may not seem so very terrible, it often means gambling, and in the Harding White House it was gambling indeed, no holds barred. Inside the venerable President's House.

One time Harding told visiting newspaperman Louis Seibold that the very fine pearl tie-pin adorning the Harding tie had been won at a poker game the previous Wednesday night. Seibold, who himself was sporting a pearl pin, could see that Harding's was worth $4,000 or more. Harding explained that he had won it with a four of spades in a side bet with one of his poker pals, against a $100 stake. As Seibold also knew, in that same poker game had been a cabinet official and other VIPs.

In his own bumbling way, it often is suggested, Warren Harding tried. He did reach out and name Charles Evans Hughes, Herbert

Hoover, and Andrew Mellon to his cabinet . . . as the stars of his cabinet. But then, as counterbalance better remembered today, there were the hacks—his attorney general, the one who said Harding's best qualification was *looking* like a president, was Harry Daugherty, a big business lobbyist.

Apparently sleepwalking through his White House years, Harding later would protest, "Some day the people will understand what some of my erstwhile friends have done to me in these critical times when I depended so much upon them."

But that was late in his administration. At first Harding was not so troubled by the failings of his friends. From the outset, he was simply a genial fellow from Ohio who welcomed public contact. He had the Marine Band play on the White House lawn, and at 12:30 most days he shook hands with unscreened visitors. To staff protests that such hospitality was too time-consuming, he simply said: "I love to meet people. It is the most pleasant thing I do; it is really the only fun I have. It does not tax me and it seems to be a very great pleasure to them."

One time, finding Harding spending valuable time answering trivial letters, Columbia University president Nicholas Murray Butler said it was silly for a president to devote himself to such minor things. "I suppose so," Harding allegedly said, "but I am not fit for this office and should never have been here."

But he was . . . and when one scandal, then another, began to come to his attention, Harding at first refused to believe the allegations against his poker pals. When one of them, Attorney General Daugherty, finally revealed the indiscretions of the Veterans Bureau chief Charlie Forbes, the worm turned.

Angry at first, Harding wouldn't communicate with Daugherty for two days. But when an investigation of Forbes showed that the charges against him were true, Harding was, in his own word, "heartsick."

How much so was revealed a day later, when a White House visitor climbing the stairs to the second floor was startled to hear Harding's voice raised in anger and, in a nearby room, to see the president himself apparently throttling a man. Harding shouted, "You yellow rat! You double-crossing bastard! If you ever—"

Harding then spotted the intruding visitor and curtly directed him to an adjacent room. On the way out later, the visitor was told the man with Harding earlier had been "Colonel Forbes of the Veterans Bureau."

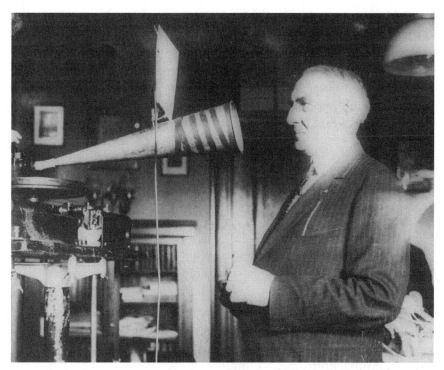

Before television and videos, phonograph recordings of a president's voice joined the written word, artistic renderings, and photography as the historical record. Here, Warren G. Harding is seen speaking into a recording machine of the 1920s. (National Photo Company Collection, American Memory Collections, Library of Congress)

Forbes then went to Europe and after Congress began to mount an investigation of his activities, he resigned while still in Paris.

Meanwhile, history may never know the substance of a coded message Harding received while traveling by ship off the West Coast in 1923. Was it about more of the still-brewing scandals? Whatever it was, Harding "suffered something of a collapse" after reading the message, wrote biographer Samuel Hopkins Adams. "For the rest of the day he seemed half stunned, muttering to himself and breaking off to ask whoever was with him what a President should do when his friends were false."

Several days later, after he made "listless" public appearances, Harding refused to go on deck when his vessel, the *Henderson,* collided with a U.S. Navy destroyer in Puget Sound. Lying in bed, hands covering his face, he said, "I hope the boat sinks."

His secretary of commerce (and later president), Herbert

Hoover, recalled frantic, endless bridge games—Harding would play with any and all willing to sit at the game table with him, around the clock. After that trip, Hoover never could play bridge again.

Arriving in Seattle, Harding stumbled through two speeches. On Sunday, July 29, he was in San Francisco, visibly ill, perhaps from stomach trouble, perhaps from a heart attack. On Friday, August 3, he died in his hotel room of an apparent stroke. No autopsy. So, who knows?

In Order to Stop Speeders

THE MANDATE FROM THE PRESIDENT to his Secret Service entourage was absolutely clear—stop those speeders on the road with the presidential limousine. Chase them down, take them into custody, and bring them back for questioning.

It was in the twilight of Wilson's presidency, after his severe stroke and before he left office. For some reason, when well enough to go out in his limousine at all, he was greatly disturbed by speed . . . his or anybody else's.

As noted in *One Night Stands with American History* by Richard Shenkman and Kurt Reiger (and *When the Cheering Stopped* by Gene Smith), Wilson told his drivers to go no faster than fifteen or twenty miles per hour. But then he noticed all those other motorists whizzing by at far greater speeds.

After enduring this development for a short while, he ordered his Secret Service escorts to take action: pursue the cars passing the presidential entourage and bring back their drivers. Bring 'em back alive, presumably.

Oddly enough, when the Secret Service agents dutifully set off in pursuit, they never seemed to get their man (or woman, for that matter). According to the Gene Smith account, "[T]hey always returned empty-handed, saying they had been unable to overtake the speeder."

Obviously, they were merely humoring the pitifully incapacitated president. But he, meanwhile, would not let the issue go. It wasn't long before he was writing his administration's attorney general to ask if a sitting president had the powers of a justice of the peace. Wilson's idea now was to arrest the speeders himself and try them on the spot . . . on the road.

Naturally, nothing ever came of that notion either. No speeders were brought before the bar in the roadside court of President Woodrow Wilson. No speeders were ever arrested by Wilson's escorts. "Eventually," wrote Smith, "the Secret Service persuaded Wilson that it would be inappropriate for a president of the United States personally to try the cases of speeding drivers."

Naturally, such odd behavior by a man in declining health was, if pitiful, also harmless enough taken by itself. The real issue that has bothered most thinking persons ever since the last months of the Wilson presidency is the frightening specter of a mentally incapacitated president occupying the White House at a time of major crisis and danger to the national interest. Obviously, a president so consumed with the notion of catching the speeders on the streets of Washington, D.C., would not inspire confidence in a major crisis.

Midcentury Melodrama

BETWEEN THE WAR OF 1812 and the Civil War, the White House and its occupants went through more improbable real-life dramas than a soap opera would ever dare to emulate. The personages who stepped in and out of the picture during the same period were "names" we now look back upon as towering, strangely unreal giants of history.

It is difficult for us today to imagine how small America once was in population, how young it was, too. In the political leadership that either resided in or passed through Washington in the first half of the nineteenth century, there were many who had known George Washington personally. Their generation was just giving way to another that would know Abraham Lincoln, Robert E. Lee, or Jefferson Davis personally. Some would have brushed elbows with them all!

Nor do we always remember how very human these legendary figures once were, the fact they were people who, like us, ate their three squares a day and enjoyed their creature comforts, even if there wasn't always running hot water.

We must assume that Henry Clay, Daniel Webster, and John C. Calhoun fell into that same category, along with the presidents, their families, and their political retinues. But . . . during those antebellum years, such intrigue, such entanglements, such real tragedy! And often, such recuperation. And . . . sadly, sometimes not. Jefferson Davis, for example: both son-in-law and confidant to presidents, cabinet member . . . there was a real study!

After graduating from West Point in 1828, he had married a young woman against her father's wishes. So adamant had been the father that they were married in an aunt's home instead of hers. Three months later, in a development typical of the day, the young bride was dead. Typhoid.

The bereaved husband and the father-in-law met years later on a battlefield of the Mexican War, by one account falling in one another's arms and weeping.

Soon after, the father-in-law, Zachary Taylor, was president and onetime son-in-law Jefferson Davis was a U.S. senator from Mississippi. By this time, Jefferson Davis had remarried. Taylor, on the other hand, had long been married to aging, aristocratic Margaret Mackall Smith of Maryland, an invalid who had opposed his presidential bid, who at first did not join her sixty-four-year-old husband at the White House, and who, when she did, was such a recluse that all kinds of rumors sprang up to explain her absence from public view. One was that she smoked a pipe!

It was Jefferson Davis's second wife, Varina, who often visited Mrs. Taylor and spoke up publicly in her defense, to say she was absolutely charming and just fine.

That was at midcentury exactly, with Taylor's famous Mexican War mount Old Whitey busily chomping the grass of the White House lawn. Six Osage Indians had appeared for Taylor's first reception in a refurbished East Room. Up on Capitol Hill, Clay, Calhoun, and Webster were debating the slavery issue almost daily—or nightly—and Millard Fillmore was presiding over the Senate as vice president. One Franklin Pierce of New Hampshire, once a congressman, was not yet back in sight.

Washington still had not forgotten Taylor's immediate predecessor, James K. Polk, who, by all accounts, had been a workaholic. He signed bills until the last possible moment. Then on his way home in the spring of 1849, he endured one smalltown parade or visiting delegation after another, until, facing a huge fish dinner in New Orleans, he begged a servant to slip him some ham and cornbread. He canceled all other public displays—and went home, only to die shortly after at age fifty-three.

Another who died later that same summer was the impoverished presidential widow and Washington social doyen Dolley Madison.

Ironically, the deceased Polk, on the day of his replacement by Taylor, had called his successor "a well-meaning old man," not to the newcomer's face, but in a diary. Ironic, in view of Polk's early demise, but . . . hold the phone!

In Washington over the next year, "old man" Taylor enjoyed the summer concerts given by the Marine Band on the south grounds of the White House. He walked among the onlookers and shook just about anyone's hand. On July 4, 1850, he took part in ceremonies at the site of the future Washington Monument, its cornerstone laid by Polk two years before. A newspaper reporter noted Taylor's "listless attitude."

Afterward, Taylor returned to the White House and enjoyed a quantity of cherries and iced milk. In five days, he was dead. History says he was a victim, not of a bowl of cherries exactly, but of *cholera morbus,* which means, in effect, gastric disaster. (An exhumation in 1991 failed to prove the alternative theory that he had been poisoned with arsenic.)

His reclusive wife, who had prayed Henry Clay would defeat her own husband in the presidential race of 1848, underwent agony during the state funeral. Said Varina Davis later:" [She] trembled silently from head to foot as one band after another blared the funeral march of the different organizations, and the heavy guns boomed in quick succession to announce the final parting."

Taking over the presidency next, Millard Fillmore also had to wait a short while before his wife joined him. She had stayed home all during his vice presidency, but they wrote each other letters every day. His wife, Abigail Powers of Buffalo, New York, once had been his teacher.

Fillmore did not move right into the White House. One newspaper said his inaction was due to malaria wafting up from the Potomac River. Fillmore himself later blamed the Taylor mourning period for delays in entertaining at the White House. Abigail Fillmore would begin a library at the White House, but she was in ill health and was mourning a recently departed sister. Their daughter Mary Abigail was acting hostess at age eighteen.

The couple finished their White House term seemingly unscathed, to be succeeded by the Franklin Pierces. With English author William Makepeace Thackery and American author Washington Irving in attendance, the Fillmores wined and dined the incoming president, then moved from the White House to the same suite Pierce had been occupying at the nearby Willard Hotel.

There they made plans to travel abroad, but Mrs. Fillmore died a month later in her hotel bed, perhaps due to catching cold on Pierce's inaugural day—while standing next to authors Thackery and Irving in the wind blowing at the Capitol.

Pierce also arrived alone at the White House, since his family, too, had just weathered a tragedy—the third of three, actually. After losing their two young sons to disease, the couple just two months before the inauguration of 1853 had seen their third and last son, eleven-year-old Benjamin, horribly injured and killed in a train wreck that left the two parents unscathed.

Even before that, Jane Means Appleton Pierce had fainted upon hearing the news that her husband was elected president and must go to Washington. Now she would only go as far as Baltimore until after the inauguration. Pierce had to visit her there.

When Jane Pierce finally took up residence in the White House, she was another recluse. But that situation—with the encouragement once more of Varina Davis—gradually changed, and Jane Pierce eventually was able to serve as hostess at major White House social occasions. Jefferson Davis, meanwhile, was Pierce's secretary of war—and one of the New Englander's closest friends.

Not even vice presidents were exempt from the grim reaper's work during this period. Vice President William R. King had gone to Cuba to recover from an illness and took his oath of office there, missing the Pierce inauguration. The Alabama senator then journeyed home. And died.

Pierce, meanwhile, was an alcoholic, history tells us. One story recounts the time, years before, when as a congressman he spent a convivial evening with a local newspaper editor, only to see his companion fall into a creek at night's end. Unable to pull him out, the drunken Pierce jumped in with him!

As President Pierce made way for his successor in 1857, neither he nor Davis, despite the latter's fierce proslavery views, could have foreseen that less than ten years later Davis would himself be a president—of the Confederate States of America.

Pierce was succeeded by a bachelor, James Buchanan, whose young, vibrant niece Harriet Lane served as his hostess. No tragedy or melodrama here ... except that a congressional friend of the president shot and killed his wife's lover in Lafayette Square, fronting the White House. The victim was Francis Scott Key's son . . . and the city's Federal prosecutor.

Except that, in another grim instance, bachelor President Buchanan thought he could rid himself of a pesky newspaper critic—a woman—by ordering her husband—a general—to Central America to deal with problems there. The newspaper woman dutifully left town with her husband. And both drowned when their ship sank in a storm.

Buchanan, of course, is best remembered today as the president who handed over the reins of government—in a most fateful exchange—to Abraham Lincoln. Then came tragedy and drama on really massive scale! The Civil War.

"Looked Like a Dead Man"

WHEN WOODROW WILSON LEFT THE White House for the peace conference in Paris less than a month after the Armistice of November 11, 1918, he seemingly was well coddled, protected, and equipped for any and all emergency.

Aboard his ship, the *George Washington,* as she steamed out of her slip at Hoboken, New Jersey, that December 4 was a Secret Service detail of eight sturdy men. He had along also his valet, his secretary of state, his chief White House usher, and two stenographers. His wife, Edith, also making the historic trip, carried along her secretary and a maid. The entourage also included Wilson's doctor, U.S. Navy captain Cary Grayson; historians; economists and, of course, lesser diplomats.

Wilson's shipboard suite was sensibly appointed—bedroom, bath, and an office. There were two telephones, one a wireless.

Forging ahead of the transport as both escort and unofficial "minesweeper" was a mighty battleship that served as the flagship of the U.S. Navy's Atlantic Fleet—the *Pennsylvania*. Additionally, a covey of ten destroyers ran alongside.

The American president, armed with his idealistic peace proposals, his Fourteen Points, was the war-weary world's man of the hour . . . and at first no one would let him forget it. When the *George Washington* (the interned German ship *Kaiser Wilhelm*, actually) reached the Azores, two additional destroyers joined the party. Two days later, as the European landmass came into view, nine U.S. battleships approached and, one-by-one, passed with a twenty-one-gun salute. Next it was more destroyers—twelve of them. Next, two French cruisers and nine more destroyers. Overhead, airplanes, and ashore, more guns firing in welcome.

When Woodrow Wilson stepped on French soil December 13, 1918, ecstatic crowds cheered and cheered. He took a train to Paris, another train arrowing ahead of his as protection.

In Paris, more of the same happy, happy crowds—masses! The Wilsons stayed at the palace of Prince Murat, safe behind high walls and guarded entranceways.

Six months in all (with a brief shipbound return to the United States), Wilson's visit was to be the longest stay abroad by any American president at any time. And while negotiations, which he had expected to go quickly, dragged on and on, his free time initially was spent in ceremonies and state visits.

In England, the Wilsons stayed at Buckingham Palace. Everywhere they went the crowds were clamorous and happy, and all events were carefully arranged, protocol flawlessly followed. One joy there for Wilson was attending the Presbyterian church his grandfather Woodrow had served as pastor. Wilson spoke from its pulpit, obviously touched to be there.

In Italy, it was more of the same. Staying with royalty, feted by the country's other leaders, a visit to the Pope and, if possible, crowds that were even more enthused than those already seen in France and England.

However coddled from human gaffes as he apparently was, and protected as he was, loved as he was at first, Wilson the Just—as the Europeans initially called him—could not forever remain immune from human fickleness or his own human frailty.

With the victorious European powers determined from the outset to punish and weaken Germany, Wilson's idealistic goals and manner simply didn't suit. The peace treaty negotiations wore him down. Political opposition to the League of Nations at home wore him even further. Indeed, much of his program simply was unacceptable in a rivalry-ridden Europe so fresh from such awesome bloodletting as the "Great War."

Secret Service Agent Edmund Starling, after watching Wilson arrive in Paris before Christmas "in fine fettle," soon was noticing an ominous decline. In mid-February, the American party headed back across the Atlantic for a two-week interim. By then, wrote Starling later, they were leaving behind in Europe, "a quagmire of misunderstanding, doubt, fear, suspicion, jealousy and greed."

Wilson reached America in late February, first going ashore at Boston. He then spent a week in Washington, where the Republicans in Congress were in revolt over the proposed League of Nations. He reboarded the *George Washington* for the trip back to Europe the evening of March 5, and on Friday the thirteenth, the ship again dropped anchor at Brest, France. Wilson's previous arrival also had been on the thirteenth—December 13, 1918. He was delighted both times, since he considered thirteen to be his lucky number.

Not so, really. That very evening, after an argument with his long-time confidant and aide, Colonel Edward M. House, Wilson looked at Starling without recognition, "his arms hanging loosely at his side." He was pale, drawn, and obviously tired. And yet they had just arrived in France again after a quiet, restful sea voyage that Wilson seemed to enjoy.

As the negotiations leading to the Versailles Treaty of 1919 resumed in earnest, Wilson deteriorated steadily. He went to bed with a cold or flu (perhaps even a mild stroke) on April 3, and Mrs. Wilson for the next few nights sometimes asked Starling to move the president's bed or raise a window. "He did not stir as the bed moved or the windows rattled, sleeping deeply and peacefully, but looking more like a dead man than the living hope of the world."

Wilson's Allied counterparts by now were more like adversaries, as they tried to enforce their interests upon the peace treaty—

almost overnight, Italian popular opinion had turned against "Wilson the Just." His political opposites from France and Britain continually picked at the treaty terms.

Wilson eventually left his sick bed, but in Starling's opinion, the president still was weak and exhausted. "He never did regain his physical strength, and his weakness of body naturally reacted upon his mind. He lacked his old quickness of grasp and tired easily."

One day, Wilson twice left behind an important briefcase full of confidential papers as he gathered his belongings after a negotiating session. Britain's Prime Minister Lloyd-George noticed Starling rescue the briefcase both times. "It was a telltale sign that the President was no longer at his peak, and was tiring fast, and since it was Lloyd-George's task to wear him down he must have felt a twinge of triumph at this indication of success," wrote Starling.

The Briton in fact reacted visibly by giving Agent Starling "something between a knowing look and a wink."

In the meantime, Wilson was giving up—compromising—on positions he had taken prior to and early in the peace conference. The pressure from the French and British was taking its toll, especially since Wilson for the most part did his own negotiating as the American spokesman, even his own typing of memoranda, while his European counterparts quite sensibly used their staffs for such purposes.

Wilson often played solitaire for hours at a time, erupted into fits of temper, and once asked to rearrange the furniture in his suite, because, "I don't like the way the colors of this furniture fight each other." His hair turned whiter and he developed a nervous twitch of the eye.

With the treaty finally signed in June, the Americans rejoined their ship for the cruise back to Hoboken. Taking a few turns about the deck with the Wilsons the day after sailing, Agent Starling was startled to see Wilson stumble three times in a row against a lifeboat ring embedded in the deck. As they approached a fourth time, Starling stepped in the way and with Mrs. Wilson's help steered their weakening charge in a safer direction.

The party arrived in the United States on July 8. For the next two months Wilson fought for ratification by the Senate of the treaty containing his beloved League of Nations. He then left Washington for his famous whistlestop railroad tour of the West, intended to drum up public support.

His physician Grayson, by now a navy admiral, warned that Wilson might not survive the demanding trip. He almost didn't. One day, Starling nearly had to lift him up to the podium for a speech. Wilson rambled weakly and even wept.

That night the train turned back to Washington. Wilson had suffered a stroke. Starling, going on furlough for a long-planned visit to his mother, said good-bye and left the Wilsons at St. Louis. By his own written account, he sat and watched as the presidential train slid on out of the rail yards, a "little red light" after a time that was fading from sight. He felt a friend's hand on his shoulder, and his friend asked, "What's the matter?"

"What do you mean what's the matter?" demanded Agent Starling. "You're crying, you damn fool!"

Another View on Wilson

BLINDS DRAWN, THE PRESIDENTIAL TRAIN passed through the rail yards of Wichita, Kansas, without making its scheduled stop for still another speech by Woodrow Wilson. Instead, it sped on toward Washington, hurrying the stricken president back to his White House quarters as rapidly as possible.

They had tried to stop him, hadn't they? His doctor. His wife. His private secretary. Admiral Cary Grayson, the presidential physician, had hinted to Joseph Tumulty, Wilson's secretary, that the speaking tour might cost Wilson his life. Edith Galt Wilson dismissed both the League of Nations and the presidency as absolute imperatives. Her only interest, she said, was "my husband and his health."

Wilson himself admitted, "I am at the end of my tether," but he was adamant—he had to lobby the American people for their approval, over Senate objection, of the Treaty of Versailles that included his plan to maintain peace, the League of Nations. To stir up public opinion in favor of Senate ratification, Wilson decided after his months in Europe he must rally the country, "swing around the circle," plunge into a nationwide speaking tour.

Launching a rail journey from Washington, D.C., to Washington State and back, Wilson set off to make forty or more speeches plugging the peacekeeping League and his conviction that the treaty containing it must be ratified by the U.S. Senate.

As if that itinerary alone were not enough strain upon the obviously exhausted Wilson, the so-called "swing" was more like a race. For behind Wilson came a squad of anti-League Senate members addressing audiences at the same stops, drawing larger and larger crowds, some greater than his own.

For twenty-two days Wilson pressed on. In one speech he could be notably forgetful of things said in another. He often was notably bitter, even depressed. Much of his imagery had to do with death. Came a day—September 25, 1919—in Pueblo, Colorado, when tears coursed down his cheeks. That afternoon he and Mrs. Wilson left the stopped train for a short walk on a country road. He was running a fever when they returned.

Tumulty, with Wilson ever since he had served as governor of New Jersey a decade before, had asked Wilson to put off the speech-making trip before they had left Washington. Even then, Tumulty had thought his longtime boss and friend was "plainly on the verge of a nervous breakdown." And now, before dawn the day after the crying incident, Tumulty heard a tapping on his sleeping compartment door.

It was Grayson knocking at four in the morning. The president! Come quick, the president is sick!

And of course he was—pale, unable to speak clearly, one side of his face frozen, an arm and leg also not functioning properly. And again tears! "My dear boy," he told Tumulty, "this has never happened to me before. I do not know what to do."

When Tumulty quite logically said the rest of the trip was to be canceled, Wilson still objected. "Don't you see," he said, "that if you cancel this trip, Senator Henry Lodge and his friends will say that I am a quitter and that the western trip was a failure and the [Versailles] Treaty will be lost?"

More concerned for Wilson's health and well-being, Tumulty and others in the presidential entourage ordered their train to speed back to Washington. They also did their best to disguise Wilson's illness, to play it down. Tumulty issued a press statement saying Wilson "so spent himself without reserve on this trip that it brought on a nervous reaction in his digestive organs."

Upon arrival in Washington, Wilson somehow summoned the strength to walk from the train. Barely a week later, he suffered a more severe and disabling stroke, also kept secret, never to recover fully from the two attacks of fall 1919. And the Senate never did ratify the Treaty of Versailles, which would have required the United States to join the League of Nations.

Two Murders Unavoided

TWO PROPHECIES OF SORTS? A pair of coincidences? Who is to say, what to say, except that the consequences were dire in both cases.

Odd, too, you might say, that Abraham Lincoln's only surviving son would reappear in American history two decades after the Lincoln era . . . but he certainly did. Robert Todd Lincoln would turn up as secretary of war for President James A. Garfield, a former Union army officer.

Just four months after his inauguration, Garfield called Robert Todd Lincoln to his side and quizzed him in great detail about his father's death at the hands of John Wilkes Booth.

That was on June 30, 1881, and on July 2, at a Washington railroad station, Garfield met his own assassin, Charles Guiteau. Two shots rang out, and Garfield fell, fatally wounded. He would survive until September 19.

Shortly after his election the year before, he had told a friend that assassination "can no more be guarded against than death by lightning; and it is best not to worry about either."

On another day, twenty years later, the last of the Union army veterans to serve as president, William McKinley, was preparing for a trip to Buffalo, New York, for the Pan-American Exposition. So was his secretary, George Corteylou, a worried man.

So worried was the presidential secretary—for his boss, not himself—that he turned down a proposed public reception for McKinley . . . only to have the president restore it to his schedule. When Corteylou protested that McKinley should avoid such public exposure, McKinley said, "Why should I? No one would want to hurt me."

As an early item in the visiting president's schedule, he gave a speech on September 5, followed by fifteen minutes of handshaking with an unscreened crowd. One onlooker was Leon Czolgosz. The next day, after a luncheon at nearby Niagara Falls, McKinley began the reception that Corteylou had feared.

It was held at the Temple of Music, its doors opened to the public exactly at 4:00 P.M. Shaking hands at an estimated rate of forty-five per minute until about 4:07, McKinley then encountered a man with a bandaged right hand. He was Leon Czolgosz, and the bandage concealed a handgun.

It was unknown to either McKinley or his secretary Corteylou that Czolgosz was a deranged malcontent from Chicago—irrational enough to have told a friend he was so displeased with society he intended to kill a priest. When the friend pointed out there were many priests, the assassin decided to go after one of a kind instead. A president.

In Buffalo, the madman fired just twice at the handshaking president. One round caromed off a button, the other, fatally, entered the president's lower torso.

McKinley died eight days later, September 14. His assassin went to the electric chair on October 23. Justice for once was swift.

★

Sickroom Cooled

★

The house on Pennsylvania Avenue was ever so still. Silent, absolutely silent. "Quiet as death," wrote a reporter staying overnight on the same floor as the president's offices and private living quarters. "I listen for every sound," added Franklin Trusdell of the National

Associated Press in a letter to his wife, Genie. "A dog barking in the distance is heard. A fountain splashes on the lawn. Not a step is heard in the mansion."

And true, silent it was that dread summer of 1881. And hot, so hot! The main floor was a mess. Some of the furniture had been taken upstairs for the convenience of visitors, aides, or family of the immobilized president. Summer covers stayed on the furniture left behind while empty spaces spoke of the pieces hastily carried upstairs. The blinds remained closed against sun and heat.

Odd, too, running up the grand staircase from a newly created ice chamber in the basement and continuing along the second-floor corridor was a series of canvas and wire tubing—ducts for cold air blown by a fan through the makeshift system to the bedroom where the president lay suffering.

Silent was the house, and silent were the crowds that stood outside in vigil for the stricken man within.

James A. Garfield had been president for less than six months when a disturbed and disappointed job-seeker shot him twice at the Baltimore and Potomac rail station on July 2 as Garfield was about to embark upon a Fourth of July stay at a New Jersey beach. He sustained a relatively harmless wound in one arm, but the real difficulty was the second bullet, now festering deep in his back. The doctors attending him in the White House could not find the spent slug. Even the famous inventor Alexander Graham Bell could not find its deadly site with an electric detector gadget he carried up to the bed in the hot, hot White House.

With no helpful medical procedure immediately in evidence, all that the doctors, family and onlooking public could do was to wait . . . wait, watch, hope, and pray for their president lying on a bamboo frame bed in great pain.

But the heat! One of his greatest discomforts was the heat that had driven previous presidents out of the mansion during Washington's summer heat waves. What could be done to relieve him of the heat on the second floor, without risking a dangerous move to cooler quarters? This was before air conditioning, of course . . . but the answer turned out to be an early and rudimentary form of that very item. *Air conditioning.*

The public had responded with all kinds of gifts for the stricken president, and among the helpful devices sent by inventors were two cooling contraptions. One, reported White House historian

William Seale, "consisted of a large closed-up vat of ice, from which tin pipes ran from the President's office in a downward slope to the President's bedroom on the opposite end of the house."

Still, the freshly cooled air at the ice end didn't get to the bedroom end quickly enough to do much good.

The second machine, for lack of a better word, incorporated a fan that blew air through a six-foot box holding a series of cheesecloth screens that were wetted down with ice-cold water. The result here was better ... but still far from perfect. Cool air did reach the uncomfortable patient at the end of the tin-pipe system, but the cool air was also humid air.

Enter now, a U.S. Navy scientist called to the scene by Garfield's doctors, one Simon Newcomb.

Intrigued by inventor R. S. Jennings's fan-powered blower apparatus, Newcomb calculated how much ice would be needed to replace the heat units normally to be found in the air in the sickroom. He also realized that putting ice between the cheesecloth box and the pipes would soak up the unwanted moisture. But Jennings still could be a useful player, and he was called in to help build a much larger, modified cooling system. So was John Wesley Powell, head of the U.S. Geological Survey, who had a first-rate scientific mind. "The three worked around the clock with a contingent of navy engineers for three days," wrote Seale. "On Monday morning, July 12, the machine was turned on. Newcomb wrote that the air that passed from the office to the sick-room was 'cool, dry and ample in supply.'"

When Garfield complained about the noise of the fan motor echoing through the tin pipes, the experts conceived of canvas-over-wire ducts to absorb the disturbing decibels. The final step was to expand the coolant capacity by using a more powerful fan engine, installing a larger ice container in the basement, and running the canvas ducts upstairs to the president's room.

For all the success achieved, however, Garfield finally died, even though a transfer to the Jersey shore in September seemed at first to benefit him mentally and physically. Before Garfield was carried out of the White House for the futile trip to his beach cottage, newsman Trusdell had spent many nights in a makeshift press center established down the hall in the waiting room to the president's office. Trusdell at first had been, "almost sure he [Garfield] will recover."

Sadly, he had been wrong, but Garfield's suffering would have one beneficial result for generations to come. As Seale pointed out in his history *The President's House,* the coolant system developed for Garfield's relief not only had given him some peace, it also amounted to "a great advance in technology." For at the White House that grim summer "had been discovered the basic principle of air conditioning."

1:00 P.M. in Dallas

DALLAS ON THE TWENTY-SECOND. Atop the Texas School Book Depository, the clock within Secret Service Agent Rufus W. Youngblood's view from the approaching motorcade said 12:30. The motorcade turned southwest onto Elm Street. The open area known as Dealey Plaza was on one side, the depository on the other.

The president waved to a crowd standing at the foot of the building.

One onlooker, Howard L. Brennan, across Elm and facing the depository, noticed a slender man about five feet, ten inches, tall, probably in his early thirties, in the sixth-floor corner window. That was a few minutes before the motorcade turned the corner and approached.

And now, quite suddenly, shots, probably three in all and "in rapid succession," according to the scenario presented in the Warren Commission report on the assassination.

Brennan actually saw the mysterious figure in the southwest corner window take aim with a rifle and fire.

It wasn't quite 12:34 P.M. in Dallas, Texas, November 22, 1963.

In the rear of his open car, the president grabbed at his neck. "He appeared to stiffen momentarily and lurch slightly forward in his seat." It later was determined that this bullet had struck him at the base of the back of his neck, right of the spine, coursed downward and out the front of his neck, tearing a nick in the knot of his tie.

Several cars behind in the motorcade, Dallas motorcycle policeman Marrion L. Baker heard a shot. Just returned from a deer-hunting trip, he was sure it came from a high-powered rifle.

Looking up, he saw pigeons bolting in the air from perches on the depository building. Gunning his motorcycle, he raced forward and dismounted at the front door.

In the presidential limousine, the governor of Texas, John Connally, had been struck a stunning blow in the back. The round passed through the right upper torso after its entry below his right armpit, then exited below his right nipple, next passed through his right wrist, just then resting on his lap, and finally wounded him in the left thigh. He was caused to spin to his right. His wife pulled him down into her lap.

Shots were still coming. "Several eyewitnesses in front of the building" would report seeing a rifle being fired from the same southeast corner window on the sixth floor.

In the limo, the president was struck for a second time after John Connally's wounding . . . all in seconds or even less. This bullet brought about "a massive and fatal wound" to the rear of the president's head. He fell leftward into his wife's lap.

One car behind in the motorcade, Secret Service Agent Clinton J. Hill had heard a "firecracker" noise and seen the president's lurch to the left. Leaping from his running-board post in the slow-moving motorcade (about eleven miles per hour), he ran to catch up with the all-important limousine before him.

Accompanying vice president Lyndon B. Johnson, one car behind Hill's follow-up vehicle, Agent Youngblood had heard an explosion and seen "unusual movements in the crowd." He also reacted quickly. "He vaulted into the rear seat and sat on the vice president in order to protect him."

Up front, in the presidential limousine two cars ahead, Secret Service Agent Roy Kellerman turned from his front-right-seat post just in time to see that his ward, the president, had been hit. "Let's get out of there; we are hit," he barked at the driver. He also radioed terse instruction to the motorcade's lead car: "Get us to the hospital immediately."

Secret Service Agent William R. Greer, driver of the presidential limo, "immediately accelerated." To the vehicle's rear, Agent Hill sprinted forward just in time to climb onto the back of the open car. He pushed forward the president's wife, who in her shock and confusion, had climbed up onto the back of the car from the rear seat. Agent Hill pushed her back down, then shielded her and her inert husband with his own body as the motorcade sped away from Dealey Plaza.

Eyewitness Brennan promptly told a policeman about his sighting of the gunman in the sixth-floor corner window. At 12:34 P.M., the Dallas Police radio named the depository building as the possible source of the shots, "and at 12:45 P.M. the police broadcast a description of the suspected assassin, based primarily on Brennan's observations."

Long before, relatively speaking, police motorman Baker had dismounted his bike and charged through the front door. He and the building superintendent, Roy Truly, first tried two elevators in the rear of the ground floor, but both lifts were somewhere above, at some upper floor. Not waiting, the two men raced up the nearby stairs. "Not more than two minutes had elapsed since the shooting," says the Warren report.

At the second-floor landing, Baker glimpsed someone through the glass window of the door in the stairway hall. Inside was a lunchroom. Gun drawn, Baker went in, followed by Truly. They encountered a lone, empty-handed young man whom Truly recognized and identified as a depository employee. Baker and Truly then resumed their dash up the stairs to the sixth floor, leaving behind, in the second-floor lunchroom, Lee Harvey Oswald.

A minute later, holding a full soft drink bottle in his hand (purchased from a lunchroom vending machine), "Oswald was seen passing through the second-floor offices."

At 12:35 P.M., the presidential limousine and other motorcade vehicles arrived at Parkland Memorial Hospital, four miles from the shooting scene. Previously alerted by the police, the emergency room staff began all-out emergency procedures to revive the stricken president, who was unconscious and barely alive . . . motor responses only.

At the depository, meanwhile, Oswald at last sight had been walking toward the front of the second-floor level. At the front, both an elevator and stairs allowed access to the first floor and its entrance below.

Seven minutes later, or at 12:40 P.M., he was seen boarding an Elm Street bus seven blocks away. Since he was then east of the depository and the bus was traveling west, it quickly ran into a traffic jam in the vicinity of the shooting scene. Having been aboard for only three or four minutes, Oswald left the bus. He had been seen by a former landlady, Mrs. Mary Bledsoe.

Minutes later, he found a taxi four blocks away and took it to the neighborhood of his rooming house quarters. He would arrive there about 1:00 P.M.

At Parkland, doctors performed a tracheotomy, used cardiac massage and intravenous cut-ins in heroic medical measures to save the president . . . but to no avail. After receiving Last Rites, John F. Kennedy was declared dead. Official time: 1:00 P.M.

In the Oak Cliff area of Dallas, meanwhile, patrolman J. D. Tippit, an eleven-year veteran of the police force, was following instructions that had been radioed to his patrol car at 12:45 P.M.—to be on the lookout for the suspect last seen at the depository window with a rifle (by Brennan's description).

At 12:54, Tippit radioed in his whereabouts, "as directed and [said he] would be available for any emergency."

At his rooming house not far away, Oswald obviously was in a hurry. Housekeeper Marlene Roberts couldn't help but notice his haste when he rushed in and didn't even reply to her greeting. He was gone in just a few minutes.

Shortly thereafter, a man was walking eastward on East Tenth Street near its intersection with Patton. Cruising the same street and approaching from behind was Tippit in his patrol car.

He pulled alongside at about 1:15 P.M. Tippit and the man talked for a moment by way of the police car's right front window, then Tippit got out of the car and started to walk around the front to approach his quarry on the sidewalk. The man drew a revolver and fired four shots at Tippit, killing him on the spot. As the assailant fled on foot, a passing witness, Domingo Benavides, used the slain policeman's patrol car radio to notify Dallas police. "The message was received shortly after 1:16 P.M."

At 1:20 P.M., Vice President Lyndon B. Johnson, waiting in a heavily protected anteroom at Parkland, was told the president was dead. Johnson now would be president, but there were fears of a possible conspiracy to kill him, too.

Shortly before 2:00 P.M., Tippit's as-yet-unnamed killer was apprehended in a movie theater, still armed with a pistol.

Back at the depository, three empty cartridge cases had been found on the floor just inside the suspicious window. Then, near the sixth-floor staircase, a bolt-action rifle with a telescopic sight was found. Soon to be identified as the murder weapon, it belonged to one Lee Harvey Oswald, further investigation revealed.

Building superintendent Truly, in the meantime, had told police that he noticed Oswald was missing from the depository's normal daily work force of fifteen men.

At 2:00 P.M., Dallas homicide chief Will Fritz returned to his headquarters with this information and was telling one of his detectives to pick up Oswald for questioning. "Standing nearby were the police officers who had just arrived with the man arrested in the Texas [movie] Theatre. When Fritz mentioned the name of the missing employee, he learned that the man was already in the interrogation room. The missing Texas School Book Depository employee and the suspect who had been apprehended in the Texas Theatre were one and the same—Lee Harvey Oswald."

On board *Air Force One* at Dallas's Love Field, Lyndon Johnson was sworn in as president by federal district court judge Sarah T. Hughes. Oswald remained in custody as *Air Force One* then took off for Washington with both the new president and the former, slain president's body aboard. Two days later, Oswald was fatally shot while being transferred from the Dallas city jail to the Dallas County jail. In full view of millions of television viewers, nightclub owner Jack Ruby stepped out of an onlooking crowd of reporters with a .38 revolver in his right hand and fired one shot that crumpled Oswald quickly to the ground, unconscious.

That was shortly after 11:20 A.M., November 24, two days after the first shooting. In seven minutes, the shooter, Oswald, also arrived at Parkland. Never regaining consciousness, he was officially pronounced dead at 1:07 P.M.

Died There

They died at the White House:

- A relative. Ulysses S. Grant's father-in-law, Judge Frederick Lincoln Dent, an unreconstructed Confederate sympathizer despite his middle name or his daughter Julia's marriage to the Union general. In 1873. Old age, essentially.

- A slave child. Infant born and died in Jefferson's White House, January of 1803.
- Second slave child born in Jefferson's White House, 1806, deceased by the end of 1808. Record kept of small coffin ordered.
- A president. The first to die in office. William Henry Harrison in April 1841, only a month after taking office. Caught cold and fever, it is thought, at his chilly inauguration in March.
- A president's wife. John Tyler's first wife, Letitia, in 1842, hardly more than a year after her husband succeeded the ill-fated William Henry Harrison. Young by today's standards, she was fifty-two and had been in ill health since moving into the White House the year before.
- Another Harrison. Same family, a later generation. Caroline, wife to President Benjamin Harrison, who was William Henry Harrison's grandson. In her late fifties, of tuberculosis in 1892. And then, misery on misery, her father, late the same year.
- Another presidential wife. Woodrow Wilson's dear Ellen. Tuberculosis of the kidneys. In her midfifties, on August 6, 1914. In Europe, World War I had just erupted.
- A president, the second to die in the presidential home. Zachary Taylor in 1850. His stomach upset after drinking ice water and eating cherries and milk on July 4, he died five days later.
- A president's son. Young Willie Lincoln, age twelve, who together with his younger brother Tad caught a raging fever (possibly typhoid) in the winter of 1862. Tad recovered, but Willie did not. After Willie's death, Abe Lincoln went to his secretary John Nicolay's office, sobbed and wept. Mary Todd Lincoln went to bed and screamed until she fell asleep. During the funeral five days later, said an onlooker, the sky was black and a fierce wind rolled up tin roofs in Washington and toppled chimneys and church steeples.
- Another presidential relative. Harry Truman's mother-in-law, Margaret Gates Wallace, on December 5, 1952, four days after a mild stroke—and a month after the American electorate chose Republican Dwight D. Eisenhower to succeed outgoing Democrat Truman.

Addenda:

- Woodrow Wilson was so affected by the death of his wife, Ellen, he wouldn't allow her remains to be placed in a coffin. He had her laid out on a sofa in the presidential bedroom, curtains pulled shut and lights low. He stayed there with her for two nights. After her funeral service in the East Room, he rode the special train to her hometown of Rome, Georgia, staying all the while in the compartment with her casket.

- Caroline Harrison's death came in the last weeks of a presidential campaign, but neither her husband nor his Democratic opponent, Grover Cleveland, had done much campaigning. Cleveland had made only one public appearance after learning of Mrs. Harrison's serious illness in 1892, and incumbent Harrison had stayed close to his dying wife all along. When it was announced that Cleveland had won the election—as the first and only president ever returned to office after leaving the White House—Harrison was visibly relieved. "For me there is no sting in it," he said. "Indeed, after the heavy blow the death of my wife dealt me, I do not think I could have stood the strain that a re-election would have brought."

- Visibly ill for several days, Zachary Taylor was treated by a doctor, Thomas Miller, often accused of having bled the dying William Henry Harrison a bit too much back in 1841, when *he* died in the White House. Taylor, in any case, was tormented by a restless delirium in which he spoke self-debasing nonsense. Congress and the public awaited the frequent White House bulletins. Mississippi senator Jefferson Davis and his wife, Varina, were repeated visitors. At the very last, for the final hours of July 9, 1850, members of the cabinet and other officials waited in an upstairs room down the hall from the president's own bedchamber.

In the bedroom itself were Taylor family members—and Jefferson Davis and Varina. By now, Taylor was very still, and barely alive. Remarkably, he suddenly spoke and said: "I am about to die. I expect my summons very soon. I have tried to discharge my duties faithfully; I regret nothing, but I am sorry I am about to leave my friends." He said this, turning to look at his wife, Margaret, and died a half-hour later, still turned in her direction.

Outlaw of Falahill

"I AM ACCUSTOMED," SAID THIS White House occupant, "to hearing malicious falsehoods about myself, but I think I have a right to object to libelous statements about my dog." Furthermore, said "the Boss," just forget the malicious rumor that he sent a U.S. navy destroyer back to the Aleutian Islands in the middle of a war to fetch an AWOL White House dog, even this very famous and popular White House dog, "at a cost to the taxpayer of two or three or twenty million dollars."

No sir, added FDR in a 1944 campaign speech before the Teamsters union, the "Republican-concocted story" did not sit well with his dog Fala. Not well at all. "His Scotch soul was furious."

Fala ("my little dog," FDR called him), of course, was a Scottie. He arrived at the White House, already housebroken, in 1940 as a present to Franklin Delano Roosevelt from his cousin Margaret Suckley, and FDR apparently fell in love with the spiky-haired pet immediately.

"He was a shaggy Scotsman, known in the books as Murray, the Outlaw of Falahill," wrote FDR's secretary, Grace Tully. He slept in the master's bedroom, he shared FDR's breakfast tray in the mornings, and during the presidential workday he "raced himself dizzy" in an outdoor pen within view of the Oval Office.

He then was seen "accompanying his master triumphantly back to the big house at the end of each day."

Among various talents, he was good at chewing the presidential trouser cuffs, just a gnaw or two, to get attention. More formally, he did tricks—rollovers, hindleg stands, and hurdles over upraised human legs.

The Boss usually handed him his dinner, presented in the presidential study in a bowl. Fala, as another trick, had to learn to beg with some decorum—too eager, and he'd have to wait for a moment.

Quite naturally, he traveled with the president, to the family home at Hyde Park, New York; to the "Little White House" at Warm

Springs, Georgia; even to the ships down at the sea, when FDR traveled by shipboard.

In that regard, though, Fala could be a major problem—a real security risk. Often pictured in the press, Fala was so well known that by appearing in public anywhere, he would reveal the fact that FDR was not far away. In wartime that could be a problem, and Tully recalled, "The secrecy would break down whenever a train stop enabled the young ruffian to persuade Arthur Prettyman, the valet, to take him out for a backside walk."

One of FDR's Secret Service entourage went so far as to call Fala "the Informer."

At the same time, Fala had a will of his own—sometimes he was where FDR wasn't, you might say. Like the day he turned up on the loose in the downtown Washington streets near the White House. Or the time he was noticed "sniffing around" at the Treasury next door.

In the latter incident, noting that it came on the fifteenth of the month, often a payday, FDR quipped, "He had probably run out of spending money—almost everybody else does on that day."

For such and other winsome ways, Fala was not only well known but loved by the general public. "Hundreds of letters came to the White House addressed to him, some signed by paw prints and many from the very old or very young lovers of dogs," said Tully.

She once found herself in hot water when she unthinkingly agreed to enroll him in the Tailwaggers Club of California, only to find out there was a chapter right in Washington, D.C.—a chapter of outraged hometown Tailwaggers!

The daily visitors to the White House, in the meantime, included people more interested in seeing Fala than the president himself.

From 1940 until the end, FDR's end in April of 1945, Fala was a part of the White House family. Of the family, period.

He only occasionally had been left behind—assuredly sulking too—when FDR traveled, and so he was present when FDR suddenly died at the Little White House in Warm Springs that fateful April day. The possibly apocryphal story, told by writer John Gunther for one, is that Fala quite suddenly sprang to life, barking in anguish, "crashed" through the screen door, ran outside, and took up a "vigil" on a nearby hilltop.

He later found some consolation as Eleanor's dog living at Hyde Park ... but, no disrespect intended, there could be no replacing FDR in little Scotsman Fala's life.

Wretched Little Sofa

THEY HAD LOVED THE WHITE House, but now it was time. Go they must. The farewells would be difficult—so difficult even for others! The intellectual Henry Adams, who lived right on Lafayette Square, would not, could not, bring himself to walk over and say good-bye. He wrote instead, "Of all earthly trials, farewells are the worst." He wrote that it would be depressing to look out the window and see the White House without its mistress of the past eight years, Edith Kermit Roosevelt, wife of Teddy the president.

And at a farewell stag luncheon for Teddy, the sheriff of Deadwood, South Dakota, Seth Bullock, was supposed to speak on behalf of the thirty-one guests—old friends from all walks of life— but the lawman from the Badlands could only choke, wordlessly, when his moment came.

Edith ordered chipped White House chinaware to be smashed and thrown away, rather than "cheapen" the august home by giving it away or selling it. Teddy went through his study in search of mementoes for friends and family, the personal things.

There was, in fact, one large "personal" item the first lady wanted to take with her when they turned over the White House to the William Howard Tafts on March 4, 1909. That was an antique mahogany sofa she had bought for $400 in 1901 for the Red Room downstairs. After the Teddy-and-Edith Roosevelt refurbishments of 1902, the same small piece wound up in the upper hall, upstairs with the family. And she loved it. She loved it so much that her adoring husband took it upon himself to write the Speaker of the House, Joe Cannon, to ask permission to take the sofa and replace it with another.

But Cannon balked, so did an official in charge of public grounds, and then the request made the newspapers, replete with implications that the "retiring" first lady was trying to take away White House furnishings that didn't belong to her.

It seemed obvious that Cannon had "leaked" the story, and Edith Roosevelt told White House military aide Archie Butt that she wouldn't leave Washington without telling the Speaker what she thought of his "little and petty" action.

"It is the first time since I have been in the White House," she declared angrily, "that I have been dragged into publicity of this kind."

As for the small piece of furniture, once so alluring, it now was that "wretched little sofa." How could she possibly want it now, "now that all the associations with it are of a most disagreeable character?"

And so, on such a sour note, the story might have ended . . . except for an unexpected assist from a key onlooker two years later.

At first, Teddy Roosevelt had been delighted to see William Howard Taft selected as their Republican Party's nominee in 1908 and then to greet him as president-elect. Their relationship later cooled, as Taft developed an agenda of his own in the presidency, but that fact did not stop the kind and thoughtful letter that one day emanated from the Taft White House, from William Howard himself.

Addressed to Edith, it concerned "a mahogany settee which you had purchased for the White House about which clustered many pleasant associations . . ." Taft made no bones of his opinion as to the steps taken before he entered the settee picture. One disapproving official he accused of "density," and Speaker of the House Cannon had merely assumed the authority "to speak" in respect to Edith Roosevelt's wish to keep the small sofa.

Taft took note of the custom by which cabinet officers could take their cabinet chairs into retirement with them, as long as they replaced them. "Why the real head of the White House, the wife of the President, should be denied the same privilege, and especially in respect to a chair or settee that she herself bought for the White House and which has not therefore acquired value by long years of use in the White House I cannot see," Taft wrote also.

Neither the disapproving official nor the Speaker "had anything to say about it," said Taft.

The final point was that he had replaced the "Roosevelt settee" at his own expense and was sending it by express as a New Year's gift. "I hope," wrote Taft on New Year's Eve 1910, "the settee will bring back to you the pleasantest hours at the White House."

Freedom at Last!

IN THE TRANSITION OF 1961, the oldest man yet to leave the White House gave way to the youngest man elected to the the presidency so far in American history—Dwight D. Eisenhower to John F. Kennedy. Unlike the Truman-Eisenhower changeover eight years before, also involving a Democrat and a Republican, this Inauguration Day was an entirely affable affair.

The two principal figures involved had met in the White House twice since Kennedy defeated Eisenhower's vice president, Richard M. Nixon, in the presidential campaign of 1960. For the most part, Ike and JFK discussed governmental policy, staffing, and transition issues in their two meetings. According to Eisenhower biographer Stephen Ambrose, the outgoing president did resent the glowing publicity that seemed to greet JFK's every move, every utterance, but Ike was pleasantly surprised when Kennedy showed up for their first White House meeting on December 6, 1960, by himself—no phalanx of supportive aides.

Kennedy arrived "sitting alone in the back seat of his limousine," wrote Ambrose in his biography, *Eisenhower.* "Eisenhower and his staff had feared he would show up with a group of assistants preparing to celebrate their victory. The President was also pleased by Kennedy's manner. As John Eisenhower [Ike's son and White House aide] recalled, Kennedy's 'warmth and modesty were impressive.' At the meeting in the Oval Office, Kennedy listened carefully and intelligently as Eisenhower explained the way the White House functioned."

Then, in another briefing the day before Kennedy's inauguration on January 20, 1961, Ike couldn't resist a bit of showing off. Like a small boy saying "watch this," he pushed a button and said into the console on his desk, "Send a chopper."

Six minutes later, reported Ambrose in his book, "a helicopter settled down on the lawn outside the Oval Office."

More seriously, Ike also told JFK about "the man with the satchel, a satchel that contained the communications equipment that connected the President with SAC [the Strategic Air Command] and the [U.S. nuclear-armed] missile forces." Eisenhower described the satchel-carrier as "an unobtrusive man who would shadow the President for all of his days in office."

On January 20 itself, the inaugural events unfolded smoothly, despite the previous night's snowfall that forced many on Eisenhower's staff to spend the night at the White House—in the basement, it seems. The next morning Ike and wife Mamie said their good-byes to the White House servants, "many" of them "with tears streaming down their faces," according to Ambrose. The Eisenhowers hosted an amicable coffee for the Kennedys, the Lyndon B. Johnsons, and a small group of fellow Democrats, then left for the major event of the day, JFK's inaugural ceremony at the Capitol.

Shortly after Kennedy's swearing-in and inaugural address, the Eisenhowers slipped out of sight with little notice. Before proceeding to their farm (and retirement home) at Gettysburg, Pennsylvania, they stopped for a private luncheon in a Washington club with Ike's cabinet members and close friends, recalled the Ambrose biography.

By now they had made a great discovery, its full impact known only to outgoing presidents before and since. Quite suddenly, wrote Ike himself later, "We were free—as only private citizens in a democratic nation can be free."

Life After the White House

PICTURE THIS. FATHER AND MOTHER in their bed one night, still awake, and teenaged daughter comes in to protest the family's proposed move from the big city to a little town in Georgia—middle-of-nowhere Georgia at that.

Could be nearly any two parents and their child, anywhere . . . any typical American home, couldn't it? Except that the stereotypical scene in this case was in the White House, and the time was late 1980, the night after Ronald Reagan was elected to succeed Jimmy

Carter. And in the bed this particular night, still stunned by their very-much-shared election loss, were Jimmy and Rosalynn.

"Amy came to our bedroom the night after the election and leaned over our high canopied bed with her head on her arms," wrote Rosalynn Carter later. "I'm sad about this election," she told her parents.

Her mother said they were sad, too, but they had tried their best to win.

In Amy's case there was another aspect to the pain. She had no desire to go back to tiny Plains, Georgia, the family's real home.

"You may be from the country," she exclaimed, "but I'm not! I've been raised in the city!"

Quite so. First Jimmy Carter had served as governor of Georgia. Headquarters, Atlanta. Then, after only a brief hiatus, it was on to Washington . . . and the White House. As Rosalynn Carter later wrote: "She was right. We had moved to the governor's mansion when she was just three years old."

Naturally, Amy was not the only family member hurting. Jimmy Carter later acknowledged that his disappointment was "great," but he "kept it bottled up for a long time." And Rosalynn, more visibly upset, just couldn't understand the rejection. "It just didn't seem fair," she felt. In her view, "We had done all we could, and somehow it had not been enough."

They would eventually develop a new life, aggressively searching out new challenges—even writing a book together about the traumatic experience: *Everything to Gain: Making the Most of the Rest of Your Life.* But those first days, weeks, even months, were difficult, and the readjustment took deep, personal reappraisals. Leaving the White House, a relief to some presidential couples, was not a welcome activity for the Carters.

There was the feeling of so much else to do before the next occupants—the Reagans—moved in. There was the feeling that life back in the small town of Plains could be pretty dull "after the exciting life of the White House and the long years of political battles," they wrote together in their book. Amy had a point!

And what readjustments when they did return! Their bungalow in an oak and hickory grove had not really been a fulltime home for ten years—outside, both topsoil and lawn had washed away. And after the White House, it offered terribly cramped quarters. Now, they wished they had put a floor in the attic so it could be more

President Jimmy Carter and his wife Rosalynn hated leaving the White House so soon. (White House Photos, American Memory Collections, Library of Congress)

fully utilized for storage. As it was, boxes and crates returning to Plains with the Carters "were stacked to the ceiling in the house and garage." Now, too, there were no servants to help in the unpacking or in the physical maintenance of their home.

Worse, after the election, the Carters discovered they were in serious financial difficulty back home—the family peanut business was in jeopardy. As the Carters explain in their book, they had placed their financial affairs in a blind trust before going to the White House in 1977, and it was only after the Reagan election that they found out "what had happened to our estate during the four years we had been in the White House."

What had happened was that the farm lands had been rented, while the family peanut warehouse had gone through various management changes. Georgia, meanwhile, had suffered three years of unremitting drought. The Carters were "deeply in debt."

To salvage the situation, they would have to sell the warehouse operation, then find something to replace it as a financial base. "Just as almost two decades of political life were about to end," they wrote, "we found that the results of the preceding twenty-three years of hard work, scrimping and saving, and plowing everything back into the business, were now also gone. No one could accuse us of becoming rich in the White House. We had not expected to, but we had hoped at least to be able to leave with what we had had when we came in. That, too, was not to be."

In the meantime, the final weeks in the White House meant, in addition to affairs of state, a last sentimental Christmas at the venerable Executive Mansion—and then all the farewells. As one related phenomenon, the old house seemed to have so many visitors! "Many close friends and relatives wanted to spend just one night in the White House while we were still there." Then, too, "Night after night we had farewell parties, along with luncheons and receptions during the day."

There were many people to thank, but sometimes the pace and the emotion could be wearing. Well-meant assurances that they were about to begin an exciting new life simply weren't true ("we'd rather not hear people say it"). And, no, they would not be happy to go home and avoid the slings and arrows of politics ("we'd thrived even with the criticisms and we loved politics").

As one welcome parting gesture, though, the Carter cabinet and its staff gave him "a complete set of tools and machinery for a wood-working shop," and if there were anything Jimmy Carter liked to do, all his own, private, relaxed self, it was to fuss around making furniture.

While there had been many issues, many political triumphs and losses, the burning issue of the Carter presidency had been the American hostages held in Iran. And now, on Inauguration Day for Ronald Reagan, they were freed—Jimmy Carter flew to Wiesbaden, Germany, to welcome them back and help to celebrate their new freedom. "Although I had not been to bed for three days during the final negotiations about the hostages, I didn't even feel the fatigue during our long trip to Germany," wrote Carter in the joint book. His return from Germany, though, was not to the White House, but to Plains, where, exhausted, he slept for almost twenty-four hours, "and then awoke to an altogether new, unwanted and potentially empty life."

Jimmy Carter at the time was fifty-six, Rosalynn, fifty-three, and Amy, thirteen. All now had to put their lives back together again. Jimmy and Rosalynn soon began on book projects—contracts with needed monetary benefit. He soon embarked upon a teaching career at Emory University in Atlanta and made plans for his Carter Center and the Jimmy Carter Library. In time, they became more and more involved in peace negotiations, election watches overseas, and health care organizations and projects, plus Habitat for Humanity, the volunteer project that provides housing for the needy.

Amy Carter at first attended school near Plains, but there were few children her own age in town, and she missed out on many school activities because no one knew what to do with her Secret Service detail ("those policemen") if she went on a weekend camping trip or an overnight "with the girls." Her parents then placed her in a boarding school in Atlanta with more girls her own age—eventually they knew her readjustment was coming along just fine when she said that if her father hadn't lost the 1980 election, she wouldn't have made those new friends at the school in Atlanta. In time Jimmy and Rosalynn could say in their shared book, "There is life after the White House!"

Additional notes: During his years in the White House, Jimmy Carter prayed on a daily basis. "Every day . . . on the way to the Oval Office from the White House living quarters," he said in January 1999, "I asked God to let the words of my mouth and the meditations of my heart be acceptable in His sight. I also prayed that I might have wisdom to make sound judgments dealing with the vicissitudes of life that I felt were on my shoulders as president of the greatest nation in the world.

"I prayed for peace and justice and for the alleviation of suffering, things of that kind."

He mentioned his daily prayer in a conference call interview with reporters at eight newspapers, the *Richmond Times-Dispatch* reported. As the newspaper also said, Carter also had cited his "daily prayer walk" in his bestselling book *Living Faith,*" based upon his experiences as a Sunday school teacher.

The book "recounts my efforts to develop and live by personal faith," Carter said that same month in a fundraising letter for the Carter Center in Atlanta and its work as "an internationally recognized force for peace and freedom."

He cited Carter Center programs such as its successful crusade against Guinea worm disease, once a threat to "100 million people from India to Africa." By early 1999 incidence of the disease had been reduced by 97 percent, his letter said.

It also recalled a place of prayer that figured in his achievement of bringing together Egyptian leader Anwar Sadat and Israel's Menachem Begin for the peace talks in 1978 that produced their Camp David Accords. "There was a little room at Camp David where Rosalynn and I worshipped on Sundays when we were away from the White House," Carter wrote in the letter. During the thirteen days of talks, Carter added, "Muslim, Christian, and Jewish officials with profound differences worshipped there during their search for peace."

Even when the peace talks hit their most difficult obstacles, "that one small room always offered peace and hope."

In Carter's view also, "It was a powerful reminder that faith can help unite us for good when worldly forces seem bent only on destruction."

Lincoln and Stanton

ABE LINCOLN AND HIS SECRETARY of war, Edwin Stanton, did not start out close friends—the outspoken Stanton once said he found "no token of any intelligent understanding by Lincoln, or the crew that govern him." As time went on, however, Lincoln worked more closely with Stanton than with any other of his cabinet members, and Stanton's esteem for his president steadily improved.

If there were any doubt as to their eventual closeness, a scene at the White House after the Battle of Gettysburg would serve to dispel it. For here, late that night of July 3, 1863, last day of the three-day battle, came a breathless Stanton pounding up the White House stairs, dispatch in hand, and then to knock on Lincoln's bedroom door.

"Who's there?" asked Lincoln, half asleep, and the simple reply was all Lincoln needed to know. "Stanton" was that reply.

Lincoln, with a light in hand, opened the door. He appeared, said the account in the *New York Tribune* of January 23, 1887, in his nightclothes—"in the shortest nightgown and the longest legs," recalled Stanton later, that he had ever witnessed on a human being.

And Lincoln knew just what Stanton wished to impart—once his war secretary caught his breath. He knew that Gettysburg had to have been a victory. Such a crucial victory, too! Lincoln "gave a shout of exultation, grabbed him [Stanton] with both arms around the waist and danced him around the chamber until they both were exhausted."

The pair then sat on a nearby trunk. Lincoln, still in his sleep-wear, read the War Department telegram again and again and stayed there until dawn as they talked over "the probabilities of the future and the results of the victory."

In the future, of course, was Lincoln's assassination, two years later, a prospect that Stanton had feared and guarded against for some time. It was the war secretary who indefatigably—even ruth-lessly—pressed the prosecution of anyone involved in the assassi-nation conspiracy.

Stanton may not really have said of Lincoln's death, "Now he belongs to the ages," as is often averred; but he certainly mourned his friend and colleague. Said Lincoln's son Robert Todd: "For more than ten days after my father's death in Washington, he [Stanton] called on me in my room, and spent the first few minutes of his vis-its weeping without saying a word."

Piece of Paper Misplaced

TO QUIT THE PRESIDENCY OR not to quit? The answer, it seemed, was on a piece of paper. And as he neared the end of his State of the Union address to a joint session of Congress, with the Supreme Court jus-tices, the diplomatic corps, and just about all the other leading lights of Washington officialdom also looking on, Lyndon Baines Johnson reached into his pocket for the piece of paper.

The draft of a statement saying that he would not run for reelec-tion wasn't there.

There is no guarantee that Johnson would have cast the die then and there, that early in 1968; but the absence of the paper was nearly a guarantee that Johnson—complex, often vacillating, often blustering, often firm, yet often impulsive—would not make his final decision then and there, in front of the country and the world.

The Vietnam War, really raging by now half a world away, was one factor, yes. But not quite the deciding factor that many suppose. It had blown up in his face, like a mine, since he assumed office upon the assassination of John F. Kennedy in 1963, true. He hated it, and it was tearing him apart, also true. But there also was his health to consider. Fears of death. A desire for time with his family . . . a yearning for peace and quiet.

In 1955, still a member of the U.S. Senate from Texas, he had suffered a nearly fatal heart attack. In 1967, as president, he underwent surgery for removal of his gallbladder and a kidney stone. By one informed account, he at first bounced back, "but then he relapsed." The same source, ABC-TV newsman William Lawrence, said: "His staff, including press secretary Bill Moyers, openly admitted his pain, his fatigue, his need for a long rest and rehabilitation."

According to his longtime friend and college classmate Willard Deason, Lyndon Johnson always had a premonition of dying young. "I believe both his father and grandfather died in their early sixties [not true, actually], and he thought that would happen to him, which of course, it did."

The thing is, "He didn't want anything like that to happen while he was President."

Johnson himself later said his mind "always" was on his 1955 heart attack. And, further, whenever he saw Woodrow Wilson's portrait in the Red Room of the White House, he recalled Wilson's last months as president—a president incapacitated by a stroke. He never looked at Wilson's face, Johnson once said, "that I didn't think that it might happen to me, that I would end another term in bed with a stroke and that the decisions of government would be taken care of by other people and that was wrong. I didn't want that to happen."

Johnson often debated the issue of running for a second term in 1968 or stepping down voluntarily. He talked it over with all kinds of advisers, official and personal . . . again and again, often appearing to have decided against seeking reelection. In fact, that's what he told his vice president, Hubert Humphrey, just a day after their landslide victory in 1964. Humphrey didn't take Johnson too seriously way back then but later conceded, "I don't doubt that he ran it in and out of his mind a hundred, maybe a thousand times."

Lady Bird Johnson also attested, "We must have discussed it hundreds of times, and the discussions began at the very beginning [of his presidency]."

By early 1968, the year Johnson would be up for a second full term, his daughter Luci had married and produced a grandson, Lyn, and Johnson loved spending time with this first grandchild. "He could play with the baby and lose himself in this," said his personal physician, Dr. James Cain. In another family development, his daughter Lynda Bird had married Charles S. Robb, a U.S. Marine Corps captain due to serve in Vietnam as of March 1968.

Wrestling with his decision, Johnson early in 1968 seemed to feel that he should step down. He apparently agreed with press secretary George Christian's view that he "had become a lightning rod for everything people in the country wanted to jump on." Especially, of course, as target of the Vietnam War protest movement.

While Johnson had his health to consider, his desire for a few quiet years with a burgeoning family, an escape from the pressures of office . . . he also was afraid the troops he had sent to Vietnam would feel betrayed if their commander in chief suddenly left the field.

What to do? The morning of January 17, 1968, the day fixed for his State of the Union address, he had studied the withdrawal statement drafted for him by George Christian. Still a big "if," it would not be something he would incorporate in the State of the Union speech itself. "If Lyndon decided to make it," said Lady Bird later, "the statement would come at the end, beginning with a line something like this: 'And now I want to speak about a personal matter. . . .'"

As late as 6:30 that evening, he paused and said to Lady Bird: "Well, what do you think? What shall I do?"

And she? "I looked at him with that hopeless feeling and said: 'Luci hopes you won't run. She wants you for herself and for Lyn and all of us. She does not want to give you up. Lynda hopes you will run. She told me so this afternoon with a sort of terrible earnestness, because her husband is going to war and she thinks there will be a better chance of getting him back alive and the war settled if you are President. Me—I don't know. I have said it all before. I can't tell you what to do.'"

And so, it might have depended upon the piece of paper that Lyndon Baines Johnson sought in his pocket as he reached the last page of his State of the Union address that evening of January 17, 1968.

What would he have done then? We'll never know, because the draft statement wasn't there.

We'll never know, but we can guess from his own explanation. He reached for it in his pocket, he later said. "I don't think I would have used it, but just to see if it was there. I don't know what I would have done if it had been there. I don't think I would have done it then, but it wasn't there, and I didn't have to confront the problem."

Later, of course, he did confront "the problem" and he did withdraw. The rest is history . . . and the night of January 17, 1968, a president of the United States did return to his White House quarters and ask his wife, "Why'd you have to keep that announcement?" And she apparently said, "I gave it back to you." And he? "No, you didn't." And then? "We both looked through my pockets and then went on, and there it was by the telephone table."

Funeral Train

"I SHALL NEVER FORGET THAT journey," wrote Secret Service Agent Edmund W. Starling. And indeed, mournfully rolling and scraping its way east on iron tracks came the funeral train. Indeed, "Sometimes it was the middle of the night when we crept slowly into a station, the bell of our locomotive clanging dolefully."

And in that doleful night, at that small station, he would see in the darkness on either side "the flicker of white garments," and he would hear "the low rolling tones of thousands of men softly singing 'Lead Kindly Light,' or 'Nearer My God to Thee.'"

They had left the West Coast—San Francisco, specifically—late on August 3 and they now would pass all the way east, practically ocean to ocean, across a nation that was obviously, clearly, "grief-stricken," exactly as Agent Starling said. Every city, every town encountered, "was in mourning."

By the long iron tracks stood the people weeping and singing hymns.

"Masons in full dress uniforms, with helmets and plumage, waited at each stopping place on the long 3,000-mile journey."

Across the continent they came, and "there seemed to be no sound but the beating of our bell and the voices, rising up and washing over our train like a tide."

And in Washington, merely more of the same. He lay in state at the White House first. Then a caisson carried the casket to the Capitol. "Never have I traveled that mile of Pennsylvania Avenue so slowly or with such an ache in my heart," wrote Starling, a White House veteran, many years later.

"Onward Christian Soldiers," played the Marine Band. "Nearer My God to Thee," enjoined "hundreds and hundreds" of school children along the route, the street strewn with their flowers. And then, after the Capitol rituals, another train, headed west to Ohio, his home.

All over again, the funeral train and its reception.

"All through the night, time after time, the locomotive slowed down and we heard the people singing."

He was on view at his father's house on Center Street. Marion, Ohio. The final rites and burial came on August 10, a procession winding through the hometown streets, past the newspaper where he once worked and his widow was his assistant, and on to the cemetery. More voices. More singing. More hymns. More throngs of mourners.

They don't say much or write much about Warren G. Harding today . . . but there was a time, obviously, when he was both mourned and loved.

First to Come, First to Go

WHEN PRESIDENT JOHN ADAMS CAME from the current national capital, Philadelphia, to see the emerging city of Washington in June of 1800, hardly 150 federal employees and only 500 or so households were there to greet him. The future Capitol was far from complete. The future White House had not yet been granted a privy.

Both the privy and a back stairs were added shortly after he moved into the shell of the presidential home that November, but Abigail Adams found only six rooms of the future mansion to be "comfortable."

Outside, in addition to the unsightly debris of construction, was a stable for seven horses, said to be somewhat advanced in years, together with a chariot, a coach, a market wagon.

For all their travels and exposure to upper-class culture in Europe, the Adams couple tended to be almost simple in taste and lifestyle. Certainly they were not extravagant or socially pretentious. An inventory of their furnishings at the White House, for instance, mentions the presidential bedroom had white dimity curtains and his parlor was "in tolerable order." The couple could boast three complete "Setable setts" of china and teaspoons to go with ladles and two fine "urns" of silver. Perhaps an extraordinary number for householders of today to consider were their thirty-three pairs of sheets.

They established their normal life on the second floor—upstairs. Here, a corner room on the west end of the southern side and the room next to it became their bedrooms. The great unfinished shell was so cold and drafty in the winter that the sun in those rooms was a warm friend. Adams made his office in the room adjoining his bedroom on its eastern side. The next room along the eastward prospect was a parlor and sitting room filled with crimson-hued pieces that once adorned their presidential drawing room in Philadelphia.

Joining the Adamses in their new home as its chief servants were John Briesler and his wife, Esther, long-term retainers who now served as the mansion's first steward and housekeeper. Normally, a grand home on the scale of the future White House would have boasted a staff of perhaps thirty servants, but the Adamses made do with the Brieslers and four added helpers—all paid from the couple's own pockets rather than from public funds. Settling in with the president and his wife for the winter of 1800–1801 were their son Thomas and their granddaughter Susannah.

The child's father was not Thomas, but rather their son Charles, who had died in New York in December. Only twenty-nine, a heavy drinker, he had suffered cirrhosis of the liver. His death, the first among presidential progeny, hit the first family hard. And on top of that sad news, John Adams lost his reelection bid in 1800 to Thomas Jefferson.

There was more bitterness during a bleak winter, with a divisive electoral college tie between Jefferson and Aaron Burr to be settled by the House of Representatives.

Inside the "castle," as Abigail Adams called it, construction work continued. The back stairway was finished in January, but only a huge space was evident at the west end of the transverse hall, to be filled during another administration by a magnificent grand stairway. The Adamses used the future Red Room, on the main floor, as a breakfast room. The kitchen was located at basement level, beneath the north entrance hall.

For the convenience of the home's first residents, architect James Hoban quickly built a wooden stairs from the balcony at the southern bow to the edge of a newly installed driveway leading southeast to Pennsylvania Avenue. Temporarily serving as an entrance hall, then, was the future Blue Room, known in its earliest days as the "oval saloon."

Probably the first major social functions held at the White House were the president's receptions for his legislators—House and Senate members. For the first one, the Adamses planned a Philadelphia-like procession of the official visitors, but Pennsylvania Avenue was a sea of mud from steady rains—few of the lawmakers could or would walk, as they had done in Philadelphia. Horse-drawn conveyances from as far away as Baltimore were pressed into service for the visitors from the Capitol. "They [then] piled out of rough, muddy vehicles, rushed across the wooden bridge in the rain into the entrance hall, where they stripped off their rain gear," wrote

William Seale in his two-volume history, *The President's House.*
"With their short-clothes, coats, shirts, hair powder and wigs, hose
and shoes relatively dry, they were joined at once by a number of
ladies."

After an exchange of greetings, Adams guided his visitors to the
refreshments awaiting them in the west end of the main floor, the
"State Room" of the early White House.

It was possibly here, too, in the White House, that one difficult
moment of the Adams denouement took place—the sharp conversation between Adams and Jefferson in which the rejected Adams
allegedly told his old ally and colleague, "You have put me out! You
have put me out!"

While they smoothed over their disagreements in later years, the
fact remained that an aging Adams was not to stay, while Jefferson
was, and they had political differences now that their young
Republic was on its feet and beginning to make its mark upon the
world.

By early 1801, Abigail Adams had left Washington for home,
while her husband, who had moved into the White House without
her, was again alone for his leavetaking. He thus was the first president to use the White House as a residence and the first to give it up
to a successor.

His time actually in residence had been very brief—only four
months. Busying himself in his upstairs office in the final weeks,
making appointments of Federalist allies that would infuriate
Jefferson before the latter's inauguration on March 4, 1801, Adams
was gone without a ripple when Washington awoke Inauguration
morning. Wagonloads of his belongings were packed and ready
when Adams mounted his coach about 4:00 A.M., long before light,
noted historian Seale. "The procession moved eastward unnoticed,
leaving the White House to Jefferson."

For the Record

ALREADY A DEEPLY DISTURBED WOMAN, Mary Todd Lincoln was so devastated by her husband's assassination that she would not attend his funeral—nor even leave the Executive Mansion for six weeks.

By then, the "funeral," actually a series of dramatic events, was over—sixteen days in the unfolding. She had had a voice in some of its planning. It was her decision, for instance, that he should be buried in their last hometown of Springfield, Illinois. And it was by her wish that little Willie Lincoln's coffin was disinterred from Oak Hill Cemetery in the Georgetown area . . . that little Willie would accompany his father on the long train trip back to Springfield and there lie beside him.

The very afternoon of his last day, Lincoln had noted the end of the rending Civil War and suggested that between that burden and "the loss of our darling Willie," he and his wife had both been "very miserable."

True, after Willie's death from a typhoid-like fever on February 20, 1862, Mary Todd had been so distraught she never again would enter the rooms in which he died and was embalmed. Now, her husband's body also had been embalmed on the premises—in the Prince of Wales Room, second floor, west hall, the very room where Willie had died.

First, nine doctors had gathered in there for the official autopsy. The spent bullet that killed Lincoln was recovered, dropping from one doctor's hands into a china basin with a clatter. Then came the embalming process. Lincoln's secretary of war, Edwin Stanton, personally dressed the body for public viewing before the burial. He rejected an offer to mask a bruise showing on the face. "No," he said, "this is part of the history of the event."

They moved the body the next night down to the East Room, the bearers shuffling along in their socks to avoid upsetting Mrs. Lincoln with the sound of their shoes while carrying out the unhappy task. Earlier, she had heard the hammering on the elaborate catafalque being built to hold the casket and thought she was hearing gunshots.

It was Tuesday, April 18, 1865, that Lincoln, clad in the suit worn at his second inauguration, went on view to the silent public filing through the East Room in two lines. He had been shot the night of April 14 and had died at 7:22 the next morning in a boardinghouse across the street from Ford's Theatre.

At noon on April 19 came the first real funeral service, the Rev. Phineas D. Gurley officiating and Lincoln's son Robert Todd in attendance ... but not Mrs. Lincoln. That afternoon the Lincoln coffin was taken to the Capitol, where it remained on view through the next day, a Thursday. On Friday morning began the train trip home to Springfield, Illinois, arranged by Stanton to nearly duplicate the route Lincoln had taken on his way to Washington from Springfield back in 1861 to become president.

So it was that this train made its major stops at Baltimore; Harrisburg, Pennsylvania; Philadelphia; New York City; Garrison's Landing near West Point; Albany; Buffalo; Cleveland; Columbus, Ohio; Indianapolis; Chicago, and, finally, Springfield. All along the route, small town or large, crowds and dignitaries marked Lincoln's passing among them, night or day. At Richmond, Indiana, just after three in the morning, some twelve thousand persons turned out—a number exceeding the local population. Funeral arches greeted the train in many towns, along with tolling bells and saluting guns. Two former presidents saw the funeral train slide by at its five-mile-per-hour pace for viewing—James Buchanan and Millard Fillmore.

In New York, local officials thought to bar representative blacks from taking part in the official procession from train to city hall and back, but Stanton quashed the unwholesome thought.

At last, on May 4, Lincoln was buried—temporarily—at Oak Ridge Cemetery in Springfield, with the Right Rev. Matthew Simpson, a Methodist bishop, giving the funeral oration. Lincoln's remains later would be placed in a permanent tomb at the National Lincoln Monument in the same cemetery in 1882 ... but not before there had been a plot to "steal" his remains and hold them hostage for the release of a counterfeiter from an Illinois prison at Joliet.

Lincoln was buried twenty days after his death. The funeral train, statisticians might wish to know, traveled exactly 1,662 miles and was only one hour late arriving in Springfield. A small fact, just for the record.

Long, Long Wait

THE WAITING FOR THIS PRESIDENT to come home to the White House is long and tedious. In the interim, there is an invitation list to consider. Four secretaries madly type up hundreds of names and then, in a room full of aides, staff members, friends, a brother-in-law in charge, the names are read out loud for approval or disapproval.

Decisions, tough decisions . . . sometimes ruthless but all necessary. Speed is absolutely mandatory. Telegrams must go out right away. Now!

Barney Ross? Old shipmate. From his navy days. Yes.

Billy Graham the evangelist? The really respected evangelist . . .

Silence.

Well?

"Billy considers himself a close friend of the president," says aide Lloyd Wright.

Somewhere in the night outside, headlights will be piercing the dark shroud over Washington. A particular vehicle will be struggling across the vale from air base to White House. A quiet and careful caravan of vehicles, actually, tires softly hissing on pavement. On his way home.

Inside, again a silence.

"By now," wrote an onlooking David Pearson years later, "there is real embarrassment in the air." And someone says they occasionally played golf together.

Finally, a voice of authority.

"No."

Next on the list?

And again the names. Yes, no. No, no, no . . . yes.

With Pearson, a high-ranking Peace Corps official, called in to help, the group headed by his boss, the brother-in-law, eventually has to move down the corridors, through darkened historic rooms, into the big room at the far east end of the main floor. The East Room.

By now it is 1:00 A.M.

They are busy studying the old Lincoln pictures. They move out the grand piano. People are draping the mirror frames, the chandelier above.

The decision is against exactly re-creating the Lincoln tableau. Too much. The great room would be "too morose and too dark." But mostly Lincolnesque, yes.

Word now comes to expect him at about 2:30 A.M.

What about a crucifix, says Pearson. They send for one, but . . . "it turns out to be pretty awful, with a bloody corpus."

The brother-in-law, Peace Corps director Sargent Shriver, says: "That's terrible. Go get the one in my bedroom."

Soon done. Danish, modern looking, and much more suitable.

New tension suddenly in the air. *Air Force One* has landed at the air base, at Andrews. He'll be here soon.

But, no, past 4:00 A.M., it turns out . . . past 4:30 A.M.

"Now, in the blackest part of the night, just before dawn, headlights begin to cut through the gloom in front of the White House. Most of us, embarrassed and feeling out of place, retreat to a corner of the East Room."

Ready. Ready as can be. . . .

Two candelabra and urns holding magnolia leaves from Andrew Jackson's tree on the south lawn now stand in the center of the large room, flanking the one dominating item—the catafalque.

It is really pretty terrible.

He is in the house, having gone on brief detour to Bethesda Naval Hospital for the necessary preparations.

Pearson would never forget. "I hear the routine sound of doors opening and closing, low voices," he wrote in the *Miami Herald* in 1967; "then come sounds that make me shiver. A military voice snaps a 'march' command; there is the clipped staccato sound of boots hitting the hard floors."

In moments, in the doorway, the strained young men, stern-faced but obviously awed by their task. They carry in the casket and set it down. And now a priest and two altar boys have materialized.

Kneeling in prayer . . .

He is here at last.

"The pallbearers step back from the casket. There is a short pause; no one quite knows what to do first. There has been no rehearsal. No one has had any experience. What do you do when you bring a dead President into the East Room of the White House at 4:30 in the morning?"

Prayers from the priest . . . and suddenly, in the doorway, she stands, his brother Bobby on one side and defense secretary Robert McNamara on the other.

An altar boy is lighting candles at each corner of the casket, and she stands there, "feet apart, the slight lean forward," eyes wide with disbelief, clothing stained still by blood . . . Jackie is back, too.

In an age, in a few minutes, the very private scene is over. One long moment she is at the casket kneeling, laying her forehead on it. "There is dead silence. Absolutely no sound of any kind." Then, she kisses the edge of the flag draped atop. She begins to stand, and then it happens. She slumps back down sobbing, sobbing, "rocked by sobs." Bobby helps, holds her . . . lets her cry. In the days ahead, noted Pearson later, she would present a regal, strong, "almost inhumanly stoic" image to the world . . . people might even wonder if she mourned, really mourned.

"But those of us in the East Room tonight know she did."

And as she is led away after her storm of grief, taken upstairs to rest and compose herself for the difficult hours and days ahead, this long night's wait is over. "They have brought John Kennedy home."

Nickel-Plated Shovel

"It was late in the evening, the cemetery was closed, it was just getting to dusk. We chased the newsmen out; they wanted to photograph the casket going in. It was just Smitty, the backhoe operator and me. We soldered the casket and backfilled the grave by hand. I felt far, far away. I was in a kind of daze looking out. It was the longest day of my life."

The day that JFK was laid to rest in Arlington National Cemetery.

Metro Kowalchick was there. A onetime coal miner from Pennsylvania, he retired in 1979 as the cemetery's operations chief and deputy superintendent. He retired back to a house in Pennsylvania atop an underground coal seam that had been on fire for more than two decades.

In 1963, the year of the Kennedy assassination, the week of the Kennedy assassination in Dallas, he was the man who lowered the casket into the ground after the crowds went away.

In fact, he and Smitty—Sylvester Smith—and a backhoe operator named Clifton Pollard dug the grave on the Arlington hillside to begin with. The Arlington cemetery staff had offered the Kennedy family one of three sites, but they "chose the first site we showed them." On the hillside it was, looking down the long vista of the Memorial Bridge leading into Washington.

"I drove the stakes in the ground," said Kowalchick years later. "They were wooden tent stakes."

Somehow he knew that JFK, himself, had passed by the site one time. "And he said something like, 'This is so peaceful. I could spend the rest of my life here'—or words to that effect."

That was something really to think about, but in the meantime there was work to do. "On Sunday, we dug the grave. We were going to do it by hand, but so many people had gathered. We put up a plywood and canvas wall."

They were trying to screen their grim work from the public, "but the news media had rented helicopters and were flying overhead."

Even so, the job was done. "We finished the sides off with a long-handled shovel. Smitty had it nickel-plated for me when I retired. It's sitting in my bedroom. It says 'From S. Smith to Big Boss' and I treasure it very much."

But back to '63, the job—"We dug down seven feet, deep enough for Mrs. Kennedy to be buried there too. The soil was hard clay; there was a big oak tree. It's still there."

Then came the day of the funeral, the burial, the crowds, the dignitaries, family, Jackie . . . *Air Force One* overhead dipping its wings in salute. Longest day in Kowalchick's life.

And at the end, every other detail done, the crowds and even the newsies gone, one more chore. His chore: "I was the one who tripped the button on the grave-site lowering device. It was chrome-plated with green straps. It's got a ratchet device that lowers the casket down."

Later, when he retired, reported Chip Brown in the *Washington Post,* a newspaper in Pennsylvania took notice. "When I retired, the *Shmokin News Item* ran a story that said 'Last Man to Touch Kennedy' or something like that. I have it in my scrapbook."

For years after his retirement, Kowalchick would visit Washington, visit the cemetery. His brother is buried there, too. "When I stop by the cemetery, they treat me like I'm part of the family. I always go by Kennedy's grave. It looks good."

Said Kowalchick also: "I don't know that I can explain my feelings. I was very touched with JFK, right from the beginning. . . ."

Wartime White House

WITH THE ADVENT OF WORLD War II, the federal city changed, the country changed, our world changed. And not far behind any of them was the White House. Before Pearl Harbor, recalled ABC-TV's David Brinkley in his book *Washington Goes to War,* a person could "walk through the White House gate and into the grounds without showing a pass or answering any questions, since the White House was not yet considered much different from any other public building in the city."

With war came security, unsurprisingly—more guards, underground bomb shelters, a war map room, unusual visitors from distant combat zones, and great secretiveness.

That first December of war, wrote presidential son Elliott Roosevelt later, albeit in a fictional murder mystery *(The White House Pantry Murder),* the windows were given blackout curtains, antiaircraft guns appeared on the roof, and "Gas masks in khaki canvas bags hung from their straps on the furniture everywhere in the house."

Winston Churchill arrived in great secrecy after crossing the Atlantic aboard a Royal Navy warship, a dangerous errand to be sure. His presence was made known only after he passed through those gates that Brinkley mentioned, just in time to help light the National Christmas Tree in 1941. A carefully kept secret for much longer was the fact that he suffered a slight cardiac episode while trying to open a stubborn White House window one night (the central heating having been a bit too much for his mostly English

With Congress declaring war on Japan December 8, 1941, the day after the Japanese attack on Pearl Harbor, President Franklin D. Roosevelt wasted no time signing the declaration of war. (Office of War Information Photograph, American Memory Collections, Library of Congress)

blood). Nevertheless, he carried right on in his planned conferences with Franklin Roosevelt, delighted to have America in the war at last as beleaguered England's ally against the Axis powers.

Churchill being Churchill, of course too, his visit gave rise to a number of colorful stories.

'Tis true, by retired Chief Usher J. B. West's later account, that Churchill constantly wore a one-piece jumpsuit, that he expected a bracing shot of Scotch for breakfast rather than a bracing orange juice, and that "the butlers wore a path in the carpet carrying trays laden with brandy to his suite."

And where in the White House did he actually stay? Well, the future Sir Winston settled that matter for himself, it seems. "Mrs. Roosevelt had arranged for him to stay in the Lincoln Bedroom, then located off the West Hall, the favorite of most male guests," wrote West. "However, he didn't like the bed, so he tried out all the beds and finally selected the Rose Suite at the east end of the second floor."

The added story is that when FDR one day was wheeled into the Rose Suite, there stood the famous British bulldog in all his altogether. Churchill didn't mind a bit, it seems, but FDR quickly backed off. "In his room," explained West later, "Mr. Churchill wore no clothes at all most of the time during the day."

Also noted by Brinkley in his book on the war's impact was the secrecy that attended various government activities, often necessary of course, but sometimes unbridled secrecy... such as the time FDR set off by train in September 1942 to visit U.S. war plants.

Only three reporters were allowed to board the special train on a hidden spur beneath the Bureau of Engraving and Printing, with the president riding along in his private car, called the "Ferdinand Magellan." "It was equipped with two elevators to lift his wheelchair on and off, an office, lounge, a bedroom, and galley. Beneath the floor were twelve inches of steel-reinforced concrete to protect him if a bomb were planted in the roadbed. The windows were bulletproof. The sides were of armor plate heavy enough to resist an artillery shell. There were three underwater escape hatches . . . to allow him to get out if the train derailed on a bridge and sank to the bottom of a river."

The reporters at first were enjoined from reporting the trip, even though—in wild contradiction to such secrecy—FDR appeared before thousands of factory workers at his secret destinations to give them encouraging pep talks.

At a ship launching in Portland, Oregon, he told fourteen thousand of them: "You know, I am not supposed to be here today. So you are the possessors of a secret that even the newspapers of the United States don't know. I hope you will keep the secret because I am under military and naval orders, and like the ship we have just seen launched today, my motions and movements are supposed to be a secret." When FDR returned to Washington, the White House reporters who had been left behind were so angry that they pounded on his office door when he was late starting an explanatory press conference.

Roosevelt may not have agreed, but usually the press corps treated him with a deference remarkable by today's standards—rarely photographing his leg braces, as one example. Sherwood Anderson, that artist with words who served as an FDR speechwriter, once explained that Roosevelt liked to "irritate" the press, "which so often had irritated him." Further, he had a small boy's fascination with mystery and he enjoyed wearing "the mantle of military security."

Such security often was needed, of course—in war, the president had to be protected. If he flew to a wartime Big Three conference in Teheran, Casablanca, or Yalta, his movements had to be clothed in secrecy and he had to be heavily guarded. All quite understandable . . . but FDR also had his visits to the hospital, using more than thirty aliases. He was a sick man before war's end, his clock winding down. At his unprecedented fourth inauguration, early in 1945, he informed his eldest son, James, that he had left instructions for his funeral in a certain safe. He also told James, "Among other things, I want you to have the family ring I wear." And it was just a few weeks later, in April, that a hastily summoned vice president Harry Truman rode the small elevator to the second floor of the White House, stepped into Eleanor Roosevelt's family sitting room, and felt her hand on his shoulder as she told him: "Harry, the President is dead."

Struggle With the Phone

LEAVING THE WHITE HOUSE AFTER years and years of coddling by staff upon staff was, for Dwight D. Eisenhower, a bit like abandoning a prettified domestic cat in the wildest of jungles. Only, he was the cat!

Here, for instance, was the man who had led the World War II

Crusade in Europe (the title of his book about the experience), who in 1961 didn't know how to pick up the telephone in his home at Gettysburg and make a simple long-distance call! Quite true, according to his biographer Stephen E. Ambrose.

The evening of January 20, 1961, just hours after leaving the White House to John F. Kennedy, Ike was back in Gettysburg, a private citizen now, and he wanted to call his son John. It was an unexpected and frustrating problem for the retired general, the former president of Columbia University, the former president of the United States. "For the past 20 years, whenever he wanted to make a call, he told a secretary to put it through for him."

In fact, he last had made a call all on his own in 1941. And back then, all he had to do was tell the operator what number he wanted, and the call went through.

Now, with a new president settling into the White House, it was fortunate for Ike that JFK had authorized an extra two weeks of duty for Ike's personal Secret Service "bodyguard," Special Agent Richard Flohr.

That night at Gettysburg, Ike tried to make his call by himself, but "[he] heard only a buzzing at the other end, shouted for the operator, clicked the receiver button a dozen times, tried dialing it like a safe, shouted again and slammed the phone down."

Enter Agent Flohr, who quickly showed the red-faced Eisenhower how the contraption worked—one small but essential lesson for the old housecat thrown back into the wild.

As Ambrose also points out, there were many other small details of everyday living that Ike had not had to deal with, things that most of us take for granted. He had never mixed frozen orange juice or paid at an automatic toll booth. Laundromats and barbershops were totally foreign to him. He hardly had ever been to a retail store, it seems. He wasn't in the habit of carrying money or credit cards on his person.

One time, Ambrose reports, while Ike was still president, he took his grandson, David, to a sporting goods store in Gettysburg and bought him an assortment of fishing gear. Then, to the owner's discomfort, he turned and walked out, "a Secret Service Agent carrying the packages." No attempt at payment!

Fortunately for all concerned, UPI's veteran White House reporter Merrimam Smith saw what happened and told the store owner simply to send a bill to the White House. Presumably, he did.

Political Know Nothings

RETIRING IN THE 1990s AS head White House gardener, Irvin Williams left behind a force of eighteen, electricians and plumbers among them. Together they tended eighteen acres of White House grounds inside the iron fences keeping the public from wandering in. They also maintained the 2.5 acres between the East Wing of the presidential home and the U.S. Treasury. Another eight gardeners did their work in an off-grounds greenhouse.

John and Abigail Adams moved in when the presidential acreage was still littered with construction debris. It was Thomas Jefferson—

Pat Nixon watches as husband Dick ceremoniously plants a tree on the South Lawn, thus joining a host of White House occupants who left behind various plantings as living legacies to their years in the Executive Mansion. (Courtesy Richard M. Nixon Library)

second official occupant, third president—who began the first real landscaping of the grounds. By the time Irwin Williams retired in 1994 after three decades of tending the White House flora, the garden force was planting one hundred thousand tulip bulbs every spring. The flower beds surrounding the fountain on the South Lawn alone "consumed," if that is the word, eight thousand Oxford red tulip bulbs.

"When the tulips at the South Fountain go, they're replaced with 1,500 geranium and salvia," he said. "That's our summer show. We'll come back in September with crysanthemums."

Overall, his domain in the middle of metropolitan Washington, D.C., contained more than 400 trees and 4,700 shrubs. As of 1994 also, 32 of the trees had been planted individually by presidents or their first ladies.

A quick tour, the *Associated Press* pointed out at the time, would include the John Quincy Adams elm, circa 1826, "dead for three years but living on as a graft on an elm sapling." Not to be missed either, "He [Williams] and his gardeners fight to prolong the life of Andrew Jackson's ancient southern Magnolia."

Before leaving his job, Williams said the hard work of producing gorgeous gardens was all worthwhile when people noticed—and commented upon—their beauty.

More wryly, having seen presidential families come and go over his time in the White House gardens, he also said: "We're here to provide what the first family needs. But what's so great about the job is that our trees, our plants, our shrubs, know nothing about politics."

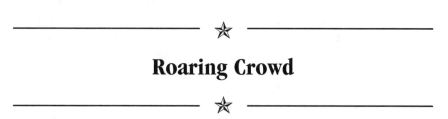

Roaring Crowd

A PARIAH TO HIS PRESIDENT and members of that official's inner circle, this was another vice president who took his oath of office in the dead of night, in a distant city, before a small group of sleepy-eyed observers rather than a roaring crowd.

A former beneficiary of the spoils system at its nineteenth-century worst, this onetime Collector of Customs for the Port of New York surprised all as president by supporting the Civil Service Reform Bill passed by Congress. Originally named to his party's presidential ticket as a sop to those disappointed by the choice for president, this man never was supposed to be president himself.

And when the new president was fatally wounded by a proclaimed follower of the Republican Stalwarts, there was suspicion that the vice president was somehow connected with the terrible deed.

As James A. Garfield then lay dying over the summer of 1881, Chester A. Arthur was greeted with little warmth by Garfield's grieving associates. He did his best to show compassion. Rather than serve as a reminder of the vice presidency's central purpose, he also kept his distance.

After Garfield's death, Arthur maintained his office in a senator's rowhouse quarters near the Capitol for another three to four months while directing a refurbishment of the rundown interior of the White House. In time, Arthur concocted a scheme to tear down the entire White House and replace it with two structures—one an office building, the other an elegant residence. His notion, thankfully, died for lack of funding. But Arthur nonetheless "redid" the East Room and other interior spaces with the help of Louis Tiffany . . . and in the process etched himself forever in history as the man who willfully sold off twenty-four wagonloads of earlier White House appurtenances. The preservationists have been hunting for most of those irreplaceable items ever since.

A surprise to Washington insiders and to the nation at large was his emergence as more of a real president than a political hack. Like John Tyler, Arthur refused to be a caretaker president—he not only endorsed early civil service reform, he generated a small tax cut, helped to reduce postage rates (from 3 cents to 2 cents for letters), presided over a tariff reduction, and refused to halt Chinese immigration. During his stewardship, the Brooklyn Bridge soared over the East River and the Washington Monument, started under James K. Polk years before, finally came to its point.

The public saw an active, energetic president . . . perhaps a bit of a New York dandy, but a man making an effort. He was a widower whose wife had died young (forty-two) of pneumonia, and he relied upon a sister, May McElroy, to serve as White House hostess.

Few were there to see when he awoke one morning at

Savannah, Georgia, bent over by abdominal pain and relieved only by a doctor's opiate. Few knew that for some years he had had kidney "trouble." Few knew that all the time he rigorously dashed around the country and about the White House in the role of president . . . that he was, in fact, dying.

He left the White House on March 4, 1885, to Grover Cleveland, returned to his home in New York—where he had been sworn in nearly four years earlier at 2:15 one September morning—and he died just a year later, age fifty-six, of Bright's disease of the kidneys. He never had really—openly at any rate—aspired to the presidency or considered a real election bid.

The day of his leavetaking, in a typical gesture by this quiet, decent man, he returned to the White House after Grover Cleveland's inaugural ceremony to inspect the State Dining Room, set for a ceremonial luncheon, and to bid each member of the staff goodbye, one by one.

When he had been officially installed in 1881, the crowd that heard his inaugural address had been hostile, silent. And so, it was nice that as Chester A. Arthur rose from Grover Cleveland's luncheon table at the White House and departed not quite four years later, a watching crowd outside bade him a fond, loud, and even roaring farewell.

Behind the dazzling white, wedding-cake facade seen by the average tourist or White House visitor lie the hard, jumbled facts of overcrowded, over-used facilities. The National Park Service hopes to fix all that with a multi-million-dollar project taking several years to accomplish. (National Park Service Photograph)

IV: As for the Future White House

"Imagine hosting four or five diplomatic receptions a week, and each time having to hire a moving company to transport the tables, chairs, and stages to the house, set them up, then take them back to a warehouse until the next event. That's the way things work at the White House, and it is confused and costly."

—THE WHITE HOUSE & PRESIDENT'S PARK,
COMPREHENSIVE DESIGN PLAN SUMMARY,
NATIONAL PARK SERVICE, DECEMBER 1998

Twenty-first Century White House

A COMPREHENSIVE TWENTY-YEAR, $300 MILLION overhaul of the White House grounds and related facilities was proposed by the National Park Service in 1998.

The proposed renovations for the eighty-two-acre "President's Park" and the immediate White House grounds would expand over-crowded facilities inside and outside the White House by digging in . . . going underground.

How else to solve the major space problems facing a twenty-first-century White House? As described by the Park Service, just on the "business side" of the presidential mansion, "The main problems are a shortage of meeting space, inadequate facilities for the White House press corps—now numbering in the thousands—and the glut of cars, trucks and delivery vans that take over President's Park."

Today's overly confined press room, built on the site of FDR's swimming pool, would be supplemented by new underground space in front of the West Wing. There, a much larger facility devot-ed solely to the media would include a new "presidential briefing room, interview rooms, and additional space for television crews, photographers and White House correspondents," plus, for the first time, separate space for foreign reporters. It all would be called the "Press Corps Center."

But that apparently does not mean the press would be shunted away from the West Wing, center of White House action. "The news media would continue to occupy the first floor of the west colon-nade."

On the residential side, the first family would be provided a recreation center, also likely to be buried out of sight north of the west wing, as a roomy relief from the often too-cramped family quar-ters. It would be a combined den, gym, and entertainment area for the White House residents of the future.

The really major aspects of the comprehensive plan, however, have more to do with parking cars and handling the flow of 1.2 mil-lion visitors who tour the White House every year. Two different underground garages for parking, plus a tunnel and moving sidewalk for the tourists would be added.

A major aim in any revamping of the White House grounds would be to resolve the chaotic delivery problems, storage problems, and entertainment problems the White House staff and occupants have struggled with for some years.

A summary of the comprehensive plan said that the presidential home is woefully ill-prepared to handle all its social functions. "Imagine hosting four or five diplomatic receptions a week, and each time having to hire a moving company to transport the tables, chairs and stages to the house, set them up, then take them back to a warehouse until the next event," said the summary. "That's the way things work at the White House, and it is confused and costly."

In addition, "Closets, corridors, and driveways overflow with furniture and equipment, as though the staff were having a tag sale. No modern hotel would put up with such chaos, yet the White House has been doing it for years because it has no choice."

One proposed change: "The convoys of trucks and vans that reg-

The visitors who line up outdoors today for the daily tours of the public White House rooms would gather indoors, out of the weather, and move into the White House grounds through an underground walking sidewalk. (National Park Service Photograph)

ularly jam the White House grounds would be redirected to loading docks beneath the New Executive Office Building, with deliveries to the White House and adjacent buildings by small vehicles similar to golf carts."

Also, "Additional storage space beneath Pennsylvania Avenue would relieve the pressure of nonstop special events—from state dinners to Easter egg rolls—that comprise daily life at the White House."

As for visitation by the general public, the physical amenities for those taking the White House tour in the twenty-first century would have an entirely new look. Instead of waiting in line, outdoors, on adjoining Fifteenth and E Streets, sometimes for hours, tourists would start their White House visit at an expanded visitor center in the nearby Commerce Building. The expansion of that now-existing facility would accommodate "a museum, four video theaters and new exhibits on the history of the White House and the American presidency." Replacing today's exhibits ("static and disconnected, providing bits and pieces of information but no overall picture"), the new displays would be interactive and computer driven. "Click on 'Gilbert Stuart' and learn the fascinating story of his famous portrait of George Washington and its dramatic rescue by Dolley Madison's servants. Click again to view the collection of White House china, or visit Monticello, the LBJ Ranch and other presidential sites around the country.

"After viewing the exhibits and watching a brief orientation film, visitors will proceed to a moving sidewalk that will carry them underneath Fifteenth and E Streets to the White House fence." There, they will resurface and "proceed directly to the East Entrance to the White House, ready to see the real thing."

As for the parking and traffic problems that have plagued Presidents' Park in recent years, clogging its small vehicular arteries, spoiling the vista once afforded by the smooth Ellipse south of the White House, the plan envisions coordinated remedies. "To reclaim President's Park from the automobile, the plan proposes two dramatic additions: a two-story, 290-car parking garage beneath Pennsylvania Avenue, and an 850-car garage under the Ellipse," said the plan's summary document. "The first would be for presidential motorcades, visiting dignitaries and senior White House staff, the second for staff during the week and possibly the public on weekends and holidays."

Overall, the proposed overhaul would "provide the space and services that are taken for granted in modern office buildings but that are currently lacking in the headquarters of American government."

It's a goal that's difficult to fault: "The plan will protect the White House's historic setting and dramatic views, while increasing the enjoyment of millions of people who visit it."

Mirror, mirror on the wall, who was the fairest of them all?
Among the first ladies of modern times, it might well have
been Jackie Kennedy, who with youthful husband Jack created
the "Camelot" image associated with the JFK White House.
Taken in 1961, this was the first official White House photo of
Jackie Kennedy. (Photo by Mark Shaw, American Memory
Collections, Library of Congress)

V: First Ladies in Review

By Ingrid Smyer

"This was I and yet not I—this was the wife of the President of the United States, and she took precedence over me."

GRACE COOLIDGE, WIFE OF CALVIN

The First Ladies

SOME, SUCH AS MARTHA, EDITH and Eleanor, came strictly from the aristocracy. Some—Rosalynn, Dolley, Eliza—were of humble beginnings. Rich, poor . . . some formally educated, most not.

Some were beautiful, some plain. Some were social leaders and trendsetters. Others were demure or even reclusive. Some were vigorous, others frail and sickly. A few were outright invalids.

And still one thread binds together all these disparate women in the tapestry of the Stars and Stripes. All, every one . . . were first ladies.

Today, it often is the husbands, the men, who are remembered. And yet "marrying up" frequently was the pattern for those very same men, whose wives later became the nation's first ladies. While young themselves, the women often saw the potential of their young men, saw promise that others just as frequently failed to perceive. Martha Custis, first of them all, chose to marry a man who had been turned down by others, her wealth a continuing bone of contention for them both. Even after he became president, the "Father of His Country" once was told to his face, "What would you have been if you hadn't married the rich widow Custis?"

But with all the power and pomp, all the fame and glory, for the most part these women fell in love with their life partners. And their stories are love stories.

✶ Martha Washington, wife of George

Martha Dandridge Custis, at twenty-six a widow with two small children, was managing her vast estate when she met the tall and elegant George Washington. It was May and apparently it was love at first sight, for by July he felt free to write to her: "I embrace the Opportunity to send a few words to one whose life is now inseparable from mine."

Accustomed to the easy life of her childhood on a plantation in Tidewater Virginia, "Patsy," as the future general and president called his bride, was a spunky young woman who once rode her horse up and down the stairs of her uncle's house. But her instinctive sense of noblesse oblige stood her well when the general led the Continental Army, and she joined him whenever she could, both to comfort his soldiers and to bolster the spirit of her "Old Man," as she fondly called him.

And when Washington became the first president of the United States after the Revolutionary War, "Lady Washington" was as diligent in her new position as she had been in every challenge. Americans, and indeed a curious world, were watching as she set a style for the new nation. She entertained formally yet set her guests at ease. Abigail Adams quickly became an admirer and friend, at one point observing that "a most becoming pleasantness sits upon her [Martha's] countenance and an unaffected deportment . . . renders her the object of veneration and respect."

Abigail even compared Martha to royalty: "I found myself much more deeply impressed than I ever did before their Majesties of Britain." And who should come next after Martha the trendsetter but Abigail herself, a first lady in her own right.

☆ Abigail Adams, wife of John

The very first "Presidentress" to live in the "cold and damp" President's House (for all of four months), she is the only woman to have been wife to one president and mother to another.

"Remember the ladies" was the plea Abigail Smith Adams wrote to her husband when he was in Philadelphia to help write the Declaration of Independence. In many ways surprisingly modern in outlook, she insisted that women were the intellectual equal of men. Though she became one of the best-read women in the country, she bemoaned her society's failure to accord women formal education. She bridled at the ridicule aimed at "Female learning." If men were trained to become "Heroes, Statesmen and Philosophers," then the other half of the population should become "Learned Women," she declared.

Neither her views nor her deportment was surprising for the daughter of a prominent Congregational minister and descendant, on her mother's side, of the Massachusetts Quincys. Like many a modern first lady, she not only was a conscientious White House hostess who gave lively levees (receptions), but she also was a champion of the president's policies, one quite comfortable in discussing the issues of the day. She was his "Lordess" (his pet name for Abigail) and helpmate throughout their long and loving life together.

☆ Dolley Madison, wife of James

Arriving in the President's House after the widower Thomas Jefferson's departure were the thoroughly compatible "survivors" of a once unlikely match. She had been raised in Philadelphia as a Quaker, widowed with a son, disowned for marrying outside the faith. He was an aristocratic Virginian, puny in stature and dour to some, but described by his future wife as the "great little Madison." And they blossomed together.

Beautiful, vivacious, and full of fun, the former Dolley Payne Todd quickly became the "Queen of Washington City," with a reign that lasted throughout a long life. She was a part-time hostess for the widowed Jefferson as wife of his secretary of state, and she then presided over the nation's first inaugural ball when her husband became president in 1809. After their White House tenure, she continued to play hostess to a parade of visitors, domestic and foreign, both at their Montpelier estate in Virginia and later, after Madison's death in 1836, at her townhouse on Lafayette Square in sight of the White House. President Zachary Taylor on the occasion of Dolley's death said: "She will never be forgotten because she was truly our First Lady for a half-century."

☆ Elizabeth Monroe, wife of James

Elegant, composed, charming, and beautiful, even regal, Elizabeth Kortright Monroe was also a bit mysterious. She came from New York City; her father had been a privateer for the British in the French and Indian War of the 1750s, but he was strangely invisible during the Revolutionary War. Monroe himself once said that his seventeen-year-old bride's father was "injured in his fortunes" during that recent rebellion.

In any case, Elizabeth's friends teased her when she chose the young lawyer from Virginia for her life partner, suggesting that she should have done better. But love won out and her husband's rising diplomatic career soon found them in the courts of Europe. The French were impressed with the stately U.S. minister's wife, referring to her as *"la belle Americaine."* She then stunned one and all by going alone by carriage through the riotous streets of Paris to visit

Madame Lafayette in her prison confines. This show of interest by the wife of the American minister often is credited with persuading leaders of the revolutionary French government to drop any thoughts of sending Lafayette's wife to the guillotine and to release her instead.

Taking up residence in the White House in 1817, the Monroes startled Washington by refusing to pay social calls, but they also instituted weekly receptions open to the public as a democratic gesture all their own. Elizabeth Monroe often suffered from poor health during her White House years, one reason given for her avoidance of the traditional social calls paid on homes scattered across a city of rough, muddy roads. In the White House, she created a formal, almost European atmosphere—oddly, some critics considered her a snob, others complained she too often hosted common riffraff.

✭ Louisa Adams, wife of John Quincy

The only first lady to be born outside the United States, the former Louisa Catherine Johnson came to this country for the first time four years after she married John Quincy Adams. Born in England, pampered and adored as a child, she seemed as a young woman to be easily drawn to the young New Englander, but in her own words, "had to be coaxed into an affection." Theirs was not quite the unabashed love story of his parents, but their differences eased in their later years.

As they traveled extensively throughout Europe in the course of her husband's diplomatic assignments, her salon became a mecca for dignitaries of all kinds. She preferred Washington society to the Yankee farm life of Quincy, Massachusetts, and was most happy to spend her allotted years in the presidential mansion (packed with family) and later to live in Washington again after the former president returned to serve as a House member for seventeen years. She managed to die in the federal city as well—and Congress adjourned in her honor.

✭ Letitia Tyler, wife of John

Shocked to find herself first lady after the sudden death of William Henry Harrison in 1841, Letitia Tyler was the first first lady to occupy the White House since the departure of Louisa Adams in 1829. Both Andrew Jackson and his successor, Martin Van Buren, were widower presidents, and Harrison died before his wife, Anna, could move into the White House with him.

Nor was Letitia Tyler anxious to fulfill her new role—a near invalid, she really couldn't do so very actively. Even in better health, she would have preferred to stay in her native Virginia tending to the plantation, the children, the neighbors, the quiet and demure life of a very gentle, genteel, and self-effacing woman. At the White House, her frail health kept her out of sight in the family quarters— her only appearance at a White House social function was for the wedding of daughter Elizabeth in early 1842. She then, later in 1842, became the first president's wife to die in the White House or during a president's term in office.

★ Julia Tyler, wife of John

Born into wealth and privilege, Julia Gardiner, "the Rose of Long Island," was in the bloom of youth and fresh from the traditional Grand Tour of Europe when she arrived in Washington for its 1843–44 social season. Here she met a grieving President Tyler . . . and soon she also was grieving, over the sudden death of her father in a freak accident aboard the U.S. Navy frigate *Princeton.*

They married the following summer, in 1844, a shock to Tyler's children by his late first wife, Letitia (mother of seven, but two died in infancy). The marriage was socially controversial as well and often ridiculed by critics. But the charming Julia had her defenders. "Under her short reign," wrote a Virginia gentleman, "society was charmed by the splendor and propriety of affairs at the White House." The ladies could be less charitable, complaining that she put on airs by receiving her White House guests on a raised platform— queenlike. Newspapers and sometimes admiring friends called her "Lady Presidentress."

Despite the great disparity in their respective ages (two decades), she stayed by Tyler's side until his death in 1862 (bearing him another seven children in the interim). And nobody ever argued with the Julia Tyler legacy calling for a rendition of "Hail to the Chief" whenever a president appears in public.

★ Sarah Polk, wife of James

Better educated than most of her female contemporaries, Sarah Childress hailed from Murfreesboro, Tennessee, the child of well-to-do parents who provided formal tutoring at home and further schooling at the Moravian "Female Academy" at Salem, North Carolina. Like Abigail Adams, she became an avid reader and later was a well-informed helpmate—if not the driving force—behind her husband, James K. Polk. With no children to take up her time and energies, she could act as his secretary, his staunch campaigner, and close adviser.

She worked hard for his election victories all the way up the political ladder—from Tennessee statehouse to governor's mansion to the White House. She loved Washington, their last such stop together, and thrived on its combination of political and social life. She impressed many with her striking "Spanish" looks, her intelligence and her charm. By all accounts, one of the most popular first ladies ever.

✱ Margaret Taylor, wife of Zachary

Margaret Mackall Smith Taylor did not want her husband to run for president in 1848. In fact, she bewailed the idea as a plot to deprive her of her husband's company and "shorten his life by unnecessary care and responsibilities." Could she have had a crystal ball? Just fifteen months later, Zachary Taylor would be dead.

"Peggy" Smith was born into a prominent family in Maryland with connections to the leading families of Virginia, but she had no desire to reign over Washington society. She had given many uncomplaining years to army life, moving from one rustic post to another, and now she preferred to settle down with "Old Zack" in a quiet little cottage in Louisiana. When she did finally arrive at the White House, she remained in the background and delegated first lady social duties to her twenty-two-year-old daughter, Betty Knox Bliss, acting hostess at the White House. They both had to leave, of course, after Zachary Taylor suddenly died in early July 1850.

✱ Abigail Fillmore, wife of Millard

Abigail Powers Fillmore was a minister's daughter, an avid reader, book lover, and teacher. When her Baptist minister father, Lemuel Powers, died, this Abigail's mother moved westward to a frontier-like village in New York State and it was here, at only sixteen, that Abigail Powers began to teach in a country schoolhouse. It was here, as well, that a determined and ambitious farm boy appeared in her classroom. Over books they fell in love and became engaged, despite objections from her family that he was beneath her socially. But love prevailed and after a long engagement she and Millard were married at the home of her brother in 1826.

The first of all the president's wives to hold a job outside the home, Abigail continued to teach until her first child was born, but she never stopped learning. Her husband valued her intellect and often asked her opinions on political matters. She is best remembered for a lasting contribution to the White House—not finding so much as a dictionary in the mansion, she began a crusade to start a White House library. She pursued her goal with such gusto that she secured an appropriation from Congress and established the nucleus of the library still filling the executive bookshelves today.

☆ Jane Pierce, wife of Franklin

"The shadow in the White House," as she came to be called, Jane Means Appleton Pierce did seem to have a gloom cloud about her. She had lost two sons earlier and just after her husband was elected to the presidency, the Pierces and their third son were on a train that derailed. They witnessed the tragic death of their eleven-year-old son Benny, while they themselves were left unscathed.

As daughter of the president of Bowdoin College, the Reverend Jesse Appleton, Jane in happier days had met a Bowdoin graduate, a young lawyer with political ambitions, Franklin Pierce. They were an unlikely pair—he an outgoing and hearty suitor who loved mingling with the rowdy politicians and she, shy, melancholy, and often in poor health. They married some years later, even though her family opposed the match. When she heard that her former congressman husband had been nominated by the Democratic Party to head the presidential ticket in 1852, she fainted. She then hoped he would not be elected, but when that, too, came to pass, she reluctantly and with considerable delay moved to the White House, where she found little pleasure.

She was a devout churchgoer, it seems. She was not easy to know—or to fathom. The author Nathaniel Hawthorne, a family friend, perhaps summed up Jane Pierce best when, on the day of her funeral, he said that she never seemed to have anything to do with "things present."

✶ Miss Harriet "Hal" Lane, niece of James Buchanan

After the gloom of the Pierce White House and two somewhat reclusive first ladies before, Washington society welcomed the bright and cheerful young "Democratic Queen" Harriet "Hal" Lane, bachelor president James Buchanan's favorite niece—also a ward whom he treated like a daughter.

Afraid she would be "spoiled outright," Buchanan was reluctant to allow her to join him in London when he was minister to the Court of Saint James, but join she did, and soon she was dancing at Buckingham Palace. In letters to her sister, she airily wrote that "Her Majesty was very gracious to me as also was the Prince."

With such happy memories in mind, Harriet returned to a United States rent with sectional controversy. In 1857, as official hostess at the White House, Harriet "glided on the tightrope of faultless social etiquette," wrote Bess Furman in her book *White House Profile,* "balancing with the parasol of discretion."

She left her art collection to the Smithsonian Institution and a generous sum to Johns Hopkins Hospital.

✶ Mary Lincoln, wife of Abraham

Mary Todd Lincoln came to the White House under the cloud of a nation in crisis—its worst ever. Several states had seceded and the Union was in jeopardy. The country stood on the brink of war. Her husband had been elected president by a narrow margin—certainly no mandate—and across the nation, he was a controversial figure at best. As further discomfort for the new mistress of the White House, a largely pro-Southern Washington society was in no mood to welcome the Republican outsiders from the Middle West . . . even if she could claim Kentucky as her birthplace.

Mary Todd's impetuous ways, along with her extravagant taste in clothes and entertainment, didn't help and soon provoked ridicule in some circles. Then she exceeded the funds appropriated by Congress for White House renovations. The press had a field day with that one—husband Abraham Lincoln was both embarrassed and displeased. Little did he know in the aftermath that she still was running up personal bills that would be difficult to meet.

Mary's critics faulted her supposed influence over the president, a concern that was neither new nor destined to fade away in the case of future first ladies. The same thing was said of Abigail

Adams and Sarah Polk in the past, and it again would be said of more recent first ladies—especially Edith Wilson, Eleanor Roosevelt, Nancy Reagan, Rosalynn Carter, and Hillary Rodham Clinton. But, few, if any, of the nation's first ladies ever were so vilified as Mary Todd Lincoln. Among other charges, this unhappy woman was even accused of treason! Hardly bearing up after the untimely deaths of two young sons, easily overwrought in any case, she found herself "surrounded on every side by people who were ready to exaggerate her shortcomings," wrote nineteenth-century author and social commentator Laura C. Holloway.

Born in Lexington, Kentucky, to Eliza and Robert Smith Todd, she had all the advantages that a fairly wealthy and well-connected father could offer, including education at Madame Mentelle's finishing school. Later she went to Springfield, Illinois, to live with her older sister and her husband. Here she met the man who would be her husband—Mary Todd and Abraham Lincoln were married in 1842. Four years later, she responded to a friend's favorable comment about Lincoln. "Yes, he is a great favorite everywhere," said Mary. "He is to be President of the United States some day; If I had not thought so, I never would have married him, for you can see he is not pretty."

The Lincolns had four sons—young Eddie died before they reached Washington; then the loss of little Willie at the White House in 1862 from typhoid fever (and brother Tad's own near death at the same time) became almost more than Mary could stand. She began to have dreams of Willie visiting her; to assuage her grief she began attending spiritualistic seances. Her excessive mourning was criticized by those whose sons were dying on the battlefields of the Civil War. There are tales, too, of her excessive jealousy—one time, she created an ugly scene over a general's wife riding horseback next to Lincoln and ahead of Mary's own carriage.

There were, however, some bright moments in her tenure at the White House, among them husband Abe's second election in November 1864 and the collapse of the Confederacy in April 1865. To celebrate the latter, Mary and Abe went for a carriage ride on the afternoon of Friday, April 14. "Dear Husband," she said, "you almost startle me by your cheerfulness." But his joy was to be shortlived. Lincoln was fatally shot that very night.

Through all their life together, Abe Lincoln's devotion to Mary was apparently undying. At one of their White House receptions (the one area in which her "press" was positive), a guest was complimenting Lincoln on Mary's social graces. "My wife is as handsome as when she was a girl," he replied. "I fell in love with her; and what is more, I have never fallen out."

Sad to say, Mary had impossible, crushing burdens heaped on her already weak shoulders—even young Tad would die within a few years of their leaving the White House in 1865. Robert Todd Lincoln, her only surviving child, later in life would serve as secretary of war under Presidents James Garfield (also assassinated) and Chester Arthur. Mary Todd Lincoln, clearly unhinged by her many trials, briefly was committed to an insane asylum (at son Robert's instigation) and died in 1882, in her midsixties.

✯ Eliza Johnson, wife of Andrew

Wife of the first president to be impeached by the House of Representatives, Eliza McCardle Johnson never wavered in her support for her husband. Nor did she even lose faith in his destiny. When a White House employee brought her news of the Senate's vote of acquittal, she cried, "I knew he'd be acquitted; I knew it."

Her parents, Sarah Phillips and John McCardle, a shoemaker, were simple folk, but they encouraged Eliza in her education. She was delighted she could use her basic education and help her "beau," as she called the young Andrew Johnson, with his writing and arithmetic.

The White House years were not happy ones for Eliza, who was ill and had to excuse herself from social duties because, "I am an invalid." Her capable daughter Martha, who as a schoolgirl had been in and out of the mansion when the Polks lived there, took over as the mistress virtually running the White House. This she did impeccably, including supervision of extensive renovations.

Eliza made only one appearance at a social function in her years at the White House: at a party for her grandchildren. She preferred to stay in the small room on the second floor that she had chosen for herself.

✯ Julia Grant, wife of Ulysses

At last a first lady was having a rollicking good time in the old mansion! After the gloom and doom of the last three presidencies—the country split asunder, the Civil War, the assassination of a president, then the impeachment trial of another—the Gilded Age (as Mark Twain called it) arrived and the Grants were right for the times.

Theirs was a story of lifelong devotion between two unlikely candidates. Julia Dent, favorite daughter of Frederick Dent, a Missouri planter and slaveowner, friendly, outgoing, and full of fun, was popular in her St. Louis society. Ulysses was the shy West Point cadet from Ohio who had shone at the academy only in horsemanship. He was a classmate of her brother Frederick. Julia and Ulysses met for the first time when he came to visit during a spring holiday.

Her father didn't think a soldier's life would be good enough for his daughter, but with cross-eyed (yes, cross-eyed) Julia and "Ulys," as she came to call him, it was love, and that was that.

They were married four years later—after the Mexican War. Grant then resigned his commission and tried his hand at various business ventures, only to meet with consistent defeat. When they were apart for any length of time, he drank heavily. Through good times and bad, though, Julia was there for him.

His salvation may have been the Civil War. Proud of her now-victorious general, she often visited him at his headquarters. An aide-de-camp said that they would sit quietly in some corner of his tent holding hands, and if anyone happened by they would blush as "two young lovers."

When the general became the president, Julia entered the "happiest period" of her life. She loved hobnobbing with the great, the near-great, even the nobodies. At her White House parties "there were ladies from Paris in elegant attire and ladies from the interior in calico," noted social commentator Ben Poore, "ladies whose cheeks were tinged with rouge, and others whose faces were weather-bronzed by outdoor work; chambermaids elbowed countesses, and all enjoyed themselves."

Fun-loving Julia showed her serious side at times and wasn't afraid to speak her mind. Grant was known to tease about having to keep his cabinet choices secret to keep her from interfering.

After they left the White House, they went on a grand tour of the world. They were popular in the courts of Europe, where they were known as America's first cheerful family to inhabit the White House in more than two decades. Sadly, Grant the private citizen lost in bad business gambles. He recouped his finances with the proceeds of his autobiography, completed just before he died of cancer.

✯ Lucy Hayes, wife of Rutherford

Madonna-like, praised for her quiet dignity and hailed by the press for simplifying the era's code of dress was Lucy Ware Webb Hayes. She also brought morning worship to the White House, and her Sunday evening "hymn-sing," drawing cabinet members and congressmen, became famous.

When the teetotaler Hayeses were making up the menu in preparation for a dinner honoring two Russian grand dukes in August 1877, the secretary of state, William Evarts, pleaded with them to serve wine. A table was set with six wine glasses at each place, but these were the last to be seen at the Hayeses' White House.

Thanks to her liquor ban, Lucy became the darling of the Women's Christian Temperance Union (WCTU), but her detractors dubbed her "Lemonade Lucy."

Born the daughter of Dr. James and Maria Webb, Lucy was interested in the feminist movement. She wrote that woman is not "the slave of man but his equal in all things, and his superior in some." But she never took an active role in the "new woman" movement nor in any way supported the WCTU, even though the leaders of both groups had solicited her endorsement. One critic, Emily Briggs, wrote to her wanting to know if the president's wife approved of "the progress of women in the high road of civilization or whether you are content because destiny lifted you to an exalted position . . . so you cannot hear the groans of the countless of our sex."

She remained aloof from all such causes, yet it was the WCTU that commissioned the portrait of Lucy Hayes presented to the White House upon her leavetaking as first lady.

✯ Lucretia Garfield, wife of James

Both Lucretia Rudolph and James Garfield took their religion seriously, accepting the Protestant work ethic without question. They were devoted to education and literature, enjoyed reading books together and attending plays, concerts, and lectures. Still, their relationship was a struggle.

During their courting days, he once "told" his diary: "There is no delirium of passion nor overwhelming power of feeling that draws me to her irresistibly." And her concern was that she loved him more than she did God. Their differences were more of personality than of circumstances. She was shy and reticent, he outgoing and gregarious . . . with strong, sometimes regrettable interests beyond home and hearth.

The "years of darkness," as the Garfields referred to their early life together became a "truce of sadness," as she forgave his indiscretions. By the time his career had taken them from Ohio to Washington for his House tenure, he could share family life with political career. His journal began to reflect deeper feeling: "she is the best woman I have ever known" and "she is the light of my life." He was an active father to their five children, too. By the time they reached the White House, "Crete," the pet name he came to call her, was deeply involved in her husband's career. Cabinet appointee James Blaine wrote to Garfield that Mrs. Garfield's backing "is more valuable to me than even the desire of the President-elect himself." Others, though, found her to be too reserved to be a social success in their short, 186-day White House stay.

The Garfield "truce" of course ended in tragedy—no sooner had "Crete" begun to recuperate from an illness than her husband was shot and fatally wounded by a crazed assassin. He clung to life for weeks, but then died.

✶ Ellen Arthur, wife of Chester

"Nell" Herndon Arthur died the year before Vice President Arthur vaulted into the Presidency; he was so remorseful for having neglected her for politics that he gave a stained-glass window in her memory to St. John's Episcopal Church in Washington, where she had sung in the choir as a young woman. He had it placed in the south side of the building so he could see it from the White House. His younger sister, Mary McElroy, served as hostess of the White House.

✶ Frances Cleveland, wife of Grover

Soon after the inauguration of the forty-eight-year-old Grover Cleveland, the widow of his former law partner, Mrs. Oscar Folsom, and her daughter Frances were invited to the White House. Washington society was atwitter, and gossip columnists naturally hailed the mother as the lady to watch. As it turned out, it was Frances whom Cleveland was courting—after "waiting for her to grow up." When law partner Oscar died in an accident years before, Cleveland became administrator of the estate and took a guardian-like interest in the eleven-year-old Folsom daughter.

She grew up, he proposed, they were married—and they even lived happily ever after. Their wedding in the Blue Room was the first presidential marriage in the White House. The couple set other "firsts" as well: Cleveland was to serve an unprecedented second term after an absence of four years, and a baby girl born to the couple during his second administration was the first to be born to a president in the White House.

"Frank," as the president called his young wife, became one of the most popular women in America. She, like Dolley Madison before her, became a role model to emulate. Newspapers and magazines of the day were filled with stories about the beautiful and elegant Mrs. Cleveland. But she had a serious side as well. A graduate of Wells College, Frances showed an interest in women's issues of the day, but she, like Lucy Hayes, refused to lend her name to any causes.

★ Caroline Harrison, wife of Benjamin

Yet another clergyman's daughter was destined to become a first lady. This time it was Caroline Lavinia Scott, whose father, Dr. John Witherspoon Scott, was a Presbyterian minister and president and founder of Oxford Female Seminary in Oxford, Ohio. One of his students was Benjamin Harrison, who would win his daughter's heart. And on October 20, 1853, Dr. Scott would perform the marriage ceremony himself.

When Harrison reached the White House in 1889, the venerable old structure was in such disrepair that Caroline ("Carrie") at once found her pet project—a campaign for a new White House. Congress granted her $35,000, a sizable amount in those days, to restore the old place instead. She went at her task with vigor, leaving not one drawer, cabinet, or closet untouched. In the process she found old, chipped, and broken china, which she sorted through—and thus she began the collection of china patterns of former first ladies that was to become a popular tourist attraction. And, using her own design—based on the four-leafed clover—she ordered a new set of china to add to the collection.

Caroline Harrison also is remembered as a founding member of the Daughters of the American Revolution (DAR) in 1890. She died of tuberculosis at the White House in October 1892, with just a few months remaining in her husband's presidency.

☆ Ida McKinley, wife of William

Of all the reclusive, sickly, or invalid wives in the White House, none was more pitiful or pampered by a husband than Ida Saxton McKinley.

As the beautiful, witty, energetic belle of Canton, Ohio, she once had every reason to expect a full active life and she was determined to spend it with the handsome young lawyer she met at a church picnic, William McKinley. Married in 1871, they were markedly devoted to one another. After a series of deaths in the family, including that of a daughter, however, Ida's health began to deteriorate. She suffered phlebitis and began to experience seizures. Although the word was never mentioned in the newspapers, it was whispered her illness was epilepsy.

When McKinley was being groomed as a presidential candidate by the Republican Party, some GOP strategists wondered if his wife were up to the job. By the time the McKinleys reached the White House, however, her health had improved and she was determined to perform her duties as first lady. Indeed, she sometimes stood in the long reception lines, but more often she received their guests while seated and holding a bouquet of flowers to avoid handshaking. And the president broke with protocol at state dinners by seating his wife at his side so that he could watch over her. If a seizure came on, it is said, he simply took out a handkerchief that he kept in his pocket for this purpose, placed it over her face, and continued with his conversation.

In time, Ida became more petulant, more dependent on him; his devotion to her earned him the title of "saint" by his friends—a term not always used with kindness. When he was shot by an assassin in September 1901, Ida amazed one and all, including her doctors, by the way she rallied, stayed by his bedside, and bolstered his spirits for the few days he lingered before death.

☆ Edith Roosevelt, wife of Theodore

A friend from childhood, raised in the same privileged New York society, Edith Kermit Carow was still there, seemingly waiting in the wings, when Teddy Roosevelt's first wife, Alice, died soon after the birth of daughter Alice (who later became the grand dame of Washington as the wife of Speaker of the House Nicholas Longworth).

Teddy's second marriage was as happy as his first, if not more so. "Edie" seemed just the stabilizing influence for the impetuous young politician. She provided the kind of understanding and warm companionship that he needed, both as widower and as a hard-driving husband, father, and career-minded man.

With her husband moving from vice president to president in the wake of William McKinley's assassination, it was a stunned but well-organized Edith who managed the move from Sagamore Hill in Oyster Bay, headquarters for the lively family of six children in all, to the new White House quarters. As TR put it, Edie was the "ideal great lady and mistress of the White House," but the self-confident first lady was even more. She often helped the president by sorting his mail, going over papers with his secretary, and scanning the major newspapers.

The Roosevelts brought an aristocratic flavor to the Executive Mansion and Edith solved some of the problems that had long plagued presidential wives—she turned to professional caterers, acquired a social secretary, discussed protocol with cabinet wives at weekly meetings. She also devised a plan for separating the president's working quarters from their personal residence, and she handled the insatiable curiosity of the press by giving out information and sometimes even pictures.

The elaborate wedding of "Princess Alice" to Nicholas Longworth and the debut of daughter Ethel under the capable management of this first lady made the Teddy Roosevelt White House a social center of the country. And at times, according to Ike Hoover (chief White House usher), the Roosevelts and their children produced "the wildest scramble in the history of the White House."

☆ Helen Taft, wife of William

The first president's wife to publish her autobiography (Julia Grant's memoirs were not made public until 1975), Helen Herron Taft set other precedents as well. On March 4, 1909, she raised eyebrows as she stepped into a waiting carriage and seated herself next to her husband—newly sworn President William Howard Taft—to ride from the Capitol to the White House. Until now, this was a privilege the incoming and outgoing presidents had reserved unto themselves. "For me," she wrote in her memoirs, "that drive was the proudest and happiest event of Inauguration Day."

And indeed the new first lady gloried in her White House role, culmination of a dream she had held since visiting her father's one-time law partner, President Rutherford Hayes, and Mrs. Hayes, when she was only seventeen. Ever since, she had set her sights on the White House—she would marry a man destined for the presidency. A likely candidate encountered soon after was "that adorable Will Taft," whom she met at a bobsled party in their native Ohio. Theirs was a meeting of the minds that blossomed into love. They were married seven years later, in 1886. Will and "Nellie" were both from Cincinnati, both from leading families of the city.

Taft's career on the bench won him a Ohio supreme court seat at the early age of twenty-nine. Though pleased for him, Helen had her eyes on greater heights yet. Then a big step forward—she became a first lady as wife of newly appointed Philippines Governor Taft in 1900. She would hone her strong personality and make an imprint on the island's style while reigning at Manila's beautiful Malacanan Palace. It was good "practice" for her ultimate role a decade later as first lady in the White House.

More than simply a social leader and an elegant party-giver, Helen Taft brought a sense of purpose to the role of first lady. Overcoming the impact of a stroke, she sponsored musicales and Shakespearean performances on the White House lawn. She arranged to have Potomac Drive converted into a park. And most visibly of all, she planned a flowering touch for the capital city that would rival the cherry-blossom festival of Tokyo. Thus the famous Japanese cherry trees planted around the Tidal Basin are a memorial to this gracious lady. When she died in 1943, she was buried next to her husband in Arlington National Cemetery—the first first lady to be interred there.

⭐ Ellen Wilson, wife of Woodrow

Her predecessor had set the stage for a more substantive role for president's wives and in the months she lived in the White House, Ellen Louise Axson Wilson involved herself in civic activities of her own. Housing reform was her special interest—and she persuaded a group of congressmen to go with her on a tour of back alleys to see for themselves the slum life right in the heart of the capital city. They came, and they saw, and they hurried "Mrs. Wilson's" bill through Congress so she would know of her success before she died in August of 1914 of tuberculosis of the kidneys.

The daughter of the Reverend S. E. Axson, a Presbyterian minister, Ellen grew up in Rome, Georgia. She believed that on the whole a person should live for others and "not for herself." As a young girl, she went off to what is now called Greenwich Village to study art at the New York Art Student's League. "I prefer painting to politics," she once said—she thought she would have become quite good at art. She instead chose marriage, and her painting activity was relegated to a back room. Actually, she set up a studio by adding a skylight in one area of the White House.

For thirty years Ellen was the "polar center" of Wilson's life. Though he had advanced degrees, he looked to her to teach him in the fields of art and literature. She was the capable homemaker, she handled the family finances and watched his diet, and she even sewed for their three daughters to save on household expenses. But she was his right hand in other areas as well, proofreading his academic work and, in politics, going over his speeches with him.

Her last wish was for her husband's happiness—she expressed hope he would marry again some day.

☆ Edith Wilson, wife of Woodrow

As a newly married first lady, Edith Bolling Galt Wilson plunged into totally uncharted water and soon was to become totally immersed in the presidency itself, after her husband, Woodrow, suffered a stroke in 1919. She was faced with a dilemma no first lady had had to face before. Should she ask her husband to resign, or should she insist that he carry on with her help? With the support of Wilson's neurologist, she devised a plan to spare her husband stress and anxiety while the business of government went on. To this end she kept visitors away and screened all documents, papers, memos, or even officials he would receive. This was, as she called it, her "stewardship." Critics complained about the "Petticoat Government," others revived that old term, "Presidentress." But she insisted that she was simply protecting her "beloved husband," trying to save his life.

Edith Wilson had shown no interest in politics or government before meeting the recently widowed Wilson in 1915. The widow of Washington businessman Norman Galt, Edith had no children and had devoted time to a family jewelry firm and been active in Washington society. When she and the grieving Wilson met, they were immediately drawn to each other. They were married, despite her objection that not enough time had lapsed since the death of the first Mrs. Wilson, on December 18, 1915. After months of gloom the White House was filled with happiness again.

Although she had demonstrated her abilities as a business-woman and had exercised real political power during her "steward-ship," she showed no sympathy for women's suffrage and never lent her name to any causes.

☆ Florence Harding, wife of Warren

"I have only one hobby—my husband," was the pat answer Florence Kling Harding gave to inquisitive interviewers. The object of her affection, Warren G. Harding, seemed to agree when he once told a reporter that his automobile was his only possession that "Florence did not have a desire to run."

She was the daughter of Marion, Ohio, banker Amos Kling, richest man in town. Strong-willed like her father, she often acted against his wishes, as in her first marriage. Educated at the Cincinnati Conservatory, she was able to support herself and her young son when that marriage ended in divorce.

Enter Warren Harding, a young man with a flair for writing who had managed to buy the local newspaper, the *Daily Star.* Again she went against her father's objections—and this time married a man who was some years younger than she. But she believed in her newspaperman and his paper. In no time she was running the business end of the company—and making it pay.

Harding's talent as a public speaker and editorial writer brought him to the attention of political wheeler-dealer Harry Daugherty, who thought Harding "looked like a President." He believed the newspaperman had a future in politics and persuaded Florence to urge him to run for the U.S. Senate. Warren won by a narrow margin, and the Hardings then were off to Washington in March 1915.

Florence reveled in her new status and loved rubbing elbows with the socially prominent Nicholas and Alice Longworth; fellow Ohioans; or millionaire Edward B. McLean and his wife, Evalyn Walsh, owner of the famous Hope Diamond. More than a social climber, however, she was an astute political strategist—Daugherty believed that she helped make Harding senator and, later, president.

Harding—not always the faithful husband—recognized her valuable contributions and with some sense of irony called her "the

Duchess," a nickname also used by his poker pals while she mixed the drinks.

Mercifully for both, perhaps, Harding died before the full airing of the Teapot Dome scandal that darkened his administration. One of his widow's last acts in the White House was to destroy papers— what they were, no one knows now.

☆ Grace Coolidge, wife of Calvin

"Public Female Favorite No. 1," Will Rogers called Grace Anna Goodhue Coolidge and "chuck plumb full of magnetism." A foreign diplomat at a reception said, "To look at her is gladness enough." Grace Coolidge's unpretentious but thoroughly winning ways had all of Washington comparing her to Dolley Madison.

It was a different tune when it came to the taciturn Cal Coolidge. In fact, most of Grace's friends—and especially her mother—could not understand what she saw in the shy, usually silent lawyer.

Grace, only child of Andrew and Lemira B. Goodhue, grew up in Burlington, Vermont. The first of the first ladies to graduate from a coed university, she received her degree from the University of Vermont, then taught at the Clarke School for the Deaf in Northampton, Massachusetts. At the school one morning, while watering flowers in a garden, she happened to notice a strange sight in a nearby window—a man in his underwear shaving with a cocked hat planted on his head. She couldn't help laughing out loud. He noticed her and soon arranged a meeting to explain his incongruous activity. The hat was there to keep a cowlick out of his face while he shaved. The man under the hat was her future husband, of course.

Grace came into her own upon her husband's ascendancy to the presidency. Even after his stint as governor of Massachusetts, she and Cal were accustomed to their no-nonsense New England frugality; but with the new allotment for entertainment, they began inviting political leaders from both parties to the White House for what soon came to be known as the "Coolidge Breakfasts."

Grace Coolidge herself took no part in politics, and her husband did not allow her to give interviews. She played a traditional role working with the Girl Scouts, hostessing receptions at the White House, managing the family affairs. Years later, reflecting on her White House years, she wrote, "This was I and yet not I—this was the wife of the President of the United States and she took precedence over me."

☆ Lou Hoover, wife of Herbert

Boy and girl born in Iowa in the same year, 1874, and only one hundred miles apart, Lou Henry and Herbert Hoover didn't cross paths until twenty years later—in far-off California.

Daughter of Florence and Charles D. Henry, the future Lou Hoover was a tomboy drawn to a father who took her camping, horseback riding, and hiking. After earning a certificate from a teacher's college, she went to work for her father's bank.

Naturally, this didn't satisfy the restless and energetic Lou. One evening she attended a lecture by a Stanford University professor that would change her life; she soon was enrolled at the school as its only woman majoring in geology. And here, in a science lab one morning, she met fellow geology student Herbert Hoover.

Shy and awkward, but extremely bright, he was an orphan raised by Quakers. At the turn of the century, mining engineers were in short supply and the young Hoover soon would be working in Australia, then in China. A telegram proposal of marriage, with honeymoon spent on the way to China, received a quick reply from the adventuresome Lou—yes!

In no time the Hoovers found themselves in the middle of the Boxer Rebellion—they and others from the international community barricaded themselves in the city of Tientsin. During one attack a flying shell fragment struck a nearby staircase while Lou calmly continued with a game of solitaire.

Soon the Hoovers—by now he was a self-made millionaire—settled in London, the world's mining capital during "the golden age of mining." Their "red roof" home became the gathering place for the international set. Then, after their two sons were born (1903 and 1907), it was off again—mother and children joined the family breadwinner in France, Russia, Burma, Korea, Japan.

Caught in Europe at the outbreak of World War I, the Hoovers assisted stranded Americans. Volunteering to help distribute food to Belgium and France, already under German occupation, the Hoovers spent four years in relief work. When America entered the war, they came back to the United States, Herbert to serve as food administrator, and Lou assisting by publicizing ways to conserve both energy and food, such as declaring "heatless" and "meatless" days.

Next, as a postwar cabinet member's wife, Lou continued her activist role. She advocated physical education for girls or women in schools of all kinds. She spoke out on women's issues, often encouraging women to seek careers. At a Girl Scouts conference in 1926, she said women who give children as their excuse for not working were simply "lazy."

When the Hoovers moved into the White House, Lou ended some of its more archaic traditions, such as leaving calling cards for cabinet wives or opening the mansion to the public on New Year's Day. She startled some onlookers by actually entertaining a black congressman's wife at a small tea—today the shock would be that the black woman and just twelve other women were invited to a tea held separately from the large reception for all the congressional wives (except that one black woman).

In general, her entertaining was lavish. "They set the best table that was ever set in the White House," wrote Chief Usher Ike Hoover later. The first lady used hand signals to communicate with the servants during formal entertaining. Most of her attendants found her silent treatment dehumanizing, and with the grim depression as backdrop, she appeared stiff, uncaring. As first lady, too, for whatever reason, she was far less open with the press than she had been in her earlier days in Washington.

☆ Eleanor Roosevelt, wife of Franklin

MRS. ROOSEVELT STILLS THE TUMULT OF 50,000, screamed one headline after Eleanor Roosevelt made a surprise appearance at the 1940 Democratic National Convention in Chicago. She had gone at husband Franklin Delano Roosevelt's request to pacify delegates balking at his choice of agricultural secretary Henry Wallace as his running mate.

Amazingly enough, it wasn't all that long since Eleanor had been an awkward, ungainly young woman with little apparent self-confidence. She had left the 1912 Democratic convention in Baltimore because it was so noisy and boring . . . far from conducive to what she considered real issues. Now, FDR's wife captured the attention of another unruly convention crowd—and held it throughout her talk.

Born into the prominent Roosevelt family of New York, Eleanor nonetheless faced childhood adversity. Her mother, Anna Hall Roosevelt, a beauty and favorite of New York society, only made little Eleanor more conscious of her own inadequacies. "She is such a funny child," Eleanor heard her mother say. And then, there was her father. Elliott Roosevelt, debonair younger brother of Theodore Roosevelt, was the light of the young girl's life, but he was an alcoholic, an on-again, off-again presence in her life. By the time she was ten, both parents had died young and Eleanor and her two brothers went to live with their strict grandmother, Mrs. Valentine Hall, once the toast of New York society.

A bright spot in Eleanor's lonely life came when she was sent abroad to the Allenswood finishing school outside of London. Under the inspiring tutelage of Marie Souvestre, Eleanor discovered talents within herself. She also saw new lifestyles from her travels on the Continent.

Much as she dreaded the thought, the still-shy Eleanor was "presented" at New York's Assembly Ball at the Waldorf-Astoria in December 1902. And during the parties of that debutante season she again met her distant cousin, the handsome and already courtly young Franklin Delano Roosevelt, a student at Harvard. Only eighteen at the time, she was thrilled by his show of interest—others were surprised. Even more surprising—startling to many—they soon became engaged. By the time FDR's mother, famously haughty as a grande dame, accepted the fact that the "apple of her eye," her only son, was determined to marry his less-than-beautiful cousin, Eleanor was teaching at a settlement house in Manhattan. Young FDR was studying law at Columbia.

They were married on St. Patrick's Day 1905, with President Teddy Roosevelt giving away his favorite niece. The young couple lived near FDR's mother, Sara Roosevelt, a domineering woman who took all the initiative from Eleanor, selecting their apartment furniture, hiring their servants, even selecting nurses after the babies began to arrive. (Eleanor would bear six children in all, five boys and a girl, but one son would die in infancy.)

Meanwhile FDR had become active in New York politics, winning a seat in the New York State Senate. Though Eleanor was not in the least interested in politics, she was impressed with her husband's forward thinking when he openly supported women's suffrage. She dutifully went to Albany to set up housekeeping for her husband and children . . . and for the first time since her marriage began to see opportunities for herself. "I had to stand on my own feet now," she would later write in her memoirs. "I was beginning to realize that something within me craved to be an individual."

With FDR's appointment in 1913 as assistant secretary of the navy came their first move to Washington and, soon, the eruption of World War I. Eleanor jumped at the chance to work for the Red Cross, knitted for servicemen (her knitting would always go with her the rest of life—her hands would never be idle). After America's entry into the war, she worked at the canteens for servicemen. She even enjoyed socializing now, with their home becoming a gathering place for FDR's political friends.

After the war, her activism only increased—Eleanor's interests now included the poor, the disenfranchised, the shell-shocked veterans and, far from last or least, the women's movement.

Then came family tragedy, it appeared. In August 1921, FDR suddenly became ill with poliomyelitis. He would never again walk unaided. His mother wanted him to retire to a quiet life at Hyde Park, the family estate up the Hudson River from New York City. But his secretary, Louis Howe, thought differently and persuaded his friend in a wheelchair to go on with his political career. Eleanor concurred.

With Howe's help, Eleanor's political education began in earnest—and she would become the "ears and eyes" of the future governor of New York and president of the United States. She traveled far and wide on his behalf. She visited institutions, prisons, hospitals, and asylums, taking copious notes on their condition and reporting what she had seen and heard.

When the Roosevelts came to the White House in 1933, Eleanor probably was the most politically astute of any first lady to occupy the Executive Mansion. She and FDR, of course, would be known for their longest tenure of any White House occupants, before or since. She took on an incredible array of causes and projects all her own—in 1935 she began her syndicated column, called "My Day." She traveled widely for the president—thirty-eight thousand miles her first year in the White House. Even when on vacation, she was taking notes on the mood of the people around the country.

This time, with FDR and Eleanor, the American public really got two for the price of one—one of them a first lady who was almost a superhuman partner to the president. She was a spokesperson for the underprivileged, civil rights, unions, and the women's movement. She became the access to the president for "little people" who otherwise had no such means. During World War II, she visited American soldiers around the world, often at recently embattled combat zones. After FDR's death in April 1945 and that war's end, she continued as a champion of political and international causes, serving as a U.S. delegate to the United Nations and as a member of the U.N. Human Rights Commission. In that capacity, she helped to draft the international body's Universal Declaration of Human Rights and then saw it adopted by the body's General Assembly. She kept up her frantic pace until her health gave out—she died in November 1962.

⋆ Bess Truman, wife of Harry

When Elizabeth Virginia "Bess" Wallace Truman became first lady, very little was known about her—and that's the way she wanted it. She had an aversion to publicity; nice ladies didn't seek it out.

Bess Wallace grew up in the comfortable world of Independence, Missouri, where her family stood high in the community. Like Lou Hoover, she was something of a tomboy, a rival to any boy who could whistle through his teeth. She was an excellent horseback rider; she climbed trees and became a local tennis champion. When a bookish young man wearing glasses began calling, Madge Wallace wasn't impressed and thought the young dirt farmer was not good enough for her daughter. But Harry Truman pursued his "one and only" anyway. After he returned from his U.S. Army combat service in France during World War I with the rank of major, they were married. In their midthirties at the time, they had been courting for fifteen years!

The low profile that Bess Truman maintained in public tended to obscure the important part she really played in her husband's life—and his success. She edited his speeches and was on the payroll for his U.S. Senate office as his secretary. Questioned about the arrangement, he told reporters, "She earns every penny of it."

They were a close-knit family, with both Bess and daughter Margaret often joining Truman on his trips. They were right there, for instance, for his famous whistle-stop campaign of 1948, standing with him on his train's rear platform in small town after small town, smiling and waving after he introduced them to them to the onlooking crowd as the "Boss" and the "Boss's Boss" (Margaret).

It was during the Truman administration that the controversial "Truman Balcony" was added to the South Portico of the White House. Architectural purists aside, it was the coolest spot in the town. Far more important in any case, a tinkling chandelier in the Blue Room's ceiling during a reception one evening had alerted

Truman to trouble above and around them—the old structure, patched up and prettied up for decades, needed strengthening, a complete overhaul, or it might come down like a house of cards. The result was complete reconstruction of the White House interior while the Trumans took up residence in Blair House, across Pennsylvania Avenue from number 1600.

Bess dutifully and graciously set up miniature Red, Blue, and Green Rooms in the traditional government guest house, even a State Dining Room, all replete with White House furniture.

When Bess Truman died in 1982, The *New York Times* headlined, BESS TRUMAN IS DEAD AT 97/WAS PRESIDENT'S "FULL PARTNER." The fact is, too, at ninety-seven, she had lived longer than any other first lady.

★ Mamie Eisenhower, wife of Dwight

Just a month after her wedding, Mamie Doud Eisenhower watched her second-lieutenant husband pack his gear. "You're not going to leave me this soon after our wedding day, are you?" she cried. His answer stunned her: "My country comes first and always will. You come second." Indeed, adjusting to the many moves of an army wife was easy compared to the anguish she suffered during their long separations. Duty and country did come first, but "I never got used to his being gone," she said toward the end of her life. "He was my husband. He was my whole life."

She was a young woman living with her parents and three sisters in Denver, Colorado, when she met her young army lieutenant—not in Colorado, but at Fort Sam Houston in Texas, where the Douds spent the winter months. The West Pointer presented her his class ring on St. Valentine's Day 1916 to mark their engagement, and they were married that summer.

Next came a series of army posts—all over the United States, in France, in the Philippines, in the Panama Canal Zone. She went through twenty-seven moves in thirty-seven years!

It was General Eisenhower, of course, who catapulted to fame during World War II as Supreme Allied Commander in Europe. Back home, though, Mamie was depressed and feared for Ike's safety. Her health deteriorated—she spent a lot of time bedridden. And while she waited, rumors drifted back from England about Ike and Kay Summersby, the young Irish woman, an ex-model, assigned as his driver. Gossip circulated in Washington, but Mamie rallied and put up a cheerful front, claiming in *Look* magazine there was nothing improper between her husband and Summersby, because, "I know Ike."

The war over, cries of "I like Ike" echoed across the land, and everyone loved the lady in pink by his side. Ike won election in 1952 by a landslide. And when they moved into the White House, Mamie quickly became a new favorite of the public. As the media soon learned, she was always good for a saucy quote. She had taken language classes with Bess Truman and other VIP women. "None of us ever really studied," said the new first lady. She made no bones about their sleeping in a double bed together, saying that she liked to be able to reach over during the night and pat Ike's familiar "bald pate."

She told reporters, "I don't understand politics." Yet she charmed everyone with her friendliness and good humor. Told that a poll had picked her husband as the greatest American, she smiled and exclaimed: "They didn't have to go to all that trouble. I could have told them."

The fashion industry experienced a shot in the arm with Mamie's interest in clothes, not to mention the fact that her coiffure sent fashionable ladies rushing to the salons to have their hair cut, colored, and in many cases "banged," like hers.

As Mamie later came to realize, times change—after a brief hiatus for Bess Truman and Mamie herself, the role of a president's wife would revert in some degree to Eleanor Roosevelt's sometimes frantic activism. So it was that Mamie told Rosalynn Carter when they met twenty years later, "I stayed busy all the time and loved being in the White House, but I was never expected to do all the things you have to do." All the same, while not so much an activist as more recent first ladies, Mamie did her dutiful bit in the White House— she and Ike entertained more heads of state and foreign leaders than most, if any, previous occupants of the White House.

★ Jackie Kennedy, wife of Jack

"Fantastically chic," pronounced the *New York Times*. "Stunning egghead," said *Newsweek*.

Jacqueline Lee Bouvier Kennedy changed forever the way we Americans look at our first ladies.

Long before she met Jack Kennedy, she stood out from the crowd. "Queen Deb of the Year is Jacqueline Bouvier," columnist Igor Cassini wrote in the *New York Journal-American,* "a regal brunette who has classic features and the daintiness of Dresden porcelain." Born into the "right" social circles, she was the daughter of John Vernon Bouvier III and his wife, Janet Lee, who later obtained a divorce and married wealthy Washington attorney Hugh D. Auchincloss in 1942.

Jackie attended the Chapin School in New York, Miss Porter's in Connecticut, then Vassar, all prestigious schools. She spent a year abroad studying at the Sorbonne in Paris, where she became fluent in French and developed a lifelong love of French art and literature. She finished her education at George Washington University in the nation's capital and later became the *Washington Times-Herald*'s "Inquiring Camera Girl." By the time she got around to interviewing the handsome young congressman from Massachusetts (and Dick Nixon also), young Jack Kennedy was already squiring her around town.

"It was a very spasmodic courtship," Jackie once told an interviewer. She held up a post card from Bermuda that read: "Wish you were here. Cheers, Jack."

"And that was my entire courtship correspondence with Jack!"

After Jack was elected to the Senate in 1952, they announced their engagement. Their wedding in Newport, Rhode Island, a year later was the social event of the season. With all the Kennedy politicos attending, it was a political event as well. After their honeymoon, the young couple settled down in Georgetown.

There, differences soon surfaced. Although Jackie took a course in American history to please her husband, she didn't find politics interesting. "Jackie is superb in her personal life," Jack once said to a friend, "but do you think she'll ever amount to anything in her political life?" To which, Jackie shot back: "Jack is superb in his political life, but do you think he will ever amount to anything in his personal life?"

The public, for its part, clamored for appearances by the glamorous wife of presidential candidate Kennedy in 1960—politically attuned or not, she was a true asset to his victorious campaign against Nixon.

As first lady, Jackie quite naturally found a project that would complement her interest in art. First, she convinced Congress to designate the White House a national historic site. Treating it as a museum, she then began the most extensive restoration of its furnishings, antiques, and objets d'art ever attempted. She spent months of study and hard work—she even scavenged through old cupboards, store-rooms, and forgotten crannies at the White House. She persuaded museum directors, various designers, and art historians to sign on to her committees and solicited anyone who owned original pieces from the mansion to return them. When the project was near completion, television cameras followed the first lady as she took the nation on a tour of the White House, which she indeed had transformed into a living museum.

Jackie of course forever will be remembered as the tragic figure at the funeral of her still-young husband, killed by an assassin's bullets in 1963, ten years after their marriage. She set grim and certainly unwilling precedent as the first president's widow to attend the swearing-in of his successor. Who can ever forget the awful image? A still-bloodstained Jackie standing by in *Air Force One* as Lyndon Baines Johnson was sworn in at Love Field in Dallas. Later married to Greek shipping magnate Aristotle Onassis, then widowed again, she died in 1994 and is buried with JFK at Arlington National Cemetery.

✫ Lady Bird Johnson, wife of Lyndon

Lady Bird and Lyndon Baines Johnson . . . like those of Jack and Jackie Kennedy, their names go well together, don't they? LBJ . . . it would be a monogram for the entire family. It even would be a president's initials, too. And who would have guessed, way back in 1934?

Home on a visit from Washington, where he served a Texas congressman as secretary, LBJ was introduced by a friend to "a lovely girl with ideals, principles, intelligence and refinement"—his own description in one of the love letters that soon followed. Theirs was a "whirlwind" courtship, as Lady Bird later recalled. Her Aunt Effie, who had helped raise Lady Bird in both Texas and Alabama after her mother's early death, responded cautiously to the tall, overpowering suitor, but the girl's father, Thomas Jefferson Taylor, took an instant liking to the frequent visitor: "This time you brought home a man," he told daughter Claudia Alta Taylor. Two months later, on November 17, 1934, they were married in San Antonio. From that day on, Lady Bird was LBJ's staunchest supporter. It was money that she had borrowed against her inheritance, in fact, that staked the start of his political career.

"Busy as a man with one hoe and two rattlesnakes," was an expression typical of the down-country girl who now joined LBJ in the nation's capital, but the thought also was fair comment on the life she had entered as the wife (and occasional office-staffer) of a young congressman in a hurry (first elected to the House in 1938 and to the Senate ten years later). She served him coffee in bed, brought him his morning paper, changed her fashions from "muley-looking" to bright yellows and reds, wore high heels, which her man preferred, laid out his clothes, and even polished his shoes at times. She ran his office when he briefly donned a uniform during World War II before all congressmen were called back to their legislative duties . . . and kept her opinions about the later Vietnam quagmire to herself. She learned always to have a well-stocked refrigerator, since LBJ often brought a crowd of political cronies in for pot-luck supper. And she never lost her equilibrium.

"She is a lot like Melanie in *Gone With the Wind*, except with more drive," daughter Lynda Bird (Mrs. Charles Robb) once said. Added younger daughter Luci Baines (Mrs. Ian Turpin), "She's really the knot of the family."

No one, of course, could ever help but notice the *L* and *B* initials that permeate the family. "Why, she's as pretty as a ladybird," was the proud proclamation of a nursemaid when Claudia was born. And Lady Bird it was from there on. LBJ was so delighted over their matching initials, he monogramed every one in the family, and every thing, including pets and their ranch.

She came to the White House under tragic circumstances and yet made the transition with grace and dignity. When her husband was elected in his own right (1964), the first lady from Texas set out to find her own project. And here, her nickname may have been prophetic—her lifelong interest had been nature and its beauty. And so, among various beautification and nature projects, one lasting contribution would be the First Lady Committee for a More Beautiful Capital, an idea that quickly spread across the nation. Meanwhile, her memoir, *A White House Diary,* published in 1970, is considered the most complete account of life in the White House by a first lady.

☆ Pat Nixon, wife of Richard

To pay her way to New York and back when she was only twenty, Pat Ryan drove a couple across the country from California. The couple were ailing, the roads were curvy, the car was cranky, and as she told a reporter later, she became, "driver, nurse, mechanic and scared." An apt prelude to her life with Richard Nixon, whom she married on June 21, 1940.

Christened Thelma Catherine Ryan, she was born on March 16—her father swung her up into his arms and called her his "St. Patrick's babe." And so, Pat it would be. Her mother died when Pat was only thirteen, leaving her to care for her father and two brothers. "Life was sort of sad," she would recall, "so I had to cheer everybody up." Her father soon died from silicosis, a lung disease he had contracted as a miner in Ely, Nevada. In New York she worked as an x-ray technician in a hospital treating patients with the same lung condition. "Haunting" as this experience was, she did it because she wanted to help. "That is what gives one the deepest pleasure in the world—helping someone," she once explained.

She was able to save enough money to return home and graduate, cum laude, in 1937 from the University of Southern California. She took a job at Whittier (California) High School, and there she met a young graduate of Duke University Law School as they both sought parts in a local theater production. Richard M. Nixon was immediately drawn to her, but she had her doubts at first. They continued to date, and at last he persuaded her to marry him. She did so in a Quaker service, since she had converted to his faith. As they drove off to Mexico for a honeymoon, the car this time was hers; she had helped pay for it.

They did not live happily ever after. In the future congressman's early days of campaigning in California, Pat pitched in every way she could—so much so that they were called the "Dick and Pat team." But politics can be wearing—and rough. In 1952, vice presidential candidate Nixon was questioned about his use of certain campaign funds; there was some doubt that Dwight Eisenhower would keep Nixon as his running mate. After making his famous televised "Checkers" speech, Nixon remained on the ticket and became vice president.

From then on, however, as Nixon himself would write later, Pat "would hate politics and dream of the day when I would leave it behind."

That day would be a long time in coming, yet Pat weathered each and every storm that seemed to plague her husband's career. Evermore careworn in appearance, she yet maintained her dignity. And as first lady, she returned to the "helping" theme of her young adulthood by encouraging volunteerism. She broke new ground by inviting visitors for nondenominational religious services in the East

Room. She encouraged further acquisition of antiques and art for the White House collection and brought in musical artists of all kinds for performances in the White House.

She was one of the most traveled first ladies, going to eighty-three nations (some crowds not so friendly; some, like the mob in Caracas when Nixon was vice president, downright life-threatening). She criss-crossed the United States many times. "I do or die," Pat was frequently quoted as saying, "I never cancel out." She must have died a lot when Nixon had to resign in 1974, but still she clung to her sense of dignity.

☆ Betty Ford, wife of Gerald

"I take a Valium every day," was the candid statement Betty Ford made in an interview as the suddenly newsworthy wife of newly appointed Vice President Gerald Ford. That sent the reporters scurrying for the phones, but it was only the beginning for this beautiful bombshell who was catapulted into the limelight by the sweeping events of the early 1970s.

First, of course, her "Jerry" was appointed by President Nixon to fill the vacancy left by the resignation of Vice President Spiro Agnew—an unprecedented event. That was in the fall of 1973 . . . with more, much more, to come. And suddenly, Betty found herself surrounded by the media; it seemed that everyone wanted to know about the woman that *Good Housekeeping* said "nobody knows." In fact, she had been around Washington a long time.

Jerry and Betty married in October 1948 in Grand Rapids, Michigan, their hometown. In November, first-time House candidate Jerry sailed into office, and the newlyweds were off to Washington. There, she was the dutiful wife doing all the right things, from teaching Sunday school to joining the appropriate wives' clubs and balancing home and hearth with four children (three sons and a daughter).

Health problems and "single-parenting" (Jerry was always away politicking or working) added to the strains. Her successful bout with dependency after they left Washington would gain her the respect of the nation. She went on to found the Betty Ford Center for Drug and Alcohol Rehabilitation, which opened in 1982 in Rancho Mirage, California.

Her mother many years earlier said daughter Elizabeth Ann "popped out of a bottle of champagne." The future first lady's happy parents were Hortense and William Bloomer; her father died when she was sixteen and she modeled to help out with the family finances. But she was able to attend the Bennington School of Dance in Vermont for two summers. Here, she was thrilled to study under the famous Martha Graham, to experience "the ecstasy of being able to dance eight hours a day." In 1975, as first lady, she had the gratification of appearing as the honored guest at the dedication of a fine arts center at Bennington College.

Only months before, she and Jerry had been suburbanites in Alexandria, Virginia—even after he moved from House minority leader to vice president. Then, just as suddenly, came President Richard Nixon's resignation in August 1974. Jerry Ford suddenly, breathtakingly, had vaulted, in less than a year, from House seat to presidency.

In the White House soon after, Betty Ford quickly established her reputation as the honest and outspoken first lady. She called the Supreme Court's ruling allowing abortion "a great, great thing." She thought it would not be surprising if the young people of the 1970s tried marijuana, and while she wouldn't condone her daughter Susan having an affair, she wouldn't make her leave home over the issue, either. Such talk shocked many but endeared her to many others who agreed.

She lobbied for the Equal Rights Amendment (ERA), and when that failed to pass she continued to work for women's causes, often by "pillowtalking" with her husband about appointments of women to more and higher positions in government.

☆ Rosalynn Carter, wife of Jimmy

A "steel magnolia blossom," is how New York Times reporter Judy Klemesrud saw this energetic campaigner from Plains, Georgia. And the name stuck, all the way to the White House.

Rosalynn Smith and Jimmy Carter grew up in the same little southwest Georgia town, alongside peanuts and cotton. Church activities were the center of life, both spiritual and social. She was a Methodist and he a Baptist. Her father, whom she adored, thought she could do anything and encouraged her every endeavor. When she was only fourteen, however, he died, an event leaving her "devastated," she wrote later, adding, "My childhood really ended at that moment."

To make ends meet, her mother took in sewing, doing piece-work for others. Rosalynn worked in the town beauty parlor and helped with the chores at home. When time came for college, she was able to attend a junior college, Georgia Southwestern.

Enter Jimmy, home from Annapolis. Rosalynn had seen his picture on the dresser of his sister Ruth, her best friend, but she thought the handsome midshipman was "out of reach" for her. His sister played matchmaker anyway and packed a picnic for the three of them. He agreed to go along, he liked her, he kissed her—and later he told his mother, "She's the girl I want to marry."

Two years later, 1946, they were married. After that, it was good-bye Plains, hello world.

Her opportunities widened as the navy moved them to places she had only dreamed about before. When her husband was off on sea duty and she was left with decisions and responsibilities, she grew in her new role as head of the household and mother of three growing boys. (Daughter Amy was born later.)

When Carter's father died in 1954, they left the navy and returned to the family company. Rosalynn hated to go back to the limiting world of Plains. Only when she began to take over the book-keeping of the wholesale peanut business did she feel she was doing something important.

Then her husband entered politics and a whole new world challenged the little girl from Plains, now dramatically coming into her own as the wife of an increasingly popular local politician. At first she was shy and afraid of making speeches for her husband, but when she realized that stumping the countryside—and later the whole country—was the name of the game, she played a major role in her husband's campaigns as he rose from the state house to the governor's mansion and finally to number 1600 Pennsylvania Avenue.

To the White House she then brought a strong sense of purpose with an agenda of her own. Heading a long list was her interest in mental health; she persuaded Jimmy to appoint a Commission on Mental Health. She lobbied for the ERA, as Betty Ford had, and worked to improve the quality of life for the aged.

In her partnership role, she sat in on cabinet meetings, rare for a first lady . . . controversial, too. She perhaps is best remembered, though, for her ambassadorial good-will tour of South America . . . if not also for her bitterness over the defeat of her husband in the 1980 election. "Nothing is more thrilling than the urgency of a campaign," she once said. The tremendous energy it takes, she added, makes victory "so sweet" but also it makes "a loss so devastating."

☆ Nancy Reagan, wife of Ronald

"Nothing can prepare you for living in the White House," wrote Nancy Davis Reagan, who along with the fortieth president of the United States spent eight years in the Executive Mansion. In fact, Nancy's life story reads pretty much like a Hollywood script and indeed could have served as preparation, as a dress rehearsal, for her strut upon the Washington stage.

As a child living with an aunt and uncle in Bethesda, Maryland, Anne Frances Robbins ("Nancy") longed to be with her stage-actress mother, Edith Luckett. Then, as in a dream come true, her divorcée mother married Dr. Loyal Davis, prominent neurosurgeon and chairman of the Department of Surgery at Northwestern University and Nancy went to live with them. She became very fond of "Dr. Loyal," as she called him, and in 1929 he legally adopted her. She later went from those comfortable circumstances to Smith College, where she majored in drama. After a debut in Chicago, she went to New York and with her mother's connections in the theater landed a few parts. Then a screen test in Hollywood came her way and earned her a seven-year contract with Metro-Goldwyn-Mayer. It was like "walking into a dream world," she later wrote, but, "You could get a severe case of insecurity when you came into makeup in the morning and found yourself seated between Elizabeth Taylor and Ava Gardner."

Now the background music reaches a crescendo—actor Ronald Reagan, divorced and single, president of the Screen Actors Guild, arrives on the scene. "From the moment I met him, Ronald Reagan has been the center of my life," she wrote in her memoir, *My Turn*. "I have been criticized for saying that, but it's true."

She and "Ronnie" married in the Little Brown Church in California's San Fernando Valley on March 4, 1952. She soon allowed her contract with M-G-M to lapse to become fulltime wife and, later, mother to Patti and Ron (born in 1952 and 1958, respectively).

In 1966, Reagan made his successful bid for the governorship of California, and Nancy was praised for the style and elegance of her clothes. A writer for *Look* magazine compared her to Jacqueline Kennedy—"she has the same spare figure, the same air of immaculate chic."

When the former first lady of California came to Washington in

1981, she utilized her keen interest in interior design for an extensive refurbishing of the White House. She was surprised to win few kudos from the press, even though no public funds had been expended—in fact, a ridiculed and costly new set of china was a private gift. It often seemed that no matter what she did, there would be critics awaiting her latest move. Even the gallantry she displayed in response to her husband's brush with death after he was shot by a would-be assassin did not seem to win her complete acceptance by the press, which always insisted upon treating her as a controversial figure.

In Reagan's second term, the critics did give her credit for her drug abuse project and her support of Foster Grandparents, a program she had begun while first lady of California. But when it became clear that Nancy was playing a substantial role in the administration, she was criticized for that, too. Before she could "retire" in 1989 with her beloved "Ronnie," the press kept up its old negative fire. It was "Fancy Nancy" here, and "frivolous clotheshorse" or "chum of the rich" there.

For all of this, Nancy still could reflect philosophically on her eight years as first lady. If nothing can prepare you for living in the White House, she now could also say, "nothing can prepare you for leaving it."

☆ Barbara Bush, wife of George

A happy grandmother, yes, and much more. One of the most popular first ladies in modern times, even Barbara Pierce Bush once was a little girl, the daughter of Marvin and Pauline Pierce. Her father was president of the McCall Corporation, and after a happy, well-to-do childhood in suburban Rye, New York, she was off to the Ashley Hall School for girls in South Carolina.

She met fellow "preppie" George Bush, a senior at Phillips Academy in Andover, Massachusetts, at a Christmas dance when she was sixteen. Just eighteen months later, they became engaged and he was off to the wars—to World War II, that is. Soon, at age eighteen, he would be the youngest man to date ever to win the U.S. Navy's aviator's wings of gold.

While his anxious fiancée waited at home for her hero's return, young George really was a hero—he experienced combat as a carrier-based pilot in the Pacific and was rescued when his Avenger torpedo plane was knocked into the sea by antiaircraft fire. About the time he returned from the war zone, safe and sound, she dropped out of Smith College and they married, in January of 1945.

After he completed his academic career at Yale University, they moved to Texas, where over the next few years he would be active in the oil business. Barbara Bush had started a career, too—as a mother, eventually, of six children. One of them, Robin, died of leukemia at age four, a traumatic experience for the still-young couple. "Because of Robin, George and I love every living human more," Barbara Bush later said.

Himself the son of a U.S. senator (Prescott Bush of Connecticut), George Bush soon would be jumping into Texas politics—he lost a race for the Senate in 1964, but bounced back two years later by winning a House seat from the Houston area.

With Barbara often by his side, he underwent another Senate debacle in 1970, then plunged into a series of public service and political posts that eventually gave him what many political pundits termed the "longest résumé in the Western World." So it was that Barbara Bush soon found herself in long-estranged Communist China as wife of the new U.S. representative to that "People's Republic."

In the seventies, she also honed her political and social skills as wife and helpmate to the American ambassador to the United Nations, to the chairman of the Republican National Committee, the director of the Central Intelligence Agency, and—in 1980—a Republican primary contender for president. And later that year, the official GOP nominee for vice president. Every one of these "title-holders" of course was her own husband, George Bush.

She and George closed out the decade with his election as vice president on the ticket headed by Ronald Reagan. Then began almost another decade in which Barbara held down a delicate political role as the wife of the man expected to seek the presidency after Reagan, but also expected to "make no waves" in the interim. They had to wait eight long years for their turn, but even so Barbara at last entered the White House in 1989 without the slightest appearance of impatience or self-consciousness.

Happy wife and helpmate, yes, and much more. She tried "to do some good every day," she once said, and many benefited from her good works. In May of 1989 she invited literacy and education experts to the White House to help organize the Barbara Bush Foundation for Family Literacy, which she then served as the honorary chairman. An advocate of volunteerism, she also supported many other groups and causes, such as the Girl Scouts of America, the Leukemia Society of America, or Reading Is Fundamental. She also encouraged school volunteer programs. She lent her support to the aged and homeless, and to victims of AIDS. At the 1992 GOP National Convention, she also went to bat for her beleaguered-appearing incumbent husband, "batting" down negative barbs in interviews and even addressing the Houston convention—and by extension, the nation—herself.

But Barbara Bush always found time for her family, too. She especially enjoyed having her crew up to Kennebunkport, Maine, the Bush summer home, for long walks along the shore or a game of tennis. And don't forget Millie, her famous springer spaniel that once even "wrote" a book (with the proceeds going to Barbara's literacy cause).

☆ Hillary Rodham Clinton, wife of Bill

They said the same things about Edith, Eleanor, Rosalynn, and others, you know, then it was Hillary's turn!

Even in 1993, at the very end of the twentieth century, America could go into a fresh tailspin over an "uppity" new woman in the White House.

Consider that at Wellesley this product of Chicago's middle-class suburbs already had cast aside her family's Republicanism, had upset the applecart of tradition by insisting that a student speak at commencement exercises—who else but class president (1967) Hillary, with a sharp attack upon the words of the great day's previous speaker, a Republican Senator?

Consider, too, that she soon had a cum laude degree from Yale Law in her feminist pocket and was off to Washington—not only joining the new wave of baby boomer women professionals on the move, but also plunging into combative politics as she signed on with the House Judiciary Committee staff (Democratic side, that is) busily drawing up papers for the impeachment of a president, Richard M. Nixon.

Marriage and a move to Arkansas proved vital to her list of accomplishments as she joined a prestigious law firm in Little Rock and became first lady of the state.

She pursued many other interests, including activities on behalf of the nonprofit National Center on Education and the Economy and as a skilled and effective crusader for her many liberal causes. True to her concerns for the poor, women, and children—her law school thesis had been on the rights of children—she worked for the Children's Defense Fund, eventually serving five years as the fund's chairperson. She received national recognition when the *National Law Journal* twice named her one of the top one hundred lawyers in the country. (She also out-earned her governor-husband, Bill, by a factor of four to five times his salary per annum.)

But not all was always hunky-dory for the little woman from Illinois, née Hillary Rodham, who chose to hitch her wagon to Arkansas and politically ambitious Bill Clinton. Controversial she was from the start, choosing to retain her maiden name and refusing to change her rebellious sixties look—sometimes wearing headbands, "Rodham" was given a large share of the blame for husband Bill Clinton's defeat for a second term as governor.

But she is also credited for learning fast—maiden name and headband disappeared in time for her husband's third and once-again successful gubernatorial run. (He would serve a total of five two-year gubernatorial terms in all.)

By the end of the 1992 presidential campaign, an entire country knew what Arkansas already knew—Hillary was a political force, with or without Bill.

Probably the most scrutinized wife of a presidential candidate ever, Hillary tried to explain that her high and often controversial visibility really wasn't her doing. In an interview with *Newsweek,* she said: "I feel like there is this great national conversation going on of which I am a part, but it is not so much about me personally but about all the changes going on in the country—about women and our roles, the choices we make in our lives."

Americans have had controversial "activist" first ladies before— Edith Wilson, Eleanor Roosevelt, Rosalynn Carter come to mind. But they were women ahead of their times, it could be said. Edith Wilson, of course, was accused of running the government while her husband, Woodrow, was incapacitated by a stroke; Eleanor Roosevelt was famous for her politicking, both by FDR's side and on behalf of her own liberal causes; and Rosalynn ruffled some feathers by taking part in Jimmy Carter's political strategy sessions, even cabinet meetings.

Would Hillary be another phenomenon like those first ladies? Or was she simply a product of her own times, as she asserted? As she "took office" early in 1993 by husband Bill's side (with an unprecedented West Wing office at that!), America anxiously waited to see what the "two for one" husband-and-wife team would accomplish. From the glamorous first lady seen at the inaugural events, to the hard-working, well-informed woman who soon headed up the Clinton administration's health care reform effort, the public indeed was treated to tantalizing repeated glimpses of a very visible White House occupant, now studiously referred to as Hillary Rodham Clinton.

But life in the Washington fishbowl is not always easy. Within two years, health reform had crashed, the Republicans had swept into control of the House of Representatives, and intimations of wheeling and dealing dogged the couple. "To a degree that seemed to leave them stunned and at times depressed," noted *Time* magazine on the eve of the 1996 presidential campaign, "the President and First Lady have been buffeted by allegations of scandal, conspiracy and cover-up."

Never mind, though. The American public disregarded all the negatives and reelected Bill Clinton to the presidency—Hillary of course going back to the White House with him as a "second-term" first lady.

Then came the Monica Lewinsky affair, Bill Clinton's transparent, tortured denials and, finally, the failed impeachment process of 1998–99. What is a wife to do? Any wife, much less a highly visible presidential wife?

Through it all, Hillary publicly defended Bill and stuck by him. She seemed to go about her business, first lady business, as usual. But ... who knows what went on inside?

By 1999, she was openly toying with the idea of moving to New York and running for the U.S. Senate. Some fans said that would be, even *should* be, a first step toward running for president herself in the year 2004 or 2008.

As is well known, Hillary indeed made the move to New York and, while husband Bill was still occupying the White House, won election to the Senate in November 2000—even as George W. Bush won his first term as president. Well known, too, is the fact that Hillary stuck to her Senate guns without uttering the slightest peep of interest in the 2004 presidential race, which she left to fellow Senate Democrat John Kerry of Massachusetts (a predictably ill-fated sacrificial lamb in the eyes of some politically attuned onlookers).

The presidential contest of 2008, however, with incumbent George W. Bush no longer a factor because of the nation's two-term limit, could be very tempting to the ambitious activist who is already the only first lady ever elected to the U. S. Senate.

Meanwhile, "Senator Hillary" kept busy on another front—adding to her laurels as a book author. While still in the White House she had produced *It Takes a Village: And Other Lessons Children Teach Us,* along with her historical look at entertaining in the presidential home, titled *An Invitation to the White House.* Next, in her post–first lady career, she turned out the 2003 tome *Living History,* a memoir that cemented her celebrity status by selling 1.5 million copies domestically and another 1.5 million copies abroad.

✫ Laura Bush, wife of George W.

She was "just born a happy little kiddo," her mother once said of her only child. Born November 4, 1946, to Texas real estate developer Harold Welch and his wife Jenna, their Laura Lane Welch would be a model child—and, in time, a model first lady.

Her formative years in Midland, Texas, so proper and so orderly, so uneventful in so many ways, could have come straight out of a fifties sitcom . . . but then came a stunning and tragic moment one autumn night. Laura, in the driver's seat, and a girlfriend had been merrily rolling along on a country road when Laura unfortunately ran an unnoticed stop sign and plowed into a car going across the same intersection. The driver of the crumpled car—a friend from high school, the golden boy of Midland, a track star—would be pronounced dead on arrival at the local hospital.

The pain was "crushing," Laura said years later to *Washington Post* reporter Ann Gerhart, who was writing about the first lady in her book *The Perfect Wife.* "I grieved a lot," Laura Bush acknowledged. "It was a horrible tragedy. . . ."

And of course, said Laura Bush also: "[It] made me have more of a perspective on life . . . maybe I would have had that perspective anyway. I just got it at seventeen."

Both before and after, books always were important to Laura, who had decided early in life that she would be a teacher just like her second-grade teacher Charlene Gnagy, whom she adored.

After graduating from Midland High School, the future first lady entered Southern Methodist University, a natural choice since she had long been active in her hometown First United Methodist

Church. In the fall of 1964, by sharp contrast with many other schools, SMU offered a squeaky-clean atmosphere perhaps a bit reminiscent of the proverbial Sunday school picnic. The girls still wore dresses to class and, as Laura told Ann Gerhart, "It was a fairly conservative campus compared to how it was just a few years after that, for [the] little brothers and sisters of my friends." Laura and her friends at SMU weren't caught up in the wildness that visited so many other college campuses during the rebellious sixties. "I mean, people smoked cigarettes—and I did," said Laura. She confessed also to some beer drinking, "and that was the way college kids were 'wild' when I was there."

Laura pledged Kappa Alpha Theta and lived in the sorority's storybook Georgian brick house, where, as described by biographer Gerhart, "the girls glided up and down a curving staircase and had their dinner served by houseboys." Laura was studious, yes, but she rarely shooed the girls out of her room, a popular gathering place. In her sophomore year in college she went home to make her debut, complete with elegant formal gown and long white kid gloves.

Through it all, though, Laura's curriculum and wider reading led her to think beyond her sheltered world. After graduation she pestered her family for permission to trek across Europe that summer with a group of girls from school, backpacks and all. Instead, her father arranged for her to join his brother, a Dallas surgeon, and his family on what Laura would later describe as a "seventeen-day, seventeen-country trip." The whirl through Europe by train and bus surely was a memorable experience for the young college graduate, but oh, what a difference three decades would make as, now the nation's first lady, she embarked on renewed foreign travel aboard the likes of *Air Force One*.

But first, back to Texas and the real world of the 1960s, when Laura Welch at the end of the summer was hired to teach third grade in a predominantly African-American school in Dallas. To a neophyte teacher like her, its twenty students to a class seemed a lot at first. But she loved it, especially that period after lunch when she could read to her students. It was through this new experience, she later said, that she "learned about the dignity of every human and every child, and how important every single child is. . . ."

In time, she was settled in Austin as a school librarian after obtaining a master's in library science at the University of Texas in the state capital. About then, too, a young man whose father sported the "longest résumé" in the Western world had moved back to Midland to seek his fortune in the oil business, just as his accomplished father had done when he returned a hero from service in Navy Air during World War II.

"Bush Boy," as the younger man's Midland friends called him, was living in a garage apartment with bedsprings held together by old neckties, or so the story goes.

More auspiciously, he had decided to run for Congress. Just as important, recalled Gerhart's book also, his friends felt he needed a helpmate . . . and soon.

Conveniently enough, it just so happened that "Bush Boy's" friend Joe O'Neill had married Laura's school chum Jan Donnelly in 1972. The O'Neill couple had been trying, without result, to get their good friends Laura and George W. together. Finally, in August of 1977, while in her hometown of Midland for a family visit, Laura agreed to join Joe and Jan for a backyard barbeque at their place. And guess who else was there? None other than "Bush Boy" himself! Asked later how the two happened to meet at their friends' barbeque, Laura somewhat wryly said, "I guess it was because we were the only two people from that era in Midland who were still single."

George and Laura liked each other almost at once. She told her mother that she had met a young man who made her laugh. For his part, young George W. Bush would write in a later autobiography that he had at last found a woman who was "gorgeous, good-humored, quick to laugh, down-to-earth and very smart." And George certainly liked his women quick-witted, as manifested years later in the form of his advisers Karen Hughes and Condaleeza Rice.

George, the extrovert of the two, has claimed they responded to love at first sight, but Laura, in her typically calm and quiet way, downplays their next step, saying, "I think it was a whirlwind romance because we were in our early thirties." Whatever the reason, to the surprise of most of their friends, the two total opposites were engaged in just three weeks and married in twelve.

A simple morning wedding in the chapel of the Midland Methodist Church where she had been baptized, and where later she would have her twin daughters Jenna and Barbara christened, was Laura's choice. A seated luncheon at the Midland Racquet Club followed.

After a brief wedding trip to Mexico, the couple began the long political journey that would take them to the Texas Governor's Mansion and on to the White House.

The two young Texans from Midland, so opposite yet so attracted to each other, began married life traveling the dusty roads of West Texas, he intent on winning the 19th Congressional District seat in the U.S. House of Representatives in Washington, and she more or less just along for the ride—for the moment. Later she would admit that those long drives from one little Texas town to the other gave them plenty of time to get to know each other. For the quiet school librarian and her talkative groom, bumping along in their open white convertible together was to be a foretaste of dramatic times that lay ahead.

As they discovered from the start, theirs was to be a marriage that works because they are best friends—and because they could agree from the start on a workable division of labor. It's their long-standing political joke that they had a prenuptial agreement saying that if she would jog with him every day, she never would have to give a political speech.

Well, as everyone soon discovered, this future first lady of Texas and the nation not only could hold her own in the political spot-light, she in fact would be a tremendous asset on the campaign trail, even when barnstorming all by her lonesome on her husband's behalf. Thus, instead of the jogging, she wound up an effective speaker and campaigner after all, but she nonetheless does love a nice long hike and bird watching. Nor does she shrink from real out-door adventure in other forms—Laura has been known to gather old school chums and take a week away from husbands and children to raft down the Grand Canyon.

Meanwhile, Laura, the only child, and George, who came from a family of spirited siblings, longed for children of their own. After four years of marriage and aware of the fact that she was not getting any younger, they had just about given up when they received the good news from her doctor that she was pregnant. They soon got an added dividend: she was carrying twins.

The result would be a difficult pregnancy, during which Laura developed toxemia, a grave condition that threatened the health of mother and babies. But Laura, with her usual sense of serenity, just took to the bed to give her babies every chance. Then on November 21, 1981, five weeks early, two beautiful and healthy baby girls were born to Laura by Caesarian section. They were given the names of their two grandmothers, Barbara and Jenna.

Although George W. had lost that race for Congress, life moved on smoothly for the young couple in Midland. George toiled in the oil business and Laura, in her usual calm way, did all the things an upper-middle class Midland matron was expected to do—drive the girls to their different activities, do her Junior League work, clean closets, rearrange the medicine cabinets, and line up her books on their shelves by the Dewey Decimal system so familiar to all good librarians.

Meanwhile George was restless, noted Mickey Herskowitz in his book *Duty, Honor, Country: The Life and Legacy of Prescott Bush* (George W.'s grandfather). After five years in the oil business "the young George ached to see that geyser of oil, hear that Niagara of noise, when the well is spouting beyond the derrick." As explained by Herskowitz, George needed what the old hands called "bagging the elephant," jargon for achieving a real gusher.

But George went in another direction. Baseball had always been of keen interest to the whole Bush clan, and young George reacted accordingly when he heard the Texas Rangers baseball team was for sale, as Herskowitz also reported. Likening himself to a pit bull, George told Laura that he was going to "grab a pants leg and not let go until the deal was done." He sold his oil company, bought the baseball team and turned it into a winner. At same time, he had met the terms of a family code established long before by family patriarch Prescott Bush, the onetime U.S. Senator from Connecticut: "Before you enter public service," the code said, "you go out and make some money and take care of your family."

Having done so, George W. now was ready to "bag" the Republican "elephant."

The twins were just twelve years old and *their* grandfather Bush (George H. W.) was a recently defeated president when their daddy ran for governor of Texas on the Republican ticket against incumbent Democrat Ann Richards. To the surprise of many in Texas, George, Laura, and the twins moved into the governor's mansion in Austin.

As first lady of Texas, Laura came to be noticed more and more widely, not because she tried to attract attention but because of her simple, quiet dignity. Her inclination was to shy away from the limelight, but in the end she very visibly chose to exert leadership in a cause close to her heart—getting people interested in reading.

During inaugural week in Austin she hosted a reading by Texas authors, and it was a tremendous success. Several months later she began her most ambitious project yet—the Texas Book Festival. Held in the Lone Star state's magnificent capitol building, it had people standing in line to meet the authors and hear the readings. Not merely a feather in Laura's cap, the book extravaganza would prove a great financial boon to Texas' public libraries. By 2002, a decade after its start, the festival had contributed $1.43 million to the public library system in Texas.

By the time George W. decided to take the plunge into presidential politics in 2000, the once-shy seeming young lady from Midland had proven her political savvy. Well known as the wife of the governor of Texas, she was just as known for her efforts to improve education and youth literacy. Laura moved into the national spotlight with considerable ease, stumping across the country and giving speeches of political significance on behalf of her husband.

Her fresh good looks of course commanded attention, but Laura also could show real firmness. One time during her husband's first run for the presidency she gave a rousing keynote address to the Texas State Republican convention, held on June 23, 2000, while her husband was campaigning elsewhere. Outside the hall, protesters were demonstrating loudly against the death penalty—and the fact that as governor, Laura's husband George had seen 135 convicts executed.

Asked by a reporter if she supported her husband's position on the death penalty, Laura wasn't about to be cornered on the controversial issue. "If I differ with my husband," she declared, "I'm not going to tell you about it; sorry." According to *USA Today,* she handled the rest of the media quizzing with similar dispatch.

There's no doubting the fact that both she and George emerged from all their campaigning as seasoned speakers, but a favorite story they still like to tell recalls those days when George W. was embarked upon his failed bid for Congress from their West Texas homeland back in the late 1970s. Pulling into their driveway after making several speeches one afternoon, he asked Laura how his speech delivery was going over. Without thinking, Laura immediately blurted, "Terrible."

George then drove his Pontiac Bonneville into the garage wall.

George W. took office in January 2001 under the cloud of court fights and Democratic challenges to a nationwide election that in the end hinged on a sparse few votes in Florida, but Laura soon was winning hearts and minds as she went about her expanded role as the nation's first lady while remaining absolutely true to herself.

Books, reading . . . her cause of expanded literacy of course came to the fore once again. As Jacqueline Leo wrote in the May 2005 *Reader's Digest,* "Laura Bush's love of reading is partly what defines her." Thus, it should have been no surprise to anyone that Laura Bush would transport her outstanding Texas book fair idea to Washington, in the form of her National Book Festival, held annually on the National Mall with the U.S. Capitol as a stunning backdrop.

The Bushes had hardly settled into the White House, of course, before that horrendous day in September 2001 dawned. Actually, it had seemed a perfectly lovely and normal morning at the executive mansion before their world—and America's—turned upside down. The first lady had bade mother-in-law Barbara Bush and father-in-law George H. W. Bush good-bye as they left the White House to fly to Minneapolis. Her husband George W. had already flown off to Florida to meet with children in an elementary school. Laura, in turn, left for the Capitol to testify on early childhood education before a Senate subcommittee.

Then came the terrorists' attack on the twin towers of the World Trade Center in New York. Not since Pearl Harbor in December of 1941 had the nation undergone such a shock, with heavy loss of life, as it experienced on September 11, 2001. "We all knew normal never again would be what we knew it to be on September 10," the first lady told *Reader's Digest* in a January 2002, article, "The Teaching of Laura Bush." Indeed, the serene lady from Texas who once tried to stay out of the limelight suddenly, together with husband George, was swept up into days of public mourning, comforting . . . and of course resolving, Never again. As was the case with husband George W., it was a transforming event in Laura's life, but she never missed a reassuring beat in her public appearances.

Still keeping steady as she goes during those dramatic days as America struck back in Afghanistan and went to war in Iraq, Laura once again would be a tremendous asset in her husband's bid for reelection in 2004. Who knows how many votes she alone may have guaranteed by appearing as a keynote speaker at the National Republican Convention in New York City, to a standing ovation, and then once more going out on the campaign trail, both in company with her husband and on her own. This time, it's worth noting,

George W. won the election with the largest number of votes any president had ever received.

Meanwhile, how to explain the ever-present radiance of Laura Bush, no matter how wearing the burden of her national role? By the time of George W.'s second term, she was dressing more boldly and fashionably than ever. She had lost weight—she confessed that she now had her own trainer—but still didn't jog with her husband. And she looked great, better than ever.

After 9/11, unsurprisingly, state dinners at the White House were limited, but the "second-term" Laura Bush definitely was more willing to open the White House to social events.

At same time, naturally, she had impact beyond the nation's borders. The war on terrorism had her full support but, at home and abroad, she continued to fight the battles of literacy and education. In the process, she served as honorary chairperson of UNESCO's Decade for Literacy.

No "desk general" satisfied with directing her causes from afar, Laura in early 2005 traveled in person to liberated Afghanistan, once the home of the dreaded Taliban regime and its terrorist allies, to promote women's education by visiting a renovation project at a women's dormitory at Kabul University, among other stops. After meeting with women planning to train teachers in rural Afghanistan, Laura said, "The United States government is wholeheartedly committed to the full participation of women in all aspects of Afghan society, not just in Kabul, but in every province."

By visiting primitive Afghanistan, not the safest place in the world, Laura scored a point on her husband, who in his first term as president had visited Iraq but not Afghanistan.

Then, too, in another news-making event rare for a first lady, Laura displayed her usual calm in the face of fierce protests by Muslim and Jewish extremists unhappy with her visit to historic religious sites in Jerusalem in May of 2005.

None of which is to say that Laura Bush has any desire to run for office herself . . . not when she can one day, after George W.'s second White House term, return with him to their ranch in their beloved Crawford, Texas, not when she can leave Washington duties behind and take up a good book instead. Or spend quality time with old friends and daughters Barbara and Jenna.

And speaking of the twins, they kept a low profile during their father's first presidential campaign, but in 2004 they spoke candidly about their parents. "I think I'm very similar to my mom in temperament," young Barbara said. "She's very level-headed. And I feel like I am, too. And she's calm and I am, too."

Jenna, for her part, said, "I'm more like my father, personality-wise. But my mom and I get along really well—obviously, because my mom and my dad get along so well."

Jenna also provided an inside view of the George-and-Laura relationship: "My dad thinks she's hilarious," said Jenna. "They laugh at each other all the time. She has a dry sense of humor. She has so many quirks in her personality and she's really cute acting; she has a really cute personality, we think."

And here's a parting thought to ponder, also from twin daughter Jenna: "I think that if he had never met my mom, there is no way that he could have been as successful as he is. Just because she is so stable."

--- ---

Acknowledgments and Further Readings

--- ---

BEFORE COMING TO HEARTFELT PERSONAL thanks for the help and encouragement received in compiling, writing and publishing all the foregoing, please allow us a grateful tip of the hat to an often faceless crowd we don't even know—those many authors and historians who wrote about the White House or its occupants in the past. For us, as researchers of secondary, previously published sources, their works have been a wonderful (and enthralling) resource. We've cited many of them in the text herein—and we would urge readers interested in following up any of our historical vignettes in greater depth to pursue those very books, most of them available in the average public library or corner bookstore.

As is apparent, many of the previously published sources we've cited for fact or occasional quote were "one-shot" books such as biographies of this or that president or first lady. Or autobiographies. Others were "insider" books by former staffers or residents of the White House, good for their detailed focus, like the biographies, but subject, quite naturally, to limitation in time frame. The more general White House histories were of course useful, but by their nature as overviews, they cannot often "zoom in" for sustained close look.

One source, however, does both, and we cannot recommend it too highly, and that is the utterly engrossing, wonderfully researched and written two-volume history of the White House by William Seale, *The President's House* (White House Historical Association, with the cooperation of the National Geographic Society, Washington, D.C., 1986—available from the White House Historical Association, 740 Jackson Place NW, Washington, D.C. 20503). No general history of the White House yet published can match Seale's work for overview or illuminating, anecdotal detail, much of which he found in his own research of old records and other primary sources. Plus, it's simply "a great read."

We can, at the same time, also steer readers to two other overview books, each a single volume, that we found to be knowledgeable in detail and highly readable as well—Bess Furman's *White House Profile* (New York and Indianapolis, 1951) and Amy LaFollette Jensen's *The White House and Its Thirty-Five Families* (New York, 1970).

Among the more focused secondary sources we consulted, a personal favorite was *Starling of the White House* by retired Secret Service Agent Edmund Starling, with Thomas Sugrue (New York, 1946), and we thank longtime friend William Fishback, special adviser to the president, University of Virginia, for lending his rare copy of this slim but indispensable volume. Another "insider" book that sat well here was former Chief Usher J. .B. West's *Upstairs at the White House: My Life With the First Ladies*, written with Mary Lynn Kotz (New York, 1973). Two more classic, "insider" books of the modern period are Chief Usher Irwin W. "Ike" Hoover's *Forty-two Years in the White House* (Boston, 1934) and Lillian Parks's *My Thirty Years Backstairs at the White House* (New York, 1961).

Most of our other sources have been named in passing, but four more that were especially useful in researching for our first ladies section were: *First Ladies: The Saga of the Presidents' Wives and their Power, Volumes I & II,* by Carl Sferrazza Anthony (New York, 1991); *First Ladies* by Margaret Truman (New York, 1995); *First Ladies* by Betty Boyd Caroli (New York, 1987) and *Presidential Wives: An Anecdotal History* by Paul F. Boller, Jr. (New York, 1988). Still another in this category was *All the Presidents' Ladies: Anecdotes of the Women Behind the Men in the White House,* by Peter Hay (New York, 1988).

We hasten to point out also that the same White House Historical Association mentioned earlier, located on Lafayette Square in front of the White House, offers not only the two-volume history by Seale but also a series of smaller, beautifully illustrated books about the first ladies, the presidents, and the White House itself. For us, they were excellent fact sources—and a pleasure simply to read or browse through for a look at the gorgeous portraits and other paintings reproduced in color on their glossy pages. A related source for two of our vignettes (Rose Garden and Paul Jennings memoir) was the Association's *White House History* journal, vol. I, no. 1 (1983).

Much of our material came from general sources too obvious and ubiquitous to mention here—American histories, for example— but a few more specific works that have gone unmentioned in full were: *Presidential Style: Giants and a Pygmy in the White House,* by Samuel and Dorothy Rosenman (New York, 1976); *Hidden Illness in the White House,* by Kenneth Crispell and Carlos Gomez (Durham, N.C., 1988); *Presidential Transitions: Eisenhower Through Reagan* by Carl M. Brauer (New York, 1986); *A Thousand Days: John F. Kennedy in the White House* by Arthur Schlesinger Jr. (New York, 1965); *The Adams Chronicles: Four Generations of Greatness,* by Jack Shepherd (Boston, 1975); *'Marse Henry: A Biography of Henry Watterson* by Isaac F. Marcosson (New York, 1951); *The Abraham Lincoln Encyclopedia* by Mark E. Neely Jr. (New York, 1982); *Plain Speaking: An Oral Biography of Harry S. Truman,* by Merle Miller (New York, 1980); *As He Saw It,* by Elliott Roosevelt (New York, 1946); and *F.D.R.: An Intimate History,* by Nathan Miller (New York, 1983).

Whether among our sources listed above or among those many others cited in the foregoing text, wherever the titles may appear herein, we are most grateful to their authors, living or deceased.

Most helpful also in reconstituting and greatly expanding our once-self-published tome of 1992 vintage was our computer guru (and University of Virginia colleague) Michael Kidd of Scottsville, Virginia. Thank you, Michael, for the many hours you put in!

Many thanks also to a pair of astute readers who spotted inadvertent errors in our earlier edition and furnished additional tidbits of White House lore now incorporated in our expanded book, with attribution for same cited in the text. Those two most helpful gentlemen are retired history Professor Earl Spangler of Waupaca, Wisconsin, and Markus Ring of Washington, D.C., consultant in dental technology—and brother, it so happens, of the telegraph operator who informed Vice President Calvin Coolidge of his abrupt ascension to the presidency.

Thanks should go also to a small legion of helpful archivists at various presidential homes and libraries who helped us to find a goodly number of the illustrations herein. Credits to originating sources will be found with the individual captions. Those with access to the Internet, for that matter, can find many more White House-related images through the American Memories Web site provided by the Library of Congress. Still others—and a wealth of information—can be found through the Web sites of many of the official presidential libraries, or the White House itself (www.whitehouse.gov).

Finally, we owe special thanks to Ron Pitkin of Cumberland House Publishing, Nashville, Tennessee, for publishing our *Best Little Stories* line of historical books—this one makes four in all, with Civil War, World War II, and American Revolution having appeared first, in that order. (And more yet to come!) We also wish to thank Mary Sanford, our astute editor at Cumberland House, for her helpfully sharp eye and red pencil. Last but far from least, many thanks also to our equally astute literary agent, Jenny Bent of Washington, D.C., for having put us all together in the first place!

The Presidents and Their Terms

George Washington (1789-1797)
John Adams (1797-1801)
Thomas Jefferson (1801-1809)
James Madison (1809-1817)
James Monroe (1817-1825)
John Quincy Adams (1825-1829)
Andrew Jackson (1829-1837)
Martin Van Buren (1837-1841)
William Henry Harrison (1841)
John Tyler (1841-1845)
James K. Polk (1845-1849)
Zachary Taylor (1849-1850)
Millard Fillmore (1850-1853)
Franklin Pierce (1853-1857)
James Buchanan (1857-1861)
Abraham Lincoln (1861-1865)
Andrew Johnson (1865-1869)
U. S. Grant (1869-1877)
Rutherford B. Hayes (1877-1881)
James A. Garfield (1881)
Chester A. Arthur (1881-1885)
Grover Cleveland (1885-1889)

Benjamin Harrison (1889-1893)
Grover Cleveland (1893-1897)
William McKinley (1897-1901)
Theodore Roosevelt (1901-1909)
William Howard Taft (1909-1913)
Woodrow Wilson (1913-1921)
Warren G. Harding (1921-1923)
Calvin Coolidge (1923-1929)
Herbert Hoover (1929-1933)
Franklin D. Roosevelt (1933-1945)
Harry S. Truman (1945-1953)
Dwight D. Eisenhower
(1953-1961)
John F. Kennedy (1961-1963)
Lyndon B. Johnson (1963-1969)
Richard M. Nixon (1969-1974)
Gerald Ford (1974-1977)
Jimmy Carter (1977-1981)
Ronald Reagan (1981-1989)
George H. W. Bush (1989-1993)
William J. Clinton (1993-2001)
George W. Bush (2001-)

The First Ladies

Martha Washington
Abigail Adams
Dolley Madison
Elizabeth Monroe
Louisa Adams
Rachel Jackson[1]
Anna Harrison[2]
Letitia Tyler
Julia Tyler
Sarah Polk
Margaret Taylor
Abigail Fillmore
Jane Pierce
Harriet Lane[3]
Mary Todd Lincoln
Eliza Johnson
Julia Grant
Lucy Hayes
Lucretia Garfield
Ellen Arthur[4]
Frances Cleveland

Caroline Harrison
Ida McKinley
Edith Roosevelt
Helen Taft
Ellen Wilson
Edith Wilson
Florence Harding
Grace Coolidge
Lou Hoover
Eleanor Roosevelt
Bess Truman
Mamie Eisenhower
Jackie Kennedy
Lady Bird Johnson
Pat Nixon
Betty Ford
Rosalynn Carter
Nancy Reagan
Barbara Bush
Hillary Rodham Clinton
Laura Bush

---

[1] Died before her husband took office.
[2] Husband died before she could join him at the White House.
[3] Niece who served as President Buchanan's "first lady."
[4] Died before her husband took office.

Index of Personalities

Authors' Note

Sometimes it's nice *not* to be an expert, and so it has been a combination of thrill, pleasure, and ongoing fascination for us to research and write our foregoing account of life in the White House and brief biographies of the women who have come and gone over the same two centuries-plus as first ladies. While we still would not claim to be expert on the subject, we surely have learned a lot, and we hope our readers will catch some of the enthusiasm with which we sat down and began writing this book. Our *First Ladies* section provides greater detail on the more recent first ladies, in part because they have tended to be more active in their White House roles, in part also because they are better documented than many of their predecessors. Whatever the case or the reader's own interest in these matters, we hope the reader can share our interest in the subject, perhaps even the frequent thrill that we experienced while putting it all together.

C. Brian Kelly
Ingrid Smyer